P9-AOR-951

NATIONAL
CULTURES
OF THE WORLD

Titles in
Cross-Cultural Statistical Encyclopedia of the World

Religious Cultures of the World: A Statistical Reference (volume 1)
Philip M. Parker

Linguistic Cultures of the World: A Statistical Reference (volume 2)
Philip M. Parker

Ethnic Cultures of the World: A Statistical Reference (volume 3)
Philip M. Parker

National Cultures of the World: A Statistical Reference (volume 4)
Philip M. Parker

NATIONAL CULTURES OF THE WORLD

A Statistical Reference

Philip M. Parker

CROSS-CULTURAL STATISTICAL
ENCYCLOPEDIA OF THE WORLD
VOLUME 4

GREENWOOD PRESS
Westport, Connecticut • London

Library of Congress Cataloging-in-Publication Data

Parker, Philip, 1960–
 National cultures of the world : a statistical reference / Philip
M. Parker.
  p. cm.—(Cross-cultural statistical encyclopedia of the
world ; v. 4)
 Includes bibliographical references and indexes.
 ISBN 0–313–29770–3 (alk. paper)
 1. Social sciences—Statistics. I. Title. II. Series: Parker,
Philip, 1960– Cross-cultural statistical encyclopedia of the world
; v. 4.
HA155.P37 1997
310—dc20 96–41974

British Library Cataloguing in Publication Data is available.

Library of Congress Catalog Card Number: 96–41974
ISBN: 0–313–29770–3 (vol. 4)
ISBN: 0–313–29768–1 (vol. 1)
ISBN: 0–313–29769–X (vol. 2)
ISBN: 0–313–29767–3 (vol. 3)

First published in 1997

Greenwood Press, 88 Post Road West, Westport, CT 06881
An imprint of Greenwood Publishing Group, Inc.

Printed in the United States of America

CONTENTS

PREFACE

Work on this book began in early 1993 when, after conversations with international managers, I began work on empirical cross-cultural consumer studies. This work has involved collecting a large quantity of statistics across the world's cultural groups (religious, linguistic, ethnic and national). While there is substantial *soft* or textual information on the world's cultural groups published in anthropological and encyclopedic works, there is no complete source of *hard* or quantitative information which might be used on a global basis for the vast majority of these *trans-national* cultural groups. This book was developed to allow quantitative comparisons across non-national cultures and is one volume of four devoted to this subject (Greenwood Press, 1997):

- Religions of the World: A Statistical Reference
- Linguistic Cultures of the World: A Statistical Reference
- Ethnic Cultures of the World: A Statistical Reference
- National Cultures of the World: A Statistical Reference

This volume presents various comparative tables across 329 variables for over 230 nations (defined in Chapter 1). Some 75,000 statistics are given covering: climatic resources, marine resources, land resources, mineral resources, cultural resources, demography and sociology, and economics. These were selected from a much larger data base of over 4000 variables covering a broader range of topics than those given here. The statistics reported were chosen from amongst the larger set for their high potential interest to economists, social scientists, or persons interested in cross-cultural studies. Economic development or strategic planners, for example, might use the variables to estimate market potential sizes, distribution efficiencies or labor force productivity levels across cultural groups. Social planners might use the variables to evaluate the impact of economic development, religion, language or political institutions on cross-cultural behavior. Across all of the areas covered in this book, the statistics provided should be seen as an initial attempt to describe national cultures along comparable and quantifiable dimensions. Should readers wish more precise or qualitative information on a given country, in-depth reviews of secondary research and primary research studies, cited in Chapter 1, are recommended.

Given the sheer volume of statistics provided (over 75,000 estimates), errors may be present in the figures reported and substantial room for improvement remains (despite great efforts to make the information as accurate as possible, as discussed in Chapter 1). Naturally, the reader uses the reported statistics at his/her own risk as neither the publisher nor the author can be held responsible for any errors in or subsequent use of the information provided here. Should the reader find important omissions/errors or have comments/questions, please feel free to contact me via the Internet (e-mail address = parker@insead.fr), or at INSEAD, Bd. de Constance, 77305 Fontainebleau, France (fax: 33-1-60-72-4242). Information on changes to the data reported can also be requested using these e-mail or postal addresses.

ACKNOWLEDGMENTS

Thanks are owed to a number of persons at the European Institute of Business Administration (INSEAD) including Marie-Louise Berry, William Fisk, and Eva Szekarez for helping me input, proof and format the information given in this book. Thanks are also owed to the Research and Development Committee at INSEAD which provided financial support for this work and to Régine, Paul and Claire who let me invest their time in this effort. Finally, thanks are given to Miklos Sarvary who acted as a sounding board for many of the ideas given in Chapter 1.

NATIONAL
CULTURES
OF THE WORLD

1

NATIONAL CULTURES

AN INTRODUCTION

Both academic and popular presses have recently stressed the importance of "borderless" markets, where national boundaries no longer become the relevant criteria in making international marketing, economic planning and business decisions. Understanding non-political borders is especially important for products and industries which are "culture bound," or those which require local adaptation. National culture is often cited as a critical factor affecting economic development, demographic behavior, and general business policies (e.g. strategies found effective in Norway may prove ineffective in Swahili populations). While there is substantial *soft* or textual information on the world's national groups published in various works, there is no complete source of *hard* or quantitative information which might be used on a global basis. This book was developed to allow quantitative comparisons across national groups which are present in multiple countries located in multiple continents. The *hard* information presented in this book allows researchers to begin to answer certain basic questions which have been relatively easy to answer at the national level, but which are illusive for national groups which are trans-national: What is the rank order of national groups by income per capita?; What percent of the population of Mexico speaks English?; Which national groups have highest consumption levels of food, or entertainment goods?; What factors best explain differences across national groups in terms of demographic, consumption and production behaviors (e.g. natural resources, political systems, or language differences)?

The book is organized into eleven chapters. This chapter briefly introduces the book's organization, and potential uses across fields (business, economics, sociology, ethnography, demography, etc.). More importantly, this chapter gives a summary of the methodologies used to generate each reported variable; caveats and limitations of the various estimation procedures used are presented. Chapter 2 provides suggestions to applied academic, business or policy researchers on how one might use the data to explain variations in behaviors across cultures (a *physioeconomic* framework). Chapters 3 to 9 present statistical profiles for each of over 200 national groups. Broadly defined, three types of estimates are given for each nation: absolute levels, average levels (e.g. per capita measures), and percentage or penetration measures. Absolute levels include such measures as population sizes. Average levels are a weighted estimate across countries where the nation is present (e.g. average life expectancy or literacy levels). Percent penetration figures indicate, for example, the percentage of a population that lives under a communist regime (or military dictatorship, etc.). In some cases the estimates are unique to the national group in question, while others are shared by multiple groups simultaneously residing in one or more countries. To the extent that the latter is true, the estimates provided reflect the *prevailing* conditions under which a national group exists (e.g. the weighted estimate of, say, literacy for a national group who's population is located in numerous countries). Estimates of prevailing conditions are most useful in studies of how certain factors affect behaviors within a given national group. Three broad classes of variables of interest to international managers or cross-cultural researchers are given: (1) business, (2) social system, and (3) physioeconomic variables.

Chapter 3 provides a number of economic and business variables. These can be used to estimate, for example, market potential sizes, distribution efficiencies or labor force productivity levels across national groups. These variables include: demographic dimensions (e.g. population sizes, population growth rates, population density, urbanization levels, labor force size, and migration levels), per capita consumption dimensions (e.g. energy, calories, protein, passenger cars, telephones, televisions, radios), production measures across industries (e.g. fish, milk, meat, electricity, coal, petroleum, automobiles), and macroeconomic and infrastructure dimensions (e.g. GNP per capita, GNP growth, highways, ports, aircraft runways, radio stations, television stations, satellite earth stations). Tables 1 to 4 illustrate the variance across some of these statistical measures across national groups. Table 1 reports the 40 most populous national cultures. Table 2 reports the top and bottom 20 national groups in terms of GNP/capita; Table 3 does the same in terms of caloric consumption per capita per day. Table 4 reports the top and bottom 20 national groups in terms of literacy.

Chapters 4 and 5 provide social variables can be used to evaluate the impact of social development, language or political institutions on behavior across national groups. There are several dimensions covered: education (e.g. number of diseases, infant mortality, female life expectancy, male life expectancy, fertility, birth rate, death rate, population/hospital ratio, literacy; political characteristics and systems (e.g. number of parties, number of administrative branches in government, number of governmental changes since 1960, percent of population living under military government, percent of population living under communist government, voting age, percent of population using the metric system, visa requirements, number of border disputes, number of civil wars, number of international wars); frequency of world languages spoken (e.g. number of languages spoken, maximum percent of any one language; percent of population speaking English, French, Spanish, Arabic, Chinese, and Portuguese); and frequency of other world national groups co-existing within the same population (e.g. number of major national groups, maximum percent representation across national groups).

Business and economics literature has long recognized the importance of physical environment on economic behavior (*physioeconomics*). National groups who's populations are land-locked, and who live in hot climates or high altitudes will have substantially different behavior than, say, a national group living in a temperate climate with an abundance of marine and mineral resources. Two sub-classes of physioeconomic dimensions are covered: (1) natural resources available (e.g. mineral reserves, natural gas reserves, crude petroleum reserves, total land area, arable land area, coastline length), and (2) climate (e.g. absolute latitude, elevation, average temperature, minimum temperature, maximum temperature, humidity, rainfall). Chapters 6 to 9 cover these areas across national groups.

Across all of the areas covered in this book, the statistics provided should be seen as an attempt to describe national groups along comparable and quantifiable dimensions. Should readers wish more precise information on a given national group, in-depth reviews of secondary research and primary research studies are strongly recommended.

Table 1. Population Sizes Across Countries

Top 40

National Groups	Population 1994
China	1,210,000
India	897,000
United States	258,000
Indonesia	195,000
Brazil	156,000
Russia	149,000
Pakistan	128,000
Japan	125,000
Bangladesh	122,000
Nigeria	107,000
Mexico	90,000
Germany (United)	80,600
Vietnam	70,100
Philippines	66,500
Iran, Islamic Republic of	63,200
Turkey	59,600
United Kingdom	57,800
Italy	57,800
France	57,400
Thailand	56,800
Egypt	56,000
Ethiopia	52,900
Ukraine	52,100
Burma	44,600
South Korea	44,500
Zaire	41,200
South Africa	39,600
Spain	39,200
Poland	38,500
Colombia	34,000
Argentina	33,500
Tanzania	28,800
Canada	28,200
Sudan	27,400
Algeria	27,100
Morocco	27,000
Kenya	26,100
Romania	23,400
North Korea	23,000
Peru	22,900

Table 2. Economic Affluence Across Countries

Top 20

National Groups	GNP/Capita
Falkland Islands	50,000
Norway	44,000
Switzerland	33,200
Liechtenstein	31,000
Brunei	30,000
Luxembourg	28,700
Japan	26,900
Finland	26,000
Sweden	25,100
Bermuda	24,500
Denmark	24,400
Iceland	23,600
United States	23,400
Cayman Islands	23,000
Germany (United)	22,300
Canada	20,800
France	20,400
Austria	20,200
San Marino	20,000
United Arab Emirates	19,900

Bottom 20

National Groups	GNP/Capita
Uganda	300
Mali	285
Cambodia	280
Laos	270
Tanzania	260
Vietnam	245
Zaire	238
Madagascar	230
Chad	229
Guinea- Bissau	219
Bangladesh	210
Burundi	210
Afghanistan	200
Bhutan	200
Malawi	200
Nepal	179
Somalia	170
Ethiopia	130
Eritrea	120
Mozambique	115

Table 3. Caloric Consumption Across Countries

Top 20

National Groups	Calories/capita/day
Belgium	3,850
Luxembourg	3,710
United Arab Emirates	3,710
Ireland	3,690
Greece	3,690
United States	3,640
Bulgaria	3,630
Libya	3,610
Hungary	3,540
Denmark	3,510
Italy	3,490
Germany (United)	3,480
Switzerland	3,430
Canada	3,420
Austria	3,420
New Zealand	3,410
Spain	3,360
Romania	3,360
Australia	3,330
Iran, Islamic Republic of	3,310

Bottom 20

National Groups	Calories/capita/day
Ecuador	2,060
Nepal	2,050
Burkina Faso	2,050
Cameroon	2,040
Bhutan	2,030
Mali	2,020
Vietnam	1,950
Central African Republic	1,940
Angola	1,930
Bangladesh	1,920
Haiti	1,900
Rwanda	1,880
Sierra Leone	1,870
Maldives	1,870
Namibia	1,840
Guinea	1,780
Ghana	1,730
Ethiopia	1,660
Chad	1,660
Mozambique	1,610

Table 4. Literacy Across Countries

Top 20

National Groups	Literacy 1994
Andorra	100
Australia	100
Belarus	100
Belgium	100
Denmark	100
Falkland Islands	100
Faroe Islands	100
Finland	100
Georgia	100
Greenland	100
Iceland	100
Ireland	100
Japan	100
Liechtenstein	100
Luxembourg	100
Tonga	100
Vatican City	100
Slovenia	99
Norway	99
Switzerland	99

Bottom 20

National Groups	Literacy 1994
Guinea-Bissau	36
Bangladesh	35
Cambodia	35
Pakistan	35
Mauritania	34
Mozambique	33
Mali	32
Chad	30
Afghanistan	29
Niger	28
Gambia	27
Sudan	27
Nepal	26
Guinea	24
Somalia	24
Benin	23
Sierra Leone	21
Eritrea	20
Burkina Faso	18
Western Sahara	15

QUANTIFYING NATIONAL CULTURES: THE METHODOLOGY

In order to correctly understand the meaning behind the various statistics provided in Chapters 3-9, the reader is advised to review the methodology described in this chapter.

ESTIMATION PROCEDURE

All of the statistics reported in Chapters 3 to 9 are estimates. The procedure used to generate these estimates involved the following steps:

- First, an exhaustive list of nations, dependencies, and territories was created in order to include all populated areas of the world.

- For each of the variables reported in Chapters 3 to 9, data were collected at the national level for as many countries as possible. For most of the variables reported in Chapters 5 to 9, which describe a country's exogenous resources, relatively precise measures were available for all countries of the world (e.g. land areas). For many variables in Chapters 3 and 4 which cover more endogenous social and economic dimensions, as complete an enumeration as possible was conducted by combining various sources, listed in the references of this chapter.

Given the volume of statistics, it should also be understood that errors are bound to have occurred during the collection procedure (though great pains were taken to proof-read and cross-validate the statistics). Given the original nature of most of the statistics reported, they should be seen, therefore, as estimates which may require external validation.

ESTIMATION TIMING

The statistics reported in Chapters 3 to 9 are based on the best estimates available during the calendar year 1994. However, in many respects, this timing should not be over emphasized . Rather the estimates should be seen as covering the countries during the period of the "early 1990s", or, especially in cases for variables reported in Chapters 3 and 4, the "later part of the 20th century". This perspective is motivated by the fact that data are often inconsistent across sources, or irregular in their availability for 1994 and were extrapolated. By combining various sources and extrapolating, the integrity of the variables was not compromised, though their exact timing (i.e. as required in time series analysis) is not exact. In cases when the variables do not reflect 1994 estimates, these are noted. A value reported as "." signifies that estimates are unavailable.

REFERENCES: INTERNATIONAL STATISTICS

Many of the following references and sources were used in generating estimates in this book.

Society, General

Bureau of Consular Affairs. *Foreign Entry Requirements*. Washington: US Department of State, 1991.

Central Intelligence Agency. *The World Factbook*. Washington: US Government Printing Office, 1994.

Crystal, David, ed. *The Cambridge Factfinder*. Cambridge: Cambridge University Press, 1994.

Dorling Kindersley. *World Reference Atlas*. London: Dorling Kindersley Limited, 1994.

Encyclopædia Britannica. *Encyclopædia Britannica World Data Annual*. Chicago: Encyclopædia Britannica, 1994.

Encyclopædia Britannica. *The New Encyclopædia Britannica*. Chicago: Encyclopædia Britannica, 1989.

Encyclopædia Universalis. *Payscope; Le nouveau paysage mondial*. Encyclopædia Universalis France S.A., 1994.

Europa Publications. *The Europa World Year Book*. London: Europa Publications Limited, annual.

Frémy, Dominique, Michèle Frémy. *Quid*. Robert Laffont, S.A., et Sté des Encyclopédies Quid, annual.

International Directory of Non-Official Statistical Sources. London: Euromonitor Plc., 1990.

NBC News. *World Atlas & Review*. 1993, Rand McNally,1993.

Paxton, John, ed. *The Statesman's Year-Book 1989-1990*. New York: St. Martin's Press, 1990.

The World Almanac and Book of Facts. Funk & Wagnalls, annual.

US Department of Health and Human Services. *Health Information for International Travel 1991*. Washington: US Government Printing Office, 1991.

US Department of State, Bureau of Public Affairs. *Background Notes*. Washington: US Government Printing Office, 1981-1991.

Geography and Climate

Financial Times International Yearbooks. *Mining 1992*. Chicago: St. James Press, 1991.

National Climatic Data Center, Asheville, North Carolina.

Rudolff, Willy. *World Climates; with tables of climatic data and practical suggestions*. Stuttgart: Weissenschaftliche, 1981.

Times Books. *The Times Books World Weather Guide*. New York: The New York Times Book Co., Inc. 1984.

US Department of the Interior, Bureau of Mines. *Minerals Yearbook,* vol. III. Washington: US Government Printing Office, annual.

World Meteorological Organization, Geneva, Switzerland.

Culture

Barreau, Daniel, ed. *Inventaire des etudes linguistiques sur les pays d'Afrique noire d'expression française et sur Madagascar.* Paris: CILF, 1978.

Comrie, Bernard. *The Languages of the Soviet Union.* Cambridge: Cambridge University Press, 1981.

Katzner, Kenneth. *The languages of the World.* London: Routledge & Kegan Paul, 1986.

Mann, Michael and David Dalby. *A Thesaurus of African Languages.* London: Saur, 1987.

O'Brien, Joanne, Martin Palmer. *Atlas des religions dans le Monde.* Paris: Editions Autrement, 1994.

Ruhlen, Merrit. *A guide to the World's Languages.* Volume 1; Classification, Stanford: Stanford University Press, 1987.

Economics

International Monetary Fund. *International Financial Statistics Yearbook.* Washington: International Monetary Fund, various issues.

The World Bank. *The World Bank Atlas 1990.* Washington: Oxford University Press.

The World Bank. *Stars.* version 2.0, World Bank Data on Diskettes, Washington: The International Bank for Reconstruction and Development/ The World Bank, annual, various years.

Business

Consumer International. London: Euromonitor Plc., 1994.

European Marketing Data and Statistics. London: Euromonitor Plc., 1994.

International Marketing Data and Statistics. London: Euromonitor Plc., 1994.

World Marketing Data and Statistics - on CD-ROM, London: Euromonitor Plc., 1994.

World Tourism Organization. *Yearbook of Tourism Statistics.* Madrid: World Tourism Organization, 1994.

2

COMPARING NATIONAL CULTURES

> No person who examines and reflects, can avoid seeing that there is but one race of
> people on the earth, who differ from each other only according to the soil and the
> climate in which they live. **J. G. Stedman** (1744–1797)[1]

This book considers the use of national social systems as a basis for cross-cultural
comparisons. As the reader will quickly surmise from the comparative statistics provided
in this book, there are wide variances in estimated economic and social behaviors across
the world's national cultures (cultures being defined by national or territorial boundaries).
Are these observed differences the result of the cultural groups themselves (e.g. national
cultures drive divergence in behaviors), by economic policies, cultural institutions, other
more fundamental mechanisms, or a combination of these? This chapter proposes a
framework which can be used to answer this question irrespective of how *culture* is
defined (e.g. based on linguistic, national, religious, or ethnic groups). The framework
explicitly integrates both *economic* and *non-economic* dimensions into comparative
studies and is an extension of earlier works which considered sources of cross-national or
cross-cultural variances in economic and social behavior as originating, in part, from
natural resources -- especially *soil* and *climate*. The statistical tables reported later are
organized following the logic presented in the framework. Before elaborating on that
logic, I will first briefly highlight a number of basic problems frequently observed in
cross-cultural or cross-national studies in economics and the social sciences in general.
These problems will likely arise in the study of cultures when these are defined as
linguistic groups. After that discussion, the *physioeconomic* framework is presented
which can overcome many of the problems highlighted.

PROBLEMS WITH CROSS-CULTURAL STUDIES

Several problems arise in cross-national studies: (1) insufficient variances in either
dependent or independent variables, or both, (2) a failure to control for sample
heterogeneity, (3) unidentified simultaneity, (4) positive spatial autocorrelation, and (5)
measurement problems. Combined, these problems result in biased explanations of cross-
national differences and/or wholly misleading statements of cause, effects, and
magnitudes. We will first review each of these before discussing possible remedies. For
the sake of illustration, we will mostly use the case of understanding variances in

---

[1] *Narrative of a Five Years' Expedition Against the Revolted Negroes of Surinam*, ch. 15 (1796; repr.
1971).

"economic performance," in the form of production, consumption, or income differences across countries.

Insufficient Variance

The Problem. The most common type of cross-cultural study consists in comparing two countries (e.g. Japan and France) and drawing certain inferences. Beyond providing simple descriptions, *comparative studies* fundamentally lack sufficient variances in or observations of behavior to draw explanatory inferences: the Japanese are different from the French because the Japanese are Japanese and the French are French.   The explanation of observed differences in behaviors across cultures is often speculative and tailored to a theory of local interest. The fallacy of *comparative studies* is the lack of degrees of freedom to rigorously test alternative explanations of observed variances; with only two observations all hypotheses are rejected, while many are suggested (e.g. the Japanese are successful due to a homogenous culture; Americans are successful due to a Protestant work ethic, etc.).

The Solution. A solution to this problem is to increase statistical power by collecting information across a large number of countries and to measure explanatory covariates across these' groups (e.g. degree of cultural homogeneity, percent of Protestants per country, etc.). If we treat the world as a natural experiment, we can learn from the wide differences in behaviors and factors affecting these behaviors only if a sufficiently large number of cultures/countries are included in the study. The increased variance in both dependent and explanatory variables can, however, lead to additional problems.

Sample Heterogeneity, Omitted Variables and Specification Errors

The Problem. As the number of observations (countries) increases within a cross-cultural study, we can begin to statistically test theories as to why certain behaviors systematically vary from one to another. This is true so long as we are able to control for factors not related to the theory which independently and exogenously affect the behavior of interest.   In essence, we hope that the sample studied is homogenous in all respects, with the exception of the covariate of interest. When dealing with cultures residing in very different parts of the globe, sample heterogeneity cannot be ignored. Consider, for example, development economists or planners who are critically interested in understanding the incremental effects of economic and social policies on various aspects of economic development. Cross-country studies which attempt to measure the incremental effects of differing policies must assume that systematic or exogenous variations which might be confounded with economic performance or behavior are controlled for. If the output of industrial minerals were used as a measure of economic performance across countries, the appropriate measure would control for the differing levels of exogenous natural reserves found in each country. Countries having no natural mineral reserves should not be considered to have ineffective economic policies due to low outputs. Likewise, policies in a country rich in reserves with positive outputs can be found less performing than alternative policies which have engendered relatively higher output levels, given a lower natural resource base.

The Solution. In order to avoid this problem, one can limit the analysis to similar countries using some matching criteria along the confounding exogenous dimension. Consider, for example, the historical study of communism and its effect on income per capita across countries. Without controlling for natural endowments, for example, the average income per capita of existing or former communist countries is compared against those of non-communist countries. Clearly, one should give more weight to comparisons such as North Korea to South Korea, North Vietnam to South Vietnam, Yugoslavia to Italy, East Germany to West Germany, Eastern Europe to Western Europe, Benin to Togo, Cuba to Jamaica, Nicaragua to Honduras, or the Soviet Union to the United States. Across these pairs we matched the samples based on various exogenous natural endowments: locality-driven climatic conditions, physical size of country, mineral and marine resources.   Proximity in location is not as critical as proximity in environmental "starting position" (e.g. we can reasonably compare the USA to the former Soviet Union which are centered on opposite sides of the northern hemisphere). Using a sample drawn from United Nations members, traditional comparisons indicate that communism had no effect on income per capita, whereas matched measures of income which control for relative starting positions in natural endowments indicate that, on average, countries governed by communist regimes suffered a average reduction in income per capita by over $3600 per year (1985 dollars). Failing to control for such exogenous factors can lead, therefore, to biased explanations of behavior.

An alternative to matching samples on exogenous dimensions is to control for these dimensions within a multivariate analysis. Only when studies include a large number of dissimilar countries or cultures can this approach be considered. In essence, it would be useful to cross-sectionally filter exogenous factors in a similar fashion to economic models which *deseasonalize* time series data (seasonality often being exogenous and independent of theories being tested).   Such a filtering is especially critical to social planners interested in measuring the incremental effect of a specific policy on economic development or progress. By proceeding with a filtering procedure, we can compare the effects of economic policies on countries like Chad, which have no mineral resources, no coastlines, no-inland waterways, desert soils, and long periods of drought, versus countries rich in marine and mineral resources with more generous climates, like the United States. In doing so, we can ascertain the extent to which countries like Chad are "poor" due to their exogenous endowment versus their economic policies. Equivalently, we can determine if Chad has higher "real" economic performance, given its endowment, than endowment rich countries having alternative policies.   The examination of the filtered data can provide insights not otherwise evident or measurable from unfiltered data (e.g. measures of economic performance or social behavior relative to each country's exogenous endowment). This option, however, generates additional modeling challenges as there can be a multitude of potential exogenous differences in the world's cultures that might affect any given economic or social behavior.

Summarizing, cross-cultural studies which have large samples assume that observations are independent panel members who's behaviors do not systematically vary via omitted exogenous factors (e.g. countries are assumed to have similar climatic, cultural, or other environmental resources). Controlling for sample heterogeneity presents the challenge of identifying factors which are (1) exogenous to the dependent variable, yet (2) independent to the theory under study. Specification errors in the form of omitted factors can lead to biases in explanation when the exogenous factor is somehow related to both the dependent and explanatory variables of interest.[1]

Simultaneity

The Problem. A problem in designing filters is that it may not be clear which variables are exogenous to the behavior in question. Consider, for example, the study of income per capita or economic wealth across countries. We might model that changes in wealth depend on and are related to population growth rates. Plausible arguments can be made, however, that population growth rates are driven by changes in wealth. This is a rather general problem within the social sciences with each discipline often treating the others' variables as exogenous to their dependent variables. In the limit, various theories from alternative schools of thought (e.g. sociological versus economic), if added together, may explain more than 100 percent of the variance of certain behaviors. In such cases, both economic and demographic forces are likely to be simultaneously driven by unidentified exogenous dimensions which have been omitted; as mentioned above this leads to biases in each school's explanation of behavior.

Consider the case of economic growth models which traditionally assume that variables such as land, labor, and capital are exogenous to economic production yet independent from one another. There have been recent calls in the economics literature that research "be directed at explaining why the variables taken to be exogenous in [economic growth] models vary so much from country to country."[2] Should the factors explaining variables held to be exogenous in the economics literature be endogenous to variables which themselves contribute to economic growth and production, then the specification errors and resulting biases may be substantial. Of particular concern is the possibility that the omitted variables may be *non-economic* in nature. In his 250-year review of the literature on economic growth models, Rostow notes[3]:

> The greatest of the unsolved problems in the analysis of economic growth is how to bring to bear in a systematic way the inescapable *non-economic* dimensions of the problem.

Rostow lists a number of non-economic dimensions as including urbanization rates, political systems, literacy rates, crude fertility rates, political strength of the military, and the predominant type of religion.[4] Including these dimensions within a general model becomes problematic in that many of these may be driven by economic processes or be drivers of variables now held to be exogenous within economic models (labor, human capital, investments, etc.). If these non-economic dimensions are included in the model, we are still left with trying to explain the origins of these dimensions. If these origins are themselves retained, then the variables traditionally held as being critical in cross-country economic models (e.g. capital and labor) may therefore have little or no incremental (independent) influence on behaviors studied (e.g. economic wealth or growth).

---

[1] Of course, including too many exogenous factors simultaneously may lead to multicollinearity and complications in understanding relationships.
[2] Mankiw, Romer and Weil 1992, *Quarterly Journal of Economics*, p.433.
[3] W.W. Rostow, *Theorists of Economic Growth from David Hume to the Present: with a Perspective on the next Century*. Oxford: Oxford University Press, 1990, p. 480.
[4] Rostow, p. 368.

The Solution. Without a formal statement of "levels of exogeneity" across a given set of variables, debates over cause, effect and explanation are endless. To avoid debates, controlling variables should be broadly seen as exogenous to both dependent and independent variables of interest (e.g. seasonality, generated by the earth's tilt and position to the sun is always seen as exogenous, say, to interest rate fluctuations and can therefore be used as a filter without much controversy). If independent variables are themselves driven by non-economic factors, these too should be filtered or eliminated from the analysis. If multiple filters are used, these should have a strict ordering of exogeneity.

Positive Spatial Autocorrelation

The Problem. The first problem mentioned above, insufficient variance, might be overcome by collecting data over a large number of countries. While this will allow researchers to observe variances and increase statistical degrees of freedom, using data collected from a large number of separate geographic locations creates an undesirable side effect not unrelated to sample heterogeneity and specification errors: spatial autocorrelation. Most comparative studies assume that each country provides as informative and independent an observation as any other. *Statistical degrees of freedom* are assumed to equal *theoretical degrees of freedom.* Yet it is difficult to believe that Belgian and Dutch economic growth would ever significantly diverge, or that substantial productivity gaps would appear within the Benelux or the countries of Central America. Observations from these countries are not independent; see Figure 1 for a graphical representation of spatial correlation. Consider, for example, a study of income per capita across 184 countries (e.g. United Nations members). If France's Departments (states) were to each declare independence and be recognized by the United Nations, we would certainly obtain some 90 new statistical observations, though the theoretical degrees of freedom are far less. In addition to proximity, shared cultural and social values (which can be proximity dependent) would reduce theoretical degrees of freedom. How many of the world's observations are actually independent panel members is difficult to say with precision. Studies which fail to recognize the low levels of theoretical degrees of freedom tend to overstate statistical relationships (i.e. fit statistics of cross-country models may be exaggerated as the "theoretical" degrees of freedom in unfiltered data are far less than the number of statistical observations -- countries -- used in the study).

The lack of independence among spatial observations (leading to spatial autocorrelation) explains, in part, why traditional empirical models of economic growth, for example, often fit well for selected sub-sets of cross-national data (e.g. the OECD countries), yet generally fail to explain under-performance in other groups. In referring to a cross-national model incorporating initial human capital, Barro finds, for example, that "the results leave unexplained a good deal of the relatively weak performances of countries in sub-Saharan Africa and Latin America. That is, the analysis does not fully capture the characteristics of the typical country on these continents that lead to below average economic growth."[1]

The Solution. Biases resulting from geographic proximity and shared histories are, once again, the result of omitted variables. To eliminate spatial correlation problems, ideally one needs to understand, in fact, why proximity leads to high interdependence across

---

[1] Barro 1991, *Quaterly Journal of Economics*, p. 437.

observations. What factors lead to this correlation? If we were able to filter the data of interest for the drivers behind proximity effects, we retain statistical degrees of freedom, but more importantly, we also increase the number of theoretical degrees of freedom and simultaneously eliminate positive spatial autocorrelation. Beyond purely statistical approaches, we need to improve the specification of the model to account for proximity.

Measurement Biases

The Problem. Not all cultures perceive the value, or utility, associated with a given behavior equally, yet we often assume so in normative cross-cultural studies, (e.g. the utility for films in Hindi varies from one culture to another). Consider cross-country economic studies which use various proxies of economic well-being (e.g. income per capita, caloric intake, ownership of consumer durables, etc.). These studies generally assume that individuals, on average, receive similar levels of utility having consumed similar levels of the proxy (e.g. calories, energy) . This assumption may be strongly violated if one considers a large number of dissimilar cultures or countries. Consider a study of food consumption (e.g. caloric intake) across all countries of the world. As caloric needs are largely dependent on human thermoregulatory needs, utilities derived from consumption will vary across populations having widely different climatic conditions. Equatorial populations obtain similar *basal utilities* to temperate populations while consuming less calories than the later. Measurement biases can exist in both dependent and independent variables, especially those linked to physical/physiological well being (e.g. food consumption, clothing, and housing -- in-door heating, air conditioning, insulation) and psychological well being (e.g. entertainment goods and services, discussed later). Furthermore, any composite index which reflects, even if only partially, differences in basal needs across countries or cultures will suffer from the same biases (e.g. income per capita which reflects consumption potential across goods having physiological and psychological benefits which may generate, at equal amounts, different utilities across cultures); this bias is analogous to composite time series which have one or more components which vary with the seasons. Cultures having lower levels of caloric consumption, housing expenditures, certain forms of entertainment consumption, or even income may therefore have equivalent or higher levels of absolute utility than those with higher levels of consumption. Likewise, the utilities or non-monetary income received from the environment directly (e.g. solar radiation/heat energy) might not be accounted for in economic measures of welfare.

The Solution. Controlling for measurement biases generated from differences in basal needs across countries is challenging. Short of changing proxies, only strong theoretical arguments can be used to give guidance on how to adjust or interpret variances in measured behaviors. For physiological behaviors, theories might come from physiology (e.g. studies of the effects of thermoregulation on the demand for food, clothing and housing).   For psychological and social behaviors, theories might be used from psychology and sociology, respectively. In general, little work has been done to adjust cross-country estimates of economic performance or social behaviors for differences is basal needs.

Figure 1
Spatial Correlation

Negative

Positive

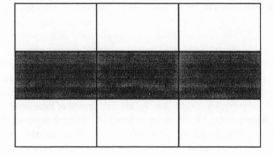

Positive

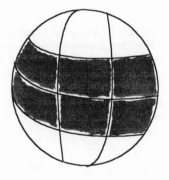

PHYSIOECONOMICS

Introduction

The problems discussed above hold irrespective of how one defines a country or a culture. The remainder of this chapter proposes a *physioeconomic* framework which can be used to overcome many of these problems. The term *physioeconomics* reflects the wedding of physiological and physical sciences with economics. The key assumption behind this framework is that all humans act within exogenous constraints imposed by nature or environmental endowments. As described later, these constraints result in physical, physiological and psychological mechanisms which affect our utilities for various goods and services, our budget constraints (assets and wealth), as well as the relative prices of alternative choices we face, especially when these are considered on a global basis across national or cultural groups. I will later argue that both dependent and independent variables in many comparative economic and social science studies are endogenous to or are dependent on natural resource endowments (many resulting from soil and climatic conditions). The failure to account for these can lead to biased estimation of tested relationships (e.g. the effect of political economy on income per capita). From this perspective, various economic and social theories can be addressed, including those which would seek to explain variances in behaviors across linguistic groups which transcend national borders. In some cases, physioeconomic models can be used to "partial out" the incremental explained variances across competing schools of thought (e.g. debates concerning the sources of economic and social well being across social systems).

My preliminary use of the framework points to a few interesting conclusions with respect to certain behaviors (e.g. economic growth) across countries/cultures: (1) societies having *absolute* differences in exogenous endowments may have *divergent* long-run *absolute* equilibrium behaviors (i.e. aggregate measures of behavior across countries), (2) societies may be *converging* over time to similar levels of behavior *relative* to their environmental endowments, (3) as time progresses, natural endowments will explain cross-country variances in social and economic behavior to a greater extent (e.g. vis-à-vis public policy, culture, or other variables), and (4) cross-national or cross-cultural studies which fail to control for these physioeconomic constraints can be systematically flawed; this is especially true for studies examining a large number of countries, cultures or social systems.

Physioeconomics: Smith and Montesquieu

It is useful to think of the proposed framework as being consistent with thoughts originating from the 18th century Enlightenment, and, in particular, those of French *philosophes* (e.g. Montesquieu and other *Encyclopedists*)[1] and classical economic thinkers (e.g. David Hume and Adam Smith). Of the philosophes, Montesquieu, a correspondent of Hume, has recently been "...regarded as a precursor of many branches of modern social science"; in particular it was the publication of his *The Spirit of the Laws (De l'esprit des lois)*, which "pioneer[ed] sociology by showing the interrelation of

---

[1] The encyclopedists include, among others, Montesquieu, Voltaire, Jean Jacques Rousseau, Friedrich Melchior, and Baron von Grimm who participated in the writing of the 18th-century *Dictionnaire Raissoné des Sciences, des Arts et des Métiers*, edited by the French philosopher Denis Diderot.

economical, geographical, political, religious, and social forces in history."[1]   The *physioeconomic* framework joins his thoughts with that of classical and neo-classical economic theories.   The framework is fundamentally based on the assumption that humans are rational utility maximizers seeking individual betterment while simultaneously exploiting, or being constrained by, natural resources.   Given this assumption and its importance later in this discussion, it is convenient to contrast the thoughts of Smith and Montesquieu as a point of departure.   While both held common views in their criticisms of earlier philosophers' careless evaluation of evidence, the two generally had independent yet complementary discussions of national characteristics and sources of economic wealth and social behavior.   Despite certain divergence's, Smith and Montesquieu held a common belief that soil and climate represent powerful forces behind cross-country (in the case of Smith) or cross-cultural (in the case of Montesquieu) variances in both economic and social behavior.   The remainder of this chapter will argue that large-scale cross-country/culture studies which systematically ignore these two forces (soil and climate) may be plagued with the problems discussed above.

Smith and Montesquieu on Soil and Climate

Montesquieu's *The Spirit of the Laws* was published in 1748, or 28 years prior to Smith's *An Inquiry into the Nature and Causes of the Wealth of Nations* in 1776.   Montesquieu devotes substantial attention, in Books 14 to 19, to the influence of physical terrain (marine biology, mineral resources and topology) and climate on capital formation, labor, technology, and general national socioeconomic conditions.   Montesquieu's basis of comparison extended to Africa, South America, Asia and the Pacific Rim. Based on several anecdotal and 18th-century scientific arguments, Montesquieu forecasted prior to the industrial revolution, among other things, that Northern Europe and Northern Asia would industrialize sooner and more so than Southern Europe and Southern Asia, respectively.   Countries with similar natural endowments would develop in similar fashions, though quite differently than countries with different environmental endowments.   Economic development occurs based on utility maximization constrained by the natural endowments one is forced to or chooses to live with. Montesquieu also conjectured that overall utility levels might be similar across countries or cultures, despite these having taken radically different development paths.   Montesquieu suggested that Southern Europeans would have equal or greater overall utilities than Northern Europeans, even though the later would have greater material/industrial wealth. This conclusion is based on the explicit assumption that endowments not only affect one's income generating capacity, but also the utility of consumption itself and the underlying motivation to generate income. Other behaviors and national characteristics attributed to variations in climate and terrain by Montesquieu include culture, work ethic, suicide, alcoholism, aggressivity, religious beliefs (superstition), mortality, fertility, stature, obesity, sexism, combativeness, and industrial development (agriculture, trade, and commerce).

Montesquieu was not unfamiliar to Smith, both having a common correspondent in David Hume. Smith rejoins Montesquieu on the first page of the *Wealth of Nations*

---

[1] Citations from Encarata electronic encyclopedia, Microsoft, 1995. Montesquieu is most known, in Anglo-Saxon literature, for his advocacy and influence on American political thought concering the separation and balance of powers within government as the best means of guaranteeing individual freedoms.

when he discusses the limit to a social system's wealth as being bounded by its " . . . soil, climate, or extent of territory..." In passages directly referring to Montesquieu, Smith repeatedly re-emphasizes that a country is affected by "the nature of its soil and climate, and its situation with respect to other countries" and "the nature of its soil, climate, and situation."[1] While Smith frequently treats social systems in a ceterus paribus setting, holding soil and climate constant, Montesquieu makes these resources his central theme in order to compare behaviors and social institutions across broader cultural dimensions. Beyond this difference in perspective, we will now consider the logic behind their emphasis of soil and climate. These discussions provide avenues to overcome measurement biases, spatial autocorrelation and other problems frequently observed in cross-cultural studies.

Soil: Economics and Sociology

Smith argues that income is generated (caused by) the need to consume, and that, in particular, "After food, clothing and lodging are the two great wants of mankind."[2] Smith's argument that land is an important input into economic models is based on the *physiological* premise that all humans must eat to survive. Since food demand is inherent, it provides a motivation to generate income and food production becomes the basic source of wealth. Food production inherently depends on the availability of *land*, labor and technology/capital. Land, therefore, becomes a necessary condition for wealth. From food demand and its subsequent supply derives profit and the satisfying of demand for other goods and services:

> Human food seems to be the only produce of *land* which always and necessarily affords some rent [profit] to the landlord. Other sorts of produce sometimes may, and sometimes may not, according to circumstances.[3]

> Food is, in this manner, not only the original source of rent [profit], but every other part of the produce of *land* which afterwards affords rent, derives that part of its value from the improvement of the powers of labor in producing food by means of the improvement and the cultivation of the land.[4]

Smith continues,

> The increasing abundance of food, in consequence of increasing improvement and cultivation, must necessarily increase the demand for every part of the produce of *land* which is not food and which can be applied either to use or to ornament[5]

The demand for "ornamental" goods or luxuries, therefore, also becomes dependent on the produce of land:

> Whatever increases the fertility of *land* in producing food, increases not only the value of the lands upon which the improvement is bestowed, but contributes likewise to increase that of many other lands, by creating a demand for their produce. The

---

[1] Smith (pp. 73-74).
[2] Smith (p. 128).
[3] Smith (p. 128), emphasis added.
[4] Smith (p. 131), emphasis added.
[5] Smith (p. 140), emphasis added.

abundance of food, of which, in consequence of the improvement of land, many people have the disposal beyond what they themselves can consume, is the great cause of the demand both for the precious metals and the precious stones, as well as for every other conveniency and ornament of dress, lodging, household furniture and equipage.[1]

Smith also argues that land becomes a source of population, labor and wages (emphasis added):

Countries are populous, not in proportion to the number of people whom their produce can clothe and lodge, but in proportion to that of those whom it can *feed*. When food is provided, it is easy to find the necessary clothing and lodging.[2]

The number of workmen increases with the increasing quantity of food, or with the growing improvement and cultivation of *land*.[3]

The high wages of labor encourages population. The cheapness and plenty of *good land* encourage improvement, and enable the proprietor to pay those high wages. In those wages consists almost the whole price of land; and though they are high, considered as the wages of labor, they are low, considered as the price of what is so very valuable. What encourages the progress of population and improvement encourages that of real wealth and greatness.[4]

Smith further emphasizes, for example, the importance of land in characterizing the success of British colonies:

In the plenty of *good land*, the European colonies established in America and the West Indies resemble, and even greatly surpass, those of ancient Greece. ... The progress of all the European colonies in wealth, population, and improvement has accordingly been very great.[5]

Not all countries, however, has equally good land endowments. For example, Smith makes a case that countries having the ability to produce potatoes have the ability to produce a wide variety of produce (emphasis added):

The *land* which is fit for potatoes, is fit for almost every other useful vegetable.[6]

Beyond land as a source of food and the subsequent demand for other goods and services, Smith notes that a country's wealth might also depend on land's ability to produce minerals. The profit and output prices from land, he argues, depend on a mine's fertility:

---

[1] Smith (p. 139), emphasis added.
[2] Smith (p. 130), emphasis added.
[3] Smith (p. 131), emphasis added.
[4] Smith (p. 437), emphasis added.
[5] Smith (p. 438), emphasis added
[6] Smith (p. 128), emphasis added.

Whether a coal mine, for example, can afford any rent, depends partly upon its fertility, and partly upon its situation. A mine of any kind may be said to be either fertile or barren, according as the quantity of mineral which can be brought from it by a certain quantity of labor, is greater or less than what can be brought by an equal quantity from the greater part of other mines of the same kind. Some coal-mines advantageously situated, cannot be wrought on account of their barrenness. The produce does not pay the expense. They can afford neither profit, nor rent.

Other coal mines in the same country sufficiently fertile, cannot be wrought on account of their situation. A quantity of mineral sufficient to defray the expense of working, could be brought from the mine by the ordinary, or even less than ordinary, quantity of labor; but in an inland country, thinly inhabited, and without either good roads or *water-carriage*, this quantity could not be sold.[1]

Smith finds that raw material prices can be affected by a country being endowed with natural reserves: "Coals, in the coal countries, are everywhere much below this highest price."[2] Smith also finds that a country's mineral wealth can affect its economic stature. Countries lacking minerals are not destined to be without minerals, however, so long as they have other land resources which can produce tradable commodities:

The quantity of the precious metals which is to be found in any country is not limited by anything in its local situation, such as the fertility or barrenness of its own mines. Those metals frequently abound in countries which possess no mines, Their quantity in every particular country seems to depend upon two different circumstances; first, upon its power of purchasing, upon the state of its industry, upon the annual produce of its *land* and labor, in consequence of which it can afford to employ a greater or a smaller quantity of labor and subsistence in bringing or purchasing such superfluities as gold and silver; and, secondly, upon the fertility or barrenness of the mines which may happen at any particular time to supply the commercial world with those metals.[3]

It was of importance to Columbus that the countries which he had discovered, whatever they were, should be represented to the court of Spain as of very great consequence; and, in what constitutes the real riches of every country, the animal and vegetable productions of the *soil*, there was at that time nothing which could well justify such a representation of them. ... Finding nothing in the animals or vegetables of the newly discovered countries which could justify a very advantageous representation of them, Columbus turned his view towards their minerals; and in the richness of the productions of this third kingdom, he flattered himself, he had found a full compensation for the insignificance of those of the other two.[4]

Montesquieu, in contrast to Smith, considers land as arable and holding mineral reserves, but also more broadly as "terrain." Montesquieu does not treat land as an abstract homogenous unit, but distinguishes between mountainous regions, maritime regions, plains, forests, and deserts (interactions of topology and climate). He holds that terrain has numerous affects on social and cultural structures: forms of government, natural

---

[1] Smith (pp. 131-132), emphasis added. Here Smith notes the importance of rivers as a natural endowment.
[2] Smith (p. 133).
[3] Smith (p. 190), emphasis added.
[4] Smith (pp. 432-433), emphasis added.

defenses, work ethics, migration and industriousness. The following passages illustrate his general philosophies:

Wealth consists in land or in movable effects; the land of each country is usually possessed by its inhabitants. Most states have laws that discourage foreigners from acquiring their lands; only the presence of the master can increase their value; therefore, this kind of wealth belongs to each state particularly. But movable effects, such as silver, notes, letters of exchange, shares in companies, ships, and all commodities, belong to the whole world, which, in this regard comprises but a single state of which all the societies are members; the people that possess the most of such movable effects in the universe are the richest.[1]

The goodness of a country's lands establishes dependence there naturally. The people in the countryside, who are the great part of the people, are not very careful of their liberty; they are too busy and too full of their individual matters of business. A countryside bursting with goods fears pillage, it fears an army.[2]

... government by one alone appears more frequently in fertile countries and government by many in the countries that are not, which is sometimes a compensation for them. The barrenness of the Attic terrain establishes popular government there, and the fertility of the Lacedaemonian terrain, aristocratic government.[3]

The fertile countries have plains where one can dispute nothing with the stronger man: therefore, one submits to him. ... But in mountainous countries, one can preserve what one has, and one has little to preserve. Therefore, it reigns more frequently in mountainous and difficult countries than in those which nature seems to have favored more.[4]

The mountain people preserve a more moderate government because they are not as greatly exposed to conquest. They defend themselves easily, they are attacked with difficulty; ammunition and provisions are brought together and transported against them at great expense, as the country provides neither. Therefore, it is more difficult to wage war against them, more dangerous to undertake it, and there is less occasion for all the law one makes for the people's security.[5]

It is natural for a people to leave a bad country in search of a better and not for them to leave a good country in search of a worse. Therefore, most invasions occur in countries nature had made to be happy, and as nothing is nearer to devastation than invasion, the best countries most often lose their population, whereas the wretched countries of the north continue to be inhabited because they are almost uninhabitable.[6]

---

[1] Montesquieu (p. 352).
[2] Montesquieu (p. 285).
[3] Montesquieu (p. 285).
[4] Montesquieu (p. 286).
[5] Montesquieu (p. 286).
[6] Montesquieu (p. 287).

The bareness of the land makes men industrious, sober, inured to work, courageous, and fit for war; they must procure for themselves what the terrain refuses them. The fertility of a country gives, along with ease, softness and a certain love for the preservation of life.[1]

Island peoples are more inclined to liberty than continental peoples. Islands are usually small; one part of the people cannot as easily be employed to oppress the other; the sea separates them from great empires, and tyranny cannot reach them; conquerors are checked by the sea; islanders are not overrun by conquest, and they preserve their laws more easily.[2]

The German and Hungarian mines make cultivating the land worthwhile, and working those of Mexico and Peru destroys that cultivation.[3]

There are so many savage nations in America because the land by itself produces much fruit with which to nourish them. If the women cultivate a bit of earth around their huts, corn grows immediately. Hunting and fishing complete their abundance. Moreover, grazing, like cattle, buffalo, etc., succeed better there than carnivorous beasts. The latter have had dominion in Africa from time immemorial. I believe one would not have all these advantages in Europe if the earth were left uncultivated; there would be scarcely anything but forest oak and of other unproductive trees.[4]

While both Montesquieu and Smith find land and terrain to provide sources of wealth and forms of culture, they also share in their appreciation of climate as playing a critical role.

Climate: Economics and Sociology

The fertility of land affects its economic value (e.g. contrasting barren deserts to fertile plains rich in minerals). Smith argues that "whatever increases the fertility of land in producing food increases not only the value of the land upon which the improvement is bestowed, but contributes likewise to increase that of many other lands, by creating a demand for their produce."[5] For both agriculture and basic living conditions, Smith and Montesquieu recognize climate as being critical inputs to fertility. For example, Smith draws a contrast between climatic conditions required for rice farming, versus grain farming:

A field of rice produces a much greater quantity of food than the most fertile field of corn. ... In Carolina, where the planters, as in other British colonies, are generally both farmers and landlords, and where rent consequently is confounded with profit, the cultivation of rice is found to be more profitable than that of corn, though their fields produce only one crop in the year, and though, from the prevalence of the customs of Europe, rice is not there the common and favorite vegetable food of the people. A good rice field is a bog as all seasons, and at one season a bog covered with water. It

---

[1] Montesquieu (p. 287).
[2] Montesquieu (p. 288).
[3] Montesquieu (p. 396).
[4] Montesquieu (p. 290).
[5] Smith (p.139).

is unfit for either corn, or pasture, or vineyard, or, indeed, for any other vegetable produce that is very useful to men; and the lands which are fit for those purposes are not fit for rice.[1]

In addition to noting that climate affects the fertility of land, Montesquieu also finds that basic needs (basal utilities) vary across climatic regions of the world and that these needs may require different social institutions to insure high welfare:

> If it is true that the character of the spirit and the passions of the heart are extremely different in the various climates, laws should be relative to the differences in these passions and the differences in these characters.[2]

> The differing needs of differing climates have formed differing ways of living, and these differing ways have found the various sorts of laws.[3]

In addition to this general view, Montesquieu, as illustrated in the following passages, relates various human endeavors, inventions, passions, and past-times to climatic variations:

> Storms and fire led us to discover that the earth contained metals. When they were once separated from the earth, it was easy to use them.[4]

> The more communicative peoples are, the more easily they change their manners, because each man is more a spectacle for another; one sees the singularities of individuals better. The climate that makes a nation like to communicate also makes it like to change, and what makes a nation like to change also makes its taste take form.[5]

> What has naturalized servitude among the southern peoples [of Europe] is that, as they can easily do without wealth, they can do even better without liberty. But the northern peoples need liberty, which procures for them more of the means of satisfying all the needs nature has given them. The northern peoples are, therefore, in a forced state unless they are either free or barbarians; almost all of the southern people are, in some fashion, in a violent state unless they are slaves.[6]

> In northern climates, the physical aspect of love has scarcely enough strength to make itself felt; in temperate climates, love, accompanied by a thousand accessories, is made pleasant by things that at first seem to be love but are still not love; in hotter climates, one makes love for itself; it is the sole cause of happiness; it is life.[7]

> In northern countries, a healthy and well-constituted but heavy machine finds its pleasures in all that can start the spirits in motion again: hunting, travels, war, and wine. You will find in the northern climates peoples who have few vices, enough virtues and much sincerity and frankness. As you move toward the countries of the

---

[1] Smith (p. 127).
[2] Montesquieu (p. 231).
[3] Montesquieu (pp. 239-240).
[4] Montesquieu (p. 292).
[5] Montesquieu (p. 311).
[6] Montesquieu (p. 355).
[7] Montesquieu (p. 234).

south, you will believe you have moved away from morality itself: the liveliest passions will increase crime; each will seek to take from others all the advantages that can favor these same passions. In temperate countries, you will see peoples whose manners, and even their vices and virtues are inconstant; the climate is not sufficiently settled to fix them.[1]

In Asia the number of dervishes, or monks, seems to increase with the heat of the climate; the Indies, where it is extremely hot, are full of them; one finds the same differences in Europe.[2]

One of the consequences of what we have just said is that it is important to a great prince to choose well the seat of his empire. He who puts it in the south will run the risk of losing the north, and he who puts it in the north will easily preserve the south. I do not speak of particular cases: as mechanics has its friction which often change or check its theoretical effects, politics, too, has its friction.[3]

Montesquieu noted that climate may affect psychological mechanisms which would affect, for example, emotions, the utilities derived from entertainment, and one's propensity to commit suicide:

In cold countries, one will have little sensitivity to pleasures; one will have more of it in temperate climates; in hot countries, sensitivity will be extreme. As one distinguishes climates by degrees of latitude, one can also distinguish them by degrees of sensitivity, so to speak. I have seen operas in England and Italy; they are the same plays with the same actors: but the same music produces such different effects in the people of the two nations that it seems inconceivable, the one so calm and the other so transported.[4]

We see in the histories that the Romans did not inflict death on themselves without cause, but the English resolve to kill themselves when one can imagine no reason for their decisions; they kill themselves in the very midst of happiness. ... It is clear that the civil laws of some countries have had reasons to stigmatize the murder of oneself, but in England one can not more punish it than one can punish the effects of madness.[5]

Smith and Montesquieu have similar thoughts with respect to climate's effect on social behaviors surrounding alcohol demand, supply and consumption. Based on certain physiological arguments, Montesquieu concludes:

The law of Mohammed that prohibits the drinking of wine is, therefore, a law of the climate of Arabia; thus, before Mohammed, water was the ordinary drink of the Arabs. The law that prohibits the Carthaginians from drinking wine was also a law of the climate; in effect, the climate of these two countries is about the same. Such a law would not be good in cold climates, where the climate seems to force a certain drunkenness of the nation quite different from drunkenness of the person.

---

[1] Montesquieu (p. 234).
[2] Montesquieu (p. 237).
[3] Montesquieu (p. 284).
[4] Montesquieu (p. 233).
[5] Montesquieu (pp. 241-242).

Drunkenness is found established around the world in proportion to the cold and dampness of the climate. As you go from the equator to our pole, you will see drunkenness increase with the degree of latitude. As you go from the same equator to the opposite pole, you will find drunkenness to the south, as on our side to the north. ... A German drinks by custom, a Spaniard by choice.[1]

Smith similarly notes a relationship between alcohol and climate:

Though individuals, besides, may sometimes ruin their fortunes by an excessive consumption of fermented liquors, there seems to be no risk that a nation should do so. Though in every country there are many people who spend upon liquors more than they can afford, there are always many more who spend less. It deserves to be remarked, too, that, if we consult experience, the cheapness of wine seems to be a cause, not of drunkenness, but of sobriety. The inhabitants of the wine countries are in general the soberest people in Europe; witness the Spaniards, the Italians, and the inhabitants of the southern provinces of France. People are seldom guilty of excess in what is their daily fare. On the contrary, in the countries which, either from excessive heat or cold, produce no grapes, and where wine consequently is dear and a rarity, drunkenness is a common vice, as among the northern nations;[2]

When a French regiment comes from some of the northern provinces of France, where wine is somewhat dear, to be quartered in the southern, where it is very cheap, the soldiers, I have frequently heard it observed, are at first debauched by the cheapness and novelty of the good wine; but after a few months' residence the greater part of them become as sober as the rest of the inhabitants.[3]

Smith's observation that individuals acclimate to local conditions is important in understanding that effects may be more generated from climate, than individual disposition, culture, race, or ethnic origin. Montesquieu makes a similar observation:

Indians are by nature without courage; even the children of Europeans born in the Indies lose courage of the European climate.[4]

Of importance to economic models is the affect of climate on labor. Here, Montesquieu holds that there are stronger disutilities to labor in hotter climates than in colder climates where there may, in fact, be positive utilities to work:

There is a kind of balance in Europe between the nations of the South and the North. The first have all sorts of the comforts of life and few needs; the second have many needs and few of the comforts of life. In the former, nature has given much and they ask but little of it; to the others nature gives little, and they ask much of it. Equilibrium is maintained by the laziness it has given to the southern nations and by the industry and activity it has given to those of the north. The latter are obliged to work much; if they did not, they would lack everything and become barbarians.[5]

---

[1] Montesquieu (p. 239).
[2] Smith (p. 376).
[3] Smith (p. 376).
[4] Montesquieu (p. 235).
[5] Montesquieu (p. 355).

...men are more vigorous in cold climates.[1]

In the time of the Romans, the peoples of northern Europe lived without arts, without education, almost without laws, and still, with only the good sense connected with the coarse fibers of these climates, they maintained themselves with remarkable wisdom against the Roman power until they came out of their forests to destroy it. [2]

The heat of the climate can be so excessive that the body there [India] will be absolutely without strength. So, prostration will pass even to the spirit; no curiosity, no noble enterprise, no generous sentiment; inclinations will be passive there; in laziness there will be happiness.[3]

In order to conquer the laziness that comes from the climate, the laws must seek to take away every means of living without labor, but in southern Europe they do the opposite: they give to those who want to be idle, places proper for the speculative life, and attach immense wealth to those places. These people who live in an abundance that is burdensome to them correctly give their excess to the common people: the common people have lost the ownership of goods; the people are repaid for it by the idleness they enjoy and they come to love their very poverty.[4]

With respect to food demand, Smith and Montesquieu differ somewhat on perspectives as Smith does not consider variances in climates across countries. To Smith, the demand for food is constant across individuals and "is limited in every man by the narrow capacity of the human stomach,"[5] and "The rich man consumes no more food that his poor neighbor. In quality it may be very different, and to select and prepare it may require more labor and art; but in quantity it is very nearly the same."[6] Montesquieu, on the other hand, notes an important climatic effect on food consumption (which, using Smith's argument, might engender a difference in the motivation to generate income). Montesquieu notes that the basic needs of populations may vary with climate, including the need for food or caloric intake:

In hot countries, relaxation of the fibers produces a great perspiration of liquids, but solids dissipate less. The fibers, which have only a very weak action and little spring, are scarcely used; little nutritious juice is needed to repair them; thus one eats little there.[7]

---

[1] Montesquieu (p. 231).
[2] Montesquieu (p. 235).
[3] Montesquieu (p. 234).
[4] Montesquieu (p. 237).
[5] Smith (p. 131).
[6] Smith (p. 131).
[7] Montesquieu (p. 239).

After Smith and Montesquieu

Smith and Montesquieu are not unique in understanding various effects of natural endowments on national or cross-cultural behavior. In the economics literature, for example, Ricardo and Maltus focus on the role of soil on production and demography. What of climatic effects? Despite a wealth of studies in agriculture, biology, physiology and psychology supporting many of Smith and Montesquieu's speculations, these effects have received far less emphasis in economics and social sciences in general.   In his review of the literature on economic growth, for example, Rostow notes Smith's focus on "soil and climate," yet in the same passage, characterizes Smith's view as consisting of three basic elements: "labor, land and capital"; climate disappears.[1] This omission persists in later works including recent exogenous and endogenous models of economic growth. Similar omissions exist in other social science disciplines.[2] Climatic effects, for whatever reason, have dropped out of 19th and 20th century analyses which basically assume that all countries or cultures have identical climates. Such reductionist approaches fly in the face of reason when one considers variances across countries with such diverse endowments in natural resources and climates as France and Chad or Mauritania. Figure 2 illustrates some of the more fundamental climatic effects on factor input prices and the utility for various goods and services as hypothesized by Smith, and, especially, Montesquieu. Failure to account for these can be a source for many of the problems mentioned earlier in this chapter.

Physioeconomics versus Environmental Determinism

Before elaborating on statistical methods to filter exogenous endowments, it is important to state that the basic philosophy of the physioeconomic approach is not deterministic. Philosophies of *determinism* hold that events, actions and decisions are deterministically the consequences of factors which are independent of human initiative or genius.[3] Determinism finds that for a given cause, events necessarily follow irrespective of chance or probability. *Environmental determinism*, in particular, holds that variances in exogenous environmental factors deterministically generate economic, social and psychological behaviors across individuals and/or societies.[4]   While biology has found that six basic factors generally determine whether life can exist within a given environment (temperature, pressure, salinity, acidity, water availability, and oxygen content), the philosophy of environmental determinism considers individuals and societies to be locked into a particular path of economic and social development, irrespective of policy or other human-generated initiatives or policies.   Policies and initiatives, themselves, are deterministically a function of a variety of environmental factors.

---

[1] Rostow (p. 35).

[2] For exceptions to this statement, please see the review in Parker (1995), *Climatic Effects on Individual, Social and Economic Behavior*, Westport, Connecticut; London: Greenwood Press.

[3] *Indeterminism*, in contrast, holds that human enterprise is free and not necessarily or at all predetermined by physiological and psychological laws. *Hereditarianism* sees heredity as the primary force in determining human behavior independent of environmental influences. *Naturalism*, especially in literature, finds that natural forces, especially *environmental*, are determining powers(see, for example, the works of Émile Zola and Guy de Maupassant in France, and Stephen Crane, Theodore Dreiser, and James T. Farrell in America).

[4] See, for examples, the work of E. Huntington (referenced in Chapter 2).

Figure 2
Certain Climatic Effects

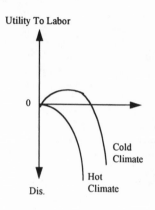

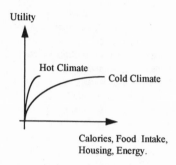

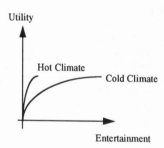

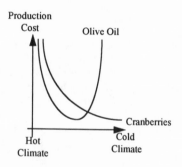

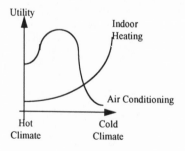

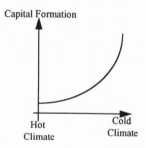

The lingering problem in most studies of natural endowments following similar arguments made by Montesquieu and Smith is attribution. During the early 20th century, certain geographers, among others, were labeled as holding a determinist view of, for example, climatic effects; climate not only correlates with cross-cultural differences in behavior, but also determined these. The lack of strong theoretical underpinnings and certain extremes in early writings, especially as directed toward individual behavior including generalizations concerning racial differences, lead to a general discredit of geography-based theories of behavior in geography, sociology and economics. Though some authors have recently argued that these early criticisms were themselves suspect of certain extremes or lacked rigor, the most important problem in attribution is the identification of physiological and psychological mechanisms. Recent work in these fields, however, fills certain gaps in identifying mechanisms, independent from race, lacking in earlier debates. Together, these would tend to suggest that climate, and other natural resources should be considered as "contributing factors" affecting behavior (rather than factors with determining roles). While some debate has occurred as to whether these effects are direct, or are mediated by social factors, the preponderance of evidence would suggest that both temporal and cross-sectional (cross-cultural) studies of behavior ignoring environmental effects may suffer from substantial specification errors. The physioeconomic framework is presented as to overcome these problems.

In contrast to environmental determinism, the physioeconomic framework blends Smith and Montesquieu by emphasizing that human initiatives can dramatically affect social and economic development, though these cannot ignore local physical environments as constraints or catalysts.[1] Both Smith and Montesquieu stressed that there are no fundamental differences across the world's races: "the difference of natural talents in different men is, in reality, much less than we are aware of."[2] Rather, laws and institutions must maximize welfare in light of natural endowments generating different supply and demand functions across geographic locations. Smith, for example, stresses the importance of individual liberty:

> Plenty of good land, and liberty to manage their own affairs their own way, seem to be the two great causes of the prosperity of all new colonies.[3]

Montesquieu has similar philosophies:

> Countries are not cultivated in proportion to their fertility, but in proportion to their liberty, and if one divides the earth in thought, one will be astonished to see that most of the time the most fertile parts are deserted and that great peoples are in those where the terrain seems to refuse everything.[4]

Montesquieu sees climate not at a determining force, but one that must be combated against or exploited for the benefit of society: "Countries [Holland and Egypt] have been made inhabitable by the industry of men,"[5] and "Men, by their good nature and their good laws, have made the earth more fit to be their home. We see rivers flowing

---

[1] Beyond a simple measurement tool, the physioeconomic framework might be seen as blending *liberalism, naturalism* and *indeterminism*.

[2] Smith (p. 12).

[3] Smith (p. 442).

[4] Montesquieu (p. 286).

[5] Montesquieu (p. 288).

where there were lakes and marshes; it is a good that nature did not make, but which is maintained by nature." [1] Montesquieu frequently proposes public policies to combat certain climatic effects:

> The cultivation of land is the greatest labor of men. The more their climate inclines them to flee this labor, the more their religion and laws should rouse them to it. Thus, the laws of the Indies, which give lands to the princes and take away from individuals the spirit of ownership, increase the bad effects of the climate, that is, natural laziness.[2]

To Smith and Montesquieu, individual and social responses vary across any two geographic areas having identical environments, even though human behavior in both are affected by physioeconomic constraints. Likewise, racial origins have no independent influences on behavior; these origins are mistakenly confounded with other mechanisms. Finally, environmental determinism would hold that the hula dance of Hawaiians was determined by the existence of ocean waves surrounding the islands; a physioeconomic approach would suggest that one's propensity to be influenced by marine resources is related to one's exposure to these resources and social institutions (culture, public policy, etc.). In all cases, individual differences and initiatives within a society allow for most behaviors to be observed in all locations of the globe. As shown in Figure 3, the frequency of behaviors can be affected by natural endowments across individuals within a population. Similarly, when one wishes to explain cross-country variances in mean behaviors using physioeconomic forces, a high explained variance does not support deterministic philosophies; see Figure 4 which relates solar climate (absolute latitude) to explained behavior and convergence.

A Physioeconomic Framework

Assumptions

The basic premise of this framework is the assumption that all human behaviors are inherently constrained to time-invariant laws of physiology, among other physical laws, which prevail irrespective of racial, religious, ethnic, cultural, sociological or economic origins and institutions. Two classes of effects encompass most physioeconomic factors: (1) soil (land, terrain, mineral resources), and (2) climate. Of the two, soil-related effects have received the most treatment in the literature. One of the more important distinctions of physioeconomic models compared to alternatives is the explicit measurement of climatic effects on behavior.

Defining Climate

Climate (e.g. tropical, polar, temperate, high-altitude, etc.) is typically defined as average meteorological conditions specific to a geographic region over a period of several years or decades (e.g. 30 years). *Weather* is typically defined as short term fluctuations in meteorology, including changes in temperature, humidity, cloudiness, rainfall, and barometric pressure. General weather patterns are associated with particular climatic

---

[1] Montesquieu (p. 289).
[2] Montesquieu (pp. 236-237).

Figure 3
Climate and Behavior: Indeterministic Effects

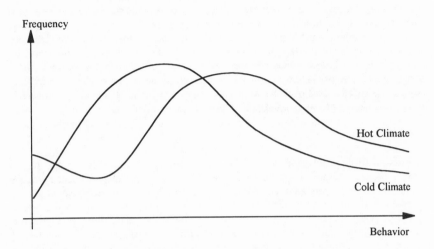

Figure 4
Explained Variance and Convergence

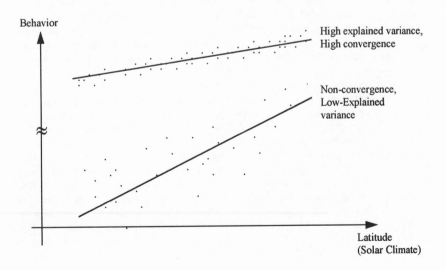

conditions (e.g. strong seasonality is highly associated with temperate climates). Climatologists recognize a hierarchy of effects in climate formation. The earth's climates originate from solar radiation which varies in relation to one's absolute latitude from the equator (a power or nonlinear function of latitude provides an approximation of radiation received; the lower the latitude the more the radiation). If the earth had no land masses, the resulting climate would be identical at all points equally distant above and below the equator. Deviations from the solar climate are generated by land areas and topology (including elevation) which result in physical climates, ocean currents and wind currents. The interactions amongst these generate prevailing weather patterns and microclimates. No two countries have identical climates. A large portion of countries, however, have similar climates across broad classifications: e.g. mostly desert, or tropical. Many have never experienced a frost over the last 10,000 years; some have almost continual rainfall, while others have virtually no rainfall at all.

Climatic Effects

In addition to direct climatic effects (e.g. rain-based agriculture is less productive in deserts than temperate climates), three climate-induced physiological constraints on human behavior in particular are noteworthy. The first results from humans being homeothermal (or homothermal) mammals (homeotherms). Humans, being warm-blooded, must constantly maintain an internal core body temperature of 37 degrees Celsius, irrespective of where they live or the environments that they face (homoiothermy or homeostatic equilibrium). Heat-exchange behavior balances incoming and outgoing heat by means of physiological processes of thermoregulation in reaction to external factors of radiation, ambient temperature, moisture/humidity, and air movement. This heat transfer relationship can be expressed as:

$$0 = M +- CD +- CV +- R - E$$

where M is the heat generated from metabolism (food consumption, physical labors, exercise), CD is heat gained/lost by conduction, CV the heat gained/lost by convection, R the heat gained/lost by radiation, and E the heat loss due to evaporation.[1] Homeostatic equilibrium, which is controlled by the hypothalamus via nervous and hormonal mechanisms, requires that the human body balance energy absorption and production. In the short-run this process may result in shivering or sweating, or, the long run, adjustments to metabolic functions. In all cases, core or deep body temperature must remain constant irrespective of the environment encountered. Reflecting the need to produce energy via metabolism, physiologists note that some 80 percent of food consumption is required for thermoregulatory needs (the rest being attributed to variety seeking and other behaviors). Failure to maintain energy balance, especially in the extremes, results in various illnesses or death (hypothermia, and heat stroke in the extremes). Bioclimatology and biometeorology attributes a number of consumption behaviors to this constraint: the use of tile floors in hot climates, dressing behaviors, an inverse relationship between caloric intake or digestive energy and ambient temperature (the hotter the climate, the less one eats, especially of foods which require high energies to digest such as meat; the colder the climate, the greater the need to install artificial heating systems and/or wear heavy/layered clothing and the higher our preferences for

---

[1] See Stanier, M.W. et al., *Energy Balance and Temperature Regulation*. Cambridge: Cambridge University Press, 1984.

alcoholic beverages).[1] This climatic effect has further been held to explain differences in physiological utility for physical work or exertion; an equivalent level physical work has greater physiological utility in temperate or polar regions than in equatorial or hot arid regions.

The second mechanism, related to the first, affects physical comfort which is dependent on changes in and long-run levels of ambient temperature and humidity. Acclimatization (or acclimation) involves an internal physiological adjustment process, also controlled by the hypothalamus. This level is typically expressed as follows:

$$TH = f(Td,Tw,Z)$$

where TH is a temperature humidity index, Td is the dry-bulb temperature, and Tw is the simultaneous wet-bulb temperature; and Z is a vector of constants, which vary by climate. For each climate there exists a temperature-humidity threshold which, if passed, generates physical discomfort or illness for those acclimated to a particular climate; in hotter climates, human physiology acclimates to allow for higher TH levels before discomfort is generated. Persons acclimated to colder climates have lower TH levels (i.e. are able to feel comfortable at lower TH levels). Persons living in the tropics, for example, have less discomfort than tourists visiting the tropics (as Scandinavian's have less discomfort than tourists coming from the tropics to Scandinavia). Thresholds are generated by both mean climatic conditions and seasonal variations.   Persons living in climates with marked seasons (very cold winters and very hot summers) have highest levels of discomfort all year round, and will have greatest physiological utility for simultaneously owning both indoor heating and summer air conditioning (non-climatic factors being held constant). Acclimation has also been used to explain variances in labor productivity for a variety of industries including mining where the underground mining environment differs substantially from the surface climate.

Based on these first two physiological mechanisms, certain climatologists and geographers argue that climate is the single most important factor generating variances in numerous human behaviors, including dietary patterns (caloric/protein intake), housing requirements (heating, insulation, architecture), and clothing requirements (light versus heavy). Since these climate-dependent activities alone represent from 30 to 50 percent of total household consumption in developed economies and up to 90 percent in lesser developed economies, climate cannot but have a substantial impact on aggregate measures of behavior which incorporate these items (e.g. cross-country measures of aggregate consumption or income per capita).

The third mechanism is the subject of recent studies in medicine and physiology which have demonstrated the role of climate in hormonal secretions, some of which result from thermoregulation, acclimatization and light absorption. Variances in hormone levels in individuals across climates are used to explain, for example, the existence of strong seasonal affective disorders in temperate or polar climates, yet weak affective disorders in equatorial climates; such disorders are commonly treated using light or phototherapy. Evidence of equatorial influences can also be seen in the seasonality of demand for mental health services. Similar tendencies have been observed for suicide and suicide ideation; persons residing closer to the poles are more likely to experience seasonal affective disorders, depression, and suicide ideation. Suicide and mood disorders rise in the winter

---

[1] For a review of the literature relating to these effects, see Chapter 2 and Parker (1995).

months in temperate or polar climates and reach their peaks toward the end of winter/early spring when cumulative imbalances are greatest.

Care must be taken not to confuse these mechanisms with direct causes of specific behaviors at the individual level.   In the case of suicide, for example, sociologists (including E. Durkheim in the late 19th century) discarded climate as a factor affecting cross-national suicide rates as climate is rarely, if ever, directly linked to a particular act of suicide. It goes without question that individual acts of suicide are frequently brought on by specific tragedy (as opposed to variations in the weather). This observance does not eliminate the possibility that climate affects one's propensity to commit suicide given a specific personal tragedy (i.e. several persons facing similar tragedies may have differing propensities to commit suicide given their respective prevailing climates -- polar versus equatorial). In some cases, climatic effects may be observed through non-meteorological factors (e.g. alcoholism) which themselves are affected by climate (polar countries generally having higher levels of alcoholism than equatorial climates). Likewise, as shown in Figure 3, a climatic effect does not prevent an individual, for example, from owning an air conditioner in a polar region (though on average, utilities are lower there than in temperate climates for this product).

Indirect Effects

To the mechanisms discussed above can be added a variety of physical constraints discussed at length by human and economic geographers.   These reflect necessary physical conditions to various behaviors at the individual or societal level. Variances in these necessary conditions, it is argued, affect equilibrium behavior. Certain sports, for example, can only be practiced in geographic areas having appropriate topologies which may interact with climate (e.g. ice fishing, coral photography, alpine skiing). Certain diseases are limited in nature to areas which have not experienced frosts over the last 10,000 years (e.g. tropical diseases, including malaria).   Virtually all animal and plant species are geographically bounded by prevailing climatic conditions (e.g. oak forests and their animal inhabitants), the proximity of which affects the economics of human consumption and transformation.   Various human activities are also directly bounded by the severity of climate: e.g. the economics of mineral extraction varies by climatic conditions; elevation and/or solar radiation prevents the cultivation of certain crops and directly affects soil fertility.   These constraints, including the availability of climate-dependent fresh water, are held to affect the supply and demand of various goods and services, certain cultural traits of populations, economic development patterns, and various vital statistics.

Figure 5 graphically summarizes the various effects discussed by identifying a simply hierarchy; Chapter 10 provides a select bibliography of works discussing various effects mentioned earlier.[1] Using this framework, one can better understand the incremental role of both exogenous climatic factors and endogenous factors which affect behavior. In this case, "exogenous" factors are meant to include all "inherited" or non-human natural resources.   Endogenous factors include any of human origin, including population, culture, religion, language, economic policies, and social systems.   Within

---

[1] See also Parker (1995), *Climatic Effects on Individual, Social, and Economic Behavior*. Westport, Connecticut; London: Greewood Press, for a more detailed summary of climatic effects.

Figure 5
Physioeconomic Framework

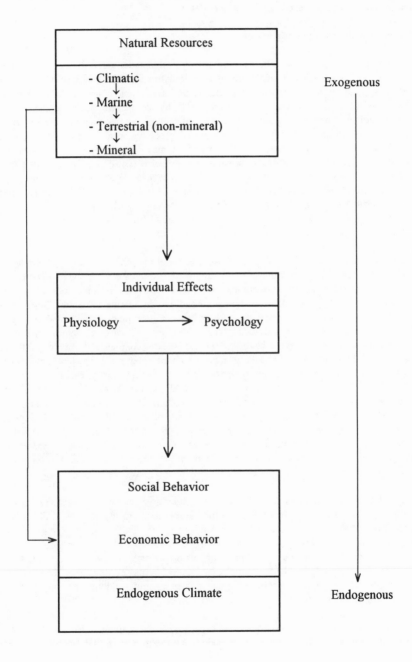

exogenous and endogenous factors, various sub-hierarchies can be considered. Figure 5 notes the existence of human-generated climate (e.g. in-door air conditioning, heating, pollution and human-induced greenhouse effects) as endogenous to natural climates which are mostly time invariant over the last ten centuries (e.g. the absolute latitude of a region, the natural existence of mineral deposits, etc.).

Estimating Physioeconomic Effects

Estimating physioeconomic effects may prove problematic given the complexity of factors affecting behavior. Climate affects water resources and temperature which affects natural vegetation, which in turn affects dietary preferences and consumption patterns. In the case of cross-national comparisons, for example, we might consider the interrelationships between income per capita, political systems, and various demographic variables (e.g. mortality levels). Each of these variables have been shown to be dependent on physioeconomic forces; many of these variables may be mediating factors to others. Short of applying numerous structural variable approaches (LISREL), one can filter each variable for physioeconomic effects in the same vein that we deseasonalize time series data (a form of multivariate "step down" analysis). In this case we are not interested in directly estimating all mediating effects (e.g. the effects of alcoholism, net of climate, on suicide), but rather the net effects of physioeconomic factors on each variable of interest (these in turn can be modeled in some dependence structure).

Figure 6 illustrates a filtering procedure based on the physioeconomic framework. Natural historians have recognized a hierarchy of exogeneity whereby certain natural phenomenon are necessary conditions (and simultaneously historical precedents) to others. Climate, for example, is a necessary condition for marine and animal/human life, which is in turn a necessary condition for culture or economic behavior. Within each level of the hierarchy are sub-hierarchies. The sun, or solar climate is the most exogenous of factors in natural history. Physical climate (continental formation) follows, resulting in land and ocean topology; again, without solar radiation, physical-induced climates would not exist. Following the hierarchy of natural history, climatic forces are generally held responsible for variances in the world's natural marine biology, vegetation and zoological resources. Again, each level in the hierarchy is a necessary condition for the next: terrestrial life depending on prior existence of marine life, which itself depends on climatic formation. Minerals are considered after these (though this might be debated) since many are formed based on the prior existence of topology (physical climate) and animal or plant life; their observance, measurement or extraction also necessarily follows, or is endogenous to, animal life.

Beyond these purely exogenous factors, difficulties arise in establishing hierarchies in human-generated factors. In contrast to the natural endowments, it may be difficult to accept that these factors are necessary conditions by order of exogeneity (e.g. religion may not be a necessary condition to language). For the sake of illustration, Figure 6 follows a hierarchy generally accepted by historians with respect to current social systems. Modern religions, for example, are generally more exogenous than modern languages which are in turn more exogenous than current economic policies, political systems or social institutions.

This framework can be operationalized for any given human behavior via sequential filtering. The dependent variable (e.g. caloric consumption) is first filtered for solar

Figure 6
Filtering Sequence
(typical incremental explained variance in parentheses)

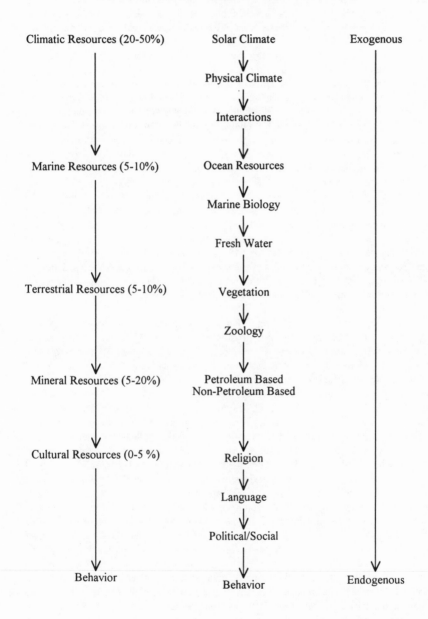

Climatic Resources (20-50%)	Solar Climate	Exogenous
	↓	
	Physical Climate	
	↓	
	Interactions	
↓	↓	
Marine Resources (5-10%)	Ocean Resources	
	↓	
	Marine Biology	
	↓	
	Fresh Water	
↓	↓	
Terrestrial Resources (5-10%)	Vegetation	
	↓	
	Zoology	
↓	↓	
Mineral Resources (5-20%)	Petroleum Based	
	Non-Petroleum Based	
	↓	
↓	↓	
Cultural Resources (0-5 %)	Religion	
	↓	
	Language	
	↓	
	Political/Social	
↓	↓	↓
Behavior	Behavior	Endogenous

climate. The resulting residuals become the transformed dependent variable which is in turn filtered for physical climate, and so forth through the hierarchy.   This process is analogous to that commonly used in time series studies which attempt to measure the short-run affects of policy on economic behavior which varies in a seasonal pattern.   An alternative approach is to simultaneously filter the original dependent variable for all exogenous factors (which may have been previously factor analyzed).   The primary advantage of the sequential filtering process is the insights gained by having a direct measure of the incremental explanatory power of each element along the filtering hierarchy.   For example, we can estimate the extent to which Protestantism (or a Protestant work ethic) explains labor productivity beyond variances explained by exogenous elements (i.e. "work ethic" may itself be explained by climate).   Similarly, we can test whether religious affiliation (Catholic versus Protestant) affects suicide rates after we control for exogenous geographic effects (given that Catholic countries are more concentrated towards the equator, compared to Protestant countries concentrated towards the poles).   Solar climate is measured as absolute latitude squared (to account for the earth's curvature).   Measures of physical climate include elevation, and total land area which simultaneously captures other terrestrial resources. Interactions are measured using climatic classifications.   Marine life is measured using coastline length. Similar measures are used for land, and mineral resources.   Cultural measures include measures of the five largest world religions, numbers of ethnic groups present, and the use of major colonial languages.   Political and economic measures include dummy variables for alternative regimes (e.g. communism, dictatorship, democracy).   It should be noted that each filter has an equal number of statistical degrees of freedom, yet, as each filter is performed in sequence of exogeneity, theoretical degrees of freedom actual increase (as discussed earlier) despite the data being transformed (re-used) across filters.

For each level of the filtering hierarchy, Figure 6 indicates in parentheses the general range of incremental percent explained variation, adjusted for degrees of freedom, across some thirty cross-national measures frequently used in demography (e.g. mortality, fertility, population, population growth rates), sociology (e.g. crime, suicide) and economics (e.g. manufacturing, mineral extraction, durables consumption, caloric intake, aggregate output, savings).   These averages should be seen as typical to many, but not general to all behaviors. These percentages are relatively invariant irrespective of how culture is defined (e.g. as nationalities, linguistic groups, religious groups, or ethno-linguistic groups).   Though infrequent, some behaviors are left unexplained by the hierarchy (e.g. short-term inflation rates across countries). Across the various levels in Figure 6, solar climate generally explains the largest variances in behavior; over 70% of the variance observed across the behaviors mentioned are explained by the exogenous factors, including income per capita. Cultural variables explain little variance beyond that already explained by natural endowments (e.g. controlling for climatic effects, religion does not have an impact on labor productivity or "work ethics"). It is interesting to note that solar climate alone (absolute latitude squared) has statistically equal or greater explanatory power than income per capita for a variety of behaviors which are typically thought of as being "development driven" or, if not development driven, "inferior" behaviors (e.g. when the consumption of a good is not positively related to income). Behaviors which are uncorrelated with income per capita but explained by solar climate include (statistically significant Pearson correlation coefficients are given in parentheses): milk consumption per capita (.53), and cereal consumption per capita (.57).   Behaviors which are better explained by solar climate than income per capita include: butter consumption per capita (.59), flour consumption per capita (.35), potato consumption per capita (.66), sugar consumption per capita (.46), caloric intake per capita (.74), coffee consumption per capita (.75), cigarette consumption per capita (.33), surface cleaner consumption per capita in Europe (.52), percent of households owning a microwave oven in Europe (.76), percent of households owning a personal stereo (e.g. Sony Walkman) in Europe (.84), percent of households owning a personal computer in Europe (.59), the number of political parties in a country (.34), suicide rates (.62), and homicide rates (-.35). Behaviors which are equally well explained by solar climate and income per capita include: average population growth rates (-.50), number of major diseases present (-.52), literacy rates (.46), the percent of homes with piped water (.66), the percent of homes with flush toilets (.73), daily newspaper circulation per capita (.76), telephones per capita (.65), beef consumption per capita (.36), pork consumption per capita (.64), egg consumption per capita (.54), beer consumption per capita (.56), steel consumption per capita (.65), toilet paper consumption per capita (.72), the percent of homes owning a video camera in Europe (.66), and the percent of homes owning cable television, in Europe (.48). In general, the correlations are higher when the data are limited to European countries, or industrial countries located in very different climatic regions (e.g. desert, polar, temperate, tropical and Mediterranean). When the entire filtering procedure is performed, explained variances are virtually always higher than using income per capita (e.g. when marine, land and mineral resources are included, considering degrees of freedom).[1]

Validation Tests

Approaches used to validate estimated effects when applying the filtering approach include replication using subsets of the data which simultaneously offer sufficient variation in climate and degrees of freedom (i.e. country observations). Clusters can include countries having non-democratic political systems, certain dominating religions, or colonial languages. One can also group the data by exogenous controls including the hemispheres, time zones, form of topology, or wealth in mineral endowments. In both cases, these validity tests must allow for sufficient variation in climate (or climate-dependent variables). Within country tests often do not provide this variation unless these have substantial variances in latitude, elevation, or other environmental factors.

Dynamics

While the percentages reported in Figure 6 are robust to the validity tests discussed above, the results are static (as is common for cross-cultural studies of climate). Two questions arise: (1) are the results robust over time, and (2) in which direction are they likely to change in the future. The first question is best evaluated using data collected over extended time periods using static samples (i.e. the same countries must be represented over time); the variables used in the exogenous filters themselves never change over time. Changes in coefficients and explained variances can address the first question. The second question is best answered by examining the dynamics of the residuals (corrected dependent variables) after the final filter of interest. Strong deviations from the mean (of zero) may foretell future dynamics reflecting a convergence or regression to the mean. In the case of zero mean shifts over time (an empirical

---

[1] Data on these behaviors are taken from primary sources or from various Euromonitor publications (European Marketing Data and Statistics; International Marketing Data and Statistics), and from various United Nations statistical reports.

question), those countries far below the mean have higher probability of increasing their behaviors toward the mean, whereas those substantially above the mean will eventually fall to the mean. Alternatively (e.g. in cases of positive mean shifts in behavior over time, driven by innovation or other growth mechanisms), those countries/cultures substantially above (or below) the mean may be on a boundary to which others converge (e.g. the saturation point on a diffusion curve); of course, this boundary may shift in time.

Some Implications

The implementation of physioeconomic models can be revealing to researchers and policy makers. The filtering of income or consumption per capita, for example, reveals that over 70 percent of variances observed internationally are explained by variances in natural endowments (e.g. countries like Chad are mostly underdeveloped due to their lacking natural resources and having equatorial or desert climates, and less due to economic policy failure). Furthermore, based on cross-sectional data which adjust for purchasing power parity and which are available back to the 1950s, this explained variance has been increasing over time. As information ubiquity and democracy progresses to such an extent that economic planning is conducted to its optimal level within each country, factors which will most explain differences across countries will be exogenous to economic policies (physioeconomic factors). In 1994, solar climate alone explained some 60 percent of the variance of income per capita across countries; also the gradual increases in explained variance has occurred while average consumption levels have substantially increased over time. Furthermore, filtered measures of development are often not correlated with unfiltered measures. When comparing each country's level of "relative development," or its level of economic performance given it exogenous endowments, one finds that resulting income differences are relatively small compared to absolute levels (e.g. within a few thousand dollars, versus tens-of-thousands of dollars). Many "lesser developed" countries (e.g. Costa Rica) have, for example, higher economic performance given their endowments relative to, say, the United States. We can conjecture that if Americans were to inherit Africa, they would do no better in developing Africa with their culture or social system than current Africans with theirs; similarly, if Japan were to have been located on the equator, its social system would have only slightly higher performance to Indonesia (as opposed to several orders of magnitude higher as estimated using absolute measures of development). By focusing on these filtered measures, therefore, one may be able to identify *"relatively* successful" countries; the policies of these countries may prove useful in other countries with relatively low performance or those having similar endowments. Tropical countries, for example, may benefit from studying social and economic policies in Costa Rica or the Cayman Islands which have managed to obtain relatively high economic performance given their natural endowments.

The concept of "relative performance" raises an interesting question concerning cross-national measures of development. There appear to be fundamental cross-country differences in both physiological and psychological utility ("basal utility") for a number of human activities including food consumption, dressing behavior, housing requirements, energy consumption, and the use of in-door entertainment. Cross-country data, including those limited to industrialized countries, seem to indicate that some portion of the observed variances in measures of development can be explained by climatic factors which may affect basal utility. For certain measures of development incorporating these behaviors (e.g. aggregate consumption per capita), holding all countries (or climatic regions) to a unique or absolute standard, regardless of where that standard is established, can be problematic. Considering the case of caloric intake, European data spanning several decades indicate substantially lower caloric consumption in warmer countries, than colder countries (consistent with thermoregulation). These levels have remained relatively constant over time, despite large increases in real income per capita. Similar observations can be made with respect to the consumption of various climate-affected behaviors (e.g. clothing, the use of internal heating, insulation, etc.). If we are interested in measuring development from a general utility perspective, differences in basal utilities should be taken into account (i.e. two divergent levels of absolute consumption may generate similar levels of utility, the difference in consumption being explained by differences in thermoregulatory functions). For example, Belgians consume some 50% more calories per capita than persons living in Bermuda (3850 versus 2545, respectively); it is difficult to imagine that all of this difference is due to economic performance or that Belgians receive that much more absolute utility from their diets. While adjustments might be made to economic development measures to account for basal utility differences across countries, these adjustments run the risk of overestimating development for those countries having the lowest absolute values on the original scale. An alternative to adjusting current measures is to place more emphasis on alternative measures not subject to basal utility shifts, or indirect physiological or psychological mechanisms. These scales should indicate relative levels of development which cannot be confounded with differences in basal utility (a lower level on the scale should always indicate lower performance and, preferably, in a linear manner). The direct or life threatening impacts of climate may also be appropriate (e.g. the prevalence of certain diseases, infant mortality, etc.).

Filtering economic data for physioeconomic factors clearly reveals that countries may develop, in equilibrium, to differing levels of behavior which may reflect, in large part, physiological effects as opposed to endogenous economic policies, culture, ethnic origins, or social institutions. Estimates of global food supply inadequacies, for example, based on temperate-climate standards are likely therefore to be exaggerated especially given the fact that most persons live closer to the equator, than in temperate climates. While shortages have occurred throughout history, it becomes paramount to objectively estimate basic requirements in order to develop appropriate policies. Otherwise, deviations from "temperate standards" may appear alarming, and result in policies detrimental to welfare. For example, food aid policies including food subsidies based on erroneous needs estimates risk destroying local farming economies. Filtered measures can also give realistic indications of the likely impact of policies on countries having different endowments (interpreting human experiences as the result of a natural experiment). For example, the application of tight (loose) monetary policy in tropical countries will not necessarily result in levels in consumption per capita as measured in temperate climates with similar policies. The same can be estimated for agricultural policies, educational policies, macroeconomic policies and general economic approaches. Likewise, the incremental influence of ethnic, religious, language or cultural differences on social behaviors can be measured (or be identified as confounding or irrelevant) using the proposed framework or similar approaches incorporating physioeconomic variables. Again, by focusing on filtered measures we can identify "relatively successful policies" which are more useful than "absolutely successful policies" which can be inappropriate or misleading.

Since climate (and other physioeconomic factors) substantially contribute to human illness (e.g. malaria) and economic poverty (e.g. due to floods or droughts), efforts might be better focused on approaches to directly combat these deleterious effects (as opposed to emphasizing or, worse, blaming confounding factors such as race or culture). Resources may be better utilized for education, for example, on pre-natal care or nutrition; malnutrition being more critical in many countries than caloric intake which appears low compared to temperate climate standards. Innovation and discovery, in the past, has demonstrated that the parameters of the model can and do change over time. Care must be taken not to interpret strong climatic effects (high explained variances) as indicating that countries will remain underdeveloped. Absolute levels of behavior have shifted over time for all countries despite physioeconomic factors playing a role in affecting variances.

Finally, by explicitly reporting noneconomic dimensions in Chapters 3 to 9 (which are presented in the order of the physioeconomic hierarchy), this book responds to calls to expand the use of non-traditional variables in comparative studies. For example, early neoclassical theories of growth suggest that economic development across countries will ultimately converge since developed economies will grow slower than lesser developed economies due to diminishing returns to reproducible capital. Weak empirical support for neoclassical models has lead to the emergence of endogenous growth models which assume constant returns to broadly defined reproducible capital. Following 18th century economic theories of national wealth, consumption, and growth, these models have historically assumed national production to be a function of capital, technology, land, and labor. More recently, both neoclassical and endogenous growth models have noted the importance of human capital, international trade, and machinery and equipment investment, among other factors, to explain cross-country differences in economic performance and growth. Across all such models, low or inconsistent explained variances across national groupings (OECD versus African countries) has lead to calls for greater inclusion of noneconomic variables. The physioeconomic variables presented later in this book will hopefully foster useful extensions of this research.

3

ECONOMICS ACROSS COUNTRIES

There are substantial variances in economic measures across the world's national cultures. This chapter provides comparative statistics for a variety of economic variables across countries. For a full discussion of the methodology used to generate these estimates, please refer to Chapter 1 which gives important caveats. This chapter first gives summary statistics of the variables reported: the number of countries for which each variable was available, weighted averages (by population) and simple averages; these averages can be used as benchmarks. Then a lengthy comparative table is presented which provides raw statistics across countries.

Most of the variables are self explanatory, though some merit commentary. All of the statistics should be considered as estimates which have undergone rounding and certain adjustments. Estimates cover macroeconomics (e.g. gross national product per capita, inflation rates, savings rates, currency convertibility), labor (percent of labor force not employed, and the percent of the population not in the labor force; employment by sector), infrastructure (roads, airports), communications (cable systems, television stations, AM/FM radio, satellite earth stations), ownership and consumption (newspaper circulation, consumer electronics, calories, sugar, energy, and electricity per capita). The estimate of "." signifies a missing value due to a lack of underlying data.

Summary Statistics:
Economic Resources

Characteristics	Number of Countries Covered	Weighted Average by Pop 1994	Simple Average	Simple Standard Deviation
Macroeconomics: GNP/capita	225	4398.83	6127.24	8208.47
: Saving rate	121	21.49	15.94	15.07
: Inflation rate	205	56.28	62.91	323.33
: Convert currency (1=yes)	192	0.74	0.64	0.48
Communist, former (1=yes)	222	0.32	0.16	0.37
Labor: Unemployment, %	188	10.45	12.46	11.79
: Nonemployment, %	207	66.79	65.60	12.04
: Agriculture, %	174	46.60	39.02	28.08
: Industry, %	145	26.40	30.45	15.28
: Services, %	120	28.30	34.69	17.62
: Unionization, %	160	27.57	23.88	23.76
Air Transportation: # of aircraft	188	552.23	79.30	604.71
: # aircraft/capita	188	2.88	9.53	33.12
: # of airports	207	1084.60	203.21	1036.20
Runways: Permanent Surface	202	384.62	55.19	342.90
: Large	201	6.71	1.12	4.85
: Medium	202	56.63	9.24	25.48
: Small	200	232.56	40.99	187.83
Roads: Total km	194	1039444.62	126023.76	516573.81
: Motorways km	215	10476.30	976.92	6264.83
: Highways total km	223	996836.40	108535.35	483947.58
: Paved km	189	289474.43	40790.88	131007.37
: Gravel km	147	447503.77	35917.98	154001.34
: Improved earth km	83	125261.90	21424.14	85921.88
: Unimproved earth km	106	47594.79	19868.46	46500.12
: Ownership car/1000 capita	188	77.05	105.30	157.42
Railways km	229	43247.53	5848.07	23836.44
Telecommunications: # AM stations	211	447.01	74.82	365.61
: # of cable systems	209	2.23	1.52	4.25
: # of TV stations	214	770.61	125.55	980.60
: # of FM stations	210	403.04	54.50	375.14
: # of SAT earth stations	220	6.45	2.03	4.38
: # of daily papers	192	871.91	56.17	244.29
: Television/1000 capita	206	148.43	175.48	187.86
: Radios/1000 population	195	268.71	356.32	329.43
: Telephones/1000 population	226	132.66	190.10	236.57
: Digital % 1993	96	43.80	68.99	31.08
: Main Lines/1000 population	183	113.37	161.93	191.05
: Cellular subs/capita	127	11.10	16.50	32.91
: Pagers/capita	39	20.27	29.47	52.62
Piped water, % dwellings	113	47.93	60.91	29.94
Food: Sugar/capita	143	138.98	207.03	132.31
: Protein 85 grm/day/capita	159	67.35	71.81	20.18
: Calories/capita/day	165	2620.71	2646.91	518.93
: Meat production/capita 1988	177	0.02	0.03	0.06
Energy: Consumption/capita	186	1631.34	2313.18	3518.71
: Electricity/capita	225	2095.27	2852.68	4022.39

Characteristics	Afghanistan	Albania	Algeria	American Samoa	Andorra	Angola	Anguilla	Antigua & Barbuda	Argentina	Armenia
Macroecon: GNP/capita	200	1250	2270	4420	15400	950	6800	6600	6800	4460
· Saving rate	13	36	37	7		28	5	8	23	
· Inflation rate			32			92		0	18	100
Convert currency (1=yes)	0	1	0	0	1	0			0	
Communist, former (1=yes)	1	1	0		0	1				1
Labor: Unemployment, %		9	25					5	7	8
· Nonemployment, %						19	5		67	
· Agriculture, %	74	55	86	12		73			12	54
· Industry, %	80	60	30	81	20	75	5	11	31	18
· Services, %		40	36		80	10	63	54	57	42
· Unionization, %			34		0	16		68	28	
Air Trans: # of aircraft	0	0	42	0		28			56	0
· # aircraft/cap	0			0		3			2	
· # of airports	41	12	141	4		309	3	2	1700	
Runways: Permanent Surf	9	5	53	2		30	1	1	137	
· Large	0		2	0					31	
· Medium	10	5	32	1		15			326	
· Small	18	5	65			54	0	0	378	
Roads: Total km	19000	16700	82000	350	220	72400	60	1170	211000	10200
· Motorways km	0	0	0			0				0
· Highways total km	21000	16700	80000	350	96	73800	60	240	208000	11300
· Paved km	2800	6700	60000	150		8580	60		47600	10500
· Gravel km	1650		20000			29400			39500	
· Improved earth km	16500	10000		200					101000	800
· Unimproved earth km	2					35900			20300	
· Ownership car/1000 cap	17	0.8	26		631	14		142	135	36
Railways km		614	4100			3190		32	34300	830
Telecom: # AM stations	5	13	26	1	1	17	3		171	
· # of cable systems	0			0	0		0			
· # of TV stations	1	1	18	1	1	6	0		231	
· # of FM stations	1	0	0			13	1			
· # of SAT earth stations	4		4	1		2	0			1
· # of daily papers	3	0	6	2					220	
· Television/1000 cap		83	73	176	149	6		290	219	45
· Radios/1000 pop	78	168	214	1320	175	19	900	256	540	113
· Telephones/1000 pop	2	16	42	182	474	5	129	95	134	172
· Digital % 93	0							100	46	
· Main Lines/1000 pop	2	16	42			5		6	143	187
· Cellular subs/cap			0.4							0.1
· Pagers/cap										
Piped water, % dwellings	25	72	35			35			75	
Food: Sugar/cap	26	164	215			70		60	208	
· Protein 85 grm/day/cap	64	83	72			45			106	
· Calories/cap/day	2290	2740	2690			1930		2090	3190	
· Meat prod/cap 88									0.1	0
Energy: Consumption/cap	232	1280	936	3210		89		1770	1900	
· Electricity/cap	69	1230	587	2130	2170	215	800	1450	1700	2660

Characteristics	Aruba	Australia	Austria	Azerbaijan	Bahamas	Bahrain	Bangla-desh	Barbados	Belarus	Belgium
Macroecon: GNP/capita	14000	17000	20200	3830	12200	7800	210	7000	6110	19200
Saving rate		21	25		6	39	5	12		14
Inflation rate	6	1	4	1350	1	2	7	6	1100	3
Convert currency (1=yes)	0	1	1	0	0	1	0		0	1
Communist, former (1=yes)	3	0	0	1		0		0	1	
Labor: Unemployment, %		10	5		6			18		9
Nonemployment, %		52	56	50	14	9	30	57	1	59
Agriculture, %		6	8	62	56	74	71	17	47	28
Industry, %		36	35	32	5	5	59	37	20	69
Services, %		58	57	26	25	85	11	32	42	70
Unionization, %		40	60		11	5	30	0		47
Air Trans: # of aircraft		150	25		38	27	15	1		5
# aircraft/cap		8	3	0	59	51	0.1	1		42
# of airports		481	55		30	3	16	1	47	24
Runways: Permanent Surf										
Large		237	20			2	12		20	
Medium		20	6		3	2		1		14
Small		268	4		26		4			3
Roads: Total km		853000	107000	30400	2400	2610	6240	1570	266000	128000
Motorways km		787	1450	0	0	0	0	0	0	1630
Highways total km		838000	95400	36700	2400	200	7240	1570	98200	103000
Paved km		244000	21800	31800	1350	200	3840	1480	66100	38000
Gravel km		228000	60800	0	1050			95	0	
Improved earth km		366000	12800							51000
Unimproved earth km				4900			3400		32100	
Ownership car/1000 cap		446	387	33	297	182	0.4	168	48	398
Railways km		40300	5830	2070			2840	0	5580	8410
Telecom: # AM stations		258	47		3	3	9	3		3
# of cable systems		134	21	151	3	3		3		5
# of TV stations		67	3	175	1	2	11	2		32
# of FM stations		10	33		2	3	6	2		39
# of SAT earth stations		3	475	98	3	3	2	1	216	2
# of daily papers		484	530		225	402	59	263	302	33
Television/1000 cap		1300	469	101	518	419	4	761		447
Radios/1000 pop		538	35	0	568	282	8	408	186	468
Telephones/1000 pop	152	500	500		100	100	19			516
Digital % 93		58	12	101	317	260	2	328	191	54
Main Lines/1000 pop		54	99	0	15	40	0	3	0.1	471
Cellular subs/cap		382	298		60	94		387		16
Pagers/cap		101	97		420		20	99		23
Piped water, % dwellings	93				78		41	3180		100
Food: Sugar/cap		54	12		2700		1920	0		293
Protein 85 grm/day/cap			99							105
Calories/cap/day	2930	3330	3420	0				1610		3850
Meat prod/cap 88		0.1	0.1				69	1770	0.1	0.1
Energy: Consumption/cap	3920	7210	4010		2580	15600	69	1610		5790
Electricity/cap	14900	8460	6400	3040	4050	6880	65	1770	3650	7010

Characteristics	Belize	Benin	Bermuda	Bhutan	Bolivia	Bosnia & Herzegov.	Botswana	Brazil	British Virgin Isl.	Brunei
Macroecon: GNP/capita	1970	430	24500	200	858	3200	2770	2680	10600	30000
..Saving rate	7	0.5	4	9	10		25	16		-5
..Inflation rate	2	1		0	10	1	15			-1
..Convert currency (1=yes)	0	1	0	0	1		1	0	0	0
Communist, former (1=yes)	0		0		1				0	
Labor: Unemployment, %	12		4		50	28	25	4		5
..Nonemployment, %	74	63	48	61	78	76	70	63	68	69
..Agriculture, %		60		93	47		59	31		
..Industry, %		38			19		23	27		2
..Services, %					34	45	18	42		4
..Unionization, %	12	75			13		16	23		14
Air Trans: # of aircraft	2	0	16	0	56	2	5	198		2
..# aircraft/cap	10	0	259	0			4			1
..# of airports	44	6	1	2	1110	45	100	3560	3	1
Runways: Permanent Surf	3	1	0	1	9		8	420		
..Large	0	0	1	0	2		0	22		0
..Medium	0	0	0	0			1			
..Small	2	4	1	2	146		27	550		0
Roads: Total km	2000	7420	0	2280	40900	21200	1350	1670000	106	2200
..Motorways km	0	0		0	0	0	0	5000		
..Highways total km	2710	5050	610	1300	38800	21200	11500	1450000		1090
..Paved km	500	920	210	418	1300	11400	1600	48000		370
..Gravel km	1600	2600	210	515	6700	8150	1700	1400000		720
..Improved earth km	300	1530		371	30800		5180			
..Unimproved earth km	310				5	1590	3040			
..Ownership car/1000 cap	85	8					14			539
Railways km		607	0	0	3670	1000	800	30100	0	16
Telecom: # AM stations	6	0	5	1	129	6	7	1220		4
..# of cable systems	0	2	3	0	0		0			0
..# of TV stations	5	2	2	0	43	2		112		
..# of FM stations		2	3	1	1		13	3		4
..# of SAT earth stations	1	1	2	0	15					2
..# of daily papers	0	0		0			1	293		
..Television/1000 cap	165	5	709	0	98		12	204	192	335
..Radios/1000 pop	506	78	1180	9	575	108	119	386	462	229
..Telephones/1000 pop	150		836	12	29		37	96	273	267
..Digital % 93	100			66			100	28		78
..Main Lines/1000 pop	157	5	676	2	27	77	43	105		209
..Cellular subs/cap		61	73		0.5			1		35
..Pagers/cap		4								
Piped water, % dwellings	28	61			35		99	55		
Food: Sugar/cap	303	25	225		177		268	377		240
..Protein 85 grm/day/cap	69	50	94		56		61	61		76
..Calories/cap/day	2580	2190	2550	2030	2130		2230	2640		2850
..Meat prod/cap 88					0					
Energy: Consumption/cap	783	50	6350	32	370	1730	425	791	1770	15600
..Electricity/cap	525	39	8150	973	280		834	1590	2800	4120

Characteristics	Bulgaria	Burkina Faso	Burma	Burundi	Cambodia	Cameroon	Canada	Cape Verde	Cayman Islands	Central Afric. Rep.
Macroecon: GNP/capita	3800	350	863	210	280	1160	20800	890	23000	440
: Saving rate	80	-2	19	5	96	20	24	8	8	-9
: Inflation rate		5		5		-2		14		6
: Convert currency (1=yes)	1	1	0	0	0	1	1	0	0	1
: Communist, former (1=yes)	1	0	0	0	1	0	0			
Labor: Unemployment, %		16	10	68	67	25	10	25		30
: Nonemployment, %	11	66	64	93	74	66	53	75	7	76
: Agriculture, %	52	82	65			74	4		74	72
: Industry, %	33		25			11	52			
: Services, %	47	1	10		16	15	44	3	2	1
: Unionization, %	86	2	59	6	5	45	31	7	64	2
Air Trans: # of aircraft	10	0.2	17	1		0.4	636	6	3	0.6
: # aircraft/cap	380	48	0.4		16	56	23	6		66
: # of airports	120	2	85	1	5	1	1420		2	66
Runways: Permanent Surf			27				455	6	0	4
: Large	20	2	3	1	2	5	4	1	2	0
: Medium	200	8	38		4	21	30	2	1	2
: Small	266	13100					338	2250	160	22
Roads: Total km	37000		23500	6290	13400	52200	884000		160	24400
: Motorways km		16500		5900	0		884000			
: Highways total km	36900	1300	27000	400	13400	65000	713000			22000
: Paved km	33500		3200	2500	2620	2680				458
: Gravel km		7400	17000	3000	7110	32300				
: Improved earth km	3370	7800					171000	5		10500
: Unimproved earth km	0.8	1	6100	3	3620	30000	493	0	0	11000
: Ownership car/1000 cap	4300	621	2		581	6	194000		2	15
Railways km	20	2	4250	2		1050	900	2	1	0
Telecom: # AM stations		0	0	0	0	10	5	1	0	1
: # of cable systems	29	2	1	1	1	1	53	2	1	0
: # of TV stations	15	1	1	2		1	29	1	0	1
: # of FM stations		3	1	1	0	1	5	6	1	1
: # of SAT earth stations	14	5	2	2	0	2	110	1	1	1
: # of daily papers	249	17	24	40	9	89	626	14	184	3
: Television/1000 cap	230	2	2	3	131	6	761	150	947	57
: Radios/1000 pop	293	92	2		3	6	780	162	406	5
: Telephones/1000 pop	290	3		4	1	6	636	100		100
: Digital % 93	0.7			0.1	0.4	0	58	41		2
: Main Lines/1000 pop	80	24	13	23	5	30	32	243		8
: Cellular subs/cap	375	34	5	72	51	26	100	66		44
: Pagers/cap	106	63	70	2270	2170	47	300	2730		1940
Piped water, % dwellings	3630	2050	2590			2040	96			0
Food: Sugar/cap	0.1		0	0	27	0	3420	0	4920	47
: Protein 85 grm/day/cap	5050	29	62	20		254	0.1	103	8200	33
: Calories/cap/day	5530	16	58	24	10	225	10900	97		
: Meat prod/cap 88							18300			
Energy: Consumption/cap										
: Electricity/cap										

Characteristics	Chad	Chile	China	Christmas Island	Cocos (Keel.) Isl.	Colombia	Comoros	Congo	Cook Island	Costa Rica
Macroecon: GNP/capita	229	2550	417			1500	540	1070	2200	2000
: Saving rate	-24	15	28			23	3	31	8	15
: Inflation rate	2	1	6			27	-1	-5		29
: Convert currency (1=yes)	1	0	1			1		1	0	1
: Communist, former (1=yes)	0	0	1			0		0		0
Labor: Unemployment, %		6	2				16			
: Nonemployment, %	66	66	53			65	69	97		73
: Agriculture, %	85	19	60			30	80	75		27
: Industry, %		36	30			24		20		35
: Services, %		45	10			46		5	68	38
: Unionization, %	20	13	65			8		20		15
Air Trans: # of aircraft		29	284	0		83	1	4		11
: # aircraft/cap	0.5	2	0.2	0	0	2	2	2	0	3
: # of airports	71	390	330	1	1	1170	4	46	6	164
Runways: Permanent Surf		48	260	0	1	70	4	0	1	28
: Large	0	0	10	0	0	8		1		1
: Medium	4	12	90			191		17		
: Small	25	58	200	1	1		3		4	10
Roads: Total km	40000	79200	1100000			129000	750	8310	187	35600
: Motorways km	0	3460	0				0	0		663
: Highways total km	31300	79000	1030000			75500	750	12000	187	15400
: Paved km	32	9910	170000			9350	210	560	35	7030
: Gravel km	7300	33100	648000			66100	540	850	35	7010
: Improved earth km		36000						5350	84	
: Unimproved earth km	24000		211000					5200		1360
: Ownership car/1000 cap	2	50	1			33	2	11	33	50
Railways km	0	7980	54000	0	0	2960		799		950
Telecom: # AM stations	6	159	274			413	2	4	0	71
: # of cable systems	0							0	2	
: # of TV stations	1	131	202		1	33	1	4	0	18
: # of FM stations	1							1		
: # of SAT earth stations	1	2	6			2		1		0
: # of daily papers	1	33	1780			32		5	1	1
: Television/1000 cap		201	27	1250	1330	108	7			136
: Radios/1000 pop	26	304	69		167	141	109	61	588	86
: Telephones/1000 pop	2	112	17			108	4	12	59	143
: Digital % 93	15		21						9	51
: Main Lines/1000 pop	0.9	124	0.6			100		9		136
: Cellular subs/cap		7				0.6				2
: Pagers/cap			8							
Piped water, % dwellings	41	70	48			54	44	97		88
Food: Sugar/cap		287				258				440
: Protein 85 grm/day/cap	53		62			56	40	51		67
: Calories/cap/day	1660	2570	2630			2550	2110	2600		2780
: Meat prod/cap 88	0	0	0							0
Energy: Consumption/cap	18	1210	819			773	47	377	556	552
: Electricity/cap	14	1330	488	17800	3370	1200	32	163	1170	1170

Characteristics	Croatia	Cuba	Cyprus	Czech Republic	Denmark	Djibouti	Dominica	Dominican Republic	Ecuador	Egypt
Macroecon: GNP/capita	6930	2460	8620	7300	24400	1030	2200	1120	1100	730
: Saving rate			22						19	17
: Inflation rate	123		26	2	2	3	6	13	60	16
: Convert currency (1=yes)	0	0	1	1	1	1			1	0
Communist, former (1=yes)	1	1	0	1	0					0
Labor: Unemployment, %	17	6	2	3	10	40	10	30	8	22
: Nonemployment, %	69	67	61	48		68	68	49	75	73
: Agriculture, %	16	20	23	12	5		37	18	34	34
: Industry, %	37	50	38	37	27		30	33	27	20
: Services, %		30	19	51	67		25	12	39	46
: Unionization, %		81	56	8	65			23	15	16
Air Trans: # of aircraft		88	11		69	1	2		23	50
: # aircraft/cap	8		15		13					0.9
: # of airports		189	14	8	121	13	2	36	143	92
Runways: Permanent Surf	7	73	12		27	2	1	3	43	66
: Large		3	0		9	2		1	1	4
: Medium		12	7		6				6	44
: Small		18	3						23	24
Roads: Total km	27400	34000	10100	55500	70900	3070	750	12000	37600	51900
: Motorways km	302	575		366	650					
: Highways total km	32100	26500	10800	55900	66500	2900	750	12000	28000	51900
: Paved km	23300	14500	5170		64600	280	370	5800	3600	17900
: Gravel km	8440	12000	5610		1930	2620	380	5600	17400	12500
: Improved earth km	0									13500
: Unimproved earth km	327							600	7000	18000
: Ownership car/1000 cap	180	23	233	245	313	18	84	21	18	19
Railways km	2560	14500	0	9440	523	99		1700	965	5110
Telecom: # AM stations	14	150	11		3	2	3	120	272	39
: # of cable systems								1	3	5
: # of TV stations	12	58	1	9	19	1	1	18	1	41
: # of FM stations	8	5	3		50	1	2		36	6
: # of SAT earth stations	0	1	1		2	2		1		4
: # of daily papers	9	4	8		49			12		17
: Television/1000 cap	221	203	141	309	528	55	49	92	82	98
: Radios/1000 pop		315	616	314	392	70	513	201	356	174
: Telephones/1000 pop	229	52	448		856	23	195	78	57	46
: Digital % 93			64		46	100	100	100	66	47
: Main Lines/1000 pop	217	33	459	218	623	18	184	82	59	
: Cellular subs/cap	5	0.1	27	2	87			2	0.5	0.3
: Pagers/cap			9		14					
Piped water,% dwellings		59	100		97	188		30	45	60
Food: Sugar/cap		510	218		284		65	266	233	233
: Protein 85 grm/day/cap		79			95			53	48	81
: Calories/cap/day		3110	3180		3510		2650	2460	2060	3310
: Meat prod/cap 88			0.1		0.3	0				0
Energy: Consumption/cap	1760	1530	2560	5990	4410	445	366	373	662	739
: Electricity/cap		1390	2430		6280	496	390	768	558	705

Characteristics	El Salvador	Equatorial Guinea	Eritrea	Estonia	Ethiopia	Falkland Islands	Faroe Islands	Fiji	Finland	France
Macroecon: GNP/capita	1190	393	120	6410	130	50000	14000	1900	26000	20400
: Saving rate	4	-0.3	12	3	4	7	2	18	24	18
: Inflation rate	12	1	10	1	8			6	2	2
: Convert currency (1=yes)	1	0		1	0	0	0	1	1	1
Communist, former (1=yes)	0			1	0			0	0	
Labor: Unemployment, %	9						6	6	20	11
: Nonemployment, %	69			50	66			68	50	58
: Agriculture, %	40	56		20	80	52	6	44		9
: Industry, %	31			42					43	45
: Services, %	29	50				36	63		48	46
: Unionization, %	15	0						19	80	20
Air Trans: # of aircraft	7	3		1	25	0	0	2	42	195
: # aircraft/cap	1				0.5	0	0	3		8
: # of airports	107	3		3	123	5	1	25	159	472
Runways: Permanent Surf	5	2				2	1	2	58	251
: Large	0	0			1	0		0	0	3
: Medium	0	1			13	1		1	23	36
: Small	4	1			38	0	1	2	22	136
Roads: Total km	12300	2630	3850	30200	39500	510	200	4560	134000	805000
: Motorways km	306								249	6680
: Highways total km	10000	2760		30300	44300	510	200	3300	103000	1555000
: Paved km	1500		807	29200	3650	30		1590	35000	803000
: Gravel km	4100		840		9650	80		1290	38000	
: Improved earth km	4400		402	0	3000					
: Unimproved earth km			1800	1100	28000	400		420		750000
: Ownership car/1000 cap	29	13	0.5	125	1			47	385	421
Railways km	602	0	307	1030	835			620	5900	34500
Telecom: # AM stations	77	2		1	4	2	1	0	6	41
: # of cable systems	0	0			0				1	24
: # of TV stations	5	1		3	1	0	3	0	235	846
: # of FM stations	0	0			0	0	3	1	105	800
: # of SAT earth stations	5				1	3	0	1		4
: # of daily papers					3	1		2	103	82
: Television/1000 cap	87	9		158	2			32	488	400
: Radios/1000 pop	412	378		380	80	789	378	597	987	859
: Telephones/1000 pop	33	7	5	238	3	211	547	99	571	693
: Digital % 93	66			5	39			96	66	86
: Main Lines/1000 pop	33	4		252	3		529		574	567
: Cellular subs/cap	0.5		0.5	9			52		124	17
: Pagers/cap										7
Piped water, % dwellings	35	4			85				95	100
Food: Sugar/cap	234				25			380	327	293
: Protein 85 grm/day/cap	52				55			64	96	111
: Calories/cap/day	2150				1660			2900	3080	3270
: Meat prod/cap 88	0			0.1	0	0.5		0	0.1	0.1
Energy: Consumption/cap	238	154			24	9000	6060	481	5840	3920
: Electricity/cap	417	49		14400	17	8080	5890	598	12500	7300

Characteristics	French Guiana	French Polynesia	Gabon	Gambia	Gaza Strip	Georgia	Germany	Ghana	Gibraltar	Greece
Macroecon: GNP/capita	4390	7030	4500	325	590	4530	22300	425	4600	8200
Saving rate			50	-8			24	2		19
Inflation rate	4	3	2	14	9			18	4	16
Convert currency (1=yes)			1	0			1	1		1
Communist, former (1=yes)	0	0	0	0	0	1	0	0	0	0
Labor: Unemployment, %	14	15			20		5	0.5		9
Nonemployment, %	81	65					54	78	53	64
Agriculture, %			90	57		48	6	55		28
Industry, %			65	75		25	41	20		29
Services, %			35	18		31	53	25		43
Unionization, %	7	6	32	30			47	13	40	15
Air Trans: # of aircraft	0	28	15	4	1		239	8	1	39
# aircraft/cap	0	43	12	4				0.5		4
# of airports	4	23	70	1			462	10	1	77
Runways: Permanent Surf	0	0	0	0	0		242	5	1	77
Large		2	0	1	0		4	1	1	0
Medium	1	2	2		0		40	7		19
Small	1		2		0		55			23
Roads: Total km	1100	600	7470	2390	0	35100	621000	28300	50	38900
Motorways km	680	600					8820			91
Highways total km	680		7500	3080		33900	466000	32300	50	38900
Paved km	510		560	431		29500		6080	50	16600
Gravel km			960	501				26200		13700
Improved earth km	170		5980				374			5630
Unimproved earth km				2150		4400				3540
Ownership car/1000 cap			14	6		78		4	1000	172
Railways km			650			1570	42000	953		2480
Telecom: # AM stations	5	5		3	0		80	4		29
# of cable systems	0	0	0	0	0		6		0	8
# of TV stations	9	6	0	0	0		225	4	4	
# of FM stations	7	2	3	0	0		470	1	6	361
# of SAT earth stations	1	1	6	2	0	149	15	1	1	17
# of daily papers			3	1			400	3		138
Television/1000 cap	158	156	36	35		96	552		241	225
Radios/1000 pop	789	503	91	129			401	185	1170	406
Telephones/1000 pop	327	229	26	17		11	575	6	313	474
Digital % 93		100		97			98		97	
Main Lines/1000 pop	494	236	28	17		97	293	3	501	485
Cellular subs/cap			0.5	0.4			0.1	0.2		16
Pagers/cap										3
Piped water, % dwellings	93	90						41		80
Food: Sugar/cap		75	119	452			293	38		293
Protein 85 grm/day/cap			57	60			101			114
Calories/cap/day	2750	2900	2490	2360			3480	1730		3690
Meat prod/cap 88	0									
Energy: Consumption/cap	2610	1440	719	104		2590	5390	115	600	3110
Electricity/cap	2690	1400	815	72			7090	322	6400	3430

Characteristics	Greenland	Grenada	Guade-loupe	Guam	Guatemala	Guernsey	Guinea	Guinea-Bissau	Guyana	Haiti
Macroecon: GNP/capita	9000	3000	4700	14300	1300		480	219	397	404
..Saving rate		3			10		8	-11	4	0.1
..Inflation rate	2	3	4	4	33	7	23	50	56	15
..Convert currency (1=yes)		1					0			
..Communist, former (1=yes)						0	0	0	0	0
Labor: Unemployment, %	0	30	0	0	13			17	15	5
..Nonemployment, %	9	59	31	3	75		62	58	67	67
..Agriculture, %		33	71	68	60		82	90	34	66
..Industry, %					26				43	9
..Services, %					14				21	25
..Unionization, %									34	
Air Trans: # of aircraft	35	31	11	13			100	2		1
..# aircraft/cap	11	20	2		0.8		10	2	4	12
..# of airports			5		448	1	15	34	54	2
Runways: Permanent Surf										
..Large	5		9	0	11	0	4			13
..Medium	2	3	8	0	3	0	0	0	5	
..Small	2	2	1	5	19	1	3	1	13	3
Roads: Total km	80	1130	2100	674	13200		30100	3500	7670	4000
..Motorways km	80			674						0
..Highways total km		1000	1940		26400		30100	3220	7670	4000
..Paved km		600	1940		2870		1150	2700	550	950
..Gravel km		300	1600		11400		13000		5000	900
..Improved earth km		100	340						1530	2150
..Unimproved earth km					12100		16000	520	590	
..Ownership car/1000 cap	0	122			27		3	4	138	4
Railways km	0				884		1040			40
Telecom: # AM stations	5	0	2	3	91	1	1	0	3	33
..# of cable systems	2	0	0	0		1		2		
..# of TV stations	4	1	9	3	25	1	1	1	3	
..# of FM stations	7	0	8	2		0	1	3		4
..# of SAT earth stations	1	0	1		25	0	1	0	3	
..# of daily papers		0	1		8	1	1	1	1	5
..Television/1000 cap	85	319	116	672	45		5		31	5
..Radios/1000 pop	365	422	119	1210	45		28	32	450	23
..Telephones/1000 pop	327	239	174	471	25		3	0.8	46	9
..Digital % 93										
..Main Lines/1000 pop	333	100		486	25		2	7	89	8
..Cellular subs/cap		200		18	0.5				48	
..Pagers/cap		4							2	
Piped water, % dwellings			29		30					
Food: Sugar/cap					296		72	32	309	94
..Protein 85 grm/day/cap		61	92		60		40	46	58	45
..Calories/cap/day		2410	2670		2300		1780	2130	2460	1900
..Meat prod/cap 88					0			0		0
Energy: Consumption/cap	3960	581	1430	5800	197		88	91	392	52
..Electricity/cap	3450	580	2000	15900	240	8320	82	17	512	75

Characteristics	Honduras	Hong Kong	Hungary	Iceland	India	Indonesia	Iran	Iraq	Ireland	Isle of Man
Macroecon: GNP/capita	1090	14600	5380	23600	369	680	6150	2300	12000	7500
Saving rate	8	26	26	24	22	20	39		15	7
Inflation rate	28	7	22	4	9	8	23		3	
Convert currency (1=yes)	1	1	1	1	1	1	0	0	1	0
Communist, former (1=yes)	0	0	1	0	0	0	0	0	0	0
Labor: Unemployment,%	15	2	15		0	3	25	5	15	1
Nonemployment,%	77	53	49	53	20	66	76	78	62	63
Agriculture,%	62	1	19		67	56	33	30	15	
Industry,%	18	60	48		19	23	27	22	28	
Services,%	20	39	33	55	14	21	40	48	57	
Unionization, %	40	16	55	60				10	58	
Air Trans: # of aircraft	6	16	28	20	93	216	48	34	23	
# aircraft/cap		3	3	71	0.1		0.8	2		1
# of airports	171	2	90	94	341	437	214	113	36	1
Runways: Permanent Surf	8	2	20	4	203	114	81	73	17	0
Large		0				12	16	8		
Medium	4	1	10	1	59	64	16	52	2	
Small	12		15	12	87		71	12	6	1
Roads: Total km	11400	1480	29800	11400	2100000	214000	139000	2550	92300	640
Motorways km	0	0	351	0	34100		490	0	8	
Highways total km	8950	1480	130000	12300	1970000	120000	140000	34700	92300	640
Paved km	1700	794	27000	166	960000		42700	17500	87400	
Gravel km		306	2330	1280	1010000		46900		4870	
Improved earth km	5000		412				49400	5500		
Unimproved earth km	2250			10900			1200	11700		
Ownership car/1000 cap		40	185	464	3	7	35	34	223	36
Railways km	870	78	7770	0	61900	6840	4730	2240	1950	
Telecom: # AM stations	176	6	32	19	96	618	77	16	9	1
# of cable systems	0	1					0			
# of TV stations	28	4	41	13	274	9	28	13	86	4
# of FM stations	2	6	15	30	4	38	3	4	45	4
# of SAT earth stations	4	3	7	1	3	2	3			
# of daily papers	4	41		6	2280	97	17	4		
Television/1000 cap	70	260	409	421	27	55	66	68	271	
Radios/1000 pop	49	514	540	586	62	140	178	186	456	323
Telephones/1000 pop	22	100	180	542	9	11	65	56	343	
Digital % 93	71	511	26	66	30	77	80		336	385
Main Lines/1000 pop	23	57	168	581	9	12		43	20	
Cellular subs/cap	0.1	164	6	73		0.4	0			
Pagers/cap		99		25					4	
Piped water, % dwellings	26	195	84	100	10	11	49	40	90	
Food: Sugar/cap	242		406	433	99	109	139	221	293	
Protein 85 grm/day/cap	52	85	102	127	54	53	86	81	106	
Calories/cap/day	2080	2780	3540	3150	2200	2510	3310	2990	3690	
Meat prod/cap 88	0		0.1	0.1			0		0.2	
Energy: Consumption/cap	179	2000	3700	5660	307	311	1650	1060	3630	
Electricity/cap	277	4900	3820	16600	319	228	886	1470	4160	2710

Characteristics	Israel	Italy	Ivory Coast	Jamaica	Japan	Jersey	Jordan	Kazakhstan	Kenya	Kiribati
Macroecon: GNP/capita	12100	18600	800	1500	26900		1620	3810	376	732
..Saving rate	2	19	17	6	32		6	84	14	6
..Inflation rate	11	7	1	61	2	8	7	0	1	1
..Convert currency (1=yes)	1	1	1	0	1	0	0	1	0	0
..Communist, former (1=yes)	0	0	0		0	0	0	1	0	0
Labor: Unemployment, %	10	11		15	2			0.4	16	3
..Nonemployment, %	74	59		58	49				65	90
..Agriculture, %	6	10	57	32	8		7	52	78	
..Industry, %	43	32	8	28	34		20	23	9	
..Services, %	51	58	7	40	58		20	32	13	
..Unionization, %	90	45	20	24	29		10		4	
Air Trans: # of aircraft	32	125	14	8	360	0	23		19	32
..# aircraft/cap	6				3		5		0.7	
..# of airports	51	137	45	36	163	1	19		249	21
Runways: Permanent Surf	26	91	7	13	131	1	14		21	4
..Large		2			2	0	1		2	0
..Medium	0	36	0	0	31	0	13		2	
..Small	6	39	3	2	51	1	0		46	5
Roads: Total km	13200	302000	55000	18200	1100000		5730	165000	54600	640
..Motorways km		6090	155		3900		0	0	0	0
..Highways total km	4750	294000	46600	18200	1110000		7500	189000	64600	640
..Paved km		261000	3600	12600	754000		5500	189000	7000	
..Gravel km		26900	32000	3200	358000		2000		4150	
..Improved earth km			11000	2400				80900	53400	
..Unimproved earth km		7010						43		
Railways km	159	19800	649	317	27300		619	14500	2390	
..Ownership car/1000 cap	565	438	15	25	283		46		16	0.8
Telecom: # AM stations	14	135	3	10	318	0	5		16	1
..# of cable systems	3	21	2	3	4	1			0	
..# of TV stations	20	83	13	8	12400	3	8		6	0
..# of FM stations	21	28	17	17	58	1	7	2	4	0
..# of SAT earth stations	3	10	2	2	5	0	5	6	2	1
..# of daily papers	22	99	2	2	125	0			5	0
..Television/000 cap	266	423	59	124	610		88		9	
..Radios/1000 pop	274	250	129	420	713		248	278	34	159
..Telephones/1000 pop	465	534	11	83	555		75	128	15	210
..Digital % 93		57	82	100						22
..Main Lines/1000 pop	314	458		83	514		96	136	10	
..Cellular subs/cap	13	35	0	6	23		1	0.1	0.1	
..Pagers/cap					64					
Piped water, % dwellings	94	92		35	98		34		32	
Food: Sugar/cap	416	293	100	398	171		294		143	68
..Protein 85 grm/day/cap	99	108	54	58	88		80		59	
..Calories/cap/day	3040	3490	2550	2580	2860		2970		2140	2940
..Meat prod/cap 88			0		0		0	0.1		
Energy: Consumption/cap	3040	3810	180	853	4000		999		106	152
..Electricity/cap	4440	4040	189	1080	6870		1060	4740	129	104

Characteristics	Kuwait	Kyrgyz-stan	Laos	Latvia	Lebanon	Lesotho	Liberia	Libya	Liechten-stein	Lithuania
Macroecon: GNP/capita	16400	3080	270	6930	2110	530	430	5800	31000	5970
: Saving rate	60		10	7		13	6	40		176
: Inflation rate	8	1500	1	1	100	13	6	8	5	1
Convert currency (1=yes)	1	0	1	1	0	1	0	0	1	1
Communist, former (1=yes)	0	1	1	1	0	0	0	0	0	1
Labor: Unemployment, %	1	2	19	6	50	0	43	2	0.1	0.5
: Agriculture, %	2	59	67	47	77	35	82	80	30	51
: Industry, %	70	33	85	16	11	63	82	18	4	18
: Services, %	2	28	6	41	79	40	82	31	54	42
: Unionization, %	53				38			51	41	
Air Trans: # of aircraft	3	0	0	0	19	0	2	28	0	
: # aircraft/cap	0	0.1	0	0.5	7	0.5	0.3	59	0	
: # of airports	9		57		9	28	66	12	0	
Runways: Permanent Surf	5		8		6	0	0	133		3
: Large	7		0		3		4	53		26
: Medium	4	1	1		2	2	5	9		1
: Small	0	144	14	419	7	2920	5410	28	250	
Roads: Total km	4210	28400	13900	58600	7190	2920	5410	32500	250	44200
: Motorways km	280	0	0	0	0	0	0	0	0	0
: Highways total km	3900	30300	27500	59500	7300	7220	10100	32500	13100	44200
: Paved km	3000	22600	1860	33000	6200	572	603	24000		35500
: Gravel km	900	0	7450	0	450	2340		8500		0
: Improved earth km					650	1810				
: Unimproved earth km		7700	18200	26500	175	2500	485	92	603	8700
: Ownership car/1000 cap	226	0.5	4	101	111	4	3	17	19	142
Railways km	0	370	0	2400	5	2	0	2		3030
Telecom: # of AM stations	3	1	0		3	3	5	12		13
: # of cable systems	1		1		13	0	4	3		
: # of TV stations	3	144	0	419	3	1	1	2	343	3
: # of FM stations	0	0.5	1		2	2	2	1	654	26
: # of SAT earth stations	1	83	2	311	40	3	18	91	846	1
: # of daily papers	7	87	5		327	28	185	211		
: Television/1000 cap	281	0	114	216	797	12	9	54		338
: Radios/1000 pop	306	0.1	20	3	120	7	2	54	99	240
: Telephones/1000 pop	201		2		127	66	45	257		346
: Digital % 93	82		0.1		2	2300	43	88		1
: Main Lines/1000 pop	167	3	11	0.1	287	0	2360	3610		
: Cellular subs/cap	48		62		82		0	0		
: Pagers/cap			2310	2160	3090		130	4290	5260	0.1
Piped water, % dwellings	58		0		0		334	4000		6610
Food: Sugar/cap	220		34		1450					
: Protein 85 grm/day/cap	92		219		1630					
: Calories/cap/day	3080									
: Meat prod/cap 88	0									
Energy: Consumption/cap	8830	0.1								
: Electricity/cap	10100	3								

Characteristics	Luxembourg	Macau	Macedonia	Madagascar	Malawi	Malaysia	Maldives	Mali	Malta	Marshall Islands
Macroecon: GNP/capita	28700	6700	3110	230	200	2960	620	285	7600	1500
..Saving rate	38	8		4	13	24		-4	26	
..Inflation rate	4		1	13		3	11	-6	3	1
..Convert currency (1=yes)	1	0	1	1	1	1	1	1	1	0
Communist, former (1=yes)	0	0	1	0	0	0	0	0	0	
Labor: Unemployment, %	1	2	20			5			4	90
..Nonemployment, %	55		75	63	96	62	72	74	65	
..Agriculture, %			8		43	22	80	72	2	
..Industry, %	42	2	40	90	23	40		12	24	
..Services, %	45	64			17	38		16	43	
..Unionization, %	56					9			40	
Air Trans: # of aircraft	13	0		4		53	0	0		17
..# aircraft/cap	3	0		0.6	0.5		1		19	4
..# of airports	3	0	5	148	48	115	4	35	1	0
Runways: Permanent Surf	2			30	6	33	2	8		0
..Large	1					1	2			0
..Medium				3	1	7		5	1	8
..Small				34	9	18	2	10	1	
Roads: Total km	5090	42	13900	34800	12200	40100		13300	1550	
..Motorways km	84		1150	0		0			0	
..Highways total km	5110	42	10600	40000	13100	29000		15700	1290	
..Paved km	5000	42	5090	4690	2360	19400		1670	1180	
..Gravel km	57		1400	811	251			3670	77	
..Improved earth km				34500	10500	4250		10400	35	
..Unimproved earth km										
..Ownership car/1000 cap	479		113	2	2	99	3	3	311	15
Railways km	271			960	789	2040	0	642	0	0
Telecom: # AM stations	2		5	17	10	28			8	
..# of cable systems	3									1
..# of TV stations	3			1		4	1	2	2	
..# of FM stations	3			3	1	33	1	2	4	1
..# of SAT earth stations						3	1	2		2
..# of daily papers	4		2			42	1	1	3	
..Television/1000 cap	430	294	189	20	2	144	24	39	741	16
..Radios/1000 pop	536	291		213	48	439	89	16	398	
..Telephones/1000 pop	559	100	170		6	153	47	2	510	
..Digital % 93	82						100		100	
..Main Lines/1000 pop	613	302	122	3	4	175	47	76	471	
..Cellular subs/cap	27	41				20		2	21	
..Pagers/cap						8				
Piped water, % dwellings	100	51		49	26	96		57	90	
Food: Sugar/cap		49		56	95		250	54	371	250
..Protein 85 grm/day/cap		62			68	61			87	
..Calories/cap/day	3710			2410	2370	2720	1870	2020	2880	
..Meat prod/cap 88										
Energy: Consumption/cap	12500	1060		39	35	1280	196	25	2050	
..Electricity/cap	13400	1810	3160	46	68	1280	125	26	3060	1580

Characteristics	Martinique	Maurita-nia	Mauritius	Mayotte	Mexico	Micronesia Federation	Moldova	Monaco	Mongolia	Montser-rat
Macroecon: GNP/capita	6000	555	2730		3660	980	3960	16000	1730	5800
: Saving rate		6	12		25		27		-1	9
: Inflation rate	4	10	5		10	1		1		
: Convert currency (1=yes)	0	0	1	0	0	0		0	0	0
Communist, former (1=yes)							1	0		
Labor: Unemployment, %	31	21					0.7		2	
: Nonemployment, %	74	79			71		52		32	3
: Agriculture, %		47	20		26		34		52	57
: Industry, %		14	70		30		21		10	
: Services, %		29	20		44					
: Unionization, %	11	6	35		35				25	30
Air Trans: # of aircraft	0	3	7	0	186			0	11	1
: # aircraft/cap				0	2					1
: # of airports	2	28	6	1	1820	6		1	81	
Runways: Permanent Surf	1	9	5	1	200	4		1	11	
: Large	0	0	2	1		0			4	0
: Medium	1	5	0	0	33	4			19	0
: Small	1	16	1	0	284				12	0
Roads: Total km	1800	7400	1820	1	237000	226	21100	50	3950	280
: Motorways km	1680	0	0		3170		0	0	0	
: Highways total km	1680	7530	1800		212000	39	20000		46700	280
: Paved km	1300	1690	1640	42	65000	39	13900		1000	200
: Gravel km	380	1040		42	30000		0			80
: Improved earth km			160	18	62000		6100			
: Unimproved earth km		4800	39		55000				45700	
Ownership car/1000 cap	0	6			69	0.5	48	706	0.8	0
Railways km	1	700	0		20400		1150	2	1780	8
Telecom: # AM stations	0	2	2	1	679	5		3	12	0
: # of cable systems	0	0	0			0				1
: # of TV stations	10	1	4	0	238	6		5	10	4
: # of FM stations	6	0	0	0		1	7	4	1	0
: # of SAT earth stations	2	3	1	0	5	4		0	1	
: # of daily papers			8		272	0			3	
: Television/1000 cap	128	23	215		127	60	126	786	56	500
: Radios/1000 cap	168	101	210	255	291		37	370	104	250
: Telephones/1000 pop	211	6	84	8	97	129	130	1660	32	
: Digital % 93		89	100		65	100			91	
: Main Lines/1000 pop		4	88		99	44			31	
: Cellular subs/cap			4		5		0.1		0.3	
Pagers/cap					2					
Piped water, % dwellings	35		33		49			100		
Food: Sugar/cap		266	278		357				173	
: Protein 85 grm/day/cap	85	96	63		82				93	
: Calories/cap/day	2780	2280	2740		3150				2830	
: Meat prod/cap 88		0	0						0.1	
Energy: Consumption/cap	1810	647	464		1740	396	0.1		1870	1230
: Electricity/cap	1720	65	694		1370		2540		1630	1010

Characteristics	Morocco	Mozam-bique	Namibia	Nauru	Nepal	Nether-lands	Netherlands Antilles	New Caledonia	New Zealand	Nicaragua
Macroecon: GNP/capita	1060	115	1300	18100	179	18300	8700	6000	14900	754
..Saving rate	10	3			9	21			21	1
..Inflation rate	6	39	12		9	2	4	4	2	432
..Convert currency (1=yes)	0	1	1		0	1	1		1	1
..Communist, former (1=yes)	0	0	0		0	0	0		0	
Labor: Unemployment,%	18	50	40		5	7	0	0	10	14
..Nonemployment, %	73	53	68		60	65	19	16	54	74
..Agriculture, %	45	85			91		51	72	11	44
..Industry, %	24	9				26			41	13
..Services, %	31	2				69			48	43
..Unionization, %	28	8	18			29	70	1	43	35
Air Trans: # of aircraft				1		98	8	6	40	9
..# aircraft/cap		0.4		0			44	29		2
..# of airports	75	195	137		37	28	7		118	228
Runways: Permanent Surf	26	27	21		5	19	6	1	34	11
..Large	2						0	0		
..Medium	13	5	4		1		2		2	2
..Small	27	26	63	6	8	11	2	2	43	12
Roads: Total km	59300	26100	42800	27	7080	118000	950	6340	93200	15100
..Motorways km			0			2050				384
..Highways total km	59200	26500	54500	27	7080	108000	950	6340	92600	25900
..Paved km	27700	4590	4080	21	2900	92500	300	634	49500	4000
..Gravel km	31500	829	2540		1660	15800	650		43100	2170
..Improved earth km				6						5430
..Unimproved earth km		21100	47900							14300
..Ownership car/1000 cap	39	3	68	159	0.8	371	0		372	12
Railways km	1890	3210	2360	4	52	2930			4380	347
Telecom: # AM stations	20	29	4	1	88	3	9	0	64	45
..# of cable systems	5			0	0		2	5	2	7
..# of TV stations	26	1	3	0	1	5	1	7	14	2
..# of FM stations	3			0	0	8	4	3		2
..# of SAT earth stations	11	4	40	1	1	12	2	1		3
..# of daily papers		5	5	0	59	4			35	
..Television/1000 cap	75	2			25	485	219	207	372	65
..Radios/1000 pop	172	21	133	750	4	793	673	566	890	278
..Telephones/1000 pop	43		36	213	88	625	168	236	717	16
..Digital % 93	37	4	49		5	93			96	
..Main Lines/1000 pop			78		5	530	9	260	466	15
..Cellular subs/cap	0.4		52			20			45	0.3
..Pagers/cap						27			17	
Piped water, % dwellings	72				66	100	87		99	45
Food: Sugar/cap	232	27	62		14	293	225	83	374	301
..Protein 85 grm/day/cap	78	28			52	97	93		110	62
..Calories/cap/day	2860	1610	1840		2050	3260	2930	2980	3410	2470
..Meat prod/cap 88					0.1	0.1		0.4	0.4	0
Energy: Consumption/cap	366	33		5900	24	6640	9790	4760	5050	280
..Electricity/cap	364	56	823	3320	35	5100	3600	7230	9140	361

Characteristics	Niger	Nigeria	Niue	Norfolk Island	North Korea	Northern Mariana Isl.	Norway	Oman	Pacific Isl. Trust	Pakistan
Macroecon: GNP/capita	310	314	1000		1390	11500	44000	6670	2260	410
: Saving rate	12	23					31	47		12
: Inflation rate	-8	45	10			7	1	-7		11
: Convert currency (1=yes)	1	1	0		0			1		0
: Communist, former (1=yes)	0	0			1		0	0		0
Labor: Unemployment, %		28					5			8
: Nonemployment, %		60					57	74		77
: Agriculture, %	47	54					41	60		53
: Industry, %	71	19					52	13		13
: Services, %	90	27					66	27		34
: Unionization, %		8					76	0		10
Air Trans: # of aircraft	0	57	1	0	0		18	19	0	40
: # aircraft/cap	0.2	0.5		0	1			11		0.3
: # of airports	29	76	1	1	58	6	103	134	20	112
Runways: Permanent Surf	8	33		0	48	3	64	6		75
: Large	0			1			0	1		
: Medium	2	15		0	17	0	12	73		31
: Small	13	22		0	28	1	16		2	43
Roads: Total km	40000	108000	123	80	23000	382	88000	24700		111000
: Motorways km	428	115		80	354	382	437			340
: Highways total km	40000	108000	123	53	30000		79500	26000		101000
: Paved km	3170	30000			450		38600	6000		40200
: Gravel km	10300	25400			29600		41000			23000
: Improved earth km										29000
: Unimproved earth km	3470	52600		27						9160
: Ownership car/1000 cap	5	4			11		403	104		6
Railways km		3510			4980		4220			12600
Telecom: # AM stations	15	35	1	0	18	0	46	2	0	19
: # of cable systems	0		0	1	0	2	4		1	0
: # of TV stations	18	28	0	0	11	0	54	7	0	29
: # of FM stations	5	17	1	0	0	1	493	3	2	8
: # of SAT earth stations	2	3	0	0	1	1		3	1	3
: # of daily papers	1		0	0	6	2	84		1	125
: Television/1000 cap	59	35			53		423	762	49	16
: Radios/1000 pop	49	29	300	1000	209		411	619	626	77
: Telephones/1000 pop	2	79	67	500	2		730	99	66	74
: Digital % 93	67	8					60	98		43
: Main Lines/1000 pop	1	3			2		568	103		16
: Cellular subs/cap		0.5					127	4		0.3
: Pagers/cap							32			0.2
Piped water, % dwellings	17	17					98			15
Food: Sugar/cap	22	23			41		298			144
: Protein 85 grm/day/cap	66	47			94		101			59
: Calories/cap/day	2350	2110			3200		3220			2240
: Meat prod/cap 88	0	0					0	0		0
Energy: Consumption/cap	60	207	333	3000	2810	732	7180	3430	638	265
: Electricity/cap	40	111	1510		2550		28200	3160	1370	343

Characteristics	Panama	Papua New Guinea	Paraguay	Peru	Philip-pines	Pitcairn Islands	Poland	Portugal	Puerto Rico	Qatar
Macroecon: GNP/capita	4410	972	1550	1430	860		4400	9000	6530	17000
:: Saving rate	19	5	19	10	24			4	1	3
:: Inflation rate	1	5	15	57			43	7		1
:: Convert currency (1=yes)	1	1	1	1	1		1	1		0
:: Communist, former (1=yes)		0	0	0	0	0	1			0
Labor: Unemployment, %	16	5	5	10	10		14	0	17	
:: Nonemployment, %	70	59	69	70	64		56	53	71	79
:: Agriculture, %	26	82	44	38	46		27	20	3	10
:: Industry, %	30	9	34	17	20		50	35	44	70
:: Services, %	44	9	22	45	34		23	45	53	20
:: Unionization, %	17			40	24		11	43	11	
Air Trans: # of aircraft	5	15	2	44	53	0	48	4	11	6
:: # aircraft/cap	2	4	9			0				4
:: # of airports	112	503	845	221	278		160	65	30	
Runways: Permanent Surf	39	18	7	36	72		85	36	19	1
:: Large	0	0	0	2	9	0	35	1	0	0
:: Medium	2	1	3	23		0	65	12	3	2
:: Small	15	39	66	43	53			8	5	
Roads: Total km	10100	19700	23600	69000	162000		363000	70200	9400	1500
:: Motorways km	545	0	700	2460	0	6	257	243	96	0
:: Highways total km	8530	19200	22200	69900	156000	6	300000	73700	13800	1500
:: Paved km	2750	640	1790	7460	29000		130000	61600	13800	1000
:: Gravel km	3270	11000	474		77000		24000			500
:: Improved earth km	2520			13500			100000	7960		
:: Unimproved earth km		7600	19700	48900	50000			4100		
:: Ownership car/1000 cap	57	4	35	17	7	0	137	225	96	226
:: Railways km	488		970	2100	592	1	26600	3580	50	0
Telecom: # AM stations	91	31	40	273	267	0	27	57		2
:: # of cable systems	1	3					6	6	9	2
:: # of TV stations	23	2	5	140	33	0	40	66		0
:: # of FM stations	0	2		0	55	0	27	66	63	3
:: # of SAT earth stations	2	1	1		3	0	1	4	60	3
:: # of daily papers	6		6	45	30		7	21		4
:: Television/1000 cap	222	2	48	95	41		292	176	300	514
:: Radios/1000 pop	160	16	80	164	45		247	171	750	459
:: Telephones/1000 pop	109	67	33	31	17	333	137	353	333	349
:: Digital % 93	53	16			36				100	
:: Main Lines/1000 pop	114	10	34	30	14		142	360	356	270
:: Cellular subs/cap	0.3	0.1	0.6	2	1		0.7	15	21	12
:: Pagers/cap					3			6	6	
Piped water, % dwellings	40		24	49	48		57	58	75	
Food: Sugar/cap	317	62	198	258	184		356	293		
:: Protein 85 grm/day/cap	60	45	79	58	53		102	91		
:: Calories/cap/day	2440	2180	2840	2190	2350		3300	3130		
:: Meat prod/cap 88	0	0	0.1				0.1	0		
Energy: Consumption/cap	600	294	229	505	295	5770	4530	1810	2980	22100
:: Electricity/cap	1190	477	518	674	402		4000	2880	4370	10200

Characteristics	Reunion	Romania	Russia	Rwanda	San Marino	Sao Tome E Principe	Saudi Arabia	Senegal	Serbia & Monten.	Seychel-les
Macroecon: GNP/capita	6000	3490	5990	322	20000	320	7050	805	3000	5590
...Saving rate						-20	65	-10		3
...Inflation rate	1	212	105	9	6	-25	5		0	1
Convert currency (1=yes)	0	0	1	1	0	0	1	1		0
Communist, former (1=yes)		1	1	0	0	0	0	0		0
Labor: Unemployment, %	35	4	3			10	0	4	25	9
...Nonemployment, %	74	53	47	54	74	79	70	68		61
...Agriculture, %		28	19	91			14	77	5	12
...Industry, %		34	39		4	2	31			19
...Services, %		38	42		81	2	55		40	32
...Unionization, %		59								
Air Trans: # of aircraft	3								5	
...# aircraft/cap	5									
...# of airports	2	165							40	
Runways: Permanent Surf		25								
...Large		0								
...Medium	1	15								2
...Small	1	15								
Roads: Total km	2800	72800	854000	13200	237	380	145000	14000	46000	302
...Motorways km	0	113	0	0		0			350	0
...Highways total km	2800	72800	879000	4890	104	300	74000	14000	46000	260
...Paved km	2200	36000	653000	460		200	35000	3780	26900	160
...Gravel km	600	27700	0	1730			39000		10400	
...Improved earth km		9100	227000							
...Unimproved earth km	0			2700				10200		
Ownership car/1000 cap			60		752		145	9		100
Railways km	0	11200	87100	0	0	0	886	1110	8700	0
Telecom: # AM stations	3	12		2		2	43	8	26	2
...# of cable systems			0				3	3	0	0
...# of TV stations	1	13	310				80	1	18	2
...# of FM stations	13	1	1050	1			13	1	9	
...# of SAT earth stations	1		4				7		1	
...# of daily papers		36	6	2				1	2	1
...Television/1000 cap	173	194	313		326		277	35	93	74
...Radios/1000 pop	230	143		52	500	250	288	70	65	359
...Telephones/1000 pop	327	118	166		680	24	152	74		209
...Digital % 93										
...Main Lines/1000 pop	349	121	171			21	125	8		
...Cellular subs/cap	10	0.1	0.1				2	0.1		
...Pagers/cap										
Piped water, % dwellings	33	82		11			47	88		23
Food: Sugar/cap								92		
...Protein 85 grm/day/cap	77	104		49		51	91	67		61
...Calories/cap/day	3010	3360		1880		2390	3030	2340		2260
...Meat prod/cap 88	0	0		0			0	0		
Energy: Consumption/cap	832	4490	6810	29		271	6360	176		1590
...Electricity/cap	1320	3490		26		126	2880	104	4	1230

Characteristics	Sierra Leone	Singapore	Slovakia	Slovenia	Solomon Islands	Somalia	South Africa	South Korea	Spain	Sri Lanka
Macroecon: GNP/capita	330	16500	6100	12400	780	170	2960	6650	13200	489
⋯Saving rate	-5	36	21	23	15		14	11	17	10
⋯Inflation rate	81	1	1	1	1		1	1	5	11
⋯Convert currency (1=yes)	1	1	1	1	1	0	0	0	1	1
Communist, former (1=yes)	0	0	1	1	0	0	0	0	0	0
Labor: Unemployment, %		2	18	13			30		18	14
⋯Nonemployment, %	70		53	60	93	77	72	62	100	63
⋯Agriculture, %	75	0	12	2	32	82	25	21	16	46
⋯Industry, %	15	48	33	46	18		39	27	28	27
⋯Services, %		61					36	52	56	27
⋯Unionization, %	35	38					17	23	10	30
Air Trans: # of aircraft	0	16				0.1	90	93	210	0.4
⋯# aircraft/cap		38		3	33	53	901	105	105	8
⋯# of airports	12	13	18	3		7	132	60	60	14
Runways: Permanent Surf										
⋯Large	4	10	53		2	2	10	23	4	12
⋯Medium	0	2	12			6	224	16	22	
⋯Small	1	4	33	3	3	15			25	7
Roads: Total km	7450	2730	17700	14500	2150	21800	181000	55800	158000	75300
⋯Motorways km		102	191	81			2040	1550	2290	
⋯Highways total km	7400	2600	17700	14600	2100	15200	188000	62900	151000	75700
⋯Paved km	1150			10500	300	2340	54000		63000	27600
⋯Gravel km	490			4030	290	2880	134000		85400	32900
⋯Improved earth km	5760			0	980	10000				14700
⋯Unimproved earth km										
Railways km	84		3670	281			95	49	294	10
⋯Ownership car/1000 cap	8	105		1200	3	1	20900	6460	15400	1950
Telecom: # AM stations	1	32		6	4	2	14	79	190	12
⋯# of cable systems	0	13		7	0	1		22	22	
⋯# of TV stations	1	3	3	5	0	1	67	256	100	5
⋯# of FM stations	1	2	2	3	0	1	286	46	406	5
⋯# of SAT earth stations	1	4	2	5	0	1		5		
⋯# of daily papers		2	9	3	1	4	19	65	102	16
⋯Television/1000 cap	10	9		266	0	14	101	207	389	32
⋯Radios/1000 pop	208	372			95	30	282	451	286	117
⋯Telephones/1000 pop	5	249	2		19	2	146	392	396	11
⋯Digital % 93		457	179	330	100				41	
⋯Main Lines/1000 pop	91	95	192	29	18	3	99	396	392	10
⋯Cellular subs/cap	4	489	1	285			0.5	12	10	0.3
⋯Pagers/cap		59		8				136	4	
Piped water, % dwellings	40	260		6	55	51	90	95	91	18
Food: Sugar/cap	30	48				66	232	131	293	128
⋯Protein 85 grm/day/cap	41	532					75	78	97	48
⋯Calories/cap/day	1870	2850			2160	2090	2940	2880	3360	2440
⋯Meat prod/cap 88	0	0						0	0.1	0
Energy: Consumption/cap	76	4980	4510		244	58	2640	2200	2490	114
⋯Electricity/cap	50	5450		6	95	41	4140	2670	3860	179

Characteristics	St. Helena	St. Kitts & Nevis	St. Lucia	St. Pierre & Miquelon	St. Vincent & Grenad.	Sudan	Suriname	Swaziland	Sweden	Switzerland
Macroecon: GNP/capita		4200	2980	9500	1850	440	3880	1200	25100	33200
: Saving rate	-1	6	4	0	6	3	10	-1	18	28
: Inflation rate		0	0	10	0	200	30	13	2	3
: Convert currency (1=yes)	0	0	0		0	0	1	1	1	1
Communist, former (1=yes)						0	0		0	0
Labor: Unemployment, %		8	16			30	17	0	3	3
: Nonemployment, %		53	70	56	40	76	76	76	47	52
: Agriculture, %			36		41	78	30	53	3	6
: Industry, %			20		30	9	15	9	28	33
: Services, %			18			13	55	9	69	61
: Unionization, %		34	20		10	0	47	10	80	20
Air Trans: # of aircraft		0	0	0	0	18	2	4	115	89
: # aircraft/cap		0	0	0	0	0.7		5	13	13
: # of airports	1	2	2	2	6	72	46	23	254	66
Runways: Permanent Surf	1	2	2	2	4	8	6	1	139	42
: Large	0	1	1	0	0	5	1	1	0	2
: Medium	1			1	1	31	2		10	5
: Small									94	18
Roads: Total km	87	300	970	120	1110	20000	9130	2740	134000	71100
: Motorways km									936	1520
: Highways total km	107	300	760	120	1000	20000	8300	2850	97400	62100
: Paved km	87	125	500	60	300	1600	500	510	51900	62100
: Gravel km		125			400	3700	5400	1230	20700	
: Improved earth km			260		300	2300	2400	1110		
: Unimproved earth km						12400			24800	
Ownership car/1000 cap	20	50	43		50	7	92	32	419	430
Railways km		58				5110	162	334	11600	5190
Telecom: # AM stations	0	2	4	0	2	11	5	7	5	7
: # of cable systems		0	0		0	0	0	0	5	0
: # of TV stations	0	4	0	1	1	3	6	10		18
: # of FM stations		0	1	0	0	2	14	6	880	265
: # of SAT earth stations	2	0	1	0	0	2	2	1	360	1
: # of daily papers			0	3				3	2	100
: Television/1000 cap		182	18	567	79	61	133	16	654	599
: Radios/1000 pop	237	467	733	667	539	243	603	154	858	367
: Telephones/1000 pop	114	79	156	533	149	4	116	29	940	882
: Digital % 93			100		100		23		67	
: Main Lines/1000 pop		282	148		134	3	111	50	726	683
: Cellular subs/cap			2		1		4	22	133	50
: Pagers/cap									27	13
Piped water, % dwellings		65	69		67	65	28		99	100
Food: Sugar/cap						135	281	486	333	326
: Protein 85 grm/day/cap						62	67	60	99	96
: Calories/cap/day		2350	2500		2780	2070	2710	2550	3050	3430
: Meat prod/cap 88			0		0	0	0		0.1	0.1
Energy: Consumption/cap	143	705	527	7000	357	64	1860	167	5070	3660
: Electricity/cap	1360	906	717	3950	421	42	3470	189	16900	8140

Characteristics	Syrian Arab Rep.	Taiwan	Tajikistan	Tanzania	Thailand	Togo	Tokelau	Tonga	Trinidad & Tobago	Tunisia
Macroecon: GNP/capita	2300	10000	2430	260	1940	421	800	1500	3800	1820
: Saving rate	4	3		12	20	14			37	24
: Inflation rate	40		100	19	6			11	17	6
: Convert currency (1=yes)	0	1	0	0	1	1		1	0	1
Communist, former (1=yes)	0	0	1	0	0	0		0	0	0
Labor: Unemployment, %	6	2		0	4	2			22	15
: Nonemployment, %	83	62	40	25	46	68		13	64	74
: Agriculture, %	32	17	66	97	59	75		75	11	26
: Industry, %	29	41	43	90	24	20		45	33	34
: Services, %	39	42	22		17				56	40
: Unionization, %	35	35		15				27	22	20
Air Trans: # of aircraft	35	0			41				14	19
: # aircraft/cap		40		0.3	0.7	0.8			11	1
: # of airports	104	36		104	115	9		6	6	29
Runways: Permanent Surf	24			12	50	9		1	2	13
: Large		16			1	2			2	0
: Medium	21	8		3	13	2		1	1	7
: Small	3			43	28	2				7
Roads: Total km	29700	20000	28500	82000	73200	7570		433	7900	29200
: Motorways km	712			0				0	50	
: Highways total km	28000	20000	29900	81900	44500	6460		198	8000	17700
: Paved km	22000	17100	24400	3600	28000	1760			4000	9100
: Gravel km	3000	2370		5600					1000	
: Improved earth km	3000	575		72700	5130	4700			3000	8600
: Unimproved earth km			8500			13				
: Ownership car/1000 cap	9	112	0.8		18		0	14	188	39
Railways km	2130	4600	480	3780	3850	520				2160
Telecom: # AM stations	9	91		12	200	3		1	2	7
: # of cable systems		9		2		0				5
: # of TV stations	55	15	2	2	11	2		0	5	19
: # of FM stations	17	23	74	4	100	1		1	4	8
: # of SAT earth stations	1		152	4	2			0	1	2
: # of daily papers	3	35		3	31					5
: Television/1000 cap	59	333	74		109	6			301	75
: Radios/1000 cap	205	269	152	29	146	214		789	309	163
: Telephones/1000 pop	58	404	51	6	44	5		37	174	155
: Digital % 93	36	71			48					58
: Main Lines/1000 pop	47	413	51		6	5			153	
: Cellular subs/cap	0	31	0.1		11				2	0.6
: Pagers/cap		80								
Piped water, % dwellings	53	42			42				42	33
Food: Sugar/cap	230			30	133	123		70	384	185
: Protein grm/day/cap	85			55	49	52			81	83
: Calories/cap/day	3260	2810		2210	2330	2220		2940	3060	2940
: Meat prod/cap 88			0							0
Energy: Consumption/cap	978	2390		36	637	70		368	6160	761
: Electricity/cap	769	4310	2930	36	813	81	194	229	2820	662

Characteristics	Turkey	Turkme-nistan	Turks & Caicos	Tuvalu	Uganda	Ukraine	United Arab Emir.	United Kingdom	United States	Uruguay
Macroecon: GNP/capita	3670	3440	5000	556	300	4840	19900	16700	23400	3600
∶ Saving rate	21	90		8	23	79	70	20	19	11
∶ Inflation rate	62			0	0		1	3	3	80
Convert currency (1=yes)	1	0		1		0	0	1	1	
Communist, former (1=yes)	0	1		0		1	0	0	0	0
Labor: Unemployment, %	10	3	0			2	2	9	7	9
∶ Nonemployment, %	65	61			90	52	68	55	51	57
∶ Agriculture, %	50		0		77	19	8	1	4	11
∶ Industry, %	21		12			41	85	27	29	31
∶ Services, %	29					40	10	72	67	58
∶ Unionization, %	10					5		40	16	15
Air Trans: # of aircraft	52			0	6		105	618	8250	11
∶ # aircraft/cap	0.9				0.3			11		4
∶ # of airports	109		7	1	35		37	498	14200	90
Runways: Permanent Surf	65		4	1	1		20	249	4820	16
∶ Large	3		0	0			7	1	63	
∶ Medium	30						5	37	325	2
∶ Small	27		4	1	3		5	133	2520	16
Roads: Total km	59100	22600	121	8	2820	247000	4360	357000	6370000	52000
∶ Motorways km	826	0		0	0	0		3090	84400	0
∶ Highways total km	49600	23000	121	8	26200	274000	2000	363000	6370000	49900
∶ Paved km	26900	18300		8	1970	236000	1800	339000		6700
∶ Gravel km	16500	0			5850	0	200			3000
∶ Improved earth km	4000	4700				37300				
∶ Unimproved earth km	2200		24	8	18400					40200
∶ Ownership car/1000 cap	25	0.5		0.8	1	56	159	367	570	116
Railways km	8420	2120			1270	22800	0	16600	270000	3000
Telecom: # AM stations	15	0	0	0	9		8	225	4890	99
∶ # of cable systems	1		3	1			4	40	7300	
∶ # of TV stations	357	2	2		1	3	12	207	5200	26
∶ # of FM stations	94		3	0	4		3	525		
∶ # of SAT earth stations	2		0	0	8		4	12	61	2
∶ # of daily papers	10		1	0	22		8		1700	9
∶ Television/1000 cap	174	2	179		2	327	109	479	814	227
∶ Radios/1000 pop	119	66		875	22		232	993	2040	586
∶ Telephones/1000 pop	208	67		125	4	166	323	523	771	178
∶ Digital % 93	58						100			
∶ Main Lines/1000 pop	226	67		19	60	180	343	492	598	187
∶ Cellular subs/cap	2	0.2			2	0.1	28	45	93	2
∶ Pagers/cap								14	95	
Piped water, % dwellings	99						54	99	99	72
Food: Sugar/cap	230				29		110	293	227	165
∶ Protein 85 grm/day/cap	88				54			88	107	80
∶ Calories/cap/day	3150				2220		3710	3220	3640	2680
∶ Meat prod/cap 88	0	0				0.1		0	0.1	0.1
Energy: Consumption/cap	1030				25		20400	5040	10100	783
∶ Electricity/cap	965	3970	818	271	31	4820	7460	5610	11800	2360

Characteristics	Uzbekistan	Vanuatu	Vatican City	Venezuela	Vietnam	Virgin Isl. US	Wallis & Futuna	West Bank	Western Samoa	Western Sahara
Macroecon: GNP/capita	2800	1180		3400	245	11000	1500	1200	900	320
: Saving rate				31						
: Inflation rate	600	4	0	33				11	10	
: Convert currency (1=yes)		0	1	0	0		0		0	0
Communist, former (1=yes)	1		0		1					
Labor: Unemployment, %	7		0	9	5	3		15		94
: Nonemployment, %		69		72	53				83	
: Agriculture, %	63			16	70	56			67	
: Industry, %	39			28	8					
: Services, %	24			56	22	8				
: Unionization, %				32	90	22				
Air Trans: # of aircraft		0		56		90				
: # aircraft/cap										
: # of airports		33	0	308	100	2	2	2	3	13
Runways: Permanent Surf				135	50		1	200	14	3
: Large	2				10	2	0		3	
: Medium	0			14	20	2	0	1		5
: Small	1			88		2	2		1	
Roads: Total km	73100	1180		101000	85700	856	100		2090	6200
: Motorways km	0	0		1290	0					6200
: Highways total km	78400	1030		77800	85000	856	100		2040	1450
: Paved km	67000	240		22800	9400		16		375	
: Gravel km	0			24500	48700					4750
: Improved earth km	11400			14500	26900					
: Unimproved earth km	37	26		15800						
: Ownership car/1000 cap			426	82	0.8		20		11	
Railways km	3460	0	3	542	2830	0	0		0	
Telecom: # AM stations		2	0	181	16	4	1		1	2
: # of cable systems		0		3	0	1	0		0	0
: # of TV stations		0	4	59	2	4	0		0	2
: # of FM stations		0	0	0	1	8	0		0	0
: # of SAT earth stations		1	1	1	3	1	0		1	2
: # of daily papers				75	4					
: Television/1000 cap	279	9		156	38	538			36	16
: Radios/1000 pop	149	242		406	52	865	17		437	195
: Telephones/1000 pop		24		109	4	471			47	6
: Digital % 93	78			43	77				100	
: Main Lines/1000 pop	76	22		110	5				43	
: Cellular subs/cap	0.2				0.1					
: Pagers/cap				4						
Piped water,% dwellings				38					9	
Food: Sugar/cap		64		275	18				132	
: Protein 85 grm/day/cap	0			69	57				63	
: Calories/cap/day		2340		2530	1950				2460	
: Meat prod/cap 88	0	0								
Energy: Consumption/cap	2350	201		3010	132	11800			357	506
: Electricity/cap		180		3080	124	9830	71		255	442

Characteristics	Yemen	Zaire	Zambia	Zimbabwe
Macroecon: GNP/capita	827	238	420	640
: Saving rate	70	21	7	13
: Inflation rate	0	4000	155	25
: Convert currency (1=yes)	0	0	1	1
Communist, former (1=yes)			0	0
Labor: Unemployment, %	13			35
: Nonemployment, %		64	72	72
: Agriculture, %	64	75	58	74
: Industry, %	22	13	11	10
: Services, %	14	12	31	16
: Unionization, %	72	45	10	17
Air Trans: # of aircraft	1	1	12	12
: # aircraft/cap	0.8			
: # of airports	46	284	117	491
Runways: Permanent Surf	10			22
: Large	0	24	13	2
: Medium	20	6	4	3
: Small	11	73	22	32
Roads: Total km	7260	145000	37400	85200
: Motorways km	0	0	0	0
: Highways total km	15500	147000	36400	85200
: Paved km	4000	2800	6500	15800
: Gravel km	.	46200	7000	39100
: Improved earth km				23100
: Unimproved earth km	11500	97500	22900	7250
Railways km		5010	1720	2750
Ownership car/1000 cap	13	2	9	29
Telecom: # AM stations	0	10	11	8
: # of cable systems		0	0	0
: # of TV stations	4	18	9	0
: # of FM stations	0	4	5	8
: # of SAT earth stations	10		3	1
: # of daily papers	1	4		2
: Television/1000 cap	6		25	27
: Radios/1000 pop	3	103	27	45
: Telephones/1000 pop	27	1	12	32
Digital % 93	15			
: Main Lines/1000 pop	14	1	10	14
: Cellular subs/cap	0.2			
: Pagers/cap				
Piped water, % dwellings		43	63	80
Food: Sugar/cap	330	24	101	227
: Protein 85 grm/day/cap	66	34	58	51
: Calories/cap/day	2270	2160	2130	2120
: Meat prod/cap 88	0	0	0	0
Energy: Consumption/cap	347	67	198	710
: Electricity/cap	137	151	909	935

4

DEMOGRAPHY & SOCIOLOGY ACROSS COUNTRIES

National cultures are often distinguished by their demographic and social behaviors. This chapter provides comparative statistics for a variety of demographic and sociological variables across countries. For a full discussion of the methodology used to generate these estimates, please refer to Chapter 1 which gives important caveats. This chapter first gives summary statistics of the variables reported: the number of countries for which each variable was available, weighted averages (by population) and simple averages; these averages can be used as benchmarks. Then a lengthy comparative table is presented which provides raw statistics across countries.

Most of the variables are self explanatory, though some merit commentary. All of the statistics should be considered as estimates which have undergone rounding and certain adjustments. Estimates in this chapter span a variety of topics, including the timing of settlements, largest cities, and political independence for each country (negative numbers signify BC). Various demographic and vital statistics are also reported. Various social and political variables are given covering migration, political systems and censorship, social unrest, and the number and prevalence of certain diseases. The estimate of "." signifies a missing value due to a lack of underlying data.

Summary Statistics:
Demographic   & Sociological Resources

Characteristics	Number of Countries Covered	Weighted Average by Pop 1994	Simple Average	Simple Standard Deviation
Population Covered 1994	234	458579.51	23871.19	102085.95
Population Covered 1993	234	453406.93	24084.44	101512.92
Population Covered 1992	234	449886.73	27057.98	106885.03
Vital Statistics: Death rate	225	9.27	9.14	4.05
: Birth rate	225	26.27	28.04	12.73
: Fertility	221	3.32	3.73	1.94
: Female life expectancy, years	225	68.77	70.02	9.94
: Male life expectancy, years	225	64.99	65.37	8.89
: Infant mortality	227	68.96	59.38	46.01
: # of major diseases	202	3.12	2.42	2.37
Demography: Migration/1000	223	0.21	0.89	19.16
: Population of Country	234	458579.51	23871.19	102085.95
: Urbanization, %	214	43.58	51.00	24.37
: Population growth	204	2.08	2.05	1.36
: Females, % of population	198	49.51	49.91	2.51
Male % ages: 0-9 years	176	51.14	50.75	1.14
: 10-19 years	176	51.28	50.78	1.56
: 20-29 years	176	50.82	50.28	3.86
: 30-39 years	176	50.69	50.18	4.26
: 40-49 years	176	50.98	50.20	3.97
: 50-59 years	176	50.97	50.21	4.88
: 60-69 years	176	48.97	48.83	4.46
: 70+ years	176	45.13	45.74	6.68
Education: Literacy, adult	230	72.78	78.81	23.46
Cities: earliest settled, year	182	-528.79	960.18	1210.75
: Largest settled, year	182	954.44	1249.24	930.30
: Largest, % population	202	5.26	17.32	15.53
Politics: # of parties	228	3.99	3.96	2.81
: Largest party, %	206	64.13	65.46	27.81
: Top two parties, %	206	79.84	82.24	20.65
: Chambers in legislation, #	229	1.52	1.38	0.49
: # of changes since 1960	202	1.82	1.57	1.43
: Independence year	231	1923.04	1886.23	185.03
Laws: Censorship (1=high)	192	0.54	0.48	0.43
: Metric system (1=yes)	222	0.10	0.20	0.40
: Visas needed (3=high)	202	2.62	2.35	0.57
: Full social security (1=yes)	192	0.27	0.37	0.48
: Military service (1=yes)	192	0.54	0.45	0.50
Crime: Murders/100k population	82	10.00	9.23	19.65
: Thefts/100k population	51	928.53	1834.12	2302.65
: Suicide/100k population	64	10.24	10.07	8.86
: Prisoners/000 population	72	0.78	1.58	2.84
: Death penalty (1=yes)	191	0.69	0.44	0.50
Unrest: Border disputes, #	233	4.75	1.23	1.87
: International wars, #	202	0.30	0.31	0.76
: # of civil wars	202	1.11	0.64	1.04
: # of civil riots	202	0.32	0.26	0.50

Characteristics	Afghan- istan	Albania	Algeria	American Samoa	Andorra	Angola	Anguilla	Antigua & Barbuda	Argentina	Armenia
Population 1994	19200	3330	27100	53	53	10300	8	66	33500	3570
Population 1993	17300	3390	27300	50	59	9340	7	65	33500	3560
Population 1992	17300	3400	26700	44	54	8900		64	33000	3600
Vital Stats: Death rate	20	5	7	4	4	19	8	18	9	7
..Birth rate	44	23	31	37	11	46	24	18	20	22
..Fertility	6	3	4	5	1	7	3	2	3	3
..Female life exp., years	44	79	68	75	81	48	77	75	75	74
..Male life exp., years	45	72	66	71	74	45	71	71	68	69
..Infant mortality	172	53	71	19	5	161	18	37	51	39
..# of major diseases	4	2	5	1	0	4			2	0
Demography: Migration	0	6	0	6	15	0	-10	8	0	-7
..Population of Country	19200	3330	27100	53	53	10300	8	66	33500	3570
..Urbanization, %	18	35	50	18	74	27	28	40	86	68
..Population growth	2	3	3	3	2	3	-2	0.4	2	0.8
..Females, % of pop	50	48	50	49	47	48	51	53	50	
Male % ages: 0-9 years	50	51	51	51	51	52		47	51	
..10-19 years	49	52	51	51	53	52		47	51	
..20-29 years	48	52	47	50	56	52		48	51	
..30-39 years	51	51	46	51	56	52		47	50	
..40-49 years	56	52	47	51	51	53		47	85	
..50-59 years	58	52	47	52	54	53		47	46	
..60-69 years	58	50	47	50	54	52		47	46	
..70+ years	29	50	57	50	50	42		47	42	
Education: Literacy, adult	29	85	57	97	100	42	95	90	95	98
Cities: earliest settled, y	-400	-1600	-300	1870		-1580		1650	1550	
..Largest settled, year	-400	1607	1000	1870		-1580		1680	1580	
..Largest, % pop	9	6	6	7	34	17	3	56	9	35
Politics: # of parties	3	4	1	2	5	5	3	3	8	4
..Largest party %		66	100		14	59		65	50	42
..Top two parties, %		93	100		25	91		94	82	69
..Chambers in leg., #	2	1		2	2	1	1	2	2	1
..# of changes 60	4			4						
Laws: Independence year	1920	1910	1960	1900	1280	1975	1980	1650	1820	1990
..Censorship (1=high)	1	1	1	1	0	1	1	1	0.5	1
..Metric system (1=yes)	0	0	0	2	1	0			2	0
..Visas needed (3=high)	2	3	3		0	3		2	0	2
..Full soc security (1=yes)	0	0	0		0	0		1	1	0
..Military service (1=yes)	0	1	1		0	1		0	2	1
Crime: Murders/100k pop										
..Thefts/100k pop									153	
..Suicide/100k pop		0.5							0.7	
..Prisoners/000 pop		0				0.5			0.8	
..Death penalty (1=yes)		2	1	0	0	0	0	1	0	
Unrest: Border disputes, #	4	0	0	0	0	0		0	4	3
..International, #	1	0	1	0	0	1		0	1	0
..# of civil wars	5	0	1	0	0	0		0	0	0
..# of civil riots	2		1		0	2				1

Characteristics	Aruba	Australia	Austria	Azerbaijan	Bahamas	Bahrain	Bangla-desh	Barbados	Belarus	Belgium
Population 1994	64	17800	7820	7350	286	532	122000	280	10300	10000
Population 1993	65	17800	7810	7470	264	570	122000	256	10400	9990
Population 1992	64	17500	7690	7250	256	554	119000	255	10300	9930
Vital Stats: Death rate	6	7	11	7	5	4	12	9	11	10
: Birth rate	16	15	12	26	19	27	36	16	15	12
: Fertility	2	2	2	3	2	4		2	2	2
: Female life exp., years	80	80	81	74	76	76	54	78	76	81
: Male life exp., years	73	74	74	70	69	71	55	72	72	74
: Infant mortality	9	13	11	47	38	32	129	27	24	8
: # of major diseases		1	1			2		1		0
Demography: Migration	-3	7	5	-3	-1		0	-6	1	1
: Population of Country	64	17800	7820	7350	286	532	122000	280	10300	10000
: Urbanization, %	53	85	58	54	70	82	18	40	65	96
: Population growth	0.6	2	0.3	2	2	5	3	0.5	0.7	0.3
: Females, % of pop	52	50	53		50	40	48	53	53	51
Male % ages: 0-9 years	49	51	51		49	50	50	50	51	51
: 10-19 years	49	51	51		52	51	51	49	50	51
: 20-29 years	49	51	50		48	66	52	48	51	51
: 30-39 years	49	51	50		50	70	51	44	50	50
: 40-49 years	48	51	49		51	64	53	43	47	49
: 50-59 years	49	47	39		49	60	55	44	45	46
: 60-69 years	49	39	34		46	57	56	43	36	37
: 70+ years	49				37	54	35	38	28	
Education: Literacy, adult	95		99	98	95	77	35	99	100	100
Cities: earliest settled, y	1820	1790	-400		1730	1510	800	1630		400
: Largest settled, year	1820	1840	-400	25	1730	1510	1610	1630	15	600
: Largest, % pop	31	20	20	5	54	28		3	2	10
Politics: # of parties		5	4	80			5	2	92	5
: Largest party %	8	54	44	80	67	100	46	64	100	18
: Top two parties, %		87	77		100	100	76	100		35
: Chambers in leg., #		2	2	1	2	1	4	1	1	2
: # of changes 60	1				1					
: Independence year	1640	1900	1920	1990	1970	1970	1970	1970	1990	1830
Laws: Censorship (1=high)		0	0	0	1	0.5	0	0.5	0	0
: Metric system (1=yes)	0	0	0	2		3	2	2		0
: Visas needed (3=high)	2	2	2	1	2	1		0	2	2
: Full soc security (1=yes)		1	1		1		2	8	1	1
: Military service (1=yes)		0	2		15	0.7	2			0
Crime: Murders/100k pop		2	2970		0.4	2	11	0.3		2620
: Thefts/100k pop		3580	27		13		0.3	0.9		22
: Suicide/100k pop		12	0.7							0.6
: Prisoners/000 pop		0.7								
: Death penalty (1=yes)	0	0	0	1	1	1	1	1	0	0
Unrest: Border disputes, #	0	0	0	0	0	0	0	0	0	0
: International, #	0	0	0	0	0	0	1	0	0	0
: # of civil wars	0	0	0	0	0	0	0	0	0	0
: # of civil riots	0	0	0	1	0	0	0	0	0	0

Characteristics	Belize	Benin	Bermuda	Bhutan	Bolivia	Bosnia & Herzegov.	Botswana	Brazil	British Virgin Isl.	Brunei
Population 1994	200	5070	62	1640	7840	4330	1350	156000	15	291
Population 1993	224	5160	60	1180	7520	4620	1330	159000	13	363
Population 1992	236	4990	59	1630	7330		1290	158000		423
Vital Stats: Death rate		15		17				7		8
:Birth rate	31	49	15	40	33	14	35	25	6	27
:Fertility	4		2	6	5	2	4	3	20	4
:Female life exp., years	73	53	78	49	64	77	65	69	75	77
:Male life exp., years	67	49	73	50	59	72	59	64	71	74
:Infant mortality	53	136	13	147	108	26	69	85	20	22
:# of major diseases	4	5		6	2		1	5	0	3
Demography: Migration					-1	0	0	0	-2	
:Population of Country	200	5070	62	1640	7840	4330	1350	156000	15	291
:Urbanization, %	50	31	100	10	50	36	26	76	15	66
:Population growth	2	3	1	2	3		4	2		6
:Females, % of pop	50	52	52	49	51		52	50		46
Male % ages: 0-9 years	50	51	51	51	50		50	50		51
:10-19 years	51	51	51	52	50		50	50		55
:20-29 years	51	38	49	51	49		45	50		52
:30-39 years	52	44	50	51	48		43	49		56
:40-49 years	51	46	48	52	48		46	49		56
:50-59 years	50	49	48	51	47		46	49		58
:60-69 years	47	50	45	51	44		47	46		53
:70+ years	47	51	39	51	78		74	46		85
Education: Literacy, adult	93	23	98	38	78	93	41	81	98	85
Cities: earliest settled, y	1640	1600	1790	1580	1550		1900	1540		1500
:Largest settled, year		1870	1790	1580			1900	1550		1500
:Largest, % pop	21		3		15	15	9	6	26	6
Politics: # of parties	2	4				5	2	5	3	
:Largest party, %	55	19			40	36	91	22		100
:Top two parties, %	100	33			67	66	100	40		100
:Chambers in leg., #	2	1	2	1	2	2	2	2	1	
:# of changes 60		7	1		4			3	1	1
Independence year	1980	1960	1610	1870	1900	1990	1970	1820	1670	1980
Laws: Censorship (1=high)	0.5	0	1	0	0.5	0	0	0	0	1
:Metric system (1=yes)	1	0	1	3	2	3	2	3	0	
:Visas needed (3=high)	2	3	2		0		0	1	0	
:Full soc security (1=yes)	1	0			1		0	8		1
:Military service (1=yes)	0				1	1			1	1
Crime: Murders/100k pop								3		
:Thefts/100k pop	0.4							0.6		1
:Suicide/100k pop	1	0			0	0	0	3	0	2
:Prisoners/000 pop	1	0	0	0	2	3	4	3	0	1
:Death penalty (1=yes)	0	0	0	0	0		0	0	0	0
Unrest: Border disputes, #	0	5	0	0	4	3	0	1	0	1
:International, #	0	0	0	0	0		0	1	0	0
:# of civil wars	0	5	0	0	0		0	0	0	0
:# of civil riots	0	0	0	0	0	3	0	0	0	0

Characteristics	Bulgaria	Burkina Faso	Burma	Burundi	Cambodia	Cameroon	Canada	Cape Verde	Cayman Islands	Central Afric. Rep.
Population 1994	8950	9780	44600	5980	9010	12600	28200	404	31	3270
Population 1993	8850	9900	43600	6100	8680	12400	27600	411	30	3090
Population 1992	8890	9650	43000	6020	7300	11700	27100	399	28	3030
Vital Stats: Death rate	12	16	10	14	15	11	7	10	5	18
..Birth rate	12	49	44	46	37	44	14	48	16	43
..Fertility	2	7	4		4	6	2	7	2	6
..Female life exp., years	76	53	64	54	52	60	81	65	80	49
..Male life exp., years	70	52	61	50	50	55	74	61	75	46
..Infant mortality	28	139	96	127	144	115	9	80	8	133
..# of major diseases	0	8	8	0	0	0	0	4	0	5
Demography: Migration	-5	-2	-2				6	-8	33	
..Population of Country	8950	9780	44600	5980	9010	12600	28200	404	31	3270
..Urbanization, %	67	9	24	6	11	41	77	32	100	42
..Population growth	0.5	2	2		0.3	3	1	1	4	2
..Females, % of pop	50	52	50	51	50	50	51	53	52	52
Male % ages: 0-9 years	51	48	50	50	50	50	51	50	48	50
..10-19 years	51	48	50	49	50	50	50	49	49	49
..20-29 years	50	48	49	48	50	50	50	49	49	48
..30-39 years	50	48	49	45	50	49	50	37	49	48
..40-49 years	49	48	49	44	50	49	49	37	48	48
..50-59 years	47	48	46	45	50	47	46	40	48	47
..60-69 years	44	47	46	50	50	45	41	44		45
..70+ years		48			50			44		43
Education: Literacy, adult	96	18	81		35	54	99	66	98	38
Cities: earliest settled, y	-600	1200	-585	1900	1370	1880	1580	1650		1890
..Largest settled, year	-100	1200	-585	1900	1370	1880	1790	1650		1890
..Largest, % pop	13	5	6	5	10	0	13	13	52	20
Politics: # of parties	3			2	4	4	5			
..Largest party %	46	73	100	80	48	49	60	71	100	40
..Top two parties, %	90	84	100	100	91	87	78	100	100	55
..Chambers in leg., #	1	1	1	1	1	1	2	1	1	2
..# of changes 60			4	6	3	2	1	2	2	
..Independence year	1910	1960	1950	1960	1950	1960	1950	1980	1670	1960
Laws: Censorship (1=high)	0	0	1	0	0	0	0	0	1	1
..Metric system (1=yes)	0						1			0
..Visas needed (3=high)	2	3	3	3	3	3	2	3	2	3
..Full soc security (1=yes)	0	0	0	0	0	0	1	0		0
..Military service (1=yes)	1		1	1	1	1	1	2		0
Crime: Murders/100k pop	3		5							
..Thefts/100k pop	593		56				5040			
..Suicide/100k pop	17						15			
..Prisoners/000 pop	1			0.5		0.5	1			
..Death penalty (1=yes)	0		1				0	0		0
Unrest: Border disputes, #	2	1	0	0	1	1	2	2		0
..International, #	0	0	0	0	1	0	0	0	0	0
..# of civil wars	0	0	3	0	2	0	0	0	0	3
..# of civil riots	0	0	1	1	1	0	0	0	0	0

Characteristics	Chad	Chile	China	Christmas Island	Cocos (Keel.) Isl.	Colombia	Comoros	Congo	Cook Island	Costa Rica
Population 1994	5990	13800	1210000	2	0.6	34000	615	2460	18	3270
Population 1993	5340	13700	1180000	2	0.6	35100	511	2420	19	3270
Population 1992	5230	13500	1170000	.	.	34500	494	2380	.	3190
Vital Stats: Death rate	21	6	7	.	.	5	12	13	6	4
: Birth rate	42	21	22	.	.	24	47	42	22	27
: Fertility	5	3	2	.	.	3	7	6	3	3
: Female life exp., years	49	77	73	.	.	74	59	56	73	79
: Male life exp., years	46	71	69	.	.	69	55	53	69	75
: Infant mortality	148	33	52	.	.	54	106	116	25	27
: # of major diseases	4	0	0	.	.	4	4	5	.	2
Demography: Migration	0	0	0	2	0.6	0	0	0	-10	1
: Population of Country	5990	13800	1210000	.	.	34000	615	2460	18	3270
: Urbanization, %	28	84	29	.	.	68	27	44	.	47
: Population growth	2	2	2	2	.	2	3	3	.	3
: Females, % of pop	52	51	49	.	.	50	50	51	48	50
Male % ages: 0-9 years	48	51	52	.	47	51	51	50	.	51
: 10-19 years	48	51	51	.	.	50	51	49	.	50
: 20-29 years	48	50	51	.	.	49	45	48	.	49
: 30-39 years	48	50	52	.	.	50	48	47	.	49
: 40-49 years	47	49	53	.	.	49	48	49	.	50
: 50-59 years	48	47	53	.	.	49	52	45	.	49
: 60-69 years	48	45	49	.	.	48	51	43	.	50
: 70+ years	47	41	43	.	.	48	51	47	.	48
Education: Literacy, adult	30	93	73	72	62	87	50	57	92	93
Cities: earliest settled, y	1900	1540	-2210	.	.	1530	48	1600	.	1740
: Largest settled, year	1900	1540	1100	.	.	1540	1890	1880	.	1740
: Largest, % pop	10	37	0.6	.	.	12	1890	26	.	9
Politics: # of parties	1	6	1	0	100	4	4	5	5	4
: Largest party %	100	31	100	100	100	50	57	38	.	49
: Top two parties, %	100	55	100	100	100	77	100	60	.	93
: Chambers in leg., #	1	2	1	.	1	2	.	.	1	1
: # of changes 60	4	4	3	.	.	1	5	3	.	0
Independence year	1960	1820	1911	1960	1960	1900	1980	1960	1900	1820
Laws: Censorship (1=high)	0.5	0	1	0	.	0.5	0.5	0.5	0	0.5
: Metric system (1=yes)	.	0	0	.	.	0	0	0	.	0
: Visas needed (3=high)	3	2	3	.	.	2	3	3	.	2
: Full soc security (1=yes)	0	0	0	.	.	1	0	0	.	1
: Military service (1=yes)	0	0	1	.	.	.	0	0	.	0
Crime: Murders/100k pop	.	.	2	.	.	62	.	.	.	4
: Thefts/100k pop	.	832	177	.	.	142	.	.	.	.
: Suicide/100k pop	.	5	.	.	.	4	.	.	.	5
: Prisoners/000 pop	.	0.2	.	.	.	1	.	.	.	.
: Death penalty (1=yes)	0	0	1	0	0	0	0	1	0	0
Unrest: Border disputes, #	1	4	1	.	.	2	1	1	.	0
: International, #	3	0	12	.	.	0	0	0	.	0
: # of civil wars	2	2	0	.	.	0	2	0	.	0
: # of civil riots	0	0	0	.	.	2	0	.	.	0

Characteristics	Croatia	Cuba	Cyprus	Czech Republic	Denmark	Djibouti	Dominica	Dominican Republic	Ecuador	Egypt
Population 1994	4850	10900	719	10400	5190	498	77	7630	11300	56000
Population 1993	4800	11000	723	10400	5160	383	88	7680	10900	58300
Population 1992	4890	10800	716		5140	355	87	7530	11000	55700
Vital Stats: Death rate	11	6	8	11	12	16	5	7	6	9
:Birth rate	12	17	18	13	13	43	24	26	28	33
:Fertility	2	2	2	2	2	6	2	3	4	4
:Female life exp., years	76	79	79	77	79	51	79	70	72	65
:Male life exp., years	70	74	74	69	73	47	74	66	67	62
:Infant mortality	21	20	18	19	10	133	28	80	76	89
:# of major diseases	0	0	0	0	0	5	0	0	0	6
Demography: Migration	0	-1	0	0	1	0	-3	-1	0	0
:Population of Country	4850	10900	719	10400	5190	498	77	7630	11300	56000
:Urbanization, %	48	73	56	77	86	80	36	59	56	45
:Population growth	0.6	1	0.3		0.5	9	0.5	3	3	2
:Females, % of pop			50		51	49	50	50	50	49
Male % ages: 0-9 years		50	52		51	51	52	49	51	51
:10-19 years		51	51		51	52	51	48	51	53
:20-29 years		51	51		51	52	53	50	50	49
:30-39 years		50	50		51	51	45	52	50	49
:40-49 years		50	49		51	51	45	54	49	51
:50-59 years		49	47		51	51	46	50	48	51
:60-69 years		51	46		50	50	38		45	50
:70+ years		50	45		47	50				45
Education: Literacy, adult	97	94	94	99	100	48	94	83	86	48
Cities: earliest settled, y		1510	1200		1000	1890	1700	1500	1000	-2570
:Largest settled, year	24	1520	1200		1040	1890	1700	1500	1540	641
:Largest, % pop	9	19	24		26	67	26	19	16	20
Politics: # of parties	62	1	4	11	8	1	3	4	7	
:Largest party %	72	100	36	38	39	49	49	43	32	77
:Top two parties, %		100	68	56	56	76	76	84	46	78
:Chambers in leg., #	1	1	2	2	1	1	1	2	1	1
:# of changes 60	0	0	2	0	0	0	0	2	4	1
:Independence year	1990	1900	1970	1990	960	1980	1980	1870	1830	1940
Laws: Censorship (1=high)	1	1	0	0	0	1	0	0.5	0	0.5
:Metric system (1=yes)	1	3	2	1	1	3	2	2	3	0
:Visas needed (3=high)	1	1	1		1	1	1	1	1	3
:Full soc security (1=yes)	1	1	1		1	1	1			0
:Military service (1=yes)	1	1						1	1	1
Crime: Murders/100k pop									10	58
:Thefts/100k pop					8370					0.5
:Suicide/100k pop			0.3	0.8	28			2	4	
:Prisoners/000 pop		1	0	1	0.7	0	1		1	1
:Death penalty (1=yes)	0	1	0	10	1	1	1	1	1	3
Unrest: Border disputes, #	2	1	0		0	0	1	0	1	2
:International, #	0	1	2		0	0	0	0	0	0
:# of civil wars	1	1				1		0	1	0
:# of civil riots	0	0			0	1		1	0	0

Characteristics	El Salvador	Equatorial Guinea	Eritrea	Estonia	Ethiopia	Falkland Islands	Faroe Islands	Fiji	Finland	France
Population 1994	5520	395	3480	1590	52900	2	48	728	5020	57400
Population 1993	5640	399	3470	1600	54900	2	48	756	5040	57300
Population 1992	5530	389		1580	54800	2		750	5010	56800
Vital Stats: Death rate		15		12	14		8	7	10	9
:Birth rate	34	42		16	45	11	17	25	12	13
:Fertility	4	5			7			3	2	2
:Female life exp., years	75	53		75	53	80	81	74	80	82
:Male life exp., years	68	49		71	50	74	74	69	72	74
:Infant mortality	61	132	175	28	134	10	7	39	6	10
:# of major diseases	6	6			4			1	0	1
Demography: Migration	-6	0		3	2		0	-10		
:Population of Country	5520	395	3480	1590	52900		48	728	5020	57400
:Urbanization, %	44	51	20	72	12	59	25	39	61	75
:Population growth	3	2		0.7		0.1			0.3	0.7
:Females, % of pop	51	52			50		48	50	51	51
Male % ages: 0-9 years	51	48			50	50		51	51	51
:10-19 years	51	48			52	55		51	51	50
:20-29 years	47	48			46	55		50	51	51
:30-39 years	48	48			47	55		50	51	51
:40-49 years	47	48			49	55		49	49	49
:50-59 years	47	49			53	55		50	41	46
:60-69 years	45	48			54	55		48	34	36
:70+ years		50			57	55		48		
Education: Literacy, adult	73	50	20	98	71	100	100	87	100	99
Cities: earliest settled, y	1530	1830			700		1600	1880	1200	-1000
:Largest settled, year	1530	1830			1890		1600	1880	1550	-300
:Largest, % pop	8	16		31	3	50		9	10	
Politics: # of parties	6	4		7			7	6	8	11
:Largest party %	46	85	100	29		100	27	44	27	43
:Top two parties, %	71	93	100	46		100	49	73	51	80
:Chambers in leg., #	2	1	1		1		1	2		2
:# of changes 60		4		1	2	3			1	1
:Independence year	1860	1970	1990	1990	1990	1830	1380	1970	1920	1690
Laws: Censorship (1=high)	1	1	1	0.5	0.5	1	0	0	0	0
:Metric system (1=yes)	0	0				2		2		0
:Visas needed (3=high)	3	3	0	2	3			0	2	2
:Full soc security (1=yes)	0	0	0	1					1	1
:Military service (1=yes)	0	0		1	0					1
Crime: Murders/100k pop	40				0	1	0	11		3
:Thefts/100k pop					7				3040	4020
:Suicide/100k pop	12			0	37				27	23
:Prisoners/000 pop				1		1			0.6	0.8
:Death penalty (1=yes)	0	1	0	0	0.3	1	0	1	0	0
Unrest: Border disputes, #	1	1		0	5					
:International, #	1	0	0	0	1	1		0	0	
:# of civil wars	1	1		0	3	0		0	0	0
:# of civil riots	0	1		0	0	0		0	0	1

Characteristics	French Guiana	French Polynesia	Gabon	Gambia	Gaza Strip	Georgia	Germany	Ghana	Gibraltar	Greece
Population 1994	122	214	1260	929	691	5490	80600	16500	31	10200
Population 1993	121	208	1120	930		5590	80400	16700	32	10300
Population 1992	105	200	1100	902		5490	79800	16100		10100
Vital Stats: Death rate	5	5	14	17	6	9	11	13	8	9
: Birth rate	27	28	29	47	46	17	11	45	18	11
: Fertility	4	3	4	6	7	2			3	2
: Female life exp., years	78	73	56	51	68	75	79	58	79	81
: Male life exp., years	71	68	52	47	66	72	73	54	73	75
: Infant mortality	17	15	118	151	41	36	11	105	6	17
: # of major diseases	1	1	5	5	4	0	1			1
Demography: Migration	24	0		0	-4	-1	0	-1	-9	0
: Population of Country	122	214	1260	929	691	5490	80600	16500	31	10200
: Urbanization, %	81	62	42	22		56	87	32	93	61
: Population growth	3	3	4	3		0.8	0.2		1	0.7
: Females, % of pop	47	49	51	50			51	51		51
Male % ages: 0-9 years	51	51	49	50			51	51		52
: 10-19 years	50	51	49	49			51	49		52
: 20-29 years	56	51	49	46			52	49		51
: 30-39 years	54	51	49	46			51	49		50
: 40-49 years	55	51	49	53			51	49		48
: 50-59 years	51	50	50	55			49	50		48
: 60-69 years	50	50	49	54			39	48		47
: 70+ years	45	50					33			43
Education: Literacy, adult	82	98	61	27		100	99	60	94	93
Cities: earliest settled, y	1660	1840	1850	1820	-1470		-500	1600	711	-1300
: Largest settled, year	1660	1840	1850	1820	-1470		1230	1600	711	-1300
: Largest, % pop	39	12	33	12		23	4	6		9
Politics: # of parties	5	4		3		5	6	4	4	4
: Largest party %			55	50		8	40	95		57
: Top two parties, %			71	62		14	76	95		94
: Chambers in leg., #	2	2	1	1		1	2	1	1	1
: # of changes 60	1	1	0	1		1	1	5		3
Independence year	1820	1850	1960	1970		1990	1990	1960	1710	1910
Laws: Censorship (1=high)			0	0.5		0	0	1	1	0.5
: Metric system (1=yes)	0	0	0	1		2	0	0		0
: Visas needed (3=high)	2	2	2	2		0	2	3		2
: Full soc security (1=yes)			0	0		0	1	0		1
: Military service (1=yes)			0	0		1	1	0		1
Crime: Murders/100k pop						1	3			1
: Thefts/100k pop							4350			475
: Suicide/100k pop							19			4
: Prisoners/000 pop							0.6			0.5
: Death penalty (1=yes)	0	0		0	1	1	0	1	0	0
Unrest: Border disputes, #	0	0	0	0		1	1	0		4
: International, #	0	0	1	1		0	0	0		0
: # of civil wars	0	0	0	0		1	0	3		2
: # of civil riots	0	0	1	0		0	0	0	0	0

Characteristics	Greenland	Grenada	Guade-loupe	Guam	Guatemala	Guernsey	Guinea	Guinea-Bissau	Guyana	Haiti
Population 1994	57	88	416	144	10000	63	6300	1030	813	6920
Population 1993	57	88	387	149	10100	63	7030	1070	739	6480
Population 1992	58	84	348	149	9500	.	7640	1050	747	6430
Vital Stats: Death rate	8	7	6	4	8	11	21	18	7	15
.. Birth rate	19	34	19	27	34	12	46	42	21	42
.. Fertility	.	5	2	3	5	2	6	6	2	6
.. Female life exp., years	69	74	80	76	67	80	46	49	74	58
.. Male life exp., years	63	69	74	72	62	75	43	45	69	55
.. Infant mortality	27	47	10	15	73	6	158	146	72	124
.. # of major diseases	0	1	1	0	4	.	.	5	.	4
Demography: Migration	0	-30	8	3	-2	5	-40	0	-20	-5
.. Population of Country	57	88	416	144	10000	63	6300	1030	813	6920
.. Urbanization, %	77	29	90	40	37	.	25	26	36	28
.. Population growth	1	2	0.1	3	3	.	2	2	1	2
.. Females, % of pop	46	52	51	48	50	5	51	52	51	52
Male % ages: 0-9 years	54	51	49	52	51	63	49	50	50	50
.. 10-19 years	54	50	49	53	51	.	48	51	50	50
.. 20-29 years	54	49	49	52	50	.	49	40	49	46
.. 30-39 years	54	48	49	52	50	.	49	44	49	46
.. 40-49 years	54	45	49	53	50	.	49	46	49	48
.. 50-59 years	55	62	49	54	50	.	48	51	50	50
.. 60-69 years	56	37	48	50	47	.	50	57	45	46
.. 70+ years	.	.	48	56	55	.	24	59	45	44
Education: Literacy, adult	100	98	90	96	55	.	24	36	96	53
Cities: earliest settled, y	1720	1650	1640	1670	1780	.	1600	1760	1630	1670
.. Largest settled, year	1720	1650	1830	1670	1780	.	1890	1760	1630	1750
.. Largest, % pop	21	2	18	30	11	.	9	12	27	8
Politics: # of parties	5	4	8	2	7	.	1	.	4	.
.. Largest party %	.	47	.	.	35	50	100	100	50	100
.. Top two parties, %	.	74	.	.	59	100	100	100	98	100
.. Chambers in leg., #	2	2	2	2	1	1	1	2	1	2
.. # of changes 60	2	4	.	1	4	.	1	3	2	3
.. Independence year	1380	1970	1640	1900	1840	1070	1960	1970	1970	1800
Laws: Censorship (1=high)	0	0.5	0	.	0.5	.	0.5	.	0.5	.
.. Metric system (1=yes)	.	0	.	1	0	1	0	0	0	0
.. Visas needed (3=high)	2	2	2	2	3	1	3	3	3	2
.. Full soc security (1=yes)	1	2	0	1	0	0	0	0	1	0
.. Military service (1=yes)	0	1	2	2	1	1	0	0	0	3
Crime: Murders/100k pop	.	.	0.9	.	0.5	.	.	.	0.5	.
.. Thefts/100k pop	.	.	.	.	.	.	.	.	.	.
.. Suicide/100k pop	.	.	10	.	.	.	.	.	.	.
.. Prisoners/000 pop	.	.	.	.	0.5	.	.	.	0.2	.
.. Death penalty (1=yes)	0	1	0	0	1	0	1	.	1	1
Unrest: Border disputes, #	0	0	0	0	1	.	0	0	0	0
.. International, #	0	1	0	0	0	.	0	0	0	1
.. # of civil wars	0	2	0	0	3	0	0	2	0	1
.. # of civil riots	0	0	0	0	.	.	0	.	0	1

Characteristics	Honduras	Hong Kong	Hungary	Iceland	India	Indonesia	Iran	Iraq	Ireland	Isle of Man
Population 1994	5650	5900	10500	283	897000	195000	63200	19900	3490	70
Population 1993	5210	5740	10400	263	901000	199000	63400	20100	3500	71
Population 1992	5090	5890	10500	263	883000	197000	61200	20300	3480	
Vital Stats: Death rate		5	13		11	8	8		9	14
:Birth rate	37	13	12	18	30	25	44	45	15	11
:Fertility	5	2	2	2	4	3	7	7	2	2
:Female life exp., years	68	84	76	81	61	64	68	68	79	78
:Male life exp., years	65	77	68	76	60	59	67	66	73	73
:Infant mortality	80	9	26	6	103	98	88	97	15	9
:# of major diseases			1	0	6	6	5	2	0	
Demography: Migration	-2	-2	0	-2	-1500	200	-1100	-3000	-4	4
:Population of Country	5650	5900	10500	283	897000	195000	63200	19900	3490	70
:Urbanization, %	42	93	61	90	27	31	55	72	53	57
:Population growth	3	2	0.4	1	2	2	3	3	1	
:Females, % of pop	50	49	52	50	48	50	48	48	50	
Male % ages: 0-9 years	50	52	51	51	52	51	52	52	52	
:10-19 years	50	52	51	51	52	51	52	51	51	
:20-29 years	50	51	51	51	51	50	52	53	51	
:30-39 years	50	53	48	50	52	49	52	52	51	
:40-49 years	50	54	47	50	52	48	52	51	51	
:50-59 years	48	53	43	49	52	48	50	51	50	
:60-69 years	47	49	37	43	52	47	48	49	48	
:70+ years		38			52	44		52	42	
Education: Literacy, adult	73	88	99	100	52	77	54	48	100	99
Cities: earliest settled, y	1540	500	-100	874	-1500	200	-1100	-3000	700	1250
:Largest settled, year	1580	500	19	874	150	500	1200	-762	836	1250
:Largest, % pop	13	41	20	37	1	3	10	24	26	
Politics: # of parties	3	1	6	5	5	4	0	1	5	0
:Largest party %	55	100	54	41	42	57	100	100	41	100
:Top two parties, %	98	100	54	62	64	69	100	100	68	100
:Chambers in leg., #	1	1	1	1	2	2	2	2	2	1
:# of changes 60		1	1	0	1	1	1	1	1	
Independence year	1840	1900	1920	1940	1950	1950	1910	1930	1920	1770
Laws: Censorship (1=high)	0.5	0.5	0.5	0	0.5	0.5	0	0	0.5	1
:Metric system (1=yes)	0	0	0	2	0	0	3	3	1	
:Visas needed (3=high)	3	2	2		3	2	0	1	2	
:Full soc security (1=yes)	0	0	1		0	0	1		1	
:Military service (1=yes)	1		1		0				0	
Crime: Murders/100k pop		1	3	0.8	4	0.9			0.8	
:Thefts/100k pop		1	2340		49	41				
:Suicide/100k pop		2	45	15		0.2			8	
:Prisoners/000 pop				0.3	1				0.6	
:Death penalty (1=yes)	0	1	0	0	3	1			0	0
Unrest: Border disputes, #	1	0	1	1	0	2	5	5		
:International, #	1	1	0	0	1	0	1	4	0	
:# of civil wars	1	0	1	0	1	1	1	2	0	
:# of civil riots	0	0	0	0	1	0	1	0	0	0

Characteristics	Israel	Italy	Ivory Coast	Jamaica	Japan	Jersey	Jordan	Kazakhstan	Kenya	Kiribati
Population 1994	5490	57800	13400	2510	125000	85	4450	17200	26100	75
Population 1993	4770	58000	13000	2530	125000	85	3760	17100	27200	75
Population 1992	4540	57900	13500	2510	125000		3560	16900	26200	72
Vital Stats: Death rate	6	10	6	6	7	10	5	8	8	12
··Birth rate	21	10	47	23	10	12	45	23	44	33
··Fertility	3	1	7	3	2	1	7	3	6	4
··Female life exp., years	80	82	57	78	82	79	73	74	64	58
··Male life exp., years	76	75	53	72	77	73	70	70	60	52
··Infant mortality	15	13	116	39	3	6	57	43	88	96
··# of major diseases			5	1			3		6	1
Demography: Migration	26	1	3	-8	0	6	1	-6		
··Population of Country	5490	57800	13400	2510	125000	85	4450	17200	26100	75
··Urbanization, %	90	69	42	50	77		69	57	24	35
··Population growth	3	0.5	4	1			4	1		2
··Females, % of pop	50	51	50	51	51		48		50	51
Male % ages: 0-9 years	51	51	51	51	51		52		50	51
··10-19 years	51	51	51	50	51		53		50	51
··20-29 years	51	51	48	50	51		53		48	47
··30-39 years	50	50	49	48	50		52		48	50
··40-49 years	49	49	50	49	49		53		48	49
··50-59 years	47	48	52	49	43		52		48	47
··60-69 years	46	46	51	47	40		50		45	45
··70+ years	47	39	46	43	40		50		45	40
Education: Literacy, adult	97	97	54	98	100		80	98	69	90
Cities: earliest settled, y	-3000	-1100	1900	1530	-700		1300		800	1790
··Largest settled, year	-1470	-1000	1900	1690	-1200		1880		1900	1790
··Largest, % pop	10	5	14	21	8		26	7	4	30
Politics: # of parties	9	10	4	2		100	6	7	6	3
··Largest party %	37	58	93	75	43	100	68	17	51	46
··Top two parties, %	64	92	98	100	57	101	88	23	66	87
··Chambers in leg., #	1	2	1	2	2	1	2	1	1	1
··# of changes 60				1					3	3
··Independence year	1950	1870	1960	1960	1870	1070	1950	1990	1960	1980
Laws: Censorship (1=high)	0	0	1	1	0	1	1	1	1	0
··Metric system (1=yes)	3	2	0	1	0		0	2	0	0
··Visas needed (3=high)	1	2	3	2	2		3	0	3	3
··Full soc security (1=yes)	1		0	0	1		0	1	0	0
··Military service (1=yes)	1		0	0				1	0	0
Crime: Murders/100k pop				2	0.9				4	
··Thefts/100k pop	2480	2800			999				42	
··Suicide/100k pop	8	8			20					
··Prisoners/000 pop	7				0.4					
··Death penalty (1=yes)	1	0	1	1	0	0	1	0	1	1
Unrest: Border disputes, #	5	2	0	0	3		2	0	2	0
··International, #	4	0	0	1	0		1	0	0	0
··# of civil wars	0	0	0	0	0		1	0	1	0
··# of civil riots	0	1	1	0	0		0	0	0	0

Characteristics	Kuwait	Kyrgyz-stan	Laos	Latvia	Lebanon	Lesotho	Liberia	Libya	Liechten-stein	Lithuania
Population 1994	1900	4570	4520	2680	2880	1860	2870	5060	29	3780
Population 1993	2030	4590	4430	2730	3520	1900	2900	4740	29	3820
Population 1992	2280	4460	4200	2700	3430	1850	2820	4480	28	3780
Vital Stats: Death rate	2	8	16	12	7	10	13	8	7	11
··Birth rate	32	31	44	15	28	35	44	36	13	15
··Fertility	4	4	6	2	4	5	7	5	2	2
··Female life exp., years	76	74	53	75	71	63	59	71	81	77
··Male life exp., years	72	68	50	71	67	60	55	66	74	72
··Infant mortality	26	58	131	26	64	105	141	89	6	21
··# of major diseases	0	0	1	0			2	5	0	0
Demography: Migration		-9	0	4	-5	0		0	0	4
··Population of Country	1900	4570	4520	2680	2880	1860	2870	5060	29	3780
··Urbanization, %	95	38	17	71	82	20	45	68	65	68
··Population growth		2		0.6	2	2	3	4	0.6	0.8
··Females, % of pop	43		50		49	52	49	47	50	
Male % ages: 0-9 years	51		50		51	48	51	53	50	
··10-19 years	51		50		51	48	50	53	50	
··20-29 years	57		50		51	48	45	53	48	
··30-39 years	64		50		51	48	48	53	52	
··40-49 years	67		51		51	48	55	53	48	
··50-59 years	67		51		51	49	58	52	46	
··60-69 years	57		50		50	48	57	53	39	
··70+ years	43		50		51	48	61			
Education: Literacy, adult	74	98	84	98	80	74	40	64	100	98
Cities: earliest settled, y	1700		1350		-700	1870	1820	-700	1100	
··Largest settled, year	1700		1350		-1500	1870	1820	-700	1150	
··Largest, % pop	7	14	9	34	44	6	16	20	18	17
Politics: # of parties	0	1	1	8	5	1	0	1	3	6
··Largest party %				36	27				51	52
··Top two parties, %				51	48				92	73
··Chambers in leg., #	1	1	1	1	1	2	1	2	1	1
··# of changes 60	0	0	0	1	0				0	
··Independence year	1960	1990	1950	1990	1940	1970	1850	1950	1720	1990
Laws: Censorship (1=high)	0.5			0.5		0				0
··Metric system (1=yes)	0	0	0	0	0	0	0	0	0	0
··Visas needed (3=high)	3	2	3	2	3	3	3	3	2	2
··Full soc security (1=yes)	1	0	0		0	0	0	0	1	0
··Military service (1=yes)	1	1	1	1	0	0	0	1	0	1
Crime: Murders/100k pop	0.5									
··Thefts/100k pop										
··Suicide/100k pop	0.9									
··Prisoners/000 pop	0.3							211		
··Death penalty (1=yes)	1	1	1	0	1	1	1	1	0	0
Unrest: Border disputes, #	1	1	1	1	3	1	1	2	0	1
··International, #	3	0	0	0	3	0	0	2	0	0
··# of civil wars	0	0	0	0	4	0	3	2	0	0
··# of civil riots	0	0	0	0	1	1	0	1	0	0

Characteristics	Luxem- bourg	Macau	Macedonia	Madagas- car	Malawi	Malaysia	Maldives	Mali	Malta	Marshall Islands
Population 1994	392	499	1990	13300	10700	19200	232	10100	360	51
Population 1993	398	466	2190	13000	9810	18900	243	8810	363	52
Population 1992	392	450		12600	9610	18400	234	8540	359	
Vital Stats: Death rate	10	4	7	14	17	6	8	21	8	8
:Birth rate	12	17	16	46	52	29	45	52	14	47
Fertility	2	2	2	6	8	4	7	7	2	7
Female life exp., years	80	84	75	57	51	73	65	48	79	75
Male life exp., years	73	78	71	54	48	69	62	45	74	70
Infant mortality	8	8	51	118	153	33	82	132	12	64
# of major diseases	0	1		5	5	5	4	5	1	
Demography: Migration	7	4	0	0	-17	0	0	-5	1	0
Population of Country	392	499	1990	13300	10700	19200	232	10100	360	51
Urbanization, %	81	97	54	23	13	39	28	20	86	26
Population growth	0.5	1		3	3	3	3	2		
Females, % of pop	52	49		51	52	50	47	51	51	
Male % ages: 0-9 years	51	52		49	50	51	51	50	51	
10-19 years	51	51		49	49	51	51	49	52	
20-29 years	50	53		49	47	49	52	49	51	
30-39 years	51	57		49	42	50	51	49	50	
40-49 years	49	51		49	47	51	57	47	48	
50-59 years	49	47		50	50	49	58	48	46	
60-69 years	42	46		50	54	47	61	39	47	
70+ years	36	37		80	42	48	69	32	42	
Education: Literacy, adult	100	90	93	80	42	78	92	32	96	93
Cities: earliest settled, y	963	100		1610	1880	200	1300	1100	1570	
Largest settled, year	963	100		1610	1880	1860	1300	1880	1570	
Largest, % pop	20	93		6	4	5	20	8	6	
Politics: # of parties	6	4	6	5	3	6	1	7	2	2
Largest party %	37		31	34	50	71	100	66	52	100
Top two parties, %	67		57	46	80	82	100	74	100	100
Chambers in leg., #	2	1	1	2	1	2	1	1	1	2
# of changes 60		0		1	1	1	2	3	1	
Independence year	1870	1560	1990	1960	1960	1970	1970	1960	1960	1990
Laws: Censorship (1=high)	0	0	0	0.5	1	0	1	0	0	0
Metric system (1=yes)	0	2		0	0	0	1	3	0	
Visas needed (3=high)	2		0	3	0	2	2	3	2	0
Full soc security (1=yes)	1		1	0	0	1	0	0	1	0
Military service (1=yes)		0.5		0	0	1	0	0		
Crime: Murders/100k pop	2	4		3	1	2	2	1	0.9	
Thefts/100k pop	20					358				
Suicide/100k pop	0.9								0.3	
Prisoners/000 pop	0.0	1		1	1	1	1	1	0.6	1
Death penalty (1=yes)	0	0	0	0	0	3	0	0	0	0
Unrest: Border disputes, #	0	0	1	1	0	0	0	0	0	0
:International, #	0			0	1	0	0	0	0	
# of civil wars	0							2	0	
# of civil riots	0			0	1	0	1	0	0	1

Characteristics	Martinique	Mauritania	Mauritius	Mayotte	Mexico	Micronesia Federation	Moldova	Monaco	Mongolia	Montserrat
Population 1994	381	2190	1110	90	90000	101	4380	29	2320	12
Population 1993	369	2120	1100	90	92200		4440	31	2370	13
Population 1992	348	2060	1090		92000		4380	30	2310	
Vital Stats: Death rate		17	7	12	5	7	9	7		10
Birth rate	19	48	19	50	29	29	19	1	7	17
Fertility	2	5	2	7	3	4	1.9	1	34	2
Female life exp., years	81	50	74	59	76	73	74	80	5	78
Male life exp., years	75	46	68	55	69	68	68	72	68	74
Infant mortality	11	111	36	84	56	51	40	14	63	11
# of major diseases	1	5	2		2				75	
Demography: Migration			-4	0	-1	12	-2	0	3	-3
Population of Country	381	2190	1110	90	90000	101	4380	9	2320	12
Urbanization, %	82	41	41		72	19	47	29	56	
Population growth	0.9	2	2		3		1	100		
Females, % of pop	52	51	50	50	50			0.9		52
Male % ages: 0-9 years	52	51	51		51			53	50	
10-19 years	50	51	51		51			51	50	
20-29 years	51	47	50		50			50	50	
30-39 years	46	46	50		50			49	50	
40-49 years	47	48	49		49			48	50	
50-59 years	47	49	51		48			48	50	
60-69 years	47	47	49		45			47	50	
70+ years	39	41	37		43			44	50	
Education: Literacy, adult	93	34	83	62	87	90	98	40	90	97
Cities: earliest settled, y	1670	1900	1740		1120			99	1650	
Largest settled, year	1670	1900	1740		1330		15	-600	1650	
Largest, % pop	54	25	13		10		4	-600	24	
Politics: # of parties	7	3	6	4	5	0	54	43	3	4
Largest party %		85	47		64	100	81	2	92	
Top two parties, %	2	86	89	3	82	100		83	97	
Chambers in leg., #	0						1	94		1
# of changes 60	0	2	1		0	1	1990	0	2	
Independence year	1640	1960	1970	1840	1840	1980	0.5	1860	1920	1630
Laws: Censorship (1=high)		1	0	0	0	0	0	0	0	
Metric system (1=yes)	0	0	0		0	0	2	2	0	1
Visas needed (3=high)	2	3	2		2		1	1	3	
Full soc security (1=yes)		0	0		0		0	0	0	
Military service (1=yes)		0	0		1				1	
Crime: Murders/100k pop	4		2		17					
Thefts/100k pop			14							
Suicide/100k pop	4		2							
Prisoners/000 pop			1		0.5		0.5			
Death penalty (1=yes)		1	2		1		0	0	0	1
Unrest: Border disputes, #	0	1	0		0	0	3	0	0	
International, #	0	1	0		0		0	0	0	
# of civil wars	0	1	0		0		0	0	0	
# of civil riots	0	1	0	1	0	0	0	0	0	0

Characteristics	Morocco	Mozambique	Namibia	Nauru	Nepal	Netherlands	Netherlands Antilles	New Caledonia	New Zealand	Nicaragua
Population 1994	27000	16000	1570	10	21100	15300	180	178	3510	4140
Population 1993	27600	16400	1590	9	20600	15200	185	179	3350	3980
Population 1992	26700	15800	1580	9	20100	15100	184	175	3320	3860
Vital Stats: Death rate	8	17	9	5	14	8	8	8	8	7
:Birth rate	29	46	45	18	38	13	18	23	16	37
:Fertility	4	6	6	5	5	2	2	3	2	5
:Female life exp., years	67	50	63	69	53	81	79	76	80	68
:Male life exp., years	63	47	58	64	54	75	74	70	73	65
:Infant mortality	89	151	97	62	115	7	11	17	14	83
:# of major diseases	3	5	4	3	5	0	1	1	0	4
Demography: Migration	-1	12	0	0	0	0	-9	1	-2	-1
:Population of Country	27000	16000	1570	10	21100	15300	180	178	3510	4140
:Urbanization, %	46	26	37	70	8	89	53	58	84	59
:Population growth	3	3	2	-1	2	0.9	2	2	1	3
:Females, % of pop	50	51	51	44	49	50	52	52	50	50
Male % ages: 0-9 years	51	49	51	52	52	51	51	52	51	54
:10-19 years	51	52	49	52	52	51	50	52	51	50
:20-29 years	50	44	49	53	50	51	48	52	51	47
:30-39 years	48	45	50	53	49	51	47	52	50	48
:40-49 years	47	49	49	54	51	50	46	52	50	49
:50-59 years	49	51	50	53	53	46	46	52	47	48
:60-69 years	51	48	48	54	53	38	47	53	40	46
:70+ years	52	50	72	99	53	99	37	54	99	45
Education: Literacy, adult	50	33			26		94	91		57
Cities: earliest settled, y	-1500	1540	1890		723	200	1530	1850	1840	1520
:Largest settled, year	-1520	1540	1890		723	900	1530	1850	1840	1520
:Largest, % pop	11	7	8	67	1	5	38	38	25	18
Politics: # of parties	5	0		0	5			8	4	
:Top two parties, %	16	100	57	100	54	25	84	84	51	55
:Chambers in leg., #	32	100	86	100	88	48	97	97	96	98
:# of changes 60	1	2	2	1	2	2	1	2	0	2
:Independence year	1960	1980	1990	1970	1770	1820	1820	1850	1950	1840
Laws: Censorship (1=high)	1	1		0	3	0	0	0	0	
:Metric system (1=yes)	0	0	0	3	0	2	2	2	0	0
:Visas needed (3=high)	2	3	3	1	0	1			2	0
:Full soc security (1=yes)	0	0	0	0	0	0				2
:Military service (1=yes)	1	1		1	0	1	1	1	1	0
Crime: Murders/100k pop	2									
:Thefts/100k pop	202					5550			4340	
:Suicide/100k pop	0.8					11			13	
:Prisoners/000 pop						0.4				
:Death penalty (1=yes)	1	0		0	1	0	0	0	0	2
Unrest: Border disputes, #	3	0	3	0	0	0	0	0	0	
:International, #	1	0	0	0	0	0	0	0	0	2
:# of civil wars	0	1	0	0	0	0	1	0	0	1
:# of civil riots	0	0	1	0	1	0		1	0	1

Characteristics	Niger	Nigeria	Niue	Norfolk Island	North Korea	Northern Mariana Isl.	Norway	Oman	Pacific Isl. Trust	Pakistan
Population 1994	8560	107000	2	3	23000	48	4320	1680	16	128000
Population 1993	8530	94500	2	3	22600	49	4310	1640	16	124000
Population 1992	8430	91200			22200		4290	1590		120000
Vital Stats: Death rate	23	16			6		10	6	7	13
:Birth rate	58	46			24	35	14	41	23	43
:Fertility	7	7			2		2	7		7
:Female life exp., years	53	54			74	69	81	69	73	59
:Male life exp., years	49	51			68	66	74	65	69	59
:Infant mortality	141	128	2		48	38	8	60	25	128
:# of major diseases	5	2			2		0	5		6
Demography: Migration	0	0	2	3	0	0	0	0	2	-1
:Population of Country	8560	107000			23000	48	4320	1680	16	128000
:Urbanization, %	20	29			62		74	10		31
:Population growth	3	3	49		2		0.6	4	49	3
Females, % of pop	51	50			50		51	47		48
Male % ages: 0-9 years	50	51			50		51	53		50
:10-19 years	49	50			50		51	53		54
:20-29 years	49	50			50		51	52		52
:30-39 years	49	51			50		51	53		51
:40-49 years	49	50			49		50	53		51
:50-59 years	48	50			50		47	52		55
:60-69 years	48	50			50		40	53		59
:70+ years	48	50			99		99	41		58
Education: Literacy, adult	28	51	96	95	99	97	99	41	92	35
Cities: earliest settled, y	1600	1100			-1120		900	1510	1520	-600
:Largest settled, year	1600	1700			-1120		1050	1510	1520	1730
:Largest, % pop	5	1	1		12	2	11	3	3	4
Politics: # of parties	10				1		1	0		6
:Largest party %	60	100	100	100	100	2	8	100	2	43
:Top two parties, %	95	100	100	100	100		41	100		79
:Chambers in leg., #	1	1	1	1	1		1	1		2
:# of changes 60	2	4			0		0	2		1
:Independence year	1960	1960	1970	1770	1950	1950	1910	1650	1	1950
Laws: Censorship (1=high)	0.5	0.5	0	0	1		0	1		1
:Metric system (1=yes)	0.0	0.0			3		2	0		3
:Visas needed (3=high)	3	3			0		1	3		0
:Full soc security (1=yes)	0	0			1	2	1	1		0
:Military service (1=yes)		1			2		2		1	78
Crime: Murders/100k pop		94			1		1			18
:Thefts/100k pop		1260					4150			
:Suicide/100k pop							16			0.3
:Prisoners/000 pop							0.5	1		
:Death penalty (1=yes)	1	0	0	0	1		0	3	0	1
Unrest: Border disputes, #	0	0			2		2	2		3
:International, #	0	4			1		0	0		0
:# of civil wars	1	0			0		0	0		1
:# of civil riots	1				0		0	0		0

Characteristics	Panama	Papua New Guinea	Paraguay	Peru	Philippines	Pitcairn Islands	Poland	Portugal	Puerto Rico	Qatar
Population 1994	2560	4170	4630	22900	66500	0.1	38500	9890	3730	489
Population 1993	2580	4100	5080	23200	68500	0.1	38200	10500	3550	537
Population 1992	2530	4000	4940	22800	67100	.	37800	10400	3300	545
Vital Stats: Death rate	5	11	5	7	7	.	10	10	8	4
: Birth rate	25	34	33	27	28	.	14	12	17	21
: Fertility	3	5	4	3	4	.	2	2	2	4
: Female life exp., years	77	57	74	67	68	.	77	78	79	74
: Male life exp., years	73	55	71	63	63	.	69	71	73	69
: Infant mortality	35	85	57	89	71	.	27	22	14	45
: # of major diseases	5	5	0	0	5	.	1	2	0	4
Demography: Migration	0	0	0	0	-1	0.1	-1	-2	0	15
: Population of Country	2560	4170	4630	22900	66500	.	38500	9890	3730	489
: Urbanization, %	53	16	47	70	42	.	61	33	72	89
: Population growth	3	2	3	3	.	.	0.8	0.4	0.1	6
: Females, % of pop	49	48	50	50	50	.	51	52	51	36
Male % ages: 0-9 years	51	52	51	51	51	.	51	51	49	51
: 10-19 years	51	54	51	51	51	.	51	51	49	54
: 20-29 years	51	51	51	51	50	.	50	50	49	71
: 30-39 years	51	51	50	50	49	.	49	49	49	73
: 40-49 years	52	51	50	49	49	.	47	47	49	72
: 50-59 years	51	51	50	47	48	.	47	47	49	73
: 60-69 years	50	51	47	43	47	.	45	45	49	71
: 70+ years	88	52	44	43	47	.	35	38	49	50
Education: Literacy, adult	88	52	90	95	90	90	99	85	89	76
Cities: earliest settled, y	1670	1870	1540	1100	1400	.	700	-2000	1520	1870
: Largest settled, year	1670	1870	1540	1530	1400	100	1000	-2000	1520	1870
Politics: # of parties	28	7	15	21	3	100	4	4	14	42
: Largest, % pop	4	4	5	6	.	1	.	5	.	.
: Largest party %	34	20	67	55	36	100	37	59	6	100
: Top two parties, %	63	34	93	100	53	100	66	90	.	100
: Chambers in leg., #	.	1	2	1	2	1	2	1	2	1
: # of changes 60	2	0	1	4	2	.	1	2	.	.
Independence year	1900	1980	1940	1820	1950	1890	1950	1640	1900	1970
Laws: Censorship (1=high)	1	0.5	0.5	1	0.5	.	0	0	1	1
: Metric system (1=yes)	0	1	1	1	0	.	0	0	1	1
: Visas needed (3=high)	2	0	2	2	2	.	2	2	2	2
: Full soc security (1=yes)	0	0	0	1	0	.	1	1	.	1
: Military service (1=yes)	0	0	1	1	0	1	0	1	1	1
Crime: Murders/100k pop	6	.	4	7	30	100	2	2	18	.
: Thefts/100k pop	4	.	2	35.1	0.5	100	1650	436	8	13
: Suicide/100k pop	.	.	.	0.5	0.2	1	13	9	.	.
: Prisoners/000 pop	.	.	.	0.8	.	.	.	0.8	.	.
: Death penalty (1=yes)	0	0	0	1	.	.	1	0	.	2
Unrest: Border disputes, #	0	0	1	1	2	0	0	2	0	1
: International, #	1	0	0	4	0	.	0	0	0	0
: # of civil wars	1	0	1	0	2	.	0	1	0	0
: # of civil riots	0	0	0	0	0	.	1	0	0	0

Characteristics	Reunion	Romania	Russia	Rwanda	San Marino	Sao Tome E Principe	Saudi Arabia	Senegal	Serbia & Monten.	Seychelles
Population 1994	642	23400	149000	7780	23	127	16500	7930	10500	71
Population 1993	635	23400	149000	8330	23	135	18500	8460	10700	71
Population 1992	619	23500	148000	8200	23	132	18600	8200	.	70
Vital Stats: Death rate	26	11	11	14	8		6	13		23
..Birth rate	3	14	15	52		38	39	44		2
..Fertility	77	75	74	55	79			6		75
..Female life exp., years	70	69	70	51	74	68	68	57	52	65
..Male life exp., years	8	40	36	129	21	64	65	54		26
..Infant mortality	1					85	88	102		
..# of major diseases	0	-3	1	0	0	5	4	5		-8
Demography: Migration					5	0	0	0		71
..Population of Country	642	23400	149000	7780	23	127	16500	7930	10500	51
..Urbanization, %	62	53	71	7	85	38	74	35	47	3
..Population growth			0.7		0.6					
..Females, % of pop	51	51		3	52	50	47	51		49
Male % ages: 0-9 years	49	51		51	52	51	53	49		51
..10-19 years	49	51		50	52	51	53	49		53
..20-29 years	49	51		49	50	49	53	49		55
..30-39 years	49	49		44	50	47	53	49		49
..40-49 years	49	49		45	51	51	53	49		45
..50-59 years	49	44		44	50	49	53	50		44
..60-69 years	50	44		47	48	49	53	50		34
..70+ years	69	42		53	42	41	62	38	89	85
Education: Literacy, adult		96	99	1940	98	57	200	1860		1770
Cities: earliest settled, y	1670	-700		1940		1490	1700	1860		1770
..Largest settled, year	1670	630		2	30	1490	8	17		33
..Largest, % pop	20	17	6	0	6	27	0	8		3
Politics: # of parties	6	15	8	100	43	4	100	70	5	82
..Largest party %		34	21	100	66	60	100	93	34	97
..Top two parties, %		58	37			98			59	
..Chambers in leg., #		2	2	3	2	1	1		2	1
..# of changes 60	2			1	1		0	1		
Independence year	0	1950	1990	1960	301	1980	1930	1960	1990	1980
Laws: Censorship (1=high)	1640		0.5			0.5			1	0
..Metric system (1=yes)		0	0	0	0	0	0	0		0
..Visas needed (3=high)	0	3	2	3	2	3	3	3	1	2
..Full soc security (1=yes)	3	1	1	0	1	0	1	0	1	1
..Military service (1=yes)		3	1	0	0	0	1	0		0
Crime: Murders/100k pop						2	0.6			
..Thefts/100k pop		140					58			15
..Suicide/100k pop	0	2	1	1	0	0		0		0
..Prisoners/000 pop	0	0	1	0	0	0	1	0	1	1
..Death penalty (1=yes)	0	0	0	2	0	0	5	0		0
Unrest: Border disputes, #	0	1	0	0	0	0	1	1		0
..International, #		1		0						
..# of civil wars										
..# of civil riots										

Characteristics	Sierra Leone	Singapore	Slovakia	Slovenia	Solomon Islands	Somalia	South Africa	South Korea	Spain	Sri Lanka
Population 1994	4510	2860	5330	1960	333	9520	39600	44500	39200	17900
Population 1993	4510	2830	5380	1990	372	6840	42800	44200	39400	17800
Population 1992	4390	2790	.	2010	359	6930	41700	43500	39500	17600
Vital Stats: Death rate	20	5	9	9	5	13	8	6	9	6
: Birth rate	46	18	15	15	40	46	34	16	11	20
: Fertility	.	2	2	2	6	7	4	2	1	2
: Female life exp., years	48	78	77	78	72	57	67	74	82	74
: Male life exp., years	43	73	68	70	67	56	62	68	75	70
: Infant mortality	163	7	20	23	68	135	72	30	11	39
: # of major diseases	7	1	.	0	4	5	.	1	0	2
Demography: Migration	-28	0	0	0	0	-12	0	1	0	-2
: Population of country	4510	2860	5330	1960	333	9520	39600	44500	39200	17900
: Urbanization, %	31	100	77	47	11	36	59	72	81	22
: Population growth	2	2	.	0.6	4	3	2	2	.	2
: Females, % of pop	50	49	.	.	48	51	49	49	51	49
Male % ages: 0-9 years	50	52	.	.	52	49	50	52	51	51
: 10-19 years	50	52	.	.	52	50	50	52	52	51
: 20-29 years	50	51	.	.	50	49	53	51	50	51
: 30-39 years	49	50	.	.	51	50	53	51	48	51
: 40-49 years	49	51	.	.	53	49	52	52	46	52
: 50-59 years	49	49	.	.	53	49	50	47	40	52
: 60-69 years	49	49	.	.	60	48	47	43	46	54
: 70+ years	50	42	.	.	62	50	40	35	40	54
Education: Literacy, adult	21	90	93	99	60	24	76	96	96	88
Cities: earliest settled, y	1790	1100	.	.	1940	908	1650	-57	-1200	-543
: Largest settled, year	1790	1100	.	.	1940	908	1650	-6	931	-543
: Largest, % pop	11	90	.	15	9	15	5	22	8	4
Politics: # of parties	0	3	7	18	5	.	.	4	11	.
: Largest party %	100	95	49	24	45	100	63	50	46	56
: Top two parties, %	100	99	69	41	60	100	84	82	86	86
: Chambers in leg., #	1	1	1	2	1	1	2	2	2	2
: # of changes 60	3	0	.	1	3	3	1	.	.	.
: Independence year	1960	1970	1990	1990	1980	1960	1930	1950	1490	1950
Laws: Censorship (1=high)	1	1	0	0	0.1	0	0.5	.	0.5	1
: Metric system (1=yes)	0	1	1	0	1	3	.	0	.	.
: Visas needed (3=high)	3	1	1	1	1	3	3	2	2	0
: Full soc security (1=yes)	0	1	.	0	0	0	0	1	1	2
: Military service (1=yes)	0	2	0	1	0	0	0	1	1	0
Crime: Murders/100k pop	.	1	.	.	.	.	9	1	1	.
: Thefts/100k pop	.	12	0	2	0	1	109	230	2040	0.8
: Suicide/100k pop	1	2	0	1	0	5	0.3	8	0.7	0
: Prisoners/000 pop	.	1	.	.	.	1	1	.	0	0
: Death penalty (1=yes)	0	1	0	0	0	2	.	1	.	0
Unrest: Border disputes, #	0	0	0	1	0	1	0	0	2	0
: International, #	2	0	0	0	0	5	0	0	1	1
: # of civil wars	2	0	0	1	0	1	0	1	0	1
: # of civil riots	0	0	0	1	0	2	2	1	.	1

Characteristics	St. Helena	St. Kitts & Nevis	St. Lucia	St. Pierre & Miquelon	St. Vincent & Grenad.	Sudan	Suriname	Swaziland	Sweden	Switzerland
Population 1994	7	43	147	6	114	27400	440	818	8670	6860
Population 1993	7	40	152	7	116	28800	415	906	8680	6930
Population 1992		40	156		116	28000	408	882	8600	6830
Vital Stats: Death rate	7	10	5	6	5	13	6	12	11	9
: Birth rate	10	22	26	9	23	44	26	44	13	12
: Fertility	1	2	3	1	2	6	3	6	2	2
: Female life exp., years	76	71	75	78	74	54	74	60	81	83
: Male life exp., years	72	66	70	75	71	53	68	56	75	76
: Infant mortality	40	44	32	10	39	105	52	121	5	6
: # of major diseases	0	1	1		1	6	1	6	0	0
Demography: Migration	7	-9	-4	1	-7	0	-5	-6	2	3
: Population of Country		43	147	6	114	27400	440	818	8670	6860
: Urbanization, %		45	46		23	26	48	30	84	60
: Population growth	48	0.4	2	51	2	3	-0.7	3	0.5	0.5
: Females, % of pop		50	52		52	50	50	53	51	51
Male % ages: 0-9 years		50	50		51	51	51	50	51	51
: 10-19 years		51	51		51	50	50	48	51	51
: 20-29 years		52	50		47	50	49	42	51	50
: 30-39 years		49	46		47	49	47	44	50	50
: 40-49 years		46	45		44	48	48	44	48	49
: 50-59 years		45	44		45	47	50	43	41	46
: 60-69 years		38	38		38	43	45	42		38
: 70+ years						27		33		
Education: Literacy, adult	98	98	88	99	96		95	68	99	99
Cities: earliest settled, y			1770		1760	1800	1540	1900	900	-3000
: Largest settled, year			1770		1760	1820	1540	1900	1260	-3000
: Largest, % pop	2	48	35	2	17		26	5	8	5
Politics: # of parties		4	2		3		6	1	8	6
: Largest party %		29	65		57	100	59	100	40	22
: Top two parties, %	1	58	100	2	71	100	82	100	63	43
: Chambers in leg., #		1	2		1		3	2	1	0
: # of changes 60										
: Independence year	1670	1980	1980	1600	1980	1960	1980	1970	1910	1820
Laws: Censorship (1=high)	1		0.5	0	1	1	0.5	1	0	0
: Metric system (1=yes)									0	0
: Visas needed (3=high)		2	2		2	3	3	2	2	2
: Full soc security (1=yes)		1	1		1		1		1	1
: Military service (1=yes)	1						1		1	1
Crime: Murders/100k pop		1	7		7	3	5	1	7	3
: Thefts/100k pop									8620	4590
: Suicide/100k pop							22		19	24
: Prisoners/000 pop									0.5	0.7
: Death penalty (1=yes)	0	1	1	0	1	1	2	1	1	0
Unrest: Border disputes, #						2			0	0
: International, #		0	0		0	1	0	0	0	0
: # of civil wars		0	0		0	2	2	0	0	0
: # of civil riots		0	0		0	0	0	0	1	0

Characteristics	Syrian Arab Rep.	Taiwan	Tajikistan	Tanzania	Thailand	Togo	Tokelau	Tonga	Trinidad & Tobago	Tunisia
Population 1994	13800	20800	5730	28800	56800	3910	2	96	1300	8580
Population 1993	14200	21100	5630	28800	58600	4100	2	104	1310	8600
Population 1992	13500	20900	5270	27800	57600	3950		103	1300	8450
Vital Stats: Death rate	7	5	8	15	6	12		7	6	5
: Birth rate	44	16	40	49	20	48		26	21	25
: Fertility					2			4	2	3
: Female life exp., years	71	78	74	51	71	58		70	74	74
: Male life exp., years	68	72	70	53	67	54		65	69	70
: Infant mortality	60	5	73	123	49	123		53	23	60
: # of major diseases	5	1	1	1	2	0				1
Demography: Migration	0	0	-1	-1	0	0		-11	-3	0
: Population of Country	13800	20800	5730	28800	56800	3910	2	96	1300	8590
: Urbanization, %	50	70	32	24	20	24		27	67	54
: Population growth	3	1	3	3	3	3		0.9	1	2
: Females, % of pop	49	48		51	50	51	51	50	50	49
Male % ages: 0-9 years	52	52		50	51	49		51	51	51
: 10-19 years	52	52		48	51	49		51	50	51
: 20-29 years	50	52		46	51	49		50	50	50
: 30-39 years	49	52		49	50	49		51	49	49
: 40-49 years	53	53		51	48	49		51	49	48
: 50-59 years	51	52		48	46	48		51	49	52
: 60-69 years	50	53		48	42	48		50	42	55
: 70+ years	50	52		48	42	50		50	42	56
Education: Literacy, adult	64	92	98	89	93	43	99	100	96	65
Cities: earliest settled, y	-1400	-1630		1600	700	1900		1860	1600	-400
: Largest settled, year	-1400	-1710		1860	1780	1900		1860	1600	-400
: Largest, % pop	10	13	12	3	10	10		28	3	7
Politics: # of parties	6	2	5	1	6	5			3	5
: Largest party,%	54	79	94	100	22	44	100		58	88
: Top two parties, %	57	97	94	100	43	87	100		94	94
: Chambers in leg., #	1	2	1	1	2	1	1	1	2	1
: # of changes 60	2	1	1	1	3	1				1
: Independence year	1950	1950	1990	1960	1880	1960	1930	1970	1960	1960
Laws: Censorship (1=high)	1	0.5	1	0.1	1	1		1		0.5
: Metric system (1=yes)	0	0	0	0	0	0		2	0	0
: Visas needed (3=high)	3	3	2	3	2	2		0	2	2
: Full soc security (1=yes)	0	0	0	0	0	0		0	1	0
: Military service (1=yes)	1	1	1	0	0	0	0	0	0	0
Crime: Murders/100k pop	2									
: Thefts/100k pop	51				10				5	349
: Suicide/100k pop					6			0.6	9	
: Prisoners/000 pop					9				2	
: Death penalty (1=yes)	1	1	1	0	1	1	0	0	1	1
Unrest: Border disputes, #	5	2	1	1	1					1
: International, #	4			1						1
: # of civil wars	1	0	0	0	0	1		0	0	0
: # of civil riots	2	0	0	0	0			0	0	0

Characteristics	Turkey	Turkme-nistan	Turks & Caicos	Tuvalu	Uganda	Ukraine	United Arab Emir.	United Kingdom	United States	Uruguay
Population 1994	59000	3980		11	19300	52100	1820	57800	258000	3130
Population 1993	61000	3860	14	9	19700	51900	2660	57900	257000	3170
Population 1992	59900	3710	13	9	19400	51900	2530	57700	255000	3140
Vital Stats: Death rate	6	9	5	9	14	12	3	11	9	6
..Birth rate	27	36	16	28	51	14	29	14	14	17
..Fertility	3	5			7	2	5	2	2	2
..Female life exp., years	72	74	77	64	55	75	74	79	80	76
..Male life exp., years	68	66	73	61	51	71	70	73	73	69
..Infant mortality	76	86	13	53	112	27	39	10	15	37
..# of major diseases	0	0			6	0	5	0	0	0
Demography: Migration	0	-3	22	0			27	0	2	-1
..Population of Country	59600	3980	14	11	19300	52100	1820	57800	258000	3130
..Urbanization, %	61	45	52	29	10	67	78	89	74	87
..Population growth	2	3			3	0.3	5	0.2	1	0.4
..Females, % of pop	49				50	54	29	51	51	51
Male % ages: 0-9 years	51			56	50	51	51	52	51	51
..10-19 years	52			47	50	51	63	51	51	51
..20-29 years	51			47	49	50	81	51	50	50
..30-39 years	50			47	49	49	82	50	49	50
..40-49 years	50			47	49	47	78	50	49	49
..50-59 years	51			48	49	45	74	49	48	47
..60-69 years	49			48	50	35	59	47	46	42
..70+ years	43			47	48	27	60	37	38	96
Education: Literacy, adult	81	98	98	96		98	68	99	98	
Cities: earliest settled, y	-3650		1770		1890		1760	-600	1540	1730
..Largest settled, year	-658				1890		1800	43	1620	1730
..Largest, % pop	9	11	3	33	2	5	11	12	3	40
Politics: # of parties	7				0	13	0	6	2	4
..Largest party %	39	100		100	100	25	100	52	60	39
..Top two parties, %	64	100		100	100	48	100	94	100	69
..Chambers in leg., #	1	1	1	1	1		2	2	2	2
..# of changes 60	2	1			3	1	1	0	0	5
Independence year	1920	1990	1770	1980	1960	1990	1971	1920	1776	1830
Laws: Censorship (1=high)	1	1	1	0		0	1	0	0	0
..Metric system (1=yes)	0	0		1		0		1	1	0
..Visas needed (3=high)	2	2	1	3	3	2	3	2	2	2
..Full soc security (1=yes)	1	0		0	0	0	1	1	1	1
..Military service (1=yes)	1	1		0	0	1		0	0	
Crime: Murders/100k pop	2							3	9	4
..Thefts/100k pop	68							6680	5350	
..Suicide/100k pop								9	13	9
..Prisoners/000 pop	0.9				0.5			0.9	0.3	0.6
..Death penalty (1=yes)	1	1	0				1	0	1	
Unrest: Border disputes, #	4	0		0	0	3	4	0	4	2
..International, #	2	0		0	0	0	0	0	2	0
..# of civil wars	0	0		0	0	0	0	0	0	2
..# of civil riots	1	0		0	2	0	0	0	0	2

Characteristics	Uzbekis-tan	Vanuatu	Vatican City	Venezuela	Vietnam	Virgin Isl., US	Wallis & Futuna	West Bank	Western Samoa	Western Sahara
Population 1994	21700	164		20600	70100	103	14	1400	221	207
Population 1993	21800	173		20600	71100	99	14	1400	199	202
Population 1992	20900	175		20700	69000	100			194	202
Vital Stats: Death rate	7	5		4	8	5	6	6	6	20
.: Birth rate	34	35		27	29	21	27	35	34	48
.: Fertility	4			3	4	3	4		4	7
.: Female life exp., years	74	72		78	67	77	71	71	70	46
.: Male life exp., years	69	67		71	63	74	70	68	65	43
.: Infant mortality	65	61		40	69	13	29	37	66	159
.: # of major diseases	1	1		5	5	0			1	
Demography: Migration	-2	0		1	-1	-26	-8	2	-4	-2
.: Population of Country	21700	164		20600	70100	103	14	1400	221	207
.: Urbanization, %	41	23	100	86	21	39			21	37
.: Population growth	3	4	0.9	4	2	0.7			0.8	3
.: Females, % of pop		47		50	52	52		50	48	
Male % ages: 0-9 years										
.: 10-19 years										
.: 20-29 years										
.: 30-39 years										
.: 40-49 years										
.: 50-59 years										
.: 60-69 years										
.: 70+ years										
Education: Literacy, adult	98	53	100	88	88	90	50		98	15
Cities: earliest settled, y		1860		1520	-200	1670		-1900	1850	1940
.: Largest settled, year		1860		1570	1700	1670		-1900	1850	1940
.: Largest, % pop	10	9	100	5	5	19	5		17	48
Politics: # of parties	1	4	0	27	1	3			2	2
.: Largest party %	100	41	100	27	100		2	100	65	
.: Top two parties, %	100	63	100	54	100			100	98	
.: Chambers in leg., #	1	1	1	2	1	2	2		1	1
.: # of changes 60		1		1						
.: Independence year	1990	1980	1930	1830	1980	1920	1840		1960	1980
Laws: Censorship (1=high)	1	0	0	0	0.5		0			
.: Metric system (1=yes)	0	1	0	0	0.3				2	0
.: Visas needed (3=high)	2	1	1	3	3				0	0
.: Full soc security (1=yes)	1	0	0	0	0				0	
.: Military service (1=yes)	1	0	0	1	1			1	0	
Crime: Murders/100k pop										
.: Thefts/100k pop				53	1					
.: Suicide/100k pop				5	6					
.: Prisoners/000 pop				2	3					
.: Death penalty (1=yes)	0	0	0	1	2	0	0		0	
Unrest: Border disputes, #	0	0	0	0	0	0	0	1	0	
.: International, #	0	0	0			0			0	2
.: # of civil wars	0	0	0			0			0	1
.: # of civil riots	0	0	0			0			0	1

Characteristics	Yemen	Zaire	Zambia	Zimbabwe
Population 1994	13000	41200	8870	10900
Population 1993	10700	40900	8990	11100
Population 1992	10400	39100	8740	11000
Vital Stats: Death rate	16	13	11	8
:Birth rate	51	45	48	40
:Fertility	7	6	7	5
:Female life exp., years	55	56	59	64
:Male life exp., years	52	53	55	60
:Infant mortality	138	112	97	80
:# of major diseases	5	2	2	2
Demography: Migration	-3	0	-2	-3
:Population of Country	13000	41200	8870	10900
:Urbanization, %	26	41	49	27
:Population growth	2	3	3	3
:Females, % of pop		51	51	51
Male % ages: 0-9 years				
:10-19 years				
:20-29 years				
:30-39 years				
:40-49 years				
:50-59 years				
:60-69 years				
:70+ years				
Education: Literacy, adult	39	72	73	67
Cities: earliest settled, y		1880	1900	1890
:Largest settled, year		1890	1910	1890
:Largest, % pop	4	7	2	6
Politics: # of parties	5	0		5
:Largest party %	40	100	83	97
:Top two parties, %	61	100	100	99
:Chambers in leg., #	1	1	2	1
:# of changes 60	3			1
Independence year	1990	1960	1960	1980
Laws: Censorship (1=high)	1	1	0.5	0
:Metric system (1=yes)	0	0	0	0
:Visas needed (3=high)	3	3	3	2
:Full soc security (1=yes)	0	0	0	0
:Military service (1=yes)	1	0	0	0
Crime: Murders/100k pop				18
:Thefts/100k pop				1450
:Suicide/100k pop	1	1		17
:Prisoners/000 pop	2	2	2	2
:Death penalty (1=yes)	1	0	0	1
Unrest: Border disputes, #	2	1	0	1
:International, #	1	2	0	0
:# of civil wars	2	0	0	0
:# of civil riots	1	1	0	1

5

CULTURAL RESOURCES ACROSS COUNTRIES

A given cultural group will rarely exist in isolation and is likely to co-exist with others within a given social or cultural milieu. This chapter provides comparative statistics for a variety of cultural variables across countries. For a full discussion of the methodology used to generate these estimates, please refer to Chapter 1 which gives important caveats. This chapter first gives summary statistics of the variables reported: the number of countries for which each variable was available, weighted averages (by population) and simple averages; these averages can be used as benchmarks. Then a lengthy comparative table is presented which provides raw statistics across countries.

Most of the variables are self explanatory, though some merit commentary. All of the statistics should be considered as estimates which have undergone rounding and certain adjustments. Culture is broadly defined as a country's ethnic, religious and linguistic heritage. The variable "Ethnic Groups: # present" measures the average number of ethnic groups co-living within the country. The higher this number, the more the country is exposed to multiple ethnic groups. The variable "Max ethnic %" estimates the percent of the highest represented ethnic group in the country. The higher this number, the more homogeneous (the less dominated by one) the country is in terms of its exposure to multiple ethnic groups; similarly for religions and colonial languages. For these latter two, estimates are given covering the percent of the population having certain religious beliefs (practiced and official) and colonial languages (spoken as mother tongues, being official, or being used, in part, in commercial settings).

Summary Statistics:
Cultural Resources

Characteristics	Number of Countries Covered	Weighted Average by Pop 1994	Simple Average	Simple Standard Deviation
Ethnic Groups: # present	234	8.19	4.95	3.20
: Maximum % present	233	73.25	70.32	23.21
Religions: # present	234	10.69	7.61	3.31
: Maximum % present	233	67.05	68.66	22.78
Beliefs: Anglican %	233	0.90	4.33	12.96
: Buddhist %	233	5.93	3.37	14.09
: Christian Total %	233	29.42	57.73	38.59
: Hindu %	233	13.67	1.89	9.54
: Jewish %	233	0.27	0.52	5.55
: Islam %	233	19.90	21.32	35.27
: Protestant Total %	233	6.63	19.83	29.16
: Roman Catholic %	234	15.89	30.06	35.53
: Traditional %	233	2.31	4.25	11.20
Official: Anglican	234	0.01	0.00	0.07
: Buddhism	234	0.01	0.01	0.11
: Christianism	234	0.00	0.00	0.07
: Greek Orthodox	234	0.00	0.00	0.07
: Hinduism	234	0.00	0.00	0.07
: Islam	234	0.11	0.11	0.31
: Lutheran-Evangelical	234	0.00	0.03	0.16
: Monotheism	234	0.03	0.00	0.07
: Orthodox	234	0.00	0.01	0.09
Languages: # present	234	7.72	3.82	3.28
: Maximum % present	233	63.78	74.29	25.81
: Number official	192	1.33	1.29	1.02
: None official (1=yes)	222	0.05	0.02	0.13
Mother Tongue: Arabic %	231	3.58	7.86	24.46
: Chinese (all) %	231	20.65	1.89	11.82
: English %	232	5.95	8.78	25.70
: French %	231	1.03	1.60	9.80
: German %	231	1.72	1.65	11.99
: Spanish %	233	5.39	7.99	25.26
Official: Arabic %	234	4.56	11.11	31.49
: Chinese %	234	22.21	1.71	12.99
: English %	234	29.61	32.91	47.09
: French %	234	4.91	17.09	37.73
: German %	234	1.89	2.56	15.84
: Spanish %	234	5.99	8.97	28.64
Commercial: Arabic %	228	0.05	0.12	0.32
: Chinese %	228	0.23	0.02	0.15
: English %	228	0.64	0.64	0.48
: French %	228	0.14	0.28	0.45
: German %	228	0.04	0.06	0.24
: Italian %	228	0.02	0.05	0.21
: Portuguese %	228	0.03	0.03	0.17
: Russian %	228	0.08	0.09	0.28
: Spanish %	228	0.11	0.13	0.33

Characteristics	Afghan-istan	Albania	Algeria	American Samoa	Andorra	Angola	Anguilla	Antigua & Barbuda	Argentina	Armenia
Ethnic Groups: # present	7	4	3	3	6	12	2	3	2	4
:Max % present	52	97	83	90	46	37	60	94	85	95
Religions: # present	7	5	7	5	4	8	7	7	9	3
:Max % present	74	65	99	50	99	69	40	44	93	94
Beliefs: Anglican %	0	0	0	0	0	0	40	44	0	0
:Buddhist %	0	0	0.4	0	0	0	0	0	0	0
:Christian Total %	0	33	0	98	100	90	88	96	95	97
:Hindu %	0	0	0	0	0	0	0	0	0.0	0
:Jewish %	0	0	0	0	0.4	0	0	0	0.0	0
:Islam %	89	65	99	0	0	0	0	0	2	3
:Protestant Total %	0	1	0	79	0.5	20	85	86	93	3
:Roman Catholic %	0	13	0.4	20	99	69	3	10	93	
:Traditional %	0	0	0	0	0	1	0	0	0.1	
Official: Anglican										
:Buddhism										
:Christianism										
:Greek Orthodox										
:Hinduism										
:Islam	1		1							
:Luthren Evangelical										
:Monotheism							1	1		
:Orthodox				2	3	9	1	1	3	4
Languages:: # present	6	2	5							
:Max % present	51	98	83	90	56	37	100	96	96	90
:Number official	2	1	1		1	1		1	1	1
:None official (1=yes)	0	0	0	0	0	0	0	0	0	0
Mother Tongue: Arabic %	0	0	83							
:Chinese (all) %	0	0	0	3						
:English %	0	0	0		8		100			
:French %	0	0	0							
:German %	0	0	0							
:Spanish %	0	0	0		56				96	
Official: Arabic %	0	0	100							
:Chinese %	0	0	0							
:English %	0	0	0	100			100	100		
:French %	0	0	0							
:German %	0	0	0							
:Spanish %	0	0	0						100	
Commercial: Arabic %	0	0	1	0	0	0	0	0	1	0
:Chinese %	0	1	0	1	1	1	1	1	1	1
:English %	1	0	0	0	0	0	0	0	1	0
:French %	0	0	1	0	0	0	0	0	1	0
:German %	0	0	0	0	0	0	0	0	0	0
:Italian %	0	1	0	0	0	0	0	0	0	0
:Portuguese %	0	0	0	0	0	1	0	0	0	0
:Russian %	0	0	0	0	0	0	0	0	0	1
:Spanish %	0	0	0	0	1	0	0	0	1	0

Characteristics	Aruba	Australia	Austria	Azerbaijan	Bahamas	Bahrain	Bangla-desh	Barbados	Belarus	Belgium
Ethnic Groups: # present	1	3	4	6	3	5	3	3	5	8
Max % present	80	95	95	81	77	65	98	86	78	55
Religions: # present	3	15	8	5	10	7	8	8	3	8
Max % present	89	26	83	60	32	60	87	40	60	79
Beliefs: Anglican %	0	25	0	0	20	0	0	40	0	0
Buddhist %	0	0	0	0	0	0	0	0	0	0
Christian Total %	97	74	88	11	83	7	0	59	68	79
Hindu %	0	0	0	0	0.1	2	12	0	0	0.3
Islam %	0	0	0.2	80	0	90	87	0	0	0.3
Jewish %	0	0.5	0.2	0	0	0	0	0	0	0
Protestant Total %	8	43	6	0	64	0	0	55	0	0
Roman Catholic %	89	26	83	0	19	0	0.1	4	8	79
Traditional %	0	0	0	0	0	0	0	0	0	0
Official: Anglican	0	0	0	0	0	0	0	0	0	0
Buddhism	0	0	0	0	0	0	0	0	0	0
Christianity	0	0	0	0	0	0	0	0	0	0
Greek Orthodox	0	0	0	0	0	0	0	0	0	0
Hinduism	0	0	0	0	0	0	0	0	0	0
Islam	0	0	0	0	0	1	1	0	0	0
Luthren Evangelical	0	0	0	0	0	0	0	0	0	0
Monotheism	0	0	0	0	0	0	0	0	0	0
Orthodox	0	0	0	0	0	0	0	0	0	0
Languages: # present	1	3	1	4	2	3	2	2	4	4
Max % present	86	89	99	78	85	81	98	90	70	59
Number official	0	1	1	1	1	1	1	1	1	3
None official (1=yes)	0	0	0	0	0	0	0	0	0	0
Mother Tongue: Arabic %	0	0	0	0	0	80	0	0	0	0
Chinese (all) %	0	0	0	0	0	0	0	0	0	0
English %	0	89	0	0	85	0	0	90	0	0
French %	0	0	0	0	0	0	0	0	0	0
German %	0	0	99	0	0	0	0	0	0	0.6
Spanish %	0	0	0	0	0	0	0	0	0	0
Official: Arabic %	0	0	0	0	0	100	0	0	0	0
Chinese %	0	0	0	0	0	0	0	0	0	0
English %	0	89	0	0	100	0	0	100	0	0
French %	0	0	0	0	0	0	0	0	0	100
German %	0	0	99	0	0	0	0	0	0	100
Spanish %	0	0	0	0	0	0	0	0	0	0
Commercial: Arabic %	0	0	0	0	0	100	0	0	0	0
Chinese %	0	0	0	0	0	0	0	0	0	0
English %	0	100	0	0	0	1	1	1	0	1
French %	0	0	0	0	0	0	0	0	0	1
German %	0	0	100	0	0	0	0	0	0	1
Italian %	0	1	1	0	0	0	0	0	0	0
Portuguese %	0	0	0	0	0	0	0	0	0	0
Russian %	0	0	0	1	0	0	0	0	1	0
Spanish %	0	0	0	0	0	0	0	0	0	0

Characteristics	Belize	Benin	Bermuda	Bhutan	Bolivia	Bosnia & Herzegov.	Botswana	Brazil	British Virgin Isl.	Brunei
Ethnic Groups: # present	6	5	2	3	4	3	5	9	2	4
Max % present	38	66	61	63	31	40	76	22	60	66
Religions: # present	16	8	9	5	8	6	7	14	10	7
Max % present	58	63	37	70	93	43	50	63	45	63
Beliefs: Anglican %	12	0	37	0	0	0	0	0	21	0
Buddhist %	0	0	0	70	0	0	0	0.3	0	13
Christian Total %	89	23	72	0	93	52	48	78	90	10
Hindu %	3	0	0	25	0	0	0	0	0	0
Jewish %	1	0	0	0	0	0	0	0.1	0	0
Islam %	0	13	0	5	0	43	0	0	0	63
Protestant Total %	31	3	58	0	0	4	27	6	84	0
Roman Catholic %	58	20	14	0	93	17	9	63	6	0
Traditional %	4	63	0	0	0.8	0	50	0	0	5
Official: Anglican	0	0	0	0	0	0	0	0	0	0
Buddhism	0	0	0	1	0	0	0	0	0	0
Christianism	0	0	0	0	0	0	0	0	0	0
Greek Orthodox	0	0	0	0	0	0	0	0	0	0
Hinduism	0	0	0	0	0	0	0	0	0	0
Islam	0	0	0	0	0	0	0	0	0	1
Luthren Evangelical	0	0	0	0	0	0	0	0	0	0
Monotheism	0	0	0	0	0	0	0	0	0	0
Orthodox	0	0	0	0	0	0	0	0	0	0
Languages: # present	4	10	1	5	3	1	3	2	1	4
Max % present	60	26	93	30	37	99	75	97	100	50
Number official	1	1	.	1	3	1	1	1	.	1
None official (1=yes)	0	0	0	0	0	0	0	0	0	0
Mother Tongue: Arabic %	0	0	0	0	0	0	0	0	0	0
Chinese (all) %	0	0	0	0	0	0	0	0	0	13
English %	0	0	93	0	0	0	0	0	0	3
French %	0	0	0	0	0	0	0	0	0	0
German %	0	0	0	0	0	0	0	0	0	0
Spanish %	25	0	0	0	35	0	0	0	0	0
Official: Arabic %	0	0	0	0	0	0	0	0	0	0
Chinese %	0	0	0	0	0	0	0	0	0	0
English %	100	0	100	0	0	0	100	0	100	0
French %	0	100	0	0	0	0	0	0	0	0
German %	0	0	0	0	0	0	0	0	0	0
Spanish %	0	0	0	0	100	0	0	0	0	0
Commercial: Arabic %	0	0	0	0	0	0	0	0	0	0
Chinese %	0	0	0	0	0	0	0	0	0	0
English %	1	1	1	1	1	.	1	1	1	1
French %	0	0	0	0	0	.	0	0	0	0
German %	0	0	0	0	0	.	0	0	0	0
Italian %	0	0	0	0	0	.	0	0	0	0
Portuguese %	0	0	0	0	0	.	0	1	0	0
Russian %	0	0	0	0	0	.	0	0	0	0
Spanish %	1	0	0	0	1	.	0	0	0	0

Characteristics	Bulgaria	Burkina Faso	Burma	Burundi	Cambodia	Cameroon	Canada	Cape Verde	Cayman Islands	Central Afric. Rep.
Ethnic Groups: # present	6	9	6	4	3	11	28	3	3	8
Max % present	85	48	69	83	88	20	34	71	40	29
Religions: # present	7	7	12	7	8	8	15	5	6	6
Max % present	77	45	89	70	88	34	45	90	36	40
Beliefs: Anglican %	0	0	0	0	0	0	5	0	0	0
Buddhist %	0	0	89	0	88	0	0	0	0	0
Christian Total %	78	12	5	79	0	52	87	97	60	69
Hindu %	0	0	0	0	0	0	0.4	0	0	0
Jewish %	0.1	0	0	0	0	0	1	0	2	0
Islam %	13	42	4	1	2	22	0.4	0	0	8
Protestant Total %	0.7	2	0	9	0	18	41	7	60	40
Roman Catholic %	0.0	10	4	70	2	34	45	90	0	29
Traditional %	0	45	0	10	0	25	0	0	0	18
Official: Anglican	0	0	0	0	0	0	0	0	0	0
Buddhism	0	0	1	0	1	0	0	0	0	0
Christianism	0	0	0	0	0	0	0	0	0	0
Greek Orthodox	0	0	0	0	0	0	0	0	0	0
Hinduism	0	0	0	0	0	0	0	0	0	0
Islam	0	0	0	0	0	0	0	0	0	0
Luthren Evangelical	0	0	0	0	0	0	0	0	0	0
Monotheism	0	0	0	0	0	0	0	0	0	0
Orthodox	1	0	0	0	0	0	0	0	0	0
Languages: # present	3	7	8	3	5	6	29	2	1	4
Max % present	85	48	69	97	80	9	60	70	100	47
Number official	1	1	1	2	1	2	2	1	0	1
None official (1=yes)	0	0	0	0	0	0	0	0	0	0
Mother Tongue: Arabic %	0	0	0	0	0	0	0.1	0	0	0
Chinese (all) %	0	0	0	0	0	0	0.9	0	0	0
English %	0	0	0	0	0	0	60	0	100	0
French %	0	0	0	0	4	0	24	0	0	0
German %	0	0	0	0	0	0	2	0	0	0
Spanish %	0	0	0	0	0	0	0.3	0	0	0
Official: Arabic %	0	0	0	0	0	0	0	0	0	0
Chinese %	0	0	0	0	0	0	0	0	0	0
English %	0	0	0	0	0	100	100	0	100	0
French %	0	100	0	100	0	100	100	0	0	100
German %	0	0	0	0	0	0	0	0	0	0
Spanish %	0	0	0	0	0	0	0	0	0	0
Commercial: Arabic %	0	0	0	0	0	0	0	0	0	0
Chinese %	0	0	0	0	0	0	0	0	0	0
English %	0	0	1	0	0	1	1	0	1	0
French %	0	1	0	1	1	0	1	0	0	1
German %	0	0	0	0	0	0	0	0	0	0
Italian %	0	0	0	0	0	0	0	0	0	0
Portuguese %	0	0	0	0	0	0	0	1	0	0
Russian %	1	0	0	0	0	0	0	0	0	0
Spanish %	0	0	0	0	0	0	0	0	0	0

Characteristics	Chad	Chile	China	Christmas Island	Cocos (Keel.) Isl.	Colombia	Comoros	Congo	Cook Island	Costa Rica
Ethnic Groups: # present	11	3	16	3	2	6	3	8	4	5
:Max % present	31	80	93	61	50	58	97	52	81	86
Religions: # present	8	9	8	11	5	9	4	8	4	8
:Max % present	43	81	59	36	90	93	99	54	98	88
Beliefs: Anglican %	0	0	0	3	0	0	0	0	0	0
:Buddhist %	0	0	6	36	0	0	0	0	0	0
:Christian Total %	33	87	0.2	18	0	93	0.6	78	98	88
:Hindu %	0	0.1	0	0	0	0	0	0	0	0.1
:Jewish %	0	0	0	0	0	0	0	0	0	0
:Islam %	43	0	2	25	90	0	99	24	0	0
:Protestant Total %	8	6	0	58	0	93	0	54	98	88
:Roman Catholic %	24	81	0.1	0	0	0.8	0.6	19	0	0
:Traditional %	0	0.7	0	0	0	0	0	10	0	0
Official: Anglican	0	0	0	0	0	0	0	0	0	0
:Buddhism	0	0	0	0	0	0	0	0	0	0
:Christianism	0	0	0	0	0	0	0	0	0	0
:Greek Orthodox	0	0	0	0	0	0	0	0	0	0
:Hinduism	0	0	0	0	0	0	0	0	0	0
:Islam	0	0	0	0	0	0	1	0	0	0
:Luthren Evangelical	0	0	0	0	0	0	0	0	0	0
:Monotheism	0	0	0	0	0	0	0	0	0	0
:Orthodox	0	0	0	0	0	0	0	0	0	0
Languages: # present	7	2	8	1	1	1	1	4	1	3
:Max % present	30	92	67	100	100	99	100	47	100	97
:Number official	1	1	1	0	0	1	2	1	1	1
:None official (1=yes)	0	0	0	1	1	0	0	0	0	0
Mother Tongue: Arabic %	30	0	0	0	0	0	100	0	0	0
:Chinese (all) %	0	0	93	0	0	0	0	0	0	0
:English %	0	0	0	0	0	0	0	0	0	0
:French %	0	0	0	0	0	0	0	0	0	0
:German %	0	0	0	0	0	0	0	0	0	0
:Spanish %	0	92	0	0	0	99	0	0	0	97
Official: Arabic %	100	0	0	0	0	0	100	0	0	0
:Chinese %	0	0	100	0	0	0	0	0	0	0
:English %	0	0	0	100	100	0	0	0	100	0
:French %	100	0	0	0	0	0	100	100	0	0
:German %	0	0	0	0	0	0	0	0	0	0
:Spanish %	0	100	0	0	0	100	0	0	0	97
Commercial: Arabic %	1	0	0	0	0	0	1	0	0	0
:Chinese %	0	0	1	0	0	0	0	0	0	0
:English %	0	0	0	1	1	0	0	0	1	0
:French %	1	0	0	0	0	0	1	1	0	0
:German %	0	0	0	0	0	0	0	0	0	0
:Italian %	0	0	0	0	0	0	0	0	0	0
:Portuguese %	0	0	0	0	0	0	0	0	0	0
:Russian %	0	0	0	0	0	0	0	0	0	0
:Spanish %	0	1	0	0	0	1	0	0	0	1

Characteristics	Croatia	Cuba	Cyprus	Czech Republic	Denmark	Djibouti	Dominica	Dominican Republic	Ecuador	Egypt
Ethnic Groups: # present	7	3	2	6	7	4	4	3	4	1
: Max % present	78	66	78	94	97	47	91	73	50	99
Religions: # present	6	10	8	14	10	7	10	6	8	7
: Max % present	77	53	76	40	88	94	77	92	92	88
Beliefs: Anglican %	0	0	0	0	0	0	0	0	0	0
··Buddhist %	0	0	0	0	0	0	0	0	0	0
··Christian Total %	89	36	78	48	89	5	92	92	92	10
··Hindu %	0	0	0	0	0	0	0	0	0	0
··Jewish %	0	0	0	0.1	0.1	0	0	0	0	0
··Islam %	1	0	19	0	0.1	94	0	0	0	88
··Protestant Total %	1	3	0	7	88	1	15	0	0	0
··Roman Catholic %	77	33	0	39	0.5	3	77	92	92	0
··Traditional %	0	0	0	0	0	0	0	0	0.5	0
Official: Anglican	0	0	0	0	0	0	0	0	0	0
··Buddhism	0	0	0	0	0	0	0	0	0	0
··Christianism	0	0	0	0	0	0	0	0	0	0
··Greek Orthodox	0	0	0	0	0	0	0	0	0	0
··Hinduism	0	0	0	0	0	0	0	0	0	0
··Islam	0	0	0	0	0	1	0	0	0	1
··Luthren Evangelical	0	0	0	0	1	0	0	0	0	0
··Monotheism	0	0	0	0	0	0	0	0	0	0
··Orthodox	0	0	0	0	0	0	0	0	0	0
Languages: # present	1	1	2	6	2	4	1	2	2	1
: Max % present	96	100	73	66	97	47	100	98	93	99
··Number official	1	1	2	1	1	2	1	1	1	1
··None official (1=yes)	0	0	0	0	0	0	0	0	0	0
Mother Tongue: Arabic %	0	0	0	0	0	0	0	0	0	99
··Chinese (all) %	0	0	0	0	0	0	0	0	0	0
··English %	0	0	0	0	0	0	100	0	0	0
··French %	0	0	0	0	0	0	0	0	0	0
··German %	0	0	0	1	0	0	0	0	0	0
··Spanish %	0	100	0	0	0	0	0	98	93	0
Official: Arabic %	0	0	0	0	0	100	0	0	0	100
··Chinese %	0	0	0	0	0	0	0	0	0	0
··English %	0	0	0	0	0	0	100	0	0	0
··French %	0	0	0	0	0	100	0	0	0	0
··German %	0	0	0	0	0	0	0	0	0	0
··Spanish %	0	100	0	0	0	0	0	100	100	0
Commercial: Arabic %	0	0	0		0	0	0	0	0	0
··Chinese %	0	0	0		0	0	0	0	0	0
··English %	1	0	1		0	1	1	1	0	1
··French %	0	0	0		0	1	0	0	0	0
··German %	1	0	0		0	0	0	0	0	0
··Italian %	1	0	0		0	0	0	0	0	0
··Portuguese %	0	0	0		0	0	0	0	0	0
··Russian %	0	0	0		0	0	0	0	0	0
··Spanish %	0	1	0		0	0	0	1	1	0

Characteristics	El Salvador	Equatorial Guinea	Eritrea	Estonia	Ethiopia	Falkland Islands	Faroe Islands	Fiji	Finland	France
Ethnic Groups: # present	3	5	4	5	9	1	5	3	2	7
: Max % present	91	78	50	62	38	100	97	50	94	90
Religions: # present	7	8	2	3	9	4	4	9	7	10
: Max % present	92	85	80	100	48	50	97	52	87	76
Beliefs: Anglican %	0	0	0	0	0	50	0	0	0	0
: Buddhist %	0	0	0	0	0	0	0	0	0	0
: Christian Total %	92	85	20	100	53	50	97	52	88	82
: Hindu %	0	0	0	0	0	0	0	38	0	0
: Jewish %	0	0	0	0.2	0	0	0	0	0	1
: Islam %	0	0.5	80	0	32	0	0	8	0	3
: Protestant Total %	0	0	0	100	0	50	97	0	87	2
: Roman Catholic %	92	85	0	0	0	0	0	0	0	76
: Traditional %	0.1	0	0	0	11	0	0	0	0	0
Official: Anglican	0	0	0	0	0	0	0	0	0	0
: Buddhism	0	0	0	0	0	0	0	0	0	0
: Christianism	0	0	0	0	0	0	0	0	0	0
: Greek Orthodox	0	0	0	0	0	0	0	0	0	0
: Hinduism	0	0	0	0	0	0	0	0	0	0
: Islam	0	0	0	0	0	0	0	0	0	0
: Luthren Evangelical	0	0	0	0	0	0	0	0	1	0
: Monotheism	0	0	0	0	0	0	0	0	0	0
: Orthodox	0	0	0	0	1	0	0	0	1	0
Languages: # present	1	4	4	3	11	1	2	3	2	8
: Max % present	100	75	50	65	31	100	97	49	94	83
: Number official	1	1	2	1	1	1	0	1	2	1
None official (1=yes)	0	0	0	0	0	0	0	0	0	0
Mother Tongue: Arabic %	0	0	3	0	0	0	0	0	0	3
: Chinese (all) %	0	0	0	0	0	0	0	0	0	0
: English %	0	0	0	0	0	100	0	0	0	0
: French %	0	0	0	0	0	0	0	0	0	83
: German %	0	0	0	0	0	0	0	0	0	2
: Spanish %	100	0	0	0	0	0	0	0	0	0
Official: Arabic %	0	0	0	0	0	0	0	0	0	0
: Chinese %	0	0	0	0	0	0	0	0	0	0
: English %	0	0	0	0	0	100	0	100	0	0
: French %	0	0	0	0	0	0	0	0	0	100
: German %	0	0	0	0	0	0	0	0	0	0
: Spanish %	100	100	0	0	0	0	0	0	0	0
Commercial: Arabic %	0	0	0	0	0	0	0	0	0	0
: Chinese %	0	0	0	0	0	0	0	0	0	0
: English %	0	0	1	0	1	100	0	1	1	1
: French %	0	0	0	0	0	0	0	0	0	1
: German %	0	0	0	0	0	0	0	0	0	0
: Italian %	0	0	0	0	0	0	0	0	0	0
: Portuguese %	0	0	0	0	0	0	0	0	0	0
: Russian %	0	0	0	1	0	0	0	0	0	0
: Spanish %	1	1	0	0	0	0	0	0	0	0

Characteristics	French Guiana	French Polynesia	Gabon	Gambia	Gaza Strip	Georgia	Germany	Ghana	Gibraltar	Greece
Ethnic Groups: # present	8	5	4	5	2	10	7	6	6	4
Max % present	43	68	36	40	100	70	93	52	66	95
Religions: # present	11	8	7	5	3	5	8	8	8	9
Max % present	80	47	65	94	99	75	43	28	74	97
Beliefs: Anglican %	0	0	0	0	0	0	0	0	8	0
Buddhist %	0	0	0	0	0	0	0	0	0	0
Christian Total %	84	97	96	4	0.7	83	61	62	85	98
Hindu %	0	0	0	0	0	0	0.1	0	0	0
Jewish %	0	0	0	0	0.3	1	0	0	1	0
Islam %	1	0	0.8	94	99	1	2	16	8	2
Protestant Total %	4	50	19	0	0	0	44	28	11	0.1
Roman Catholic %	80	39	65	0	0	0	15	21	74	0.4
Traditional %	0.9	0	3	0.9	0	0	0	0	0	0
Official: Anglican	0	0	0	0	0	0	0	0	0	0
Buddhism	0	0	0	0	0	0	0	0	0	0
Christianism	0	0	0	0	0	0	0	0	0	0
Greek Orthodox	0	0	0	0	0	0	0	0	0	1
Hinduism	0	0	0	0	0	0	0	0	0	0
Islam	0	0	0	0	0	0	0	0	0	0
Luthren Evangelical	0	0	0	0	0	0	1	0	0	0
Monotheism	0	0	0	0	0	0	0	0	0	0
Orthodox	0	0	0	0	0	1	0	0	0	0
Languages: # present	2	5	5	4	2	4	2	9	5	4
Max % present	90	69	29	40	99	69	98	44	86	95
Number official			1	1		1	1	1		1
None official (1=yes)	0	0	0	0	0	0	0	0	0	0
Mother Tongue: Arabic %	0	0	0	0	99	0	0	0	0	0
Chinese (all) %	0	0	0	0	0	0	0	0	0	0
English %	0	0	0	0	0	0	0	0	2	0
French %	0	90	6	0	0	0	0	0	0	0
German %	0	0	0	0	0	0	98	0	0	0
Spanish %	0	0	0	0	0	0	0	0	11	0
Official: Arabic %	0	0	0	0	100	0	0	0	0	0
Chinese %	0	0	0	0	0	0	0	0	0	0
English %	0	0	0	100	0	0	0	100	86	0
French %	100	100	100	0	0	0	0	0	0	0
German %	0	0	0	0	0	0	100	0	0	0
Spanish %	0	0	0	0	0	0	0	0	0	0
Commercial: Arabic %	0	0	0	0	100	0	0	0	0	0
Chinese %	0	0	0	0	0	0	0	0	0	0
English %	0	0	0	1	1	0	1	1	100	1
French %	1	1	1	0	0	0	0	0	0	1
German %	0	0	0	0	0	0	1	0	0	0
Italian %	0	0	0	0	0	0	0	0	0	0
Portuguese %	0	0	0	0	0	0	0	0	0	0
Russian %	0	0	0	0	0	1	0	0	0	0
Spanish %	0	0	0	0	0	0	0	0	1	0

Characteristics	Greenland	Grenada	Guadeloupe	Guam	Guatemala	Guernsey	Guinea	Guinea-Bissau	Guyana	Haiti
Ethnic Groups: # present	1	4	4	6	4	2	5	5	4	3
: Max % present	83	84	77	42	55	80	39	27	51	95
Religions: # present	5	8	6	3	9	7	7	7	12	11
: Max % present	98	64	89	80	74	63	80	58	37	80
Beliefs: Anglican %	0	20				63			15	0
: Buddhist %										
: Christian Total %	98	94	89	96	98	95	2	6	41	94
: Hindu %	0	0	0	0	0	0	0	0	37	0
: Jewish %	0	0	0	0	0	0	0	0	0	0
: Islam %	0	0	0	0	0	0	80	34	2	0
: Protestant Total %	98	30	5	16	24	77			41	14
: Roman Catholic %	0	64	89	80	74	18				80
: Traditional %	0						5	58		
Official: Anglican	0	0	0	0	0	0	0	0	0	0
: Buddhism	0	0	0	0	0	0	0	0	0	0
: Christianism	0	0	0	0	0	0	0	0	0	0
: Greek Orthodox	0	0	0	0	0	0	0	0	0	0
: Hinduism	0	0	0	0	0	0	0	0	0	0
: Islam	0	0	0	0	0	0	0	0	0	0
: Luthren Evangelical	1	0	0	0	0	0	0	0	0	0
: Monotheism	0	0	0	0	0	0	0	0	0	0
: Orthodox	0	0	0	0	0	0	0	0	0	0
Languages: # present	2	2	1	4	6		6	6	3	2
: Max % present	86	97	100	50	66	100	40	30	78	99
: Number official		1	1	1	1	1	1	1	1	2
: None official (1=yes)						0				
Mother Tongue: Arabic %		0	0	0	0		0	0	0	0
: Chinese (all) %		0	0	0	0		0	0	0	0
: English %		0	0	25	0		0	0	100	0
: French %		0	100	0	0		0	0	0	0
: German %		0	0	0	0		0	0	0	0
: Spanish %		0	0	0	66		0	0	0	0
Official: Arabic %		0	0	0	0	0	0	0	0	0
: Chinese %		0	0	0	0	0	0	0	0	0
: English %		100	0	100	0	100	0	0	100	0
: French %		0	100	0	0	0	100	0	0	100
: German %		0	0	0	0	0	0	0	0	0
: Spanish %		0	0	0	100	0	0	0	0	0
Commercial: Arabic %		0	0	0	0	0	0	0	0	0
: Chinese %		0	0	0	0	0	0	0	0	0
: English %		1	0	1	0	1	0	0	1	0
: French %		0	1	0	0	0	1	0	0	1
: German %		0	0	0	0	0	0	0	0	0
: Italian %		0	0	0	0	0	0	0	0	0
: Portuguese %		0	0	0	0	0	0	1	0	0
: Russian %		0	0	0	0	0	0	0	0	0
: Spanish %	0	0	0	0	1	0	0	0	0	0

Characteristics	Honduras	Hong Kong	Hungary	Iceland	India	Indonesia	Iran	Iraq	Ireland	Isle of Man
Ethnic Groups: # present	4	9	7	5	3	4	11	5	1	4
: Max % present	90	97	97	97	72	39	46	77	94	89
Religions: # present	1	9	10	8	14	12	12	12	8	6
: Max % present	90	43	57	93	80	81	91	60	93	61
Beliefs: Anglican %	0	0	0	0	0	0	0	0	0	61
: Buddhist %	0	34	0	0	0.7	0.9	0	0	0	0
: Christian Total %	98	9	82	97	2	9	0.7	4	96	91
: Hindu %	0	0	0	0	80	2	0	0	0	0
: Jewish %	0	0	0.8	0	0	0	0	0	0	0.1
: Islam %	0	0	0	0	11	81	98	94	0	0
: Protestant Total %	8	0	21	96	1	5	0	3	3	80
: Roman Catholic %	90	0	57	1	1	4	0	3	93	11
: Traditional %	0.1	0	0	0	0	4	0	0	0	0
Official: Anglican	0	0	0	0	0	0	0	0	0	0
: Buddhism	0	0	0	0	0	0	0	0	0	0
: Christianism	0	0	0	0	0	0	0	0	0	0
: Greek Orthodox	0	0	0	0	0	0	0	0	0	0
: Hinduism	0	0	0	0	1	0	0	0	0	0
: Islam	0	0	0	0	0	1	1	1	0	0
: Luthren Evangelical	0	0	0	1	0	0	0	0	0	0
: Monotheism	0	0	0	0	0	0	0	0	0	0
: Orthodox	0	0	0	0	0	0	0	0	0	0
Languages: # present	3	2	5	1	14			5	2	3
: Max % present	97	97	99	100	28	42	50	78	95	89
: Number official	1	2	1	1	2	1	1	1	2	0
: None official (1=yes)	0	0	0	0	0	0	0	0	0	0
Mother Tongue: Arabic %	0	0	0	0	0	0	0	78	0	0
: Chinese (all) %	0	97	0	0	0	2	0	0	0	0
: English %	1	2	0	0	0	0	0	0	95	89
: French %	0	0	0	0	0	0	0	0	0	0
: German %	0	0	0.4	0	0	0	0	0	0	0
: Spanish %	97	0	0	0	0	0	0	0	0	0
Official: Arabic %	0	0	0	0	0	0	0	100	0	0
: Chinese %	0	100	0	0	0	0	0	0	0	0
: English %	0	100	0	0	100	0	0	0	100	100
: French %	0	0	0	0	0	0	0	0	0	0
: German %	0	0	1	0	0	0	0	0	0	0
: Spanish %	100	0	0	0	0	0	0	0	0	0
Commercial: Arabic %	0	0	0	0	0	0	0	1	0	0
: Chinese %	0	0	0	0	0	0	0	0	0	0
: English %	0	1	0	1	1	1	1	0	1	1
: French %	0	0	0	0	0	0	0	0	0	0
: German %	0	0	1	0	0	0	0	0	0	0
: Italian %	0	0	0	0	0	0	0	0	0	0
: Portuguese %	0	0	0	0	0	0	0	0	0	0
: Russian %	0	0	0	0	0	0	0	0	0	0
: Spanish %	1	0	0	0	0	0	0	0	0	0

Characteristics	Israel	Italy	Ivory Coast	Jamaica	Japan	Jersey	Jordan	Kazakhstan	Kenya	Kiribati
Ethnic Groups: # present	2	1	7	4	1	2	5	9	10	4
: Max % present	82	98	20	76	99	80	99	42	21	96
Religions: # present	8	6	9	15	9	7	6	4	13	7
: Max % present	84	82	37	18	55	63	92	47	26	53
Beliefs: Anglican %	0	0	0	0	0	63	0	0	7	0
: Buddhist %	0	0	0	0	55	0	0	0	0	0
: Christian Total %	2	82	20	58	2	95	5	17	73	95
: Hindu %	0	0.1	0	0	0	0	0	0	0	0
: Jewish %	84	0	0	0	0	0	0	0	0	0
: Islam %	10	0	20	0	0	0	92	47	6	0
: Protestant Total %	0	0	5	53	0	77	0	2	29	43
: Roman Catholic %	0	82	15	5	0	18	0	0	26	53
: Traditional %	0	0	37	0	0	0	0	0	1	0
Official: Anglican	0	0	0	0	0	0	0	0	0	0
: Buddhism	0	0	0	0	0	0	0	0	0	0
: Christianism	0	0	0	0	0	0	0	0	0	0
: Greek Orthodox	0	0	0	0	0	0	0	0	0	0
: Hinduism	0	0	0	0	0	0	0	0	0	0
: Islam	0	0	0	0	0	0	0	0	0	0
: Luthren Evangelical	0	0	0	0	0	0	0	0	0	0
: Monotheism	0	0	0	0	0	0	0	0	0	0
: Orthodox	0	0	0	0	0	0	0	0	0	0
Languages: # present	5	5	5	3	1	0	2	4	8	2
: Max % present	69	94	41	70	99	.	98	50	20	97
: Number official	1	1	1	1	1	.	1	1	1	1
: None official (1=yes)	0	0	0	0	0	.	0	0	0	0
Mother Tongue: Arabic %	18	0	0	0	0	0	98	0	0	0
: Chinese (all) %	0	0	0	0	0	0	0	0	0	0
: English %	0	0	0	27	0	0	0	0	0	3
: French %	0	0	0	0	0	0	0	0	0	0
: German %	0	0	0	0	0	0	0	4	0	0
: Spanish %	0	0	0	0	0	0	0	0	0	0
Official: Arabic %	100	0	0	0	0	0	100	0	0	0
: Chinese %	0	0	0	0	0	0	0	0	0	0
: English %	0	0	0	100	0	100	0	0	100	0
: French %	0	0	100	0	0	0	0	0	0	0
: German %	0	0	0	0	0	0	0	0	0	0
: Spanish %	0	0	0	0	0	0	0	0	0	0
Commercial: Arabic %	0	0	0	0	0	0	1	0	0	0
: Chinese %	0	0	0	0	0	0	0	0	0	0
: English %	1	1	1	1	1	1	1	1	1	1
: French %	0	1	1	0	0	0	0	0	0	0
: German %	1	1	0	0	0	0	0	0	0	0
: Italian %	0	0	0	0	0	0	0	0	0	0
: Portuguese %	1	1	0	0	0	0	0	0	0	0
: Russian %	0	0	0	0	0	0	0	1	0	0
: Spanish %	0	0	0	0	0	0	0	0	0	0

Characteristics	Kuwait	Kyrgyz-stan	Laos	Latvia	Lebanon	Lesotho	Liberia	Libya	Liechten-stein	Lithuania
Ethnic Groups: # present	3	8	5	6	3	1	10	8	4	6
: Max % present	42	52	67	52	83	100	19	89	64	80
Religions: # present	5	5	9	5	12	9	5	5	6	4
: Max % present	45	70	58	35	30	44	67	97	86	80
Beliefs: Anglican %	0	0	0	0	0	12	0	0	0	0
: Buddhist %	0	0	58	0	0	0	0	0	0	0
: Christian Total %	0	20	2	65	15	93	67	0	95	95
: Hindu %	0	0	0	0	0	0	0	0	0	0
: Jewish %	0	0	0	0	0	0	0	0	0.1	0.3
: Islam %	85	70	1	0	50	0	14	97	0	0
: Protestant Total %	0	0	0	25	0	41	0	0	9	15
: Roman Catholic %	0	0	0	20	4	44	0	0	86	80
: Traditional %	0	0	33	0	0	6	19	0	0	0
Official: Anglican	0	0	0	0	0	0	0	0	0	0
: Buddhism	0	0	0	0	0	0	0	0	0	0
: Christianism	0	0	0	0	0	0	0	0	0	0
: Greek Orthodox	0	0	0	0	0	0	0	0	0	0
: Hinduism	0	0	0	0	0	0	0	0	0	0
: Islam	1	0	0	0	0	0	0	1	0	0
: Luthren Evangelical	0	0	0	0	0	0	0	0	0	0
: Monotheism	0	0	0	0	0	0	0	0	0	0
: Orthodox	0	0	0	0	0	0	0	0	0	0
Languages: # present	1	5	4	2	2	2	8	2	1	5
: Max % present	85	48	79	54	93	85	23	95	100	80
: Number official	1	2	1	1	1	2	1	1	1	1
: None official (1=yes)	0	0	0	0	0	0	0	0	0	0
Mother Tongue: Arabic %	85	0	0	0	93	0	0	95	0	0
: Chinese (all) %	0	0	0	0	0	0	0	0	0	0
: English %	0	0	0	0	0	0	0	0	0	0
: French %	0	0	0	0	0	0	0	0	0	0
: German %	0	0	0	0	0	0	0	0	100	0
: Spanish %	0	0	0	0	0	0	0	0	0	0
Official: Arabic %	100	0	0	0	100	0	0	100	0	0
: Chinese %	0	0	0	0	0	0	0	0	0	0
: English %	0	0	0	0	0	100	100	0	0	0
: French %	0	0	0	0	0	0	0	0	0	0
: German %	0	0	0	0	0	0	0	0	100	0
: Spanish %	0	0	0	0	0	0	0	0	0	0
Commercial: Arabic %	1	0	0	0	1	0	0	1	0	0
: Chinese %	0	0	0	0	0	0	0	0	0	0
: English %	1	0	0	0	0	1	1	1	0	0
: French %	0	0	1	0	1	0	0	0	0	0
: German %	0	0	0	0	0	0	0	0	100	0
: Italian %	0	0	0	0	0	0	0	1	0	0
: Portuguese %	0	0	0	0	0	0	0	0	0	0
: Russian %	0	1	0	1	0	0	0	0	0	1
: Spanish %	0	0	0	0	0	0	0	0	0	0

Characteristics	Luxem-bourg	Macau	Macedonia	Madagas-car	Malawi	Malaysia	Maldives	Mali	Malta	Marshall Islands
Ethnic Groups: # present	6	3	6	11	4	3	4	11	2	1
:Max % present	71	74	67	27	58	61	40	32	96	100
Religions: # present	7	8	5	10	8	11	4	6	6	3
:Max % present	92	49	59	47	34	53	100	89	97	90
Beliefs: Anglican %	0	0	0	0	0	0	0	0	0	0
:Buddhist %	0	16	0	0	0	17	0	0	0	0
:Christian Total %	93	17	64	50	64	6	0	1	97	99
:Hindu %	0.3	0	0	0	0	7	0	0	0	0
:Jewish %	0.0	0	0	0	0	0	0	0	0	0
:Islam %	1	0	26	3	16	53	100	89	0	0
:Protestant Total %		1	1	26	34	0	0	0	0	90
:Roman Catholic %	92	6	4	47	28	4	0	9	97	9
:Traditional %	0	0	0	0	19	0	0	0	0	0
Official: Anglican	0	0	0	0	0	0	0	0	0	0
:Buddhism	0	0	0	0	0	0	0	0	0	0
:Christianity	0	0	0	0	0	0	0	0	0	0
:Greek Orthodox	0	0	0	0	0	0	0	0	0	0
:Hinduism	0	0	0	0	0	0	0	0	0	0
:Islam	0	0	0	0	0	0	1	0	0	0
:Luthren Evangelical	0	0	0	0	0	0	0	0	0	0
:Monotheism	0	0	0	0	0	0	0	0	0	0
:Orthodox	0	0	0	0	0	0	0	0	0	0
Languages: # present	1	2	4	1	4	10	1	9	3	4
:Max % present	100	99	70	99	50	47	100	38	96	80
:Number official	1		0	2	2	1	1	1	2	2
:None official (1=yes)	0	0	0	0	0	0	0	0	0	0
Mother Tongue: Arabic %	0	0	0	0	0	0	0	0	0	0
:Chinese (all) %	0	99	0	0	0	28	0	0	0	0
:English %	0	0	0	0	0	0	0	0	0	0
:French %	0	0	0	0	0	0	0	0	0	0
:German %	0	0	0	0	0	0	0	0	0	0
:Spanish %	0	0	0	0	0	0	0	0	0	0
Official: Arabic %	0	0	0	0	0	0	0	0	0	0
:Chinese %	0	99	0	0	0	0	0	0	0	0
:English %	0	0	0	0	100	0	0	0	100	100
:French %	100	0	0	100	0	0	0	100	0	0
:German %	100	0	0	0	0	0	0	0	0	0
:Spanish %	0	0	0	0	0	0	0	0	0	0
Commercial: Arabic %	0	0	.	0	0	0	0	0	0	0
:Chinese %	0	1	.	0	0	1	0	0	0	0
:English %	0	1	.	0	1	1	1	0	1	1
:French %	1	0	.	1	0	0	0	1	0	0
:German %	1	0	.	0	0	0	0	0	0	0
:Italian %	0	0	.	0	0	0	0	0	1	0
:Portuguese %	0	1	.	0	0	0	0	0	0	0
:Russian %	0	0	.	0	0	0	0	0	0	0
:Spanish %	0	0	.	0	0	0	0	0	0	0

Characteristics	Martinique	Mauritania	Mauritius	Mayotte	Mexico	Micronesia Federation	Moldova	Monaco	Mongolia	Montserrat
Ethnic Groups: # present	3	5	4	5	4	0	7	11	6	4
: Max % present	94	82	56	97	55	0	63	52	79	96
Religions: # present	7	6	9	3	8	.	6	4	6	8
: Max % present	89	99	53	97	93	.	96	90	49	38
Beliefs: Anglican %	0	0	0.4	0	0	.	0	0	0	38
: Buddhist %	0	0	0	0	0	.	0	0	2	0
: Christian Total %	93	0.4	30	3	96	.	97	90	0	98
: Hindu %	0	0	53	0	0.1	.	0	0	0	0
: Islam %	0	99	13	97	0	.	2	2	1	0
: Jewish %	0	0	0	0	0	.	0	0	0	0
: Protestant Total %	5	0	4	3	3	.	0	0	0	86
: Roman Catholic %	89	0	26	3	93	50	0	90	0	12
: Traditional %	0	0	0	0	0.1	.	0	0	0	0
Official: Anglican	0	0	0	0	0	0	0	0	0	0
: Buddhism	0	0	0	0	0	0	0	0	0	0
: Christianism	0	0	0	0	0	0	0	0	0	0
: Greek Orthodox	0	0	0	0	0	0	0	0	0	0
: Hinduism	0	0	0	0	0	0	0	0	0	0
: Islam	0	1	0	0	0	0	0	0	0	0
: Luthren Evangelical	0	0	0	0	0	0	0	0	0	0
: Monotheism	0	0	0	0	0	0	0	0	0	0
: Orthodox	0	0	0	0	0	0	1	0	0	0
Languages: # present	1	5	7	3	9	0	5	5	4	1
: Max % present	100	80	54	80	84	1	62	58	90	100
Number official	.	1	1	.	1	0	1	1	1	.
None official (1=yes)	.	0	0	.	0	1	0	0	0	.
Mother Tongue: Arabic %	0	80	0	0.7	0	0	0	0	0	0
: Chinese (all) %	0	0	0	0	0	0	0	0	0	0
: English %	0	0	4	0	0	20	0	5	0	100
: French %	0	0	0	0	0	0	0	58	0	0
: German %	0	0	0	0	0	0	0	0	0	0
: Spanish %	0	0	0	0	84	0	0	0	0	0
Official: Arabic %	0	100	0	0	0	0	0	0	0	0
: Chinese %	0	0	0	0	0	0	0	0	0	0
: English %	0	0	100	0	0	100	0	0	0	100
: French %	100	0	100	100	0	0	0	100	0	0
: German %	0	0	0	0	0	0	0	0	0	0
: Spanish %	0	0	0	0	100	0	0	0	0	0
Commercial: Arabic %	0	1	0	0	0	0	0	0	0	0
: Chinese %	0	0	0	0	0	0	0	0	0	0
: English %	1	0	1	1	0	1	0	1	0	100
: French %	1	0	1	0	0	0	0	1	0	0
: German %	0	0	0	0	0	0	0	0	0	0
: Italian %	0	0	0	0	0	0	0	1	0	0
: Portuguese %	0	0	0	0	0	0	0	0	0	0
: Russian %	0	0	0	0	0	0	1	0	1	0
: Spanish %	0	0	0	0	1	0	0	0	0	0

Characteristics	Morocco	Mozam-bique	Namibia	Nauru	Nepal	Nether-lands	Netherlands Antilles	New Caledonia	New Zealand	Nicaragua
Ethnic Groups: # present	2	5	6	4	7	4	4	6	3	5
: Max % present	70	47	50	58	58	95	84	43	86	69
Religions: # present	7	7	8	8	10	10	9	9	14	11
: Max % present	99	48	51	54	86	36	85	72	22	87
Beliefs: Anglican %	0	0	5	3	0	0	0	0	22	0
: Buddhist %	0	0	0	2	8	0	0	0	0	0
: Christian Total %	1	31	82	81	0.2	62	97	88	63	92
: Hindu %	0	0	0	0	86	0.2	0.4	0	0.1	0
: Jewish %	0	0	0.1	0	0	0.3	0	0.3	0	0
: Islam %	99	13	0	0	3	0	0.4	0	0.1	0
: Protestant Total %	0	0	62	57	0	26	12	16	48	5
: Roman Catholic %	0	31	20	24	0	36	85	72	15	87
: Traditional %	0	48	3	0	0.6	0	0	0.1	0.2	0
Official: Anglican	0	0	0	0	0	0	0	0	0	0
: Buddhism	0	0	0	0	0	0	0	0	0	0
: Christianism	0	0	0	0	0	0	0	0	0	0
: Greek Orthodox	0	0	0	0	0	0	0	0	0	0
: Hinduism	0	0	0	0	1	0	0	0	0	0
: Islam	1	0	0	0	0	0	0	0	0	0
: Luthren Evangelical	0	0	0	0	0	0	0	0	0	0
: Monotheism	0	0	0	0	0	0	0	0	0	0
: Orthodox	0	0	0	0	0	0	0	0	0	0
Languages: # present	4	9	9	6	10	2	2	3	2	3
: Max % present	65	38	47	58	51	93	86	42	93	95
: None official	0	0	0	0	0	0	0	0	0	0
: Number official (1=yes)	1	1	1	1	1	1	1	0	1	1
Mother Tongue: Arabic %	65	0	0	0	0	0	0	0	0	0
: Chinese (all) %	0	0	0	0	0	0	0	0	0	0
: English %	0	0	1	9	0	0	0	0	93	0
: French %	0	0	0	0	0	0	0	35	0	0
: German %	0	0	3	0	0	0	0	0	0	0
: Spanish %	0	0	0	0	0	0	0	0	0	95
Official: Arabic %	100	0	0	0	0	0	0	0	0	0
: Chinese %	0	0	0	0	0	0	0	0	0	0
: English %	0	0	100	0	0	0	8	0	100	0
: French %	0	0	0	0	0	0	0	100	0	0
: German %	0	0	0	0	0	0	0	0	0	0
: Spanish %	0	0	0	0	0	0	0	0	0	100
Commercial: Arabic %	1	0	0	0	0	0	0	0	0	0
: Chinese %	0	0	0	0	0	0	0	0	0	0
: English %	1	0	1	1	0	0	0	0	1	0
: French %	1	0	0	0	0	0	0	1	0	0
: German %	0	0	1	0	0	0	0	0	0	0
: Italian %	0	0	0	0	0	0	0	0	0	0
: Portuguese %	0	1	0	0	0	0	0	0	0	0
: Russian %	0	0	0	0	0	0	0	0	0	0
: Spanish %	1	0	0	0	0	0	1	0	0	1

Characteristics	Niger	Nigeria	Niue	Norfolk Island	North Korea	Northern Mariana Isl.	Norway	Oman	Pacific Isl. Trust	Pakistan
Ethnic Groups: # present	6	11	2	3	2	6	7	4	4	5
:Max % present	52	21	97	85	100	45	97	74	40	66
Religions: # present	4	9	9	6	5	5	7	6	4	12
:Max % present	90	45	75	39	71	49	88	72	97	77
Beliefs: Anglican %	0	0	1	39	0	0	0	0	0	0
:Buddhist %	0	0	0	0	0	0	0	0	0	0
:Christian Total %	0	49	98	71	0.9	95	92	0	0	2
:Hindu %	0	0	0	0	0	0	0	13	0	2
:Jewish %	0	0	0	0	0	0	0	0	0	0
:Islam %	90	45	0	0	0	0	0	87	0	97
:Protestant Total %	0	26	90	60	0	49	88	0	0	0
:Roman Catholic %	0	12	7	12	0	46	0	0	0.9	0
:Traditional %	0	6	0	0	15	4	0	0	0	0
Official: Anglican	0	0	0	0	0	0	0	0	0	0
:Buddhism	0	0	0	0	0	0	0	0	0	0
:Christianism	0	0	0	0	0	0	0	0	0	0
:Greek Orthodox	0	0	0	0	0	0	0	0	0	0
:Hinduism	0	0	0	0	0	0	0	0	0	0
:Islam	0	0	0	0	1	0	0	1	0	1
:Luthren Evangelical	0	0	0	0	0	0	1	0	0	0
:Monotheism	0	0	0	0	0	0	0	0	0	0
:Orthodox	0	0	0	0	0	0	0	0	0	0
Languages: # present	5	12	2	3	1	3	2	6	3	8
:Max % present	46	21	95	50	100	43	99	68	45	48
:Number official	1	1			1		1	1		1
:None official (1=yes)										
Mother Tongue: Arabic %	0	0	0	0	0	0	0	68	0	0
:Chinese (all) %	0	0	0	0	0	0	0	0	0	0
:English %	0	0	3	50	0	0	0	0	15	0
:French %	0	0	0	0	0	0	0	0	0	0
:German %	0	0	0	0	0	0	0	0	0	0
:Spanish %	0	0	0	0	0	0	0	0	0	0
Official: Arabic %	0	0	0	0	0	0	0	100	0	0
:Chinese %	0	0	0	0	0	0	0	0	0	0
:English %	0	100	100	100	0	100	0	0	100	0
:French %	100	0	0	0	0	0	0	0	0	0
:German %	0	0	0	0	0	0	0	0	0	0
:Spanish %	0	0	0	0	0	0	0	0	0	0
Commercial: Arabic %	0	0	0	0	0	0	0	1	0	0
:Chinese %	0	0	0	0	0	0	0	0	0	0
:English %	0	1	1	1	0	1	1	0	1	1
:French %	1	0	0	0	0	0	0	0	0	0
:German %	0	0	0	0	0	0	0	0	0	0
:Italian %	0	0	0	0	0	0	0	0	0	0
:Portuguese %	0	0	0	0	0	0	0	0	0	0
:Russian %	0	0	0	0	0	0	0	0	0	0
:Spanish %	0	0	0	0	0	0	0	0	0	0

Characteristics	Panama	Papua New Guinea	Paraguay	Peru	Philip-pines	Pitcairn Islands	Poland	Portugal	Puerto Rico	Qatar
Ethnic Groups: # present	7	2	3	5	3	1	2	8	2	5
Max % present	30	84	91	47	92	100	99	99	80	25
Religions: # present	11	13	7	9	11	1	6	7	9	6
Max % present	84	35	96	92	84	100	89	92	85	92
Beliefs: Anglican %	0	0	0	0	0	0	0	0	0	0
Buddhist %	0	0	0	0	0	0	0	0	0	0
Christian Total %	89	91	98	98	88	100	90	94	90	6
Hindu %	0.3	0	0	0	0	0	0	0	0	1
Jewish %	0.2	0.2	0	0	0	0	0	0.1	0.1	0
Islam %	5	0	0	0	4	0	0	0.6	5	92
Protestant Total %	5	58	2	0	4	100	0	0	0	0
Roman Catholic %	84	33	96	92	84	0	89	92	85	0
Traditional %	0.2	3	0.4	0.8	0.6	0	0	0	0	0
Official: Anglican	0	0	0	0	0	0	0	0	0	0
Buddhism	0	0	0	0	0	0	0	0	0	0
Christianism	0	0	0	0	0	0	0	0	0	0
Greek Orthodox	0	0	0	0	0	0	0	0	0	0
Hinduism	0	0	0	0	0	0	0	0	0	0
Islam	0	0	0	0	0	0	0	0	0	0
Luthren Evangelical	0	0	0	0	0	0	0	0	0	0
Monotheism	0	0	0	0	0	0	0	0	0	0
Orthodox	0	0	0	0	0	0	0	0	0	0
Languages: # present	5	4	4	3	8	1	2	1	1	3
Max % present	81	73	89	68	29	50	98	100	99	56
Number official	1	2	2	3	2	.	1	1	1	1
None official (1=yes)	0	0	0	0	0	0	0	0	0	0
Mother Tongue: Arabic %	0	0	0	0	0	0	0	0	0	56
Chinese (all) %	0	0	0	0	0	0	0	0	0	0
English %	0	0	1	0	0	50	0	0	0	0
French %	0	0	0	0	0	0	0	0	0	0
German %	0	0	0	0	0	0	0	0	0	0
Spanish %	81	0	60	68	0	0	0	0	0	0
Official: Arabic %	0	0	0	0	0	0	0	0	0	100
Chinese %	0	0	0	0	0	0	0	0	0	0
English %	0	100	0	0	100	100	0	0	0	0
French %	0	0	0	0	0	0	0	0	0	0
German %	0	0	0	0	0	0	0	0	0	0
Spanish %	100	0	100	100	0	0	0	0	100	0
Commercial: Arabic %	0	0	0	0	0	0	0	0	0	1
Chinese %	0	0	0	0	0	0	0	0	0	0
English %	1	1	0	0	1	1	0	0	1	1
French %	0	0	0	0	0	0	0	0	0	0
German %	0	0	0	0	0	0	1	0	0	0
Italian %	0	0	0	0	0	0	0	0	0	0
Portuguese %	0	0	0	0	0	0	0	1	0	0
Russian %	0	0	0	0	0	0	0	0	0	0
Spanish %	1	0	1	1	0	0	0	0	1	0

Characteristics	Reunion	Romania	Russia	Rwanda	San Marino	Sao Tome E Principe	Saudi Arabia	Senegal	Serbia & Monten.	Seychelles
Ethnic Groups: # present	5	5	8	3	2	5	3	8	4	5
:Max % present	64	88	82	90	80	60	82	36	63	89
Religions: # present	7	9	6	6	4	5	6	5	5	6
:Max % present	90	70	75	65	95	81	99	91	65	89
Beliefs: Anglican %	0	0	0	0	0	0	0	0	0	0
:Buddhist %	0	0	0	0	0	0	0	0	0	0
:Christian Total %	90	90	84	74	95	98	0.8	5	70	97
:Hindu %	0	0.1	0	0	0	0	0	0	0	0.4
:Jewish %	2	0.2	1	0	0	0	0	0	0	0
:Islam %	0	0	5	9	0	0	99	91	19	0
:Protestant Total %	0	7	5	9	0	7	0	0	1	9
:Roman Catholic %	90	5	4	65	95	81	0	3	4	89
:Traditional %	0	0	0	17	0	0	0	0	0	0
Official: Anglican	0	0	0	0	0	0	0	0	0	0
:Buddhism	0	0	0	0	0	0	0	0	0	0
:Christianism	0	0	0	1	1	1	0	0	0	0
:Greek Orthodox	0	0	0	0	0	0	0	0	0	0
:Hinduism	0	0	0	0	0	0	0	0	0	0
:Islam	0	0	0	0	0	0	1	0	0	0
:Luthren Evangelical	0	0	0	0	0	0	0	0	0	0
:Monotheism	0	0	0	0	0	0	0	0	0	0
:Orthodox	0	0	0	0	0	0	0	0	0	0
Languages: # present	2	4	4	3	1	1	1	7	2	3
:Max % present	86	87	87	100	100	100	99	44	95	94
:Number official		1	1	2	1	1	1	1	1	1
:None official (1=yes)	0	0	0	0	0	0	0	0	0	0
Mother Tongue: Arabic %	0	0	0	0	0	0	99	0	0	0
:Chinese (all) %	0	0	0	0	0	0	0	0	0	0
:English %	0	0	0	0	0	0	0	0	0	2
:French %	10	0	0	0	0	0	0	0	0	3
:German %	0	2	0	0	0	0	0	0	0	0
:Spanish %	0	0	0	0	0	0	0	0	0	0
Official: Arabic %	0	0	0	0	0	0	100	0	0	0
:Chinese %	0	0	0	0	0	0	0	0	0	0
:English %	0	0	0	0	0	0	0	0	0	100
:French %	100	0	0	100	0	0	0	100	0	100
:German %	0	0	0	0	0	0	0	0	0	0
:Spanish %	0	0	0	0	0	0	0	0	0	0
Commercial: Arabic %	0	0	0	0	0	0	100	0	0	0
:Chinese %	0	0	0	0	0	0	0	0	0	0
:English %	1	1	1	1	1	1	1	1		1
:French %	100	0	0	100	0	0	0	0		0
:German %	0	0	0	0	0	0	0	0		0
:Italian %	0	0	0	0	100	0	0	0		0
:Portuguese %	0	0	0	0	0	100	0	0		0
:Russian %	0	0	1	0	0	0	0	0		0
:Spanish %	0	0	0	0	0	0	0	0		0

Characteristics	Sierra Leone	Singapore	Slovakia	Slovenia	Solomon Islands	Somalia	South Africa	South Korea	Spain	Sri Lanka
Ethnic Groups: # present	9	3	9	5	5	3	9	1	4	3
. Max % present	34	76	86	91	93	98	24	100	73	74
Religions: # present	7	14	8	4	11	6	17	12	7	12
. Max % present	52	53	60	94	33	100	34	23	95	67
Beliefs: Anglican %	1	0.6	0	0	33	0	4	0	0	0
. Buddhist %	0	0	0	0	0	0	0	23	0	67
. Christian Total %	8	7	80	96	93	0.1	68	33	96	8
. Hindu %	0	16	0	0	0	0	0.2	0	0	16
. Jewish %	0	0	0	0	0	0	0.6	0	0.3	0
. Islam %	39	16	0	1	0	100	1	0	0	8
. Protestant Total %	6	4	16	0	74	0	13	23	0.4	0
. Roman Catholic %	2	0	60	94	19	0	8	10	95	0
. Traditional %	52	0	0	0	3	0	20	0	0	0
Official: Anglican	0	0	0	0	0	0	0	0	0	0
. Buddhism	0	0	0	0	0	0	0	0	0	0
. Christianism	0	0	0	0	0	0	0	0	0	0
. Greek Orthodox	0	0	0	0	0	0	0	0	0	0
. Hinduism	0	0	0	0	0	0	0	0	0	0
. Islam	0	0	0	0	0	1	0	0	0	0
. Luthren Evangelical	0	0	0	0	0	0	0	0	0	0
. Monotheism	0	0	0	0	0	0	0	0	0	0
. Orthodox	0	0	0	0	0	0	0	0	0	0
Languages: # present	12	6	2	2	6	3	10	1	4	2
. Max % present	31	45	85	91	67	97	25	100	70	66
. Number official	1	4	1	1	1	2	13	1	4	1
. None official (1=yes)	0	0	0	0	0	0	0	0	0	0
Mother Tongue: Arabic %	0	0	0	0	0	1	0	0	0	0
. Chinese (all) %	0	56	0	0	0	0	0	0	0	0
. English %	0	9	0	0	0	0	9	0	0	0
. French %	0	0	0	0	0	0	0	0	0	0
. German %	0	0	0	0	0	0	0	0	0	0
. Spanish %	0	0	0	0	0	0	0	0	70	0
Official: Arabic %	0	0	0	0	0	100	0	0	0	0
. Chinese %	0	100	0	0	0	0	0	0	0	0
. English %	100	100	.	0	100	0	9	0	0	0
. French %	0	0	.	0	0	0	0	0	0	0
. German %	0	0	.	0	0	0	0	0	0	0
. Spanish %	0	0	.	0	0	0	0	0	70	0
Commercial: Arabic %	0	0	.	0	0	1	0	0	0	0
. Chinese %	0	0	.	0	0	0	0	0	0	0
. English %	1	1	.	1	1	1	100	0	1	1
. French %	0	0	.	0	0	0	0	0	0	0
. German %	0	0	.	1	0	0	0	0	0	0
. Italian %	0	0	.	1	0	0	0	0	0	0
. Portuguese %	0	0	.	0	0	0	0	0	0	0
. Russian %	0	0	.	0	0	0	0	0	0	0
. Spanish %	0	0	.	0	0	0	0	0	100	0

Characteristics	Switzerland	Sweden	Swaziland	Suriname	Sudan	St. Vincent & Grenad.	St. Pierre & Miquelon	St. Lucia	St. Kitts & Nevis	St. Helena
Ethnic Groups: # present	6	2	6	8	10	5	2	4	4	1
·Max % present	65	90	84	31	49	74	50	90	91	100
Religions: # present	8	7	6	11	8	11	3	8	5	7
·Max % present	48	78	37	27	73	36	98	86	36	90
Beliefs: Anglican %	0	0	0	0	0	36	0	3	36	90
··Buddhist %	0	0	0	0	0	0	0	0	0	0
··Christian Total %	92	80	77	41	8	90	99	95	87	99
··Hindu %	0	0	0	27	0	0	0	0	0	0
··Islam %	0.3	0.2	0	20	73	0	0	0	0	0
··Jewish %	2	0.2	0	0.1	0	0	0.9	0	0	0
··Protestant Total %	44	79	37	18	2	67	0.9	9	76	99
··Roman Catholic %	48	1	11	23	6	19	98	86	11	0.7
··Traditional %	0	0	21	5	17	2	0	0	0	0
Official: Anglican	0	0	0	0	0	0	0	0	0	1
··Buddhism	0	0	0	0	0	0	0	0	0	0
··Christianism	0	0	0	0	0	0	0	0	0	0
··Greek Orthodox	0	0	0	0	0	0	0	0	0	0
··Hinduism	0	0	0	0	0	0	0	0	0	0
··Islam	0	0	0	0	1	0	0	0	0	0
··Luthren Evangelical	0	1	0	0	0	0	0	0	0	0
··Monotheism	0	0	0	0	0	0	0	0	0	0
··Orthodox	0	0	0	0	0	0	0	0	0	0
Languages: # present	6	2	2	6	7	1	1	1	1	1
·Max % present	65	93	91	33	51	100	100	100	100	100
·Number official	3	0	2	1	1	1	1	1	1	1
·None official (1=yes)	0	1	0	0	0	0	0	0	0	0
Mother Tongue: Arabic %	0	0	0	0	51	0	0	0	0	0
··Chinese (all) %	0	0	0	0	0	0	0	0	0	0
··English %	0	0	0	0	0	100	0	100	100	100
··French %	18	0	0	0	0	0	100	0	0	0
··German %	65	0	0	0	0	0	0	0	0	0
··Spanish %	0	0	0	0	0	0	0	0	0	0
Official: Arabic %	0	0	0	0	100	0	0	0	0	0
··Chinese %	0	0	0	0	0	0	0	0	0	0
··English %	0	0	100	0	0	100	0	100	100	100
··French %	100	0	0	0	0	0	100	0	0	0
··German %	100	0	0	0	0	0	0	0	0	0
··Spanish %	0	0	0	0	0	0	0	0	0	0
Commercial: Arabic %	0	0	0	0	1	0	0	0	0	0
··Chinese %	0	0	0	0	0	0	0	0	0	0
··English %	0	1	100	1	0	1	0	1	1	1
··French %	1	0	0	0	0	0	1	0	0	0
··German %	1	0	0	0	0	0	0	0	0	0
··Italian %	1	0	0	0	0	0	0	0	0	0
··Portuguese %	0	0	0	0	0	0	0	0	0	0
··Russian %	0	0	0	0	0	0	0	0	0	0
··Spanish %	0	0	0	0	0	0	0	0	0	0

Characteristics	Syrian Arab Rep.	Taiwan	Tajikistan	Tanzania	Thailand	Togo	Tokelau	Tonga	Trinidad & Tobago	Tunisia
Ethnic Groups: # present	2	3	5	5	5	6	2	1	6	4
:Max % present	89	84	65	21	53	45	99	98	41	98
Religions: # present	8	10	3	12	11	7	4	4	12	7
:Max % present	74	49	80	33	92	50	67	43	33	99
Beliefs: Anglican %	0	0	0	0	0	0	0	0	15	0
:Buddhist %	0	43	0	0	92	0	0	0	0	0.3
:Christian Total %	8	7	0	34	1	35	92	93	55	0
:Hindu %	0	0	0	0	0	0	0	0	24	0
:Jewish %	0	0	0	0	0	0	0	0	0	0
:Islam %	90	0.5	85	33	4	12	0	0	6	99
:Protestant Total %	0	0	0	0	0	9	67	54	0	0
:Roman Catholic %	0	0	0	26	0.5	26	25	16	22	0
:Traditional %	0	0.1	0	32	0	50	0	0	3	0
Official: Anglican	0	0	0	0	0	0	0	0	0	0
:Buddhism	0	0	0	0	1	0	0	0	0	0
:Christianism	0	0	0	0	0	0	0	1	0	0
:Greek Orthodox	0	0	0	0	0	0	0	0	0	0
:Hinduism	0	0	0	0	0	0	0	0	0	0
:Islam	1	0	0	0	0	0	0	0	0	1
:Luthren Evangelical	0	0	0	0	0	0	0	0	0	0
:Monotheism	0	0	0	0	0	0	0	0	0	0
:Orthodox	0	0	0	0	0	0	0	0	0	0
Languages: # present	4	3	3	10	7	11	3	0	3	0
:Max % present	88	69	59	13	41	22	80	98	53	99
:Number official	1	1	1	2	1	3	.	1	1	0
:None official (1=yes)	0	0	0	0	0	0	.	0	0	0
Mother Tongue: Arabic %	88	0	0	0	0	0	0	0	0	99
:Chinese (all) %	0	31	0	0	2	0	0	0	0	0
:English %	0	0	0	0	0	0	5	0	53	0
:French %	0	0	0	0	0	0	0	0	0	0
:German %	0	0	0	0	0	0	0	0	0	0
:Spanish %	0	0	0	0	0	0	0	0	0	0
Official: Arabic %	100	0	0	0	0	0	0	0	0	100
:Chinese %	0	100	0	0	0	0	0	0	0	0
:English %	0	0	0	100	0	0	100	100	100	0
:French %	0	0	0	0	0	100	0	0	0	0
:German %	0	0	0	0	0	0	0	0	0	0
:Spanish %	0	0	0	0	0	0	0	0	0	0
Commercial: Arabic %	1	0	0	0	0	0	0	0	0	1
:Chinese %	0	1	0	0	1	0	0	0	0	0
:English %	1	1	0	1	1	0	1	1	1	1
:French %	1	0	0	0	0	1	0	0	1	1
:German %	0	0	0	0	0	0	0	0	0	0
:Italian %	0	0	0	0	0	0	0	0	0	1
:Portuguese %	0	0	0	0	0	0	0	0	0	0
:Russian %	0	0	1	0	0	0	0	0	0	0
:Spanish %	0	0	0	0	0	0	0	0	1	0

Characteristics	Turkey	Turkme-nistan	Turks & Caicos	Tuvalu	Uganda	Ukraine	United Arab Emir.	United Kingdom	United States	Uruguay
Ethnic Groups: # present	7	7	3	3	11	8	9	11	18	5
Max % present	86	73	77	91	18	74	56	81	71	86
Religions: # present	9	3	6	5	8	4	6	15	29	7
Max % present	99	87	41	93	50	76	79	57	23	60
Beliefs: Anglican %	0	0	18	0	26	0	0	57	0	0
Buddhist %	0	0	0	0	0	0	0	0.2	0	0
Christian Total %	0.3	11	80	94	76	90	4	87	62	62
Hindu %	0	0	0	0	0	0	0	0.7	0	0
Jewish %	0	0	0	0	0	0	0	0.5	2	1
Islam %	99	87	0	0	7	8	95	1	2	0
Protestant Total %	0	0	80	94	26	0	0	72	35	2
Roman Catholic %	0	0	0	0.2	50	14	0	13	23	60
Traditional %	0	0	0	0	13	0	0	0	0	0
Official: Anglican	0	0	0	0	0	0	0	1	0	0
Buddhism	0	0	0	0	0	0	0	0	0	0
Christianism	0	0	0	0	0	0	0	0	0	0
Greek Orthodox	0	0	0	0	0	0	0	0	0	0
Hinduism	0	0	0	0	0	0	0	0	0	0
Islam	0	0	0	0	0	0	1	0	0	0
Luthren Evangelical	0	0	0	0	0	0	0	0	0	0
Monotheism	0	0	0	0	0	0	0	0	0	0
Orthodox	0	0	0	0	0	0	0	0	0	0
Languages: # present	2	4	1	2	10	2	9	2	14	1
Max % present	90	68	100	97	16	66	48	98	89	100
Number official	1	1	0	0	1	1	1	0	1	0
None official (1=yes)	0	0	0	0	0	0	0	0	0.1	0
Mother Tongue: Arabic %	0	0	0	0	0	0	48	0	0.5	0
Chinese (all) %	0	0	0	0	0	0	0	0	89	0
English %	0	0	100	100	0	0	0	98	0.7	0
French %	0	0	0	0	0	0	0	0	0.6	0
German %	0	0	0	0	0	0	0	0	0.7	0
Spanish %	0	0	0	0	0	0	0	0	0	100
Official: Arabic %	0	0	0	0	0	0	100	0	0	0
Chinese %	0	0	0	0	0	0	0	0	0	0
English %	0	0	100	100	100	0	0	98	0	0
French %	0	0	0	0	0	0	0	0	0	0
German %	0	0	0	0	0	0	0	0	0	0
Spanish %	0	0	0	0	0	0	0	0	0	100
Commercial: Arabic %	0	0	0	0	0	0	1	0	0	0
Chinese %	0	0	0	0	0	0	0	0	0	0
English %	0	0	100	100	0	0	0	100	100	0
French %	1	0	0	0	0	0	0	0	0	0
German %	1	0	0	0	0	0	0	0	0	0
Italian %	0	0	0	0	0	0	0	0	0	0
Portuguese %	0	0	0	0	0	0	0	0	0	0
Russian %	0	1	1	1	1	1	1	1	1	0
Spanish %	0	0	0	0	0	0	0	0	0	1

Characteristics	Uzbekistan	Vanuatu	Vatican City	Venezuela	Vietnam	Virgin Isl. US	Wallis & Futuna	West Bank	Western Samoa	Western Sahara
Ethnic Groups: # present	8	7	2	4	7	3	1	2	3	1
: Max % present	71	95	98	69	88	74	98	88	88	99
Religions: # present	3	10	2	8	10	7	2	3	6	3
: Max % present	88	37	100	91	55	42	99	80	47	100
Beliefs: Anglican %	0	14	0	0	0	0	0	0	0	0
: Buddhist %	0	0	0	0	55	0	0	0	0	0
: Christian Total %	9	76	100	91	7	93	99	8	93	0
: Hindu %	0	0	0	0.1	0	0.3	0	0	0	0
: Jewish %	0	0	0	0	0	0	0	12	0	0
: Islam %	88	0	0	0	0	0	0	80	0	100
: Protestant Total %	0	61	0	0	0	59	0	0	71	0
: Roman Catholic %	0	15	100	91	7	34	99	0	22	0
: Traditional %	0	1	0	1	3	0	0	0	0	0
Official: Anglican	0	0	0	0	0	0	0	0	0	0
: Buddhism	0	0	0	0	0	0	0	0	0	0
: Christianism	0	0	1	0	0	0	0	0	0	0
: Greek Orthodox	0	0	0	0	0	0	0	0	0	0
: Hinduism	0	0	0	0	0	0	0	0	0	0
: Islam	0	0	0	0	0	0	0	0	0	1
: Luthren Evangelical	0	0	0	0	0	0	0	0	0	0
: Monotheism	0	0	0	0	0	0	0	0	0	0
: Orthodox	0	0	0	0	0	0	0	0	0	0
Languages: # present	5	1	1	2	6	3	2	2	2	1
: Max % present	69	94	95	97	90	81	80	88	99	100
: Number official	1	2	2	1	1	1	0	0	2	0
: None official (1=yes)	0	0	0	0	0	0	0	0	0	1
Mother Tongue: Arabic %	0	0	0	0	0	0	0	88	0	100
: Chinese (all) %	0	0	0	0	0	0	0	0	0	0
: English %	0	0	0	0	0	81	0	0	0	0
: French %	0	0	0	0	0	3	0.9	0	0	0
: German %	0	0	0	0	0	0	0	0	0	0
: Spanish %	0	0	0	97	0	13	0	0	0	0
Official: Arabic %	0	0	0	0	0	0	0	100	0	100
: Chinese %	0	0	0	0	0	0	0	0	0	0
: English %	0	100	0	0	0	100	0	100	100	0
: French %	0	100	0	0	0	0	100	0	0	0
: German %	0	0	0	0	0	0	0	0	0	0
: Spanish %	0	0	0	97	0	0	0	0	0	0
Commercial: Arabic %	0	0		0	0	0	0	100	0	100
: Chinese %	0	0		0	0	0	0	0	0	0
: English %	0	0		0	0	100	0	0	0	0
: French %	0	0		0	0	0	0	0	0	0
: German %	0	0		0	0	0	0	0	0	0
: Italian %	0	0		0	0	0	0	0	0	0
: Portuguese %	0	0		0	0	0	0	0	0	0
: Russian %	1	1		1	1	1	1	1	1	1
: Spanish %	0	0		1	0	0	0	0	0	0

Characteristics	Yemen	Zaire	Zambia	Zimbabwe
Ethnic Groups: # present	5	13	7	4
:Max % present	95	18	35	71
Religions: # present	2	9	9	10
:Max % present	53	48	34	40
Beliefs: Anglican %	0	0	0	0
:Buddhist %	0	0	0	0
:Christian Total %	0	94	69	43
:Hindu %	0	0	0	0
:Islam %	100	1	0.3	0
:Jewish %	0	0	0	0
:Protestant Total %	0	29	34	18
:Roman Catholic %	0	48	26	12
:Traditional %	0	3	27	40
Official: Anglican	0	0	0	0
:Buddhism	0	0	0	0
:Christianism	0	0	0	0
:Greek Orthodox	0	0	0	0
:Hinduism	0	0	0	0
:Islam	1	0	0	0
:Luthren Evangelical	0	0	0	0
:Monotheism	0	0	0	0
:Orthodox	0	0	0	0
Languages: # present	3	4	8	6
:Max % present	93	7	25	55
:Number official	1	1	1	1
:None official (1=yes)	0	0	0	0
Mother Tongue: Arabic %	93	0	0	0
:Chinese (all) %	0	0	0	0
:English %	0	0	1	7
:French %	0	0	0	0
:German %	0	0	0	0
:Spanish %	0	0	0	0
Official: Arabic %	100	0	0	0
:Chinese %	0	0	0	0
:English %	0	0	100	100
:French %	0	100	0	0
:German %	0	0	0	0
:Spanish %	0	0	0	0
Commercial: Arabic %	1	0	0	0
:Chinese %	0	0	0	0
:English %	1	0	1	1
:French %	0	1	0	0
:German %	0	0	0	0
:Italian %	0	0	0	0
:Portuguese %	0	0	0	0
:Russian %	0	0	0	0
:Spanish %	0	0	0	0

6

MINERAL RESOURCES ACROSS COUNTRIES

This chapter provides comparative statistics for a variety of variables covering each country's mineral resources. For a full discussion of the methodology used to generate these estimates, please refer to Chapter 1 which gives important caveats. This chapter first gives summary statistics of the variables reported: the number of countries for which each variable was available, weighted averages (by population) and simple averages; these averages can be used as benchmarks. Then a lengthy comparative table is presented which provides raw statistics across countries.

Most of the variables are self explanatory, though some merit commentary. All of the statistics should be considered as estimates which have undergone rounding and certain adjustments. First, across 44 minerals, each country is characterized as living in areas holding a given percent of the world's known reserves. A value of "0" should be interpreted as a negligible level or a very small percentage of known world reserves. These reserves may not be economically viable, so the measure reflects an exogenous presence, rather than a mining activity. For example, South Africa contains 89% of the world's known reserves of platinum. The sum of these percentages is then reported as "Total minerals: % sum." The number of minerals which are heavily mined are then given: "Number of Minerals." Finally, per capita oil reserves are estimated. Some national cultures do not reside in areas with these mineral resources.

Summary Statistics:
Mineral Resources

Characteristics	Number of Countries Covered	Weighted Average by Pop 1994	Simple Average	Simple Standard Deviation
World Reserves %: Bauxite	234	1.49	0.40	2.44
: Antimony	234	11.58	0.37	3.48
: Barytes	234	9.16	0.37	2.34
: Beryllium	234	4.13	0.36	2.76
: Bismuth	234	4.94	0.36	2.06
: Boron	234	3.76	0.36	3.24
: Cadmium	234	2.08	0.33	1.66
: Chromium	234	1.24	0.39	4.66
: Cobalt	234	0.51	0.41	3.45
: Copper	234	1.09	0.34	2.19
: Fluorspar	234	2.80	0.28	1.85
: Gold	234	0.93	0.29	3.14
: Indium	234	2.98	0.33	2.20
: Ind. diamond	234	0.35	0.13	1.30
: Iron ore	234	2.40	0.21	1.32
: Kaolin	234	3.04	0.30	2.52
: Lead	234	3.28	0.35	1.92
: Lithium	234	1.00	0.43	4.08
: Magnesium	234	6.91	0.28	2.32
: Manganese	234	1.13	0.27	3.01
: Mercury	234	2.40	0.34	3.92
: Molybdenum	234	4.38	0.39	3.56
: Nickel	234	0.82	0.37	2.76
: Niobium	234	2.24	0.36	5.12
: Phosphate	234	1.06	0.34	2.60
: Platinum group	234	0.65	0.38	5.79
: Potash	234	1.11	0.25	3.07
: Rare minerals	234	12.28	0.33	3.51
: Rhenium	234	0.87	0.31	3.63
: Selenium	234	1.15	0.33	2.04
: Silver	234	0.86	0.24	1.62
: Sulphur	234	2.33	0.28	1.50
: Talc	234	1.95	0.19	2.31
: Tantalum	234	0.77	0.33	2.40
: Tellurium	234	1.00	0.31	2.17
: Tin	234	6.65	0.40	2.58
: Titanium A	234	6.07	0.41	2.36
: Titanium B	234	6.27	0.48	5.20
: Tungsten	234	10.21	0.36	3.06
: Uranium	234	0.81	0.10	0.62
: Vanadium	234	3.37	0.16	1.62
: Vermiculite	234	2.79	0.41	4.20
: Zinc	234	2.90	0.35	1.70
: Zirconium	234	1.63	0.39	3.66
Total minerals: % sum	234	139.36	14.36	58.27
Number of Minerals	234	13.88	1.91	5.19
Oil reserves (/cap bbl)	187	138990.93	556236.87	4166311.50

Characteristics	Afghan- istan	Albania	Algeria	American Samoa	Andorra	Angola	Anguilla	Antigua & Barbuda	Argentina	Armenia
World Reserves %: Bauxite	0	0	0	0	0	0	0	0	0	0
: Antimony	0	0	0	0	0	0	0	0	0	0
: Barytes	0	0	1	0	0	0	0	0	0	0
: Beryllium	0	0	0	0	0	0	0	0	7	0
: Bismuth	0	0	0	0	0	0	0	0	0	0
: Boron	0	0	0	0	0	0	0	0	1	0
: Cadmium	0	0	0	0	0	0	0	0	0	0
: Chromium	0	0.5	0	0	0	0	0	0	0	0
: Cobalt	0	0	0	0	0	0	0	0	0	0
: Copper	0	0	0	0	0	0	0	0	0	0
: Fluorspar	0	0	0	0	0	0	0	0	0	0
: Gold	0	0	0	0	0	0	0	0	0	0
: Indium	0	0	0	0	0	0	0	0	0	0
: Ind. diamond	0	0	0	0	0	0	0	0	0	0
: Iron ore	0	0	0	0	0	0	0	0	0	0
: Kaolin	0	0	0	0	0	0	0	0	0	0
: Lead	0	0	0	0	0	0	0	0	0	0
: Lithium	0	0	0	0	0	0	0	0	0	0
: Magnesium	0	0	0	0	0	0	0	0	0	0
: Manganese	0	0	0	0	0	0	0	0	0	0
: Mercury	0	0.4	2	0	0	0	0	0	0	0
: Molybdenum	0	0	0	0	0	0	0	0	0	0
: Nickel	0	0	0	0	0	0	0	0	0	0
: Niobium	2	0	0	0	0	0	0	0	0	0
: Phosphate	0	0	0	0	0	0	0	0	0	0
: Platinum group	0	0	0	0	0	0	0	0	0	0
: Potash	0	0	0	0	0	0	0	0	0	0
: Rare minerals	0	0	0	0	0	0	0	0	0	0
: Rhenium	0	0	0	0	0	0	0	0	0	0
: Selenium	0	0	0	0	0	0	0	0	0	0
: Silver	0	0	0	0	0	0	0	0	0	0
: Sulphur	0	0	0	0	0	0	0	0	0	0
: Talc	0	0	0	0	0	0	0	0	0	0
: Tantalum	0	0	0	0	0	0	0	0	0	0
: Tellurium	0	0	0	0	0	0	0	0	0	0
: Tin	0	0	0	0	0	0	0	0	0	0
: Titanium A	0	0	0	0	0	0	0	0	0	0
: Titanium B	0	0	0	0	0	0	0	0	0	0
: Tungsten	0	0	0	0	0	0	0	0	0.4	0
: Uranium	0	0	0	0	0	0	0	0	0	0
: Vanadium	0	0	0	0	0	0	0	0	0	0
: Vermiculite	0	0	0	0	0	0	0	0	0	0
: Zinc	0	0	0	0	0	0	0	0	0	0
: Zirconium	0	0	0	0	0	0	0	0	0	0
Total minerals: % sum	2	0.9	3	0	0	0	0	0	8	0
Number of Minerals	1	2	2	0	0	0	0	0	3	0
Oil reserves (/cap bbl)	0	49500	339000	.	0	146000	.	0	46900	0

Characteristics	Aruba	Australia	Austria	Azerbaijan	Bahamas	Bahrain	Bangla-desh	Barbados	Belarus	Belgium
World Reserves %: Bauxite		21								
: Antimony		2								
: Barytes										
: Beryllium		3								
: Bismuth		17								
: Boron										
: Cadmium		1								
: Chromium		0								
: Cobalt		0.7								
: Copper		2								
: Fluorspar		3								
: Gold		8								
: Indium		16								
: Ind. diamond										
: Iron ore		2								
: Kaolin		17								
: Lead		6								
: Lithium		5								
: Magnesium		0	0.6							
: Manganese		5								
: Mercury										
: Molybdenum		0								
: Nickel		0								
: Niobium		6								
: Phosphate		3								
: Platinium group		9								
: Potash		0								
: Rare minerals										
: Rhenium		18								
: Selenium		3								
: Silver		12								
: Sulphur		6								
: Talc		2								
: Tantalum										
: Tellurium										
: Tin		0.9								
: Titanium A		0.7	0.4							
: Titanium B										
: Tungsten		12								
: Uranium		48								
: Vanadium										
: Vermiculite										
: Zinc										
: Zirconium										
Total minerals: % sum		257	1							
Number of Minerals		28	2							
Oil reserves (/cap bbl)		99100	11900	177000	0	131000	0	21000	0	0

Characteristics	Belize	Benin	Bermuda	Bhutan	Bolivia	Bosnia & Herzegov.	Botswana	Brazil	British Virgin Isl.	Brunei
World Reserves %: Bauxite								13		
Antimony					7			0		
Barytes								1		
Beryllium								37		
Bismuth					5			0		
Boron					1			0.9		
Cadmium								0.6		
Chromium								0.5		
Cobalt							0.2			
Copper										
Fluorspar								2		
Gold										
Indium								0.5		
Ind. diamond							13	0.1		
Iron ore								0.7		
Kaolin										
Lead					2			0.1		
Lithium								2		
Magnesium								3		
Manganese								1		
Mercury										
Molybdenum										
Nickel							1			
Niobium								78		
Phosphate								0.2		
Platinum group										
Potash								0.5		
Rare minerals								0.3		
Rhenium										
Selenium								0		
Silver					2			4		
Sulphur								4		
Talc								0		
Tantalum								20		
Tellurium								1		
Tin								78		
Titanium A								0.9		
Titanium B								6		
Tungsten					3			0		
Uranium								7		
Vanadium										
Vermiculite								1		
Zinc										
Zirconium								2		
Total minerals: % sum			.		20		14	271		
Number of Minerals					6		3	28		
Oil reserves (/cap bbl)		3930	.		14300		0	19400	.	4640000

Characteristics	Bulgaria	Burkina Faso	Burma	Burundi	Cambodia	Cameroon	Canada	Cape Verde	Cayman Islands	Central Afric. Rep.
World Reserves %: Bauxite	0	0	0	0	0	3	0	0	0	0
Antimony	0	0	0	0	0	0	2	0	0	0
Barytes	0	0	0	0	0	0	2	0	0	0
Beryllium	0	0	0	0	0	0	0	0	0	0
Bismuth	0	0	0	0	0	0	0	0	0	0
Boron	0	0	0	0	0	0	5	0	0	0
Cadmium	0	0	0	0	0	0	0	0	0	0
Chromium	0	0	0	0	0	0	15	0	0	0
Cobalt	0	0	0	0	0	0	0	0	0	0
Copper	0	0	0	0	0	0	1	0	0	0
Fluorspar	0	0	0	0	0	0	0	0	0	0
Gold	0	0	0	0	0	0	4	0	0	0
Indium	0	0	0	0	0	0	0.8	0	0	0
Ind. diamond	0	0	0	0	0	0	4	0	0	0.6
Iron ore	4	0	0	0	0	0	27	0	0	0
Kaolin	4	0	0	0	0	0	0	0	0	0
Lead	0	0	0	0	0	0	7	0	0	0
Lithium	0	0	0	0	0	0	0	0	0	0
Magnesium	0	0	0	0	0	0	0.8	0	0	0
Manganese	0	0	0	0	0	0	10	0	0	0
Mercury	0	0	0	0	0	0	8	0	0	0
Molybdenum	0	0	0	0	0	0	1	0	0	0
Nickel	0	0	0	0	0	0	0	0	0	0
Niobium	0	0	0	0	0	0	0	0	0	0
Phosphate	0	0	0	0	0	0	8	0	0	0
Platinium group	0	0	0	0	0	0	13	0	0	0
Potash	0	0	0	0	0	0	3	0	0	0
Rare minerals	0	0	0	0	0	0	0.4	0	0	0
Rhenium	0	0	0	0	0	0	47	0	0	0
Selenium	0	0	0	0	0	0	1	0	0	0
Silver	0	0	0	0	0	0	0	0	0	0
Sulphur	0	0	0	0	0	0	1	0	0	0
Talc	0	0	0	0	0	0	10	0	0	0
Tantalum	0	0	0	0	0	0	13	0	0	0
Tellurium	0	0	0	0	0	0	11	0	0	0
Tin	0	0	0.3	0	0	0	0	0	0	0
Titanium A	0	0	0	0	0	0	7	0	0	0
Titanium B	0	0	0	0	0	0	4	0	0	0
Tungsten	0	0	0.6	0	0	0	0	0	0	0
Uranium	0	0	0	0	0	0	13	0	0	0
Vanadium	0	0	0	0	0	0	0	0	0	0
Vermiculite	0	0	0	0	0	0	11	0	0	0
Zinc	0.2	0	0	0	0	0	15	0	0	0
Zirconium	0	0	0	0	0	0	0	0	0	0
Total minerals: % sum	0.2	0	0.9	0	0	3	246	0	0	0.6
Number of Minerals	8	0	2	0	0	1	30	0	0	1
Oil reserves (/cap bbl)	34	0	0	0	0	31900	185000	0	.	0

Characteristics	Chad	Chile	China	Christmas Island	Cocos (Keel.) Isl.	Colombia	Comoros	Congo	Cook Island	Costa Rica
World Reserves %: Bauxite	0	0	0.7	0	0	0	0	0	0	0
: Antimony	0	1	52	0	0	0	0	0	0	0
: Barytes	0	0	24	0	0	0	0	0	0	0
: Beryllium	0	0	0	0	0	0	0	0	0	0
: Bismuth	0	3	19	0	0	0	0	0	0	0
: Boron	0	0	8	0	0	0	0	0	0	0
: Cadmium	0	0	3	0	0	0	0	0	0	0
: Chromium	0	0	0	0	0	0	0	0	0	0
: Cobalt	0	0	0	0	0	0	0	0	0	0
: Copper	0	27	11	0	0	0	0	0	0	0
: Fluorspar	0	0	0	0	0	0	0	0	0	0
: Gold	0	0	9	0	0	0	0	0	0	0
: Indium	0	0	0	0	0	0	0	0	0	0
: Ind. diamond	0	0	1	0	0	0	0	0	0	0
: Iron ore	0	0	5	0	0	0	0	0	0	0
: Kaolin	0	0	1	0	0	0	0	0	0	0
: Lead	0	0	9	0	0	0	0	0	0	0
: Lithium	0	58	0	0	0	0	0	0	0	0
: Magnesium	0	0	30	0	0	0	0	0	0	0
: Manganese	0	0	2	0	0	0	0	0	0	0
: Mercury	0	0	8	0	0	0	0	0	0	0
: Molybdenum	0	21	9	0	0	0	0	0	0	0
: Nickel	0	0	2	0	0	1	0	0	0	0
: Niobium	0	0	0	0	0	0	0	0	0	0
: Phosphate	0	0	2	0.1	0	0	0	0	0	0
: Platinium group	0	0.1	0	0	0	0	0	0	0	0
: Potash	0	0	3	0	0	0	0	0	0	0
: Rare minerals	0	0	51	0	0	0	0	0	0	0
: Rhenium	0	53	0	0	0	0	0	0	0	0
: Selenium	0	23	0	0	0	0	0	0	0	0
: Silver	0	0	7	0	0	0	0	0	0	0
: Sulphur	0	0	0	0	0	0	0	0	0	0
: Talc	0	0	0	0	0	0	0	0	0	0
: Tantalum	0	0	0	0	0	0	0	0	0	0
: Tellurium	0	25	0	0	0	0	0	0	0	0
: Tin	0	0	25	0	0	0	0	0	0	0
: Titanium A	0	0	15	0	0	0	0	0	0	0
: Titanium B	0	0	15	0	0	0	0	0	0	0
: Tungsten	0	0	45	0	0	0	0	0	0	0
: Uranium	0	0	2	0	0	0	0	0	0	0
: Vanadium	0	0	14	0	0	0	0	0	0	0
: Vermiculite	0	0	0	0	0	0	0	0	0	0
: Zinc	0	0	3	0	0	0	0	0	0	0
: Zirconium	0	0	0	0	0	0	0	0	0	0
Total minerals: % sum	0	210	375	0.1		1	0	0	0	0
Number of Minerals	0	9	29	1		1	0	0	0	0
Oil reserves (/cap bbl)	0	21700	19800			57		338000		

Characteristics	Croatia	Cuba	Cyprus	Czech Republic	Denmark	Djibouti	Dominica	Dominican Republic	Ecuador	Egypt
World Reserves %: Bauxite										
Antimony										
Barytes										
Beryllium										
Bismuth										
Boron										
Cadmium										
Chromium		0.2								
Cobalt		31								
Copper										
Fluorspar										
Gold										
Indium										
Ind. diamond										
Iron ore										
Kaolin										
Lead										
Lithium										
Magnesium										
Manganese										
Mercury										
Molybdenum										
Nickel		38						1		
Niobium										
Phosphate										
Platinium group										
Potash										
Rare minerals										
Rhenium										
Selenium										
Silver										
Sulphur										
Talc										
Tantalum										
Tellurium										
Tin										
Titanium A										
Titanium B										
Tungsten										
Uranium										
Vanadium										
Vermiculite										
Zinc										
Zirconium										
Total minerals: % sum		70						1		
Number of Minerals		3						1		
Oil reserves (/cap bbl)	.	9170	0	0	141000	0	0	0	141	111000

Characteristics	El Salvador	Equatorial Guinea	Eritrea	Estonia	Ethiopia	Falkland Islands	Faroe Islands	Fiji	Finland	France
World Reserves %: Bauxite	0	0	0	0	0	0	0	0	0	0
: Antimony	0	0	0	0	0	0	0	0	0	0
: Barytes	0	0	0	0	0	0	0	0	0	1
: Beryllium	0	0	0	0	0	0	0	0	0	0
: Bismuth	0	0	0	0	0	0	0	0	0	0
: Boron	0	0	0	0	0	0	0	0	0	0
: Cadmium	0	0	0	0	0	0	0	0	0	0
: Chromium	0	0	0	0	0	0	0	0	0.7	0
: Cobalt	0	0	0	0	0	0	0	0	0	0
: Copper	0	0	0	0	0	0	0	0	0	0
: Fluorspar	0	0	0	0	0	0	0	0	0	0
: Gold	0	0	0	0	0	0	0	0	0	0
: Indium	0	0	0	0	0	0	0	0	0	4
: Ind. diamond	0	0	0	0	0	0	0	0	0	0
: Iron ore	0	0	0	0	0	0	0	0	0	5
: Kaolin	0	0	0	0	0	0	0	0	0	0
: Lead	0	0	0	0	0	0	0	0	0	0
: Lithium	0	0	0	0	0	0	0	0	0	1
: Magnesium	0	0	0	0	0	0	0	0	0	0
: Manganese	0	0	0	0	0	0	0	0	0	0
: Mercury	0	0	0	0	0	0	0	0	0	0
: Molybdenum	0	0	0	0	0	0	0	0	0	0
: Nickel	0	0	0	0	0	0	0	0	0.2	0
: Niobium	0	0	0	0	0	0	0	0	0	0
: Phosphate	0	0	0	0	0	0	0	0	0	0
: Platinum group	0	0	0	0	0	0	0	0	0	0
: Potash	0	0	0	0	0	0	0	0	0	0.2
: Rare minerals	0	0	0	0	0	0	0	0	0	0
: Rhenium	0	0	0	0	0	0	0	0	0	0
: Selenium	0	0	0	0	0	0	0	0	0	0
: Silver	0	0	0	0	0	0	0	0	0	0
: Sulphur	0	0	0	0	0	0	0	0	0	0
: Talc	0	0	0	0	0	0	0	0	0	0.7
: Tantalum	0	0	0	0	0	0	0	0	0	0
: Tellurium	0	0	0	0	0	0	0	0	0.5	0
: Tin	0	0	0	0	0	0	0	0	0	0
: Titanium A	0	0	0	0	0	0	0	0	0	0
: Titanium B	0	0	0	0	0	0	0	0	0	0
: Tungsten	0	0	0	0	0	0	0	0	0	0
: Uranium	0	0	0	0	0	0	0	0	0	0.8
: Vanadium	0	0	0	0	0	0	0	0	0	0
: Vermiculite	0	0	0	0	0	0	0	0	0	0
: Zinc	0	0	0	0	0	0	0	0	0	0
: Zirconium	0	0	0	0	0	0	0	0	0	0
Total minerals: % sum	0	0	0	0	0	0	0	0	3	14
Number of Minerals	0	0	0	0	0	0	0	0	4	7
Oil reserves (/cap bbl)	0	9130	0	·	·	·	·	0	0	3090

Characteristics	French Guiana	French Polynesia	Gabon	Gambia	Gaza Strip	Georgia	Germany	Ghana	Gibraltar	Greece
World Reserves %: Bauxite	0	0	0	0	0	0	0	0	0	3
: Antimony	0	0	0	0	0	0	0	0	0	0
: Barytes	0	0	0	0	0	0	1	0	0	0
: Beryllium	0	0	0	0	0	0	0	0	0	0
: Bismuth	0	0	0	0	0	0	0	0	0	0
: Boron	0	0	0	0	0	0	0	0	0	0
: Cadmium	0	0	0	0	0	0	0	0	0	0
: Chromium	0	0	0	0	0	0	0	0	0	0
: Cobalt	0	0	0	0	0	0	0	0	0	0.1
: Copper	0	0	0	0	0	0	0	0	0	0
: Fluorspar	0	0	0	0	0	0	0	0	0	0
: Gold	0	0	0	0	0	0	0	0.1	0	0
: Indium	0	0	0	0	0	0	2	0	0	0
: Ind. diamond	0	0	0	0	0	0	0	0	0	0
: Iron ore	0	0	0	0	0	0	0	0	0	0
: Kaolin	0	0	0	0	0	0	0	0	0	0
: Lead	0	0	0	0	0	0	0	0	0	1
: Lithium	0	0	0	0	0	0	0	0	0	0
: Magnesium	0	0	0	0	0	0	0	0	0	0
: Manganese	0	0	7	0	0	0	0	0	0	0
: Mercury	0	0	0	0	0	0	0	0	0	0
: Molybdenum	0	0	0	0	0	0	0	0	0	0
: Nickel	0	0	0	0	0	0	0	0	0	1
: Niobium	0	0	0	0	0	0	0	0	0	0
: Phosphate	0	0	0	0	0	0	0	0	0	0
: Platinium group	0	0	0	0	0	0	0	0	0	0
: Potash	0	0	0	0	0	0	5	0	0	0
: Rare minerals	0	0	0	0	0	0	0	0	0	0
: Rhenium	0	0	0	0	0	0	0	0	0	0
: Selenium	0	0	0	0	0	0	0	0	0	0
: Silver	0	0	0	0	0	0	0	0	0	0
: Sulphur	0	0	0	0	0	0	1	0	0	0
: Talc	0	0	0	0	0	0	0	0	0	0
: Tantalum	0	0	0	0	0	0	0	0	0	0
: Tellurium	0	0	0	0	0	0	0	0	0	0
: Tin	0	0	0	0	0	0	0	0	0	0
: Titanium A	0	0	0	0	0	0	0	0	0	0
: Titanium B	0	0	0	0	0	0	0	0	0	0
: Tungsten	0	0	0	0	0	0	0	0	0	0
: Uranium	0	0	0.6	0	0	0	0	0	0	0
: Vanadium	0	0	0	0	0	0	0	0	0	0
: Vermiculite	0	0	0	0	0	0	0	0	0	0
: Zinc	0	0	0	0	0	0	0	0	0	0
: Zirconium	0	0	0	0	0	0	0	0	0	0
Total minerals: % sum	0	0	8	0	0	0	10	0.1	0	5
Number of Minerals	0	0	2	0	0	0	4	1	0	4
Oil reserves (/cap bbl)	.	.	579000	0	.	0	5580	30	.	4010

Characteristics	Greenland	Grenada	Guade-loupe	Guam	Guatemala	Guernsey	Guinea	Guinea-Bissau	Guyana	Haiti
World Reserves %: Bauxite							26		3	
: Antimony										
: Barytes										
: Beryllium										
: Bismuth										
: Boron										
: Cadmium										
: Chromium										
: Cobalt										
: Copper										
: Fluorspar										
: Gold					0.3					
: Indium										
: Ind. diamond										
: Iron ore										
: Kaolin										
: Lead										
: Lithium										
: Magnesium										
: Manganese										
: Mercury										
: Molybdenum										
: Nickel										
: Niobium										
: Phosphate										
: Platinium group										
: Potash										
: Rare minerals										
: Rhenium										
: Selenium										
: Silver										
: Sulphur										
: Talc										
: Tantalum										
: Tellurium										
: Tin										
: Titanium A										
: Titanium B										
: Tungsten										
: Uranium										
: Vanadium										
: Vermiculite										
: Zinc										
: Zirconium										
Total minerals: % sum					0.3		26		3	
Number of Minerals					1		1		1	
Oil reserves (/cap bbl)					2700		0		0	

Characteristics	Honduras	Hong Kong	Hungary	Iceland	India	Indonesia	Iran	Iraq	Ireland	Isle of Man
World Reserves %: Bauxite	0	0	1	0	5	4	0	0	0	0
Antimony	0	0	0	0	0	0	0	0	0	0
Barytes	0	0	0	0	18	0	0	0	1	0
Beryllium	0	0	0	0	17	0	0	0	0	0
Bismuth	0	0	0	0	0	0	0	0	0	0
Boron	0	0	0	0	3	0	0	0	0	0
Cadmium	0	0	0	0	4	0	0	0	0	0
Chromium	0	0	0	0	0.5	0	0	0	0	0
Cobalt	0	0	0	0	0	0	0	0	0	0
Copper	0	0	0	0	0	0.7	0	0	0	0
Fluorspar	0	0	0	0	0	0	0	0	0	0
Gold	0	0	0.1	0	0	0	0.9	0	0	0
Indium	0	0	0	0	0	0	0	0	0	0
Ind. diamond	0	0	0	0	0	0	0	0	0	0
Iron ore	0	0	0	0	5	0	0	0	0	0
Kaolin	0	0	0	0	5	0	0	0	0	0
Lead	0	0	0	0	3	0	0	0	3	0
Lithium	0	0	0	0	0	0	0	0	0	0
Magnesium	0	0	0	0	1	0	0	0	0	0
Manganese	0	0	0	0	2	0	0	0	0	0
Mercury	0	0	0	0	0	0	0	0	0	0
Molybdenum	0	0	0	0	0	0	0	0	0	0
Nickel	0	0	0	0	0	7	0	0	0	0
Niobium	0	0	0	0	0	0	0	0	0	0
Phosphate	0	0	0	0	0	0	0	1	0	0
Platinium group	0	0	0	0	0	0	0	0	0	0
Potash	0	0	0	0	0	0	0	0	0	0
Rare minerals	0	0	0	0	0	0	0	0	0	0
Rhenium	0	0	0	0	0	0	0	0	0	0
Selenium	0	0	0	0	0	0	0	0	0	0
Silver	0	0	0	0	3	0	0	0	0	0
Sulphur	0	0	0	0	0.8	0	0	9	0	0
Talc	0	0	0	0	0	0	0	0	0	0
Tantalum	0	0	0	0	0	0	0	0	0	0
Tellurium	0	0	0	0	0	0	0	0	0	0
Tin	0	0	0	0	1	12	0	0	0	0
Titanium A	0	0	0	0	15	0	0	0	0	0
Titanium B	0	0	0	0	15	0	0	0	0	0
Tungsten	0	0	0	0	2	0	0	0	0	0
Uranium	0	0	0	0	0	0	0	0	0	0
Vanadium	0	0	0	0	0	0	0	0	0	0
Vermiculite	0	0	0	0	0	0	0	0	0	0
Zinc	0	0	0	0	7	0	1	0	3	0
Zirconium	0	0	0	0	0	0	0	0	0	0
Total minerals: % sum	0	0	1	0	101	22	2	10	7	0
Number of Minerals	0	0	2	0	19	4	2	2	3	0
Oil reserves (/cap bbl)	0	0	14000	0	6750	29700	1470	5020000	0	0

Characteristics	Israel	Italy	Ivory Coast	Jamaica	Japan	Jersey	Jordan	Kazakh-stan	Kenya	Kiribati
World Reserves %: Bauxite				9						
Antimony		0								
Barytes		1								
Beryllium		1								
Bismuth		0			8					
Boron					2					
Cadmium										
Chromium										
Cobalt										
Copper		3			3					
Fluorspar		3								
Gold									0.8	
Indium										
Ind. diamond										
Iron ore										
Kaolin										
Lead										
Lithium										
Magnesium										
Manganese										
Mercury		0.2								
Molybdenum										
Nickel										
Niobium										
Phosphate	0.6						0.7			
Platinium group										
Potash							0.6			
Rare minerals										
Rhenium										
Selenium					0.3					
Silver					1					
Sulphur		0.7								
Talc										
Tantalum										
Tellurium										
Tin										
Titanium A										
Titanium B										
Tungsten										
Uranium										
Vanadium										
Vermiculite										
Zinc					3					
Zirconium										
Total minerals: % sum	0.6	5	3	9	3		1	0	0.8	0
Number of Minerals	1	5	3	9	18		2	0	1	0
Oil reserves (/cap bbl)	0	12900	7460	0	480	.	899	0	0	0

Characteristics	Kuwait	Kyrgyz-stan	Laos	Latvia	Lebanon	Lesotho	Liberia	Libya	Liechten-stein	Lithuania
World Reserves %: Bauxite										
: Antimony										
: Barytes										
: Beryllium										
: Bismuth										
: Boron										
: Cadmium										
: Chromium										
: Cobalt										
: Copper										
: Fluorspar										
: Gold										
: Indium										
: Ind. diamond										
: Iron ore							0.8			
: Kaolin										
: Lead										
: Lithium										
: Magnesium										
: Manganese										
: Mercury										
: Molybdenum										
: Nickel										
: Niobium										
: Phosphate										
: Platinium group										
: Potash										
: Rare minerals										
: Rhenium										
: Selenium										
: Silver										
: Sulphur										
: Talc										
: Tantalum										
: Tellurium										
: Tin										
: Titanium A										
: Titanium B										
: Tungsten										
: Uranium										
: Vanadium										
: Vermiculite										
: Zinc										
: Zirconium										
Total minerals: % sum	0	0	0	0	0	0	0.8	0	0	0
Number of Minerals	0	0	0	0	0	0	1	0	0	0
Oil reserves (/cap bbl)	0	0	0	0	0	0	0	4500000	0	0

Characteristics	Luxem-bourg	Macau	Macedonia	Madagas-car	Malawi	Malaysia	Maldives	Mali	Malta	Marshall Islands
World Reserves %: Bauxite										
Antimony										
Barytes										
Beryllium										
Bismuth										
Boron										
Cadmium										
Chromium				0.5						
Cobalt										
Copper										
Fluorspar										
Gold										
Indium										
Ind. diamond										
Iron ore										
Kaolin										
Lead										
Lithium										
Magnesium										
Manganese										
Mercury										
Molybdenum										
Nickel						0.1				
Niobium										
Phosphate										
Platinium group										
Potash										
Rare minerals										
Rhenium										
Selenium						2				
Silver										
Sulphur						19				
Talc										
Tantalum										
Tellurium										
Tin						0.7				
Titanium A										
Titanium B										
Tungsten										
Uranium										
Vanadium										
Vermiculite										
Zinc										
Zirconium										
Total minerals: % sum				0.3		21				
Number of Minerals				0.8		5				
Oil reserves (/cap bbl)				2		192000				

Characteristics	Martini-que	Maurita-nia	Mauritius	Mayotte	Mexico	Micronesia Federation	Moldova	Monaco	Mongolia	Montser-rat
World Reserves %: Bauxite										
∴ Antimony					4					
∴ Barytes					4					
∴ Beryllium										
∴ Bismuth					9					
∴ Boron										
∴ Cadmium					7					
∴ Chromium										
∴ Cobalt					4					
∴ Copper					8					
∴ Fluorspar									0.9	
∴ Gold					3				2.1	
∴ Indium										
∴ Ind. diamond										
∴ Iron ore										
∴ Kaolin										
∴ Lead					4					
∴ Lithium										
∴ Magnesium					0.5					
∴ Manganese					4					
∴ Mercury					2					
∴ Molybdenum										
∴ Nickel										
∴ Niobium										
∴ Phosphate										
∴ Platinium group										
∴ Potash										
∴ Rare minerals										
∴ Rhenium										
∴ Selenium					5					
∴ Silver					13					
∴ Sulphur					5					
∴ Talc										
∴ Tantalum										
∴ Tellurium										
∴ Tin										
∴ Titanium A					0.3					
∴ Titanium B					0.3					
∴ Tungsten										
∴ Uranium										
∴ Vanadium					4					
∴ Vermiculite										
∴ Zinc										
∴ Zirconium										
Total minerals: % sum					78				2.2	
Number of Minerals					17				2	
Oil reserves (/cap bbl)	.	0	0	.	570000	0	0	0	0	.

Characteristics	Morocco	Mozam-bique	Namibia	Nauru	Nepal	Nether-lands	Netherlands Antilles	New Caledonia	New Zealand	Nicaragua
World Reserves %: Bauxite										
Antimony	2									
Barytes	6									
Beryllium		1								
Bismuth										
Boron										
Cadmium										
Chromium								7		
Cobalt										
Copper										
Fluorspar			1							
Gold										
Indium										
Ind. diamond										
Iron ore										
Kaolin	3									
Lead			1							
Lithium	0.1									
Magnesium					2					
Manganese										
Mercury										
Molybdenum										
Nickel								10		
Niobium										
Phosphate	24									
Platinium group										
Potash										
Rare minerals										
Rhenium										
Selenium										
Silver										
Sulphur										
Talc										
Tantalum		1	1							
Tellurium										
Tin			4							
Titanium A										
Titanium B										
Tungsten										
Uranium										
Vanadium										
Vermiculite										
Zinc										
Zirconium										
Total minerals: % sum	34	2	6	0	2			16	0.3	
Number of Minerals	5	2	3	0	1			2	0.3	
Oil reserves (/cap bbl)	0	0	0	0	0	9460			48300	0

Characteristics	Niger	Nigeria	Niue	Norfolk Island	North Korea	Northern Mariana Isl.	Norway	Oman	Pacific Isl. Trust	Pakistan
World Reserves %: Bauxite	0	0	0	0	0	0	0	0	0	0
: Antimony	0	0	0	0	0	0	0	0	0	0
: Barytes	0	0	0	0	0	0	0	0	0	0
: Beryllium	0	0	0	0	0	0	0	0	0	0
: Bismuth	0	0	0	0	0	0	0	0	0	0
: Boron	0	0	0	0	0	0	0	0	0	0
: Cadmium	0	0	0	0	0	0	0	0	0	0
: Chromium	0	0	0	0	0	0	0	0	0	0
: Cobalt	0	0	0	0	0	0	0	0	0	0
: Copper	0	0	0	0	0	0	0	0	0	0
: Fluorspar	0	0	0	0	0	0	0	0	0	0
: Gold	0	0	0	0	0	0	0	0	0	0
: Indium	0	0	0	0	0	0	0	0	0	0
: Ind. diamond	0	0	0	0	0	0	0	0	0	0
: Iron ore	0	0	0	0	0	0	0	0	0	0
: Kaolin	0	0	0	0	0	0	0	0	0	0
: Lead	0	0	0	0	0	0	0	0	0	0
: Lithium	0	0	0	0	0	0	0	0	0	0
: Magnesium	0	0	0	0	18	0	0	0	0	0
: Manganese	0	0	0	0	0	0	0	0	0	0
: Mercury	0	0	0	0	0	0	0	0	0	0
: Molybdenum	0	0	0	0	0	0	0	0	0	0
: Nickel	0	0	0	0	0	0	0	0	0	0
: Niobium	0	2	0	0	0	0	0	0	0	0
: Phosphate	0	0	0	0	0	0	0	0	0	0
: Platinium group	0	0	0	0	0	0	0	0	0	0
: Potash	0	0	0	0	0	0	0	0	0	0
: Rare minerals	0	0	0	0	0	0	0	0	0	0
: Rhenium	0	0	0	0	0	0	0	0	0	0
: Selenium	0	0	0	0	0	0	0	0	0	0
: Silver	0	0	0	0	0	0	0	0	0	0
: Sulphur	0	0	0	0	0	0	0	0	0	0
: Talc	0	0	0	0	0	0	0	0	0	0
: Tantalum	0	12	0	0	0	0	0	0	0	0
: Tellurium	0	0	0	0	0	0	0	0	0	0
: Tin	0	0.3	0	0	0	0	0	0	0	0
: Titanium A	0	0	0	0	0	0	16	0	0	0
: Titanium B	0	0	0	0	0	0	0	0	0	0
: Tungsten	0	0	0	0	3	0	0	0	0	0
: Uranium	6	0	0	0	0	0	0	0	0	0
: Vanadium	0	0	0	0	0	0	0	0	0	0
: Vermiculite	0	0	0	0	0	0	0	0	0	0
: Zinc	0	0	0	0	3	0	0	0	0	0
: Zirconium	0	0	0	0	0	0	0	0	0	0
Total minerals: % sum	6	14	0	0	24	0	16	0	0	0
Number of Minerals	1	3	0	0	3	0	1	0	0	0
Oil reserves (/cap bbl)	0	168000	.	.	0	.	2040000	2670000	.	3220

Characteristics	Panama	Papua New Guinea	Paraguay	Peru	Philippines	Pitcairn Islands	Poland	Portugal	Puerto Rico	Qatar
World Reserves %: Bauxite	0	0	0	0	0	0	0	0	0	0
Antimony	0	0	0	2	0	0	0	0	0	0
Barytes	0	0	0	1	0	0	0	0	0	0
Beryllium	0	0	0	0	0	0	0	0.3	0	0
Bismuth	0	0	0	10	0	0	0	0	0	0
Boron	0	0	0	0	0	0	0	0	0	0
Cadmium	0	0	0	2	0	0	2	0	0	0
Chromium	0	0	0	0	0.6	0	0	0	0	0
Cobalt	0	0	0	0	3	0	0	0	0	0
Copper	0	2	0	5	0	0	3	0.9	0	0
Fluorspar	0	0	0	0	0	0	0	0	0	0
Gold	0	0.8	0	3	0.9	0	0	0	0	0
Indium	0	0	0	5	0	0	0	0	0	0
Ind. diamond	0	0	0	0	0	0	0	0	0	0
Iron ore	0	0	0	0	0	0	0	0	0	0
Kaolin	0	0	0	0	0	0	0	0	0	0
Lead	0	0	0	3	0	0	3	0	0	0
Lithium	0	0	0	0	0	0	0	0	0	0
Magnesium	0	0	0	0	0	0	0	0	0	0
Manganese	0	0	0	0	0	0	0	0	0	0
Mercury	0	0	0	3	0	0	0	0	0	0
Molybdenum	0	0	0	3	0	0	0.4	0	0	0
Nickel	0	2	0	0	3	0	0	0	0	0
Niobium	0	0	0	0	0	0	0	0	0	0
Phosphate	0	0	0	0	0	0	0	0	0	0
Platinum group	0	0	0	0	0	0	0	0	0	0
Potash	0	0	0	0	0	0	0	0	0	0
Rare minerals	0	0	0	0	0	0	0	0	0	0
Rhenium	0	0	0	0	3	0	3	0	0	0
Selenium	0	0	0	2	0	0	0	0	0	0
Silver	0	0	0	9	0	0	9	0	0	0
Sulphur	0	0	0	0	0	0	0	0	0	0
Talc	0	0	0	0	0	0	0	0	0	0
Tantalum	0	0	0	0	0	0	0	0	0	0
Tellurium	0	0	0	3	0	0	0	0	0	0
Tin	0	0	0	2	0	0	0	1	0	0
Titanium A	0	0	0	0	0	0	0	0	0	0
Titanium B	0	0	0	0	0	0	0	0	0	0
Tungsten	0	0	0	0	0	0	0	1	0	0
Uranium	0	0	0	0	0	0	0	0	0	0
Vanadium	0	0	0	0.1	0	0	0	0	0	0
Vermiculite	0	0	0	0	0	0	0	0	0	0
Zinc	0	0	0	5	0	0	2	0	0	0
Zirconium	0	0	0	0	0	0	0	0	0	0
Total minerals: % sum	0	5	0	52	10	0	22	3	0	0
Number of Minerals	0	3	0	15	5	0	7	4	0	0
Oil reserves (/cap bbl)	0	81500	0	16600	2220	.	1100	0	.	7630000

Characteristics	Reunion	Romania	Russia	Rwanda	San Marino	Sao Tome E Principe	Saudi Arabia	Senegal	Serbia & Monten.	Seychelles
World Reserves %: Bauxite	0	0.2	0	0	0	0	0	0	0	0
Antimony	0	0	0	0	0	0	0	0	0	0
Barytes	0	0	0	0	0	0	0	0	0	0
Beryllium	0	0	0	0	0	0	0	0	0	0
Bismuth	0	0	0	0	0	0	0	0	0	0
Boron	0	0	0	0	0	0	0	0	0	0
Cadmium	0	0	0	0	0	0	0	0	0	0
Chromium	0	0	0	0	0	0	0	0	0	0
Cobalt	0	0	0	0	0	0	0	0	0	0
Copper	0	0	0	0	0	0	0	0	0	0
Fluorspar	0	0	0	0	0	0	0	0	0	0
Gold	0	0	0	3	0	0	0	0	0	0
Indium	0	0	0	0	0	0	0	0	0	0
Ind. diamond	0	0	0	0	0	0	0	0	0	0
Iron ore	0	0	0	0	0	0	0	0	0	0
Kaolin	0	0	0	0	0	0	0	0	0	0
Lead	0	0	0	0	0	0	0	0	0	0
Lithium	0	0	0	0	0	0	0	0	0	0
Magnesium	0	0	0	0	0	0	0	0	0	0
Manganese	0	0	0	0	0	0	0	0	0	0
Mercury	0	0	0	0	0	0	0	0	0	0
Molybdenum	0	0	0	0	0	0	0	0	0	0
Nickel	0	0	0	0	0	0	0	0	0	0
Niobium	0	0	0	0	0	0	0	0	0	0
Phosphate	0	0	0	0	0	0	0	0	0	0
Platinium group	0	0	0	0	0	0	0	0	0	0
Potash	0	0	0	0	0	0	0	0	0	0
Rare minerals	0	0	0	0	0	0	0	0	0	0
Rhenium	0	0	0	0	0	0	0	0	0	0
Selenium	0	0	0	0	0	0	0	0	0	0
Silver	0	0	0	0	0	0	0	0	0	0
Sulphur	0	0	0	0	0	0	7	0	0	0
Talc	0	0	0	0	0	0	0	0	0	0
Tantalum	0	0	0	0	0	0	0	0	0	0
Tellurium	0	0	0	0	0	0	0	0	0	0
Tin	0	0	0	0	0	0	0	0	0	0
Titanium A	0	0.6	0	0	0	0	0	0	0	0
Titanium B	0	0	0	0	0	0	0	0	0	0
Tungsten	0	0	0	0	0	0	0	0	0	0
Uranium	0	0	0	0	0	0	0	0	0	0
Vanadium	0	0	0	0	0	0	0	0	0	0
Vermiculite	0	0	0	0	0	0	0	0	0	0
Zinc	0	0	0	0	0	0	0	0	0	0
Zirconium	0	0	0	0	0	0	0	0	0	0
Total minerals: % sum	0	0.8	0	3	0	0	7	0	0	0
Number of Minerals	.	2	.	1	0	0	1	0	0	0
Oil reserves (/cap bbl)	.	68000	.	0	0	0	15700000	0	0	0

Characteristics	Sierra Leone	Singapore	Slovakia	Slovenia	Solomon Islands	Somalia	South Africa	South Korea	Spain	Sri Lanka
World Reserves %: Bauxite	0.6	0	0	0	0	0	0	0	0	0
: Antimony	0	0	0	0	0	0	6	0	0	0
: Barytes	0	0	0	0	0	0	4	0	0	0
: Beryllium	0	0	0	0	0	0	0	0	0	0
: Bismuth	0	0	0	0	0	0	0	4	4	0
: Boron	0	0	0	0	0	0	0	0	0	0
: Cadmium	0	0	0	0	0	0	0	0	0	0
: Chromium	0	0	0	0	0	0	71	0	0	0
: Cobalt	0	0	0	0	0	0	0.6	0	0	0
: Copper	0	0	0	0	0	0	0.6	0	3	0
: Fluorspar	0	0	0	0	0	0	13	0	0.8	0
: Gold	0	0	0	0	0	0	47	0	0.3	0
: Indium	0	0	0	0	0	0	0	0	0	0
: Ind. diamond	0	0	0	0	0	0	4	0	0	0
: Iron ore	0	0	0	0	0	0	2	0	0	0
: Kaolin	0	0	0	0	0	0	3	0	0.4	0
: Lead	0	0	0	0	0	0	0.2	0	0	0
: Lithium	0	0	0	0	0	0	0	0	0	0
: Magnesium	0	0	0	0	0	0	0	0	0	0
: Manganese	0	0	0	0	0	0	45	0	0	0
: Mercury	0	0	0	0	0	0	0	0	59	0
: Molybdenum	0	0	0	0	0	0	0	0.3	0	0
: Nickel	0	0	0	0	0	0	5	0	0	0
: Niobium	0	0	0	0	0	0	0	0	0	0
: Phosphate	0	0	0	0	0	0	0	0	0	0
: Platinum group	0	0	0	0	0	0	89	0	0	0
: Potash	0	0	0	0	0	0	0	0	0.3	0
: Rare minerals	0	0	0	0	0	0	0	0	0	0
: Rhenium	0	0	0	0	0	0	0	0	0	0
: Selenium	0	0	0	0	0	0	0	0	0	0
: Silver	0	0	0	0	0	0	0.5	0	4	0
: Sulphur	0	0	0	0	0	0	0	0	0	0
: Talc	0	0	0	0	0	0	0	0	0	0
: Tantalum	0	0	0	0	0	0.2	0	0	0	0
: Tellurium	0	0	0	0	0	0	0	0	0	0
: Tin	0.5	0	0	0	0	0	0	0	0	0
: Titanium A	0.2	0	0	0	0	0	18	0	0	0.9
: Titanium B	0	0	0	0	0	0	4	0	0	0
: Tungsten	0	0	0	0	0	0	0	3	0	0
: Uranium	0	0	0	0	0	0	0	0.4	0	0
: Vanadium	0	0	0	0	0	0	20	0	0	0
: Vermiculite	0	0	0	0	0	0	40	0	0	0
: Zinc	0	0	0	0	0	0	2	3	3	0
: Zirconium	0	0	0	0	0	0	28	0	0	0
Total minerals: % sum	1	0	0	0	0	0.2	428	10	77	3
Number of Minerals	4	0	0	0	0	1	23	4	9	2
Oil reserves (/cap bbl)	0	0	.	0	0	0	0	0	575	0

Characteristics	St. Helena	St. Kitts & Nevis	St. Lucia	St. Pierre & Miquelon	St. Vincent & Grenad.	Sudan	Suriname	Swaziland	Sweden	Switzerland
World Reserves %: Bauxite	0	0	0	0	0	0	3	0	0	0
Antimony										
Barytes										
Beryllium										
Bismuth										
Boron										
Cadmium										
Chromium										
Cobalt										
Copper										
Fluorspar										
Gold										
Indium										
Ind. diamond										
Iron ore										
Kaolin										
Lead										
Lithium										
Magnesium									3	
Manganese									3	
Mercury										
Molybdenum										
Nickel										
Niobium										
Phosphate										
Platinium group										
Potash										
Rare minerals										
Rhenium										
Selenium										
Silver										
Sulphur										
Talc										
Tantalum										
Tellurium										
Tin										
Titanium A										
Titanium B										
Tungsten										
Uranium										
Vanadium										
Vermiculite										
Zinc										
Zirconium										
Total minerals: % sum	0	0	0	0	0	0	3	0	5	0
Number of Minerals	.	0	0	0	0	0	1	0	2	0
Oil reserves (/cap bbl)	.	0	0	.	0	10900	0	0	0	0

Characteristics	Syrian Arab Rep.	Taiwan	Tajikistan	Tanzania	Thailand	Togo	Tokelau	Tonga	Trinidad & Tobago	Tunisia
World Reserves %: Bauxite										
Antimony					6					
Barytes					4					
Beryllium										
Bismuth										
Boron										
Cadmium										
Chromium										
Cobalt										
Copper										
Fluorspar					0.4					
Gold				0.5						
Indium										
Ind. diamond										
Iron ore										
Kaolin										
Lead										
Lithium										
Magnesium										
Manganese										
Mercury										
Molybdenum										
Nickel										
Niobium										
Phosphate										
Platinium group										
Potash										
Rare minerals										
Rhenium										
Selenium										
Silver										
Sulphur										
Talc					28					
Tantalum					5					
Tellurium										
Tin					0					
Titanium A					1					
Titanium B										
Tungsten										
Uranium										
Vanadium										
Vermiculite										
Zinc										
Zirconium										
Total minerals: % sum				0.5	45					
Number of Minerals				1	7					
Oil reserves (/cap bbl)	123000			0	4260				442000	198000

Characteristics	Turkey	Turkme-nistan	Turks & Caicos	Tuvalu	Uganda	Ukraine	United Arab Emir.	United Kingdom	United States	Uruguay
World Reserves %: Bauxite	0	0	0	0	0	0	0	0	0	0
Antimony	2	0	0	0	0	0	0	0	0.2	0
Barytes	2	0	0	0	0	0	0	0	2	0
Beryllium	0	0	0	0	0	0	0	0	18	0
Bismuth	0	0	0	0	0	0	0	0	5	0
Boron	31	0	0	0	0	0	0	0	8	0
Cadmium	0	0	0	0	0	0	0	0	0	0
Chromium	0.6	0	0	0	0	0	0	0	38	0
Cobalt	0	0	0	0	4	0	0	0	0	0
Copper	0	0	0	0	0	0	0	0	13	0
Fluorspar	0	0	0	0	0	0	0	0.8	0	0
Gold	0	0	0	0	0	0	0	0	17	0
Indium	0	0	0	0	0	0	0	0	0.4	0
Ind. diamond	0	0	0	0	0	0	0	0	11	0
Iron ore	0	0	0	0	0	0	0	0	14	0
Kaolin	0	0	0	0	0	0	0	9	6	0
Lead	0	0	0	0	0	0	0	0	36	0
Lithium	0	0	0	0	0	0	0	0	16	0
Magnesium	3	0	0	0	0	0	0	0	16	0
Manganese	3	0	0	0	0	0	0	0	0.4	0
Mercury	3	0	0	0	0	0	0	0	3	0
Molybdenum	0	0	0	0	0	0	0	0	49	0
Nickel	0	0	0	0	0	0	0	0	0.1	0
Niobium	0	0	0	0	0	0	0	0	0	0
Phosphate	0	0	0	0	0	0	0	0	0	0
Platinium group	0	0	0	0	0	0	0	0	0	0
Potash	0	0	0	0	0	0	0	0.3	1	0
Rare minerals	0	0	0	0	0	0	0	0	0	0
Rhenium	0	0	0	0	0	0	0	0	0.4	0
Selenium	0	0	0	0	0	0	0	0	0.8	0
Silver	0	0	0	0	0	0	0	0	15	0
Sulphur	0	0	0	0	0	0	0	0	16	0
Talc	0	0	0	0	0	0	0	0	15	0
Tantalum	0	0	0	0	0	0	0	0	11	0
Tellurium	0	0	0	0	0	0	0	0	10	0
Tin	0	0	0	0	0	0	0	2	35	0
Titanium A	0	0	0	0	0	0	0	0	17	0
Titanium B	0	0	0	0	0	0	0	0	0.3	0
Tungsten	3	0	0	0	0	0	0	3	0.4	0
Uranium	0	0	0	0	0	0	0	0	0.6	0
Vanadium	0	0	0	0	0	0	0	0	0	0
Vermiculite	0	0	0	0	0	0	0	0	3	0
Zinc	0	0	0	0	0	0	0	0	50	0
Zirconium	0	0	0	0	0	0	0	0	13	0
Total minerals: % sum	44	0	.	0	4	.	0	15	467	0
Number of Minerals	7	0	0	0	1	0	0	5	37	0
Oil reserves (/cap bbl)	7970	0	.	0	0	.	53800000	71700	95700	0

Characteristics	Uzbekistan	Vanuatu	Vatican City	Venezuela	Vietnam	Virgin Isl. US	Wallis & Futuna	West Bank	Western Samoa	Western Sahara
World Reserves %: Bauxite	0	0	0	2	0	0	0	0	0	0
Antimony	0	0	0	0	0	0	0	0	0	0
Barytes	0	0	0	0	0	0	0	0	0	0
Beryllium	0	0	0	0	0	0	0	0	0	0
Bismuth	0	0	0	0	0	0	0	0	0	0
Boron	0	0	0	0	0	0	0	0	0	0
Cadmium	0	0	0	0	0	0	0	0	0	0
Chromium	0	0	0	0	0	0	0	0	0	0
Cobalt	0	0	0	0	0	0	0	0	0	0
Copper	0	0	0	0	0	0	0	0	0	0
Fluorspar	0	0	0	0	0	0	0	0	0	0
Gold	0	0	0	0	0	0	0	0	0	0
Indium	0	0	0	0	0	0	0	0	0	0
Ind. diamond	0	0	0	0	0	0	0	0	0	0
Iron ore	0	0	0	2	0	0	0	0	0	0
Kaolin	0	0	0	0	0	0	0	0	0	0
Lead	0	0	0	0	0	0	0	0	0	0
Lithium	0	0	0	0	0	0	0	0	0	0
Magnesium	0	0	0	0	0	0	0	0	0	0
Manganese	0	0	0	0	0	0	0	0	0	0
Mercury	0	0	0	0	0	0	0	0	0	0
Molybdenum	0	0	0	0	0	0	0	0	0	0
Nickel	0	0	0	0	0	0	0	0	0	0
Niobium	0	0	0	0	0	0	0	0	0	0
Phosphate	0	0	0	0	0	0	0	0	0	23
Platinum group	0	0	0	0	0	0	0	0	0	0
Potash	0	0	0	0	0	0	0	0	0	0
Rare minerals	0	0	0	0	0	0	0	0	0	0
Rhenium	0	0	0	0	0	0	0	0	0	0
Selenium	0	0	0	0	0	0	0	0	0	0
Silver	0	0	0	0	0	0	0	0	0	0
Sulphur	0	0	0	0	0	0	0	0	0	0
Talc	0	0	0	0	0	0	0	0	0	0
Tantalum	0	0	0	0	0	0	0	0	0	0
Tellurium	0	0	0	0	0	0	0	0	0	0
Tin	0	0	0	0	0	0	0	0	0	0
Titanium A	0	0	0	0	0	0	0	0	0	0
Titanium B	0	0	0	0	0	0	0	0	0	0
Tungsten	0	0	0	0	0	0	0	0	0	0
Uranium	0	0	0	0	0	0	0	0	0	0
Vanadium	0	0	0	0	0	0	0	0	0	0
Vermiculite	0	0	0	0	0	0	0	0	0	0
Zinc	0	0	0	0	0	0	0	0	0	0
Zirconium	0	0	0	0	0	0	0	0	0	0
Total minerals: % sum	0	0	0	3	0	0	0	.	0	23
Number of Minerals	0	0	0	2	0	0	0	.	0	1
Oil reserves (/cap bbl)	0	0	0	3040000	7140	.	.	.	0	.

Characteristics	Yemen	Zaire	Zambia	Zimbabwe
World Reserves %: Bauxite	0	0	0	0
: Antimony	0	0	0	0
: Barytes	0	0	0	0
: Beryllium	0	0	0	0
: Bismuth	0	0	0	0.3
: Boron	0	0	0	0
: Cadmium	0	0	0	0
: Chromium	0	2	0	0
: Cobalt	0	0	11	0
: Copper	0	0	4	0
: Fluorspar	0	4	0	1
: Gold	0	0	0	0.1
: Indium	0	0	0	0
: Ind. diamond	0	41	0	0
: Iron ore	0	8	0	0
: Kaolin	0	0	0	0
: Lead	0	0	0	0
: Lithium	0	0	0	0
: Magnesium	0	0	0	0
: Manganese	0	15	0	0
: Mercury	0	0	0	0
: Molybdenum	0	0	0	0
: Nickel	0	0	0	1
: Niobium	0	0	0	0
: Phosphate	0	0	0	0
: Platinium group	0	0	0	0
: Potash	0	0	0	0
: Rare minerals	0	0	0	0
: Rhenium	0	0	0	0
: Selenium	0	0.8	4	0
: Silver	0	0	0	0
: Sulphur	0	0	0	0.2
: Talc	0	0	0	0
: Tantalum	0	0	0	0
: Tellurium	0	0	0	0
: Tin	0	1	0	0
: Titanium A	0	0	0	0
: Titanium B	0	0	0	0
: Tungsten	0	7	9	0.3
: Uranium	0	0	0	0
: Vanadium	0	8	0	0
: Vermiculite	0	0.3	0	0.2
: Zinc	0	0	0	0
: Zirconium	0	0.1	0	0
Total minerals: % sum	0	99	27	12
Number of Minerals	0	12	4	17
Oil reserves (/cap bbl)	309000	4540	0	0

7

LAND RESOURCES ACROSS COUNTRIES

Many cultural teachings are directly related to local terrain. This chapter provides comparative statistics for a variety of variables characterizing each country's land-based resources (excluding minerals, covered in Chapter 6). For a full discussion of the methodology used to generate these estimates, please refer to Chapter 1 which gives important caveats. This chapter first gives summary statistics of the variables reported: the number of countries for which each variable was available, weighted averages (by population) and simple averages; these averages can be used as benchmarks. Then a lengthy comparative table is presented which provides raw statistics across countries.

Most of the variables are self explanatory, though some merit commentary. All of the statistics should be considered as estimates which have undergone rounding and certain adjustments. Land-related estimates cover the amount of land available, its current use, the degree to which it is protected by law, and the extent to which it may be exposed to earthquakes, volcanism, soil degradation, overgrazing, and deforestation. Elevation and time zone location are also given; these statistics are estimated for inhabited regions. Then, each country is characterized as being located in or exposed to the earth's tectonic plates, vegetation zones (Biomes), and zoological zones.

Summary Statistics:
Land Resources

Characteristics	Number of Countries Covered	Weighted Average by Pop 1994	Simple Average	Simple Standard Deviation
Land: Total Area (km sq)	234	4202557.66	580200.63	1761242.55
: Density (pop/km sq)	234	161.62	403.43	2330.33
: # of boundaries	233	6.55	2.55	2.59
: Total boundary (km)	234	10513.13	2114.62	3165.84
: Terrain (3=mountains)	234	2.17	1.81	1.13
Land Usage: Arable %	232	22.57	13.16	14.59
: Permanent crops %	232	1.46	3.73	8.22
: Meadows & pastures %	232	18.58	17.16	19.42
: Forest & woodland %	232	25.33	22.89	23.27
: Other %	232	29.01	36.52	29.76
: Irrigated %	221	5.57	2.38	8.43
: % Protected	191	3.63	4.56	8.71
: % Partially Protected	192	3.13	2.46	5.25
Risks: Earthquake (1=high)	234	0.43	0.18	0.38
: Volcanism	234	0.12	0.10	0.30
: Soil degradation	234	0.54	0.21	0.40
: Desertification	234	0.61	0.22	0.41
: Overgrazing	234	0.21	0.09	0.29
: Deforestation	234	0.61	0.27	0.45
Elevation: average (m)	234	209.68	244.61	463.61
: Highest point (m)	193	5840.48	2722.96	2025.86
: Lowest point (m)	193	-34.13	40.54	189.27
Timezone (GMT)	233	3.93	1.59	4.89
Tectonic plate: African	234	0.17	0.32	0.47
: Eurasian	234	0.72	0.35	0.48
: Indo-Australian	234	0.28	0.12	0.33
: Pacific	234	0.08	0.10	0.30
: American	234	0.13	0.14	0.34
: Nasca	234	0.00	0.01	0.11
: Caribbean	234	0.02	0.02	0.13
Biome: Desert (1=yes)	234	0.25	0.20	0.40
: Monsoon	234	0.46	0.14	0.35
: Tropical rain forest	234	0.36	0.32	0.47
: Savanna	234	0.36	0.23	0.42
: Mediterranean	234	0.09	0.14	0.34
: Temperate grassland	234	0.43	0.18	0.38
: Temperate forest	234	0.45	0.21	0.41
: Mountain	234	0.40	0.13	0.34
: Taiga	234	0.04	0.03	0.17
: Tundra	234	0.03	0.01	0.09
: Polar	234	0.03	0.02	0.13
Zoology: Neotropical	234	0.08	0.21	0.40
: Nearctic	234	0.08	0.12	0.32
: Ethiopian	234	0.13	0.26	0.44
: Oriental	234	0.52	0.10	0.30
: Palearctic	234	0.64	0.35	0.48
: Australian	234	0.04	0.08	0.27

Characteristics	Afghanistan	Albania	Algeria	American Samoa	Andorra	Angola	Anguilla	Antigua & Barbuda	Argentina	Armenia
Land: Total Area (km sq)	648000	28800	2380000	199	450	1250000	91	440	2770000	29800
: Density (pop/km sq)	30	116	11	267	118	8	82	149	12	120
: # of boundaries	4	7	7	0	7	4	0	0	5	5
: Total boundary (km)	5830	768	6340	0	125	5200	0	0	9670	1250
: Terrain (3=mountains)	4	3	2	4	2	2	0	0	3	3
Land Usage: Arable %	12	21	3	10	2	2	0	18	9	10
: Permanent crops %		4		10					4	
: Meadows & pastures %	46	15	13		56	23		7	52	
: Forest & woodland %	3	38	2	70	22	43		16	22	
: Other %	39	22	82	10	20	32		59	13	
: Irrigated %		1								
: % Protected	0.3	2	0.1			2			3	7
: % Partially Protected	0.2	0.8				1			2	
Risks: Earthquake (1=high)	1	1	1			1			1	1
: Volcanism										
: Soil degradation	1						1		1	
: Desertification	1		1			1				
: Overgrazing	1								1	
: Deforestation	1	1	1	5	1	1				
Elevation: average (m)	1820	127	59		1080	43	40	6	25	990
: Highest point (m)	7480	2750	2910		2950	2620		402	6960	4090
: Lowest point (m)	259	0	-40		840	0		0	-42	390
Timezone (GMT)		1	1	-11	1	1	-4	-4	-3	3
Tectonic plate: African	0	0	1	0	0	1	0	0	0	0
: Eurasian	1	1	0	0	1	0	0	0	0	1
: Indo-Australian	0	0	0	0	0	0	0	0	0	0
: Pacific	0	0	0	1	0	0	0	0	0	0
: American	0	0	0	0	0	0	1	0	1	0
: Nasca	0	0	0	0	0	0	0	0	1	0
: Caribbean	0	0	0	0	0	0	0	1	0	0
Biome: Desert (1=yes)	0	0	1	0	0	0	0	0	0	0
: Monsoon	0	0	0	0	0	0	0	0	0	0
: Tropical rain forest	0	0	0	1	0	1	0	0	0	0
: Savanna	0	0	0	0	0	1	0	0	0	0
: Mediterranean	0	1	1	0	0	0	0	0	0	0
: Temperate grassland	0	0	0	0	0	0	0	0	1	0
: Temperate forest	0	0	0	0	0	0	0	0	0	0
: Mountain	1	0	0	0	1	0	0	0	0	1
: Taiga	0	0	0	0	0	0	0	0	0	0
: Tundra	0	0	0	0	0	0	0	0	0	0
: Polar	0	0	0	0	0	0	0	0	0	0
Zoology: Neotropical	0	0	0	0	0	0	1	1	1	0
: Nearctic	0	0	0	0	0	0	0	0	0	0
: Ethiopian	0	0	0	0	0	1	0	0	0	0
: Oriental	1	0	1	0	0	0	0	0	0	0
: Palearctic	1	1	1	0	1	0	0	0	1	1
: Australian	0	0	0	1	0	0	0	0	0	0

Characteristics	Aruba	Australia	Austria	Azerbaijan	Bahamas	Bahrain	Bangla-desh	Barbados	Belarus	Belgium
Land: Total Area (km sq)	193	7690000	83900	86600	13900	620	144000	430	208000	30500
:Density (pop/km sq)	329	2	93	85	21	857	849	651	50	328
:# of boundaries	0	0	7	2	0	0	2	0	5	4
:Total boundary (km)	1	1	2640	2010	0	0	4250	1	3100	1390
:Terrain (3=mountains)	0	1	4	1	1	0	1	1	1	2
Land Usage: Arable %	0	6	17	18	1	2	67	77	29	24
:Permanent crops %	0	0	1	0	0	6	2	0	0	1
:Meadows & pastures %	0	58	24	25	0	6	4	9	15	20
:Forest & woodland %	0	14	39	0	32	0	16	0	0	21
:Other %	100	22	19	57	67	90	11	14	56	34
:Irrigated %	.	0	0	70	0	1	14	1	1	0
:% Protected	.	6	25	2	9	0	0.7	0	0	2
:% Partially Protected	0	2	0	0	0	0	0	0	0	0
Risks: Earthquake (1=high)	0	0	0	0	0	0	0	0	0	0
:Volcanism	0	1	0	0	0	0	0	0	0	0
:Soil degradation	0	0	0	0	0	0	0	0	0	0
:Desertification	0	0	0	0	0	0	0	0	0	0
:Overgrazing	0	0	0	0	0	0	0	0	0	0
:Deforestation	0	0	0	0	0	1	1	0	0	0
Elevation: average (m)	16	200	910	384	5	0.9	8	55	156	76
:Highest point (m)	.	2230	3800	4470	63	134	957	340	345	694
:Lowest point (m)	0	-16	115	-28	-5	0	0	0	85	0
Timezone (GMT)	-4	9	1	3	-5	3	6	-4	3	1
Tectonic plate: African	0	0	0	0	0	0	0	0	0	0
:Eurasian	0	0	1	1	0	0	0	0	1	1
:Indo-Australian	0	1	0	0	0	0	1	0	0	0
:Pacific	0	0	0	0	0	0	0	0	0	0
:American	1	0	0	0	1	0	0	0	0	0
:Nasca	0	0	0	0	0	0	0	0	0	0
:Caribbean	0	0	0	0	0	0	0	1	0	0
Biome: Desert (1=yes)	1	1	0	0	0	1	0	0	0	0
:Monsoon	0	0	0	0	0	0	1	0	0	0
:Tropical rain forest	0	1	0	0	1	0	1	1	0	0
:Savanna	0	1	0	0	0	0	0	0	0	0
:Mediterranean	0	1	0	0	0	0	0	0	0	0
:Temperate grassland	0	1	0	1	0	0	0	0	0	0
:Temperate forest	0	0	1	0	0	0	0	0	1	1
:Mountain	0	0	1	1	0	0	0	0	0	0
:Taiga	0	0	0	0	0	0	0	0	0	0
:Tundra	0	0	0	0	0	0	0	0	0	0
:Polar	0	0	0	0	0	0	0	0	0	0
Zoology: Neotropical	1	0	0	0	1	0	0	1	0	0
:Nearctic	0	0	0	0	0	0	0	0	0	0
:Ethiopian	0	0	0	0	0	0	0	0	0	0
:Oriental	0	0	0	0	0	0	1	0	0	0
:Paleartic	0	0	1	1	0	1	0	0	1	1
:Australian	0	1	0	0	0	0	0	0	0	0

Characteristics	Belize	Benin	Bermuda	Bhutan	Bolivia	Bosnia & Herzegov.	Botswana	Brazil	British Virgin Isl.	Brunei
Land: Total Area (km sq)	23000	113000	50	47000	1100000	51200	600000	8510000	150	5770
: Density (pop/km sq)	9	45	1240	35	7	85	2	18	102	50
: # of boundaries	2	4	0	2	5	3	3	10	0	
:: Total boundary (km)	516	1990		1080	6740	1370	4010	14700	1	381
:: Terrain (3=mountains)	1	2	1	3	3	3	2	2	1	2
Land Usage: Arable %	2	12	0	2	2	20	2	7	20	1
: Permanent crops %	2	4	0	0	0	2	0	1	7	1
: Meadows & pastures %	44	4	0	5	25	25	75	19	33	
: Forest & woodland %	52	35	20	70	52	36	2	67	7	79
: Other %	0	45	80	23	20	17	21	6	33	18
: Irrigated %	0	0	0	0	0	0	0	3	0	0
: % Protected	5	7		19	9	0	17	0		14
:: % Partially Protected	0	0	0	18	5	1	2	0	0	5
Risks: Earthquake (1=high)	0	0	0	0	1	0	0	1	0	1
: Volcanism	0	0	0	0	1	0	0	0	0	0
: Soil degradation	0	0	0	0	0	0	0	0	0	0
: Desertification	0	0	0	0	0	0	1	0	0	0
: Overgrazing	0	0	0	0	0	0	1	0	0	0
: Deforestation	5	0	0	0	1	0	0	1	0	3
Elevation: average (m)			48		2420	125	1010	990		
: Highest point (m)	1120	681	79	7550	6320		1510	3010	40	1850
: Lowest point (m)	0	0	0	97	90	0	513	0	0	0
Timezone (GMT)	-6	1	-4	6	-4	1	2	-3	-4	8
Tectonic plate: African	0	1	0	0	0	0	1	0	0	0
: Eurasian	0	0	0	0	0	1	0	0	0	1
: Indo-Australian	0	0	0	1	0	0	0	0	0	0
: Pacific	0	0	0	0	0	0	0	0	0	0
: American	0	0	1	0	1	0	0	1	0	0
: Nasca	0	0	0	0	1	0	0	0	0	0
: Caribbean	1	0	0	0	0	0	0	0	1	0
Biome: Desert (1=yes)	0	0	0	0	0	0	1	0	0	0
: Monsoon	0	0	0	0	0	0	0	0	0	0
: Tropical rain forest	1	1	0	0	1	0	0	1	1	1
: Savanna	0	1	0	0	0	0	1	1	0	0
: Mediterranean	0	0	0	0	0	1	0	0	0	0
: Temperate grassland	0	0	0	0	0	0	0	0	0	0
: Temperate forest	0	0	1	0	0	1	0	0	0	0
: Mountain	0	0	0	1	1	1	0	0	0	0
: Taiga	0	0	0	0	0	0	0	0	0	0
: Tundra	0	0	0	0	0	0	0	0	0	0
: Polar	0	0	0	0	0	0	0	0	0	0
Zoology: Neotropical	1	0	0	0	1	0	0	1	1	0
: Nearctic	0	0	1	0	0	0	0	0	0	0
: Ethiopian	0	1	0	0	0	0	1	0	0	0
: Oriental	0	0	0	1	0	0	0	0	0	1
: Paleartic	0	0	0	0	0	1	0	0	0	0
: Australian	0	0	0	0	0	0	0	0	0	0

Characteristics	Bulgaria	Burkina Faso	Burma	Burundi	Cambodia	Cameroon	Canada	Cape Verde	Cayman Islands	Central Afric. Rep.
Land: Total Area (km sq)	111000	274000	677000	27800	181000	475000	9980000	4030	260	623000
: Density (pop/km sq)	81	36	66	215	50	26	3	100	120	5
: # of boundaries	4	6	5	3	3	6	1	0	0	5
: Total boundary (km)	1880	3190	5880	974	2570	4590	8890	0	0	5200
: Terrain (3=mountains)	3	1	3	2	2	2	2	4	0	1
Land Usage: Arable %	34	10	15	43	16	13	5	9	0	3
: Permanent crops %	3	0	1	8	1	2	0	0	0	0
: Meadows & pastures %	18	37	1	35	3	18	3	6	8	5
: Forest & woodland %	35	26	49	2	76	54	35	0	23	64
: Other %	10	27	34	12	4	13	57	85	69	28
: Irrigated %	11	0	2	0	1	0	0	1	0	0
: % Protected	2	10	0.3	3	0	4	5	0	.	9
: % Partially Protected	0	8	1	0	0	2	2	0	0	4
Risks: Earthquake (1=high)	1	0	1	1	0	0	0	1	0	0
: Volcanism	0	0	0	0	0	1	0	0	0	0
: Soil degradation	0	0	0	0	0	0	0	0	0	0
: Desertification	0	1	0	0	0	1	0	1	0	1
: Overgrazing	0	1	0	1	0	1	0	0	0	0
: Deforestation	1	1	1	1	1	1	0	1	0	0
Elevation: average (m)	564	304	6	783	11	387	85	28	34	381
: Highest point (m)	2920	747	5880	2670	1810	4100	5950	2830		1410
: Lowest point (m)	0	135	0	772	0	0	0	0		335
Timezone (GMT)	2	0	7	2	7	1	-6	-1	-5	1
Tectonic plate: African	0	1	0	1	0	1	0	1	0	1
: Eurasian	1	0	1	0	1	0	0	0	0	0
: Indo-Australian	0	0	1	0	1	0	0	0	0	0
: Pacific	0	0	0	0	0	0	0	0	0	0
: American	0	0	0	0	0	0	1	0	0	0
: Nasca	0	0	0	0	0	0	0	0	0	0
: Caribbean	0	0	0	0	0	0	0	0	1	0
Biome: Desert (1=yes)	0	0	0	0	0	0	0	1	0	0
: Monsoon	0	0	1	0	1	0	0	0	0	0
: Tropical rain forest	0	0	1	0	1	1	0	0	1	1
: Savanna	0	1	0	1	0	1	0	0	0	1
: Mediterranean	1	0	0	0	0	0	0	0	0	0
: Temperate grassland	1	0	0	0	0	0	1	0	0	0
: Temperate forest	0	0	0	0	0	0	1	0	0	0
: Mountain	0	0	0	0	0	0	1	0	0	0
: Taiga	0	0	0	0	0	0	1	0	0	0
: Tundra	0	0	0	0	0	0	1	0	0	0
: Polar	0	0	0	0	0	0	0	0	0	0
Zoology: Neotropical	0	0	0	0	0	0	0	0	1	0
: Nearctic	0	0	0	0	0	0	1	0	0	0
: Ethiopian	0	1	0	1	0	1	0	1	0	1
: Oriental	0	0	1	0	1	0	0	0	0	0
: Paleartic	1	0	0	0	0	0	0	0	0	0
: Australian	0	0	0	0	0	0	0	0	0	0

Characteristics	Chad	Chile	China	Christmas Island	Cocos (Keel.) Isl.	Colombia	Comoros	Congo	Cook Island	Costa Rica
Land: Total Area (km sq)	1280000	757000	9600000	135	14	1140000	2170	342000	240	50900
:Density (pop/km sq)	5	18	126	12	42	30	283	7	75	64
:# of boundaries	6	6	13	0	0	4	0	5	0	2
:Total boundary (km)	5970	6170	23200	0	0	7410	0	5500	0	639
:Terrain (3=mountains)	2	4	3	3	0	3	3	2	2	3
Land Usage: Arable %	2	7	10	0	0	4	35	0	4	6
:Permanent crops %	0	0	0	0	0	2	7	0	22	7
:Meadows & pastures %	36	16	31	0	0	29	16	29	0	45
:Forest & woodland %	11	21	14	0	0	49	34	62	74	34
:Other %	51	56	45	100	100	16		7	0	8
:Irrigated %	0.3	2	5	0	0	8	0	0	0	1
:% Protected	0	18	0	0	0	8	0	0		12
:% Partially Protected	0	7	3	0	0	0	0	4		3
Risks: Earthquake (1=high)	0	1	1	0	0	1	0	0	0	1
:Volcanism	1	1	0	0	0	0	1	0	0	1
:Soil degradation	0	1	1	0	0	0	0	0	0	0
:Desertification	1	0	1	0	0	1	0	0	0	1
:Overgrazing	0	0	0	0	0	0	0	0	0	0
:Deforestation	0	0	1	0	0	0	0	0	0	0
Elevation: average (m)	300	268	28			1560	59	513		1170
:Highest point (m)	3410	6890	8850	27	2	5800	2360	981	2	3820
:Lowest point (m)	160	0	-154			0	3	1	12	0
Timezone (GMT)	1	-4	8	1	1	-5	3	1		-6
Tectonic plate: African	1	0	0	0	0	0	1	1	0	0
:Eurasian	0	0	1	0	0	0	0	0	0	0
:Indo-Australian	0	0	0	1	1	0	0	0	0	0
:Pacific	0	0	0	0	0	0	0	0	1	0
:American	0	1	0	0	0	1	0	0	0	0
:Nasca	0	0	0	0	0	0	0	0	0	0
:Caribbean	0	0	0	0	0	1	0	0	0	1
Biome: Desert (1=yes)	1	0	1	0	0	0	0	0	0	0
:Monsoon	0	0	1	0	0	0	0	0	0	0
:Tropical rain forest	0	0	0	1	1	1	1	1	1	1
:Savanna	0	0	0	0	0	1	0	1	0	1
:Mediterranean	0	1	0	0	0	0	0	0	0	0
:Temperate grassland	0	0	1	0	0	0	0	0	0	0
:Temperate forest	0	1	1	0	0	0	0	0	0	0
:Mountain	0	1	1	0	0	1	0	0	0	1
:Taiga	0	0	1	0	0	0	0	0	0	0
:Tundra	0	0	0	0	0	0	0	0	0	0
:Polar	0	0	0	0	0	0	0	0	0	0
Zoology: Neotropical	0	1	0	0	0	1	0	0	0	1
:Nearctic	0	0	0	0	0	0	0	0	0	0
:Ethiopian	1	0	0	0	0	0	1	1	0	0
:Oriental	0	0	1	1	1	0	0	0	0	0
:Paleartic	0	0	1	0	0	0	0	0	0	0
:Australian	0	0	0	0	1	0	0	0	0	0

Characteristics	Croatia	Cuba	Cyprus	Czech Republic	Denmark	Djibouti	Dominica	Dominican Republic	Ecuador	Egypt
Land: Total Area (km sq)	56500	111000	9250	78400	43100	22000	750	48700	284000	1000000
: Density (pop/km sq)	86	98	78	132	121	23	103	157	40	56
: # of boundaries	6	1	0	3	1	3	0	1	2	4
: Total boundary (km)	1840	29	0		68	517	0	275	2010	2690
: Terrain (3=mountains)	2			3	0	1	3		3	
Land Usage: Arable %	32	23	40		61			23	6	3
: Permanent crops %	2	6	7		0	0	13	7	3	
: Meadows & pastures %	20	23	10		6	9		43	17	2
: Forest & woodland %	18	17	18		12		41	13	51	
: Other %	15	31	25	100	21		34	14	23	95
: Irrigated %	9	6	10		9			4		
: % Protected	5	6	0.2	6	10	0.4	9	20	6	0.8
: % Partially Protected	6	2			9			10		0.7
Risks: Earthquake (1=high)	1	0	1	1	0	0	0	0	1	0
: Volcanism	0	0	0	0	0	0	0	0	1	1
: Soil degradation	0	0	0	0	0	0	0	0	1	1
: Desertification	0	0	0	0	0	0	0	0	0	0
: Overgrazing	0	0	0	0	0	0	0	0	0	0
: Deforestation	1	0	0	9	5	0	0	0	1	0
Elevation: average (m)	132	49	155		5			14	1410	24
: Highest point (m)	1910	1970	1950	.	173	2060	1430	3180	6310	2640
: Lowest point (m)	0	-5	0		-7	-153	0	-40	0	-133
Timezone (GMT)	1	-5	2	1	1	3	-4	-4	-5	2
Tectonic plate: African	0	0	0	0	0	1	0	0	0	1
: Eurasian	1	0	1	1	1	0	0	0	0	0
: Indo-Australian	0	0	0	0	0	0	0	0	0	0
: Pacific	0	0	0	0	0	0	0	0	0	0
: American	0	1	0	0	0	0	1	1	1	0
: Nasca	0	0	0	0	0	0	0	0	1	0
: Caribbean	0	1	0	0	0	0	1	1	0	0
Biome: Desert (1=yes)	0	0	0	0	0	1	0	0	0	1
: Monsoon	0	0	0	0	0	0	0	0	0	0
: Tropical rain forest	0	1	0	0	0	0	1	1	1	0
: Savanna	0	0	0	0	0	0	0	0	0	0
: Mediterranean	1	0	1	0	0	0	0	0	0	0
: Temperate grassland	0	0	0	0	0	0	0	0	0	0
: Temperate forest	1	0	0	1	1	0	0	0	0	0
: Mountain	0	0	0	0	0	0	0	0	1	0
: Taiga	0	0	0	0	0	0	0	0	0	0
: Tundra	0	0	0	0	0	0	0	0	0	0
: Polar	0	0	0	0	0	0	0	0	0	0
Zoology: Neotropical	0	1	0	0	0	0	1	1	1	0
: Nearctic	0	0	0	0	0	0	0	0	0	0
: Ethiopian	0	0	0	0	0	1	0	0	0	1
: Oriental	0	0	0	0	0	0	0	0	0	0
: Palearctic	1	0	1	1	1	0	0	0	0	1
: Australian	0	0	0	0	0	0	0	0	0	0

Characteristics	El Salvador	Equatorial Guinea	Eritrea	Estonia	Ethiopia	Falkland Islands	Faroe Islands	Fiji	Finland	France
Land: Total Area (km sq)	21000	28100	93700	45100	1220000	12200	1400	18300	337000	547000
: Density (pop/km sq)	262	14	37	35	43	0.2	34	40	15	105
: # of boundaries	2	2		2	4	0	0	0	3	8
: Total boundary (km)	545	539		557	5140				2580	2890
: Terrain (3=mountains)	3				3	2	1	3		2
Land Usage: Arable %	27	5		22	12	0	2	8	8	32
: Permanent crops %	8	4		0	1	0	0	5	0	2
: Meadows & pastures %	29	4		11	41	99	0	3	0	23
: Forest & woodland %	6	61		31	24	0	0	65	76	27
: Other %	30	26		21	22	1	98	19	16	16
: Irrigated %	5	0		0	0	0	0	0.3	0	2
: % Protected	0.1	0			3			0.3	2	9
: % Partially Protected	1	0							1	
Risks: Earthquake (1=high)	1	0		0	1	0	0	1	0	0
: Volcanism	1	0		0	1	0	0	0	0	0
: Soil degradation	0	0		0	1	0	0	0	0	0
: Desertification	0	0		0	1	0	0	0	0	0
: Overgrazing	0	0		0	1	0	0	0	0	0
: Deforestation	1	0		0	1	0	0	1	0	0
Elevation: average (m)	698	20		46	2140				12	60
: Highest point (m)	2730	3010		318	4620	705	24	1320	1330	4810
: Lowest point (m)	0	0		0	-125	0		0	0	-3
Timezone (GMT)	-6	1	3	2	3	-4	0	11	2	1
Tectonic plate: African	0	1	1	0	1	0	0	0	0	0
: Eurasian	0	0	0	1	0	0	1	0	1	1
: Indo-Australian	0	0	0	0	0	0	0	1	0	0
: Pacific	0	0	0	0	0	0	0	0	0	0
: American	0	0	0	0	0	1	0	0	0	0
: Nasca	0	0	0	0	0	0	0	0	0	0
: Caribbean	1	0	0	0	0	0	0	0	0	0
Biome: Desert (1=yes)	0	0	0	0	1	0	0	0	0	0
: Monsoon	0	0	0	0	0	0	0	0	0	0
: Tropical rain forest	1	1	0	0	0	0	0	1	0	0
: Savanna	1	0	0	0	1	0	0	1	0	0
: Mediterranean	0	0	0	0	0	0	0	0	0	1
: Temperate grassland	0	0	0	0	0	1	0	0	0	0
: Temperate forest	0	0	0	1	0	0	0	0	1	1
: Mountain	1	0	0	0	1	0	0	0	0	1
: Taiga	0	0	0	0	0	0	0	0	1	0
: Tundra	0	0	0	0	0	0	1	0	0	0
: Polar	0	0	0	0	0	0	0	0	0	0
Zoology: Neotropical	1	0	0	0	0	1	0	0	0	0
: Nearctic	1	0	0	0	0	0	0	0	0	0
: Ethiopian	0	1	1	0	1	0	0	0	0	0
: Oriental	0	0	0	0	0	0	0	0	0	0
: Palearctic	0	0	0	1	0	0	1	0	1	1
: Australian	0	0	0	0	0	0	0	1	0	0

Characteristics	French Guiana	French Polynesia	Gabon	Gambia	Gaza Strip	Georgia	Germany	Ghana	Gibraltar	Greece
Land: Total Area (km sq)	91000	3940	268000	11300	380	69700	357000	239000	7	132000
: Density (pop/km sq)	1	54	5	82	1820	79	226	69	4810	77
: # of boundaries	2	0	3	1	2	4	9	3	1	4
: Total boundary (km)	1180		2550	740	62	1460	4260	2090	1	1230
: Terrain (3=mountains)	1	2	1	1	1	3	1	2		3
Land Usage: Arable %	0		1	16	13		30	5	0	23
: Permanent crops %	0	19	1	0	32		1		0	8
: Meadows & pastures %		5	18	9	0		19	15	0	40
: Forest & woodland %	82	31	78	20	0		30	37	0	20
: Other %	18	44	2	55	55		20	36	100	9
: Irrigated %	0	0	0	3			1	0		7
: % Protected			4	2		3	0	5		0.8
: % Partially Protected							16	0		0.2
Risks: Earthquake (1=high)										1
: Volcanism	0	0	0	0	0	0	0	0	0	0
: Soil degradation	0	0	0	0	0	0	0	0	0	0
: Desertification	0	0	0	0	1	0	0	0	0	0
: Overgrazing	0	0	0	0	1	0	0	0	0	0
: Deforestation	0	0	1	1	0	0	0	1	0	0
Elevation: average (m)						490	47	65		5
: Highest point (m)	830	2240	1020	53	48	5070	2960	885	3	2920
: Lowest point (m)	0	0	0	0	0	0	-2	0	0	0
Timezone (GMT)	-4	-6	1	0	2	3	1	0	1	2
Tectonic plate: African	0	0	1	1	1	0	0	1	0	0
: Eurasian	0	0	0	0	0	1	1	0	1	1
: Indo-Australian	0	0	0	0	0	0	0	0	0	0
: Pacific	0	1	0	0	0	0	0	0	0	0
: American	1	0	0	0	0	0	0	0	0	0
: Nasca	0	0	0	0	0	0	0	0	0	0
: Caribbean	0	0	0	0	0	0	0	0	0	0
Biome: Desert (1=yes)	0	0	0	0	0	0	0	0	0	0
: Monsoon	0	0	0	0	0	0	0	0	0	0
: Tropical rain forest	1	1	1	0	0	0	0	1	0	0
: Savanna	0	0	0	1	0	0	0	0	0	0
: Mediterranean	0	0	0	0	1	0	0	0	1	1
: Temperate grassland	0	0	0	0	0	0	0	0	0	0
: Temperate forest	0	0	0	0	0	1	1	0	0	0
: Mountain	0	0	0	0	0	1	0	0	0	0
: Taiga	0	0	0	0	0	0	0	0	0	0
: Tundra	0	0	0	0	0	0	0	0	0	0
: Polar	0	0	0	0	0	0	0	0	0	0
Zoology: Neotropical	1	0	0	0	0	0	0	0	0	0
: Nearctic	0	0	0	0	0	0	0	0	0	0
: Ethiopian	0	0	1	1	0	0	0	1	0	0
: Oriental	0	0	0	0	0	0	0	0	0	0
: Palearctic	0	0	0	0	1	1	1	0	1	1
: Australian	0	1	0	0	0	0	0	0	0	0

Characteristics	Greenland	Grenada	Guade-loupe	Guam	Guatemala	Guernsey	Guinea	Guinea-Bissau	Guyana	Haiti
Land: Total Area (km sq)	2180000	340	1780	541	109000	194	246000	36100	215000	27800
: Density (pop/km sq)	0	259	234	267	92	325	26	28	4	249
: # of boundaries	0	0	0	0	4	0	6	2	3	1
: Total boundary (km)					1690		3400	724	2460	275
: Terrain (3=mountains)	1		3	3	3			9	1	3
Land Usage: Arable %	0	15	18	11	12		6	11	3	20
: Permanent crops %	0	26	5	11	4			1	0	13
: Meadows & pastures %	1	3	13	15	12		12	46	6	18
: Forest & woodland %		9	40	18	40		42	38	83	4
: Other %	99	47	24	45	32		40	6	8	45
: Irrigated %	0	0	1	0	1		0.7	0	1	0.3
: % Protected					0.5					0.4
: % Partially Protected										
Risks: Earthquake (1=high)	0	0	0	0	1	0	0	0	0	1
: Volcanism	0	0	0	0	1	0	0	0	0	0
: Soil degradation	0	0	0	0	0	0	0	0	0	0
: Desertification	0	0	0	0	0	0	0	0	0	0
: Overgrazing	0	0	0	0	0	0	0	0	0	0
: Deforestation	0	0	0	0	1	0	1	0	0	1
Elevation: average (m)	25	92	14	78	1500	5	46	20	2	41
: Highest point (m)	3700	840			4220		1750	4250	2870	2670
: Lowest point (m)	0	0	0	0	0	0	0	0	0	0
Timezone (GMT)	-3	-4	-4	10	-6	0	0	0	-4	-5
Tectonic plate: African	0	0	0	0	0	0	1	1	0	0
: Eurasian	0	0	0	0	0	1	0	0	0	0
: Indo-Australian	0	0	0	0	0	0	0	0	0	0
: Pacific	0	0	0	1	0	0	0	0	0	0
: American	1	0	0	0	0	0	0	0	1	0
: Nasca	0	0	0	0	0	0	0	0	0	0
: Caribbean	0	1	1	0	1	0	0	0	0	1
Biome: Desert (1=yes)	0	0	0	0	0	0	0	0	0	0
: Monsoon	0	0	0	0	0	0	0	0	0	0
: Tropical rain forest	0	1	1	1	1	0	1	1	1	1
: Savanna	0	0	0	0	0	0	1	0	0	0
: Mediterranean	0	0	0	0	0	0	0	0	0	0
: Temperate grassland	0	0	0	0	0	0	0	0	0	0
: Temperate forest	0	0	0	0	0	1	0	0	0	0
: Mountain	0	0	0	0	1	0	0	0	0	0
: Taiga	0	0	0	0	0	0	0	0	0	0
: Tundra	1	0	0	0	0	0	0	0	0	0
: Polar	1	0	0	0	0	0	0	0	0	0
Zoology: Neotropical	0	1	1	0	1	0	0	0	1	1
: Nearctic	1	0	0	0	0	0	0	0	0	0
: Ethiopian	0	0	0	0	0	0	1	1	0	0
: Oriental	0	0	0	0	0	0	0	0	0	0
: Paleartic	1	0	0	0	0	1	0	0	0	0
: Australian	0	0	0	1	0	0	0	0	0	0

Characteristics	Honduras	Hong Kong	Hungary	Iceland	India	Indonesia	Iran	Iraq	Ireland	Isle of Man
Land: Total Area (km sq)	112000	1040	93000	103000	3290000	1920000	1650000	435000	70300	588
:Density (pop/km sq)	50	5670	113	3	273	101	38	46	50	119
:# of boundaries	3	1	5	0	6	2	5	2	1	0
:Total boundary (km)	1520	30	2250	0	14100	2670	5490	3450	360	0
:Terrain (3=mountains)	3	2	0	1	1	1	3	2	1	0
Land Usage: Arable %	14	7	54	0	55	8	8	12	14	1
:Permanent crops %	2	1	3	0	1	7	0	0	0	0
:Meadows & pastures %	30	1	14	23	4	7	27	9	71	0
:Forest & woodland %	34	12	18	1	23	67	11	3	5	0
:Other %	20	79	11	76	17	15	54	75	10	0
:Irrigated %	1	3	2	0	13	1	5	4	0	0
:% Protected	6	0	6	9	4	10	3	0	0	0
:% Partially Protected	1	36	5	7	3	3	0	0	0.4	·
Risks: Earthquake (1=high)	1	0	0	1	1	1	1	1	0	0
:Volcanism	0	0	0	1	1	1	1	0	0	0
:Soil degradation	0	0	0	0	1	0	0	0	0	0
:Desertification	1	0	0	0	1	0	0	0	0	0
:Overgrazing	0	0	0	0	0	0	0	0	0	0
:Deforestation	1	0	0	0	1	7	1	0	1	0
Elevation: average (m)	587	33	115	28	114		913	34	16	87
:Highest point (m)	2850	957	1010	2120	8600	5030	5600	3610	1040	
:Lowest point (m)	0	0	78	0	0	0	-28	0	0	0
Timezone (GMT)	-6	8	1	0	6	8	4	3	0	0
Tectonic plate: African	0	0	0	0	0	0	0	0	0	0
:Eurasian	0	1	1	1	0	0	1	1	1	1
:Indo-Australian	0	0	0	0	1	1	0	0	0	0
:Pacific	0	0	0	0	0	1	0	0	0	0
:American	0	0	0	1	0	0	0	0	0	0
:Nasca	0	0	0	0	0	0	0	0	0	0
:Caribbean	1	0	0	0	0	0	0	0	0	0
Biome: Desert (1=yes)	0	0	0	0	0	0	1	1	0	0
:Monsoon	0	1	0	0	1	1	0	0	0	0
:Tropical rain forest	1	0	0	0	0	1	0	0	0	0
:Savanna	0	0	0	0	1	0	0	0	0	0
:Mediterranean	0	0	0	0	0	0	1	0	0	0
:Temperate grassland	0	0	1	0	0	0	0	0	0	0
:Temperate forest	0	0	1	0	0	0	0	0	1	1
:Mountain	1	0	0	0	1	1	1	0	0	0
:Taiga	0	0	0	0	0	0	0	0	0	0
:Tundra	0	0	0	1	0	0	0	0	0	0
:Polar	0	0	0	0	0	0	0	0	0	0
Zoology: Neotropical	1	0	0	0	0	0	0	0	0	0
:Nearctic	0	0	0	0	0	0	0	0	0	0
:Ethiopian	0	0	0	0	0	0	0	0	0	0
:Oriental	0	1	0	0	1	1	0	0	0	0
:Paleartic	0	0	1	1	0	0	1	1	1	1
:Australian	0	0	0	0	0	1	0	0	0	0

Characteristics	Israel	Italy	Ivory Coast	Jamaica	Japan	Jersey	Jordan	Kazakhstan	Kenya	Kiribati
Land: Total Area (km sq)	20800	301000	322000	11000	372000	117	91900	2720000	583000	717
::Density (pop/km sq)	264	192	42	228	335	730	48	6	45	105
::# of boundaries	6	5	5	0	0	0	5	5	5	0
::Total boundary (km)	1010	1900	3110	0	0	0	1590	12000	3480	0
::Terrain (3=mountains)	1	3	2	3	3	1	1	2	3	0
Land Usage: Arable %	17	32	9	19	11		4	15	3	0
::Permanent crops %	5	10	4	6	1		0.5		1	51
::Meadows & pastures %	40	17	9	18	2		0.5	57	7	0
::Forest & woodland %	6	22	26	28	68		0.5	4	4	3
::Other %	32	19	52	29	17		94	24	85	46
::Irrigated %	1	10		3	60		0.5	0		0
::% Protected	0	7	6	3	6		1	0	6	39
::% Partially Protected	0	6	0.3	0	1		1	0	0	0
Risks: Earthquake (1=high)	0	1	0	0	1		1	0	1	0
::Volcanism	0	1	0	0	1		0	0	1	0
::Soil degradation	0	0	0	0	0		0	0	1	0
::Desertification	0	0	0	0	0		1	1	0	0
::Overgrazing	0	0	0	0	0		1	1	1	0
::Deforestation	0	0	1	1	0		0	0	1	0
Elevation: average (m)	407			32		5	700	63	887	
::Highest point (m)	1210	4810	1750	2260	3780		1750	6990	5200	75
::Lowest point (m)	-403	0	0	0	-4		-403	-132	0	-12
::Timezone (GMT)	2	1	0	-5	9	0	2	5	3	12
Tectonic plate: African	1	0	1	0	0	0	1	0	1	0
::Eurasian	0	1	0	0	1	1	0	1	0	0
::Indo-Australian	0	0	0	0	0	0	0	0	0	0
::Pacific	0	0	0	0	1	0	0	0	0	1
::American	0	0	0	0	0	0	0	0	0	0
::Nasca	0	0	0	0	0	0	0	0	0	0
::Caribbean	0	0	0	1	0	0	0	0	0	0
Biome: Desert (1=yes)	1	0	0	0	0	0	1	1	0	0
::Monsoon	0	0	0	0	1	0	0	0	0	0
::Tropical rain forest	0	0	1	1	0	0	0	0	1	1
::Savanna	0	0	1	0	0	0	0	0	1	0
::Mediterranean	1	1	0	0	0	0	1	0	0	0
::Temperate grassland	0	0	0	0	0	0	0	1	0	0
::Temperate forest	0	1	0	0	1	1	0	0	0	0
::Mountain	0	1	0	0	1	0	0	0	0	0
::Taiga	0	0	0	0	0	0	0	0	0	0
::Tundra	0	0	0	0	0	0	0	0	0	0
::Polar	0	0	0	0	0	0	0	0	0	0
Zoology: Neotropical	0	0	0	1	0	0	0	0	0	0
::Nearctic	0	0	0	0	0	0	0	0	0	0
::Ethiopian	0	0	1	0	0	0	0	0	1	0
::Oriental	0	0	0	0	0	0	0	0	0	0
::Palearctic	1	1	0	0	1	1	1	1	0	0
::Australian	0	0	0	0	0	0	0	0	0	1

Characteristics	Kuwait	Kyrgyz-stan	Laos	Latvia	Lebanon	Lesotho	Liberia	Libya	Liechten-stein	Lithuania
Land: Total Area (km sq)	17800	199000	237000	64100	10400	30400	111000	1760000	160	65200
:Density (pop/km sq)	106	23	19	42	277	61	26	3	178	58
:# of boundaries	2	4	5	4	2	1	3	6	2	4
:Total boundary (km)	462	3880	5080	1080	454	909	1590	4380	78	1270
:Terrain (3=mountains)	0	3	3	0	3	0	0	0	3	0
Land Usage: Arable %	0		4	27	21	10	1	1	25	49
:Permanent crops %	0		0	0	9	0	3	0	0	
:Meadows & pastures %	8		3	13	1	66	2	8	38	22
:Forest & woodland %	0		58	39	8	0	39	0	19	16
:Other %	92		35	21	61	24	55	91	18	12
:Irrigated %	0	1	1	0	8	0	0	0	0	
:% Protected	0		0	3	0.3	0.2	1	0.1	38	2
:% Partially Protected	1		0	0	0	0	0	0	0	0
Risks: Earthquake (1=high)	0	1	0	0	1	0	0	0	0	0
:Volcanism	0	0	0	0	0	0	0	0	0	0
:Soil degradation	0	0	0	0	0	0	0	0	0	0
:Desertification	1	0	0	0	0	0	0	1	0	0
:Overgrazing	0	0	0	0	1	1	0	1	0	1
:Deforestation	0	0	1	0	0	0	1	0	0	0
Elevation: average (m)	5	775		46	17	1570	23		465	46
:Highest point (m)	281	7130	2820	311	3080	3480	1380	2270	2600	292
:Lowest point (m)	0	550	70	0	0	1520	0	-47	430	0
:Timezone (GMT)	3	5	7	2	2	2	0	1	1	2
Tectonic plate: African	0	0	0	0	0	1	1	1	0	0
:Eurasian	1	1	1	1	1	0	0	0	1	1
:Indo-Australian	0	0	0	0	0	0	0	0	0	0
:Pacific	0	0	0	0	0	0	0	0	0	0
:American	0	0	0	0	0	0	0	0	0	0
:Nasca	0	0	0	0	0	0	0	0	0	0
:Caribbean	0	0	0	0	0	0	0	0	0	0
Biome: Desert (1=yes)	1	0	0	0	0	0	0	1	0	0
:Monsoon	0	0	1	0	0	0	0	0	0	0
:Tropical rain forest	0	0	0	0	0	0	1	0	0	0
:Savanna	0	0	0	0	0	0	0	0	0	0
:Mediterranean	0	0	0	0	1	0	0	0	0	0
:Temperate grassland	0	1	0	0	0	1	0	0	0	0
:Temperate forest	0	0	0	1	0	0	0	0	0	1
:Mountain	0	0	0	0	0	0	0	0	1	0
:Taiga	0	0	0	0	0	0	0	0	0	0
:Tundra	0	0	0	0	0	0	0	0	0	0
:Polar	0	0	0	0	0	0	0	0	0	0
Zoology: Neotropical	0	0	0	0	0	0	0	0	0	0
:Nearctic	0	0	0	0	0	0	0	0	0	0
:Ethiopian	0	0	0	0	0	1	1	0	0	0
:Oriental	0	0	1	0	0	0	0	0	0	0
:Palearctic	1	1	0	1	1	0	0	1	1	1
:Australian	0	0	0	0	0	0	0	0	0	0

Characteristics	Luxem-bourg	Macau	Macedonia	Madagas-car	Malawi	Malaysia	Maldives	Mali	Malta	Marshall Islands
Land: Total Area (km sq)	2590	16	25300	587000	118000	330000	300	1240000	320	181
:Density (pop/km sq)	151	31200	79	23	90	58	773	8	1130	279
:# of boundaries	3	1	5	0	3	4	0	7	0	0
:Total boundary (km)	359	0.3	748	0	2880	2690	0	7240	0	0
:Terrain (3=mountains)	1	0	2	2	2	2	0	1	0	0
Land Usage: Arable %	24	0	5	4	25	3	10	2	38	0
:Permanent crops %	1	0	5	1	0	10	3	0	3	60
:Meadows & pastures %	20	0	20	58	20	0	0	25	0	0
:Forest & woodland %	21	0	30	26	50	63	3	7	0	0
:Other %	34	100	40	11	5	24	84	66	59	40
:Irrigated %	0		6	2	1		0	3	3	
:% Protected	0			2	1			0		
:% Partially Protected	0		1	1	4			1		1
Risks: Earthquake (1=high)	0	0	0	0	0	0	0	0	0	0
:Volcanism	0	0	0	0	0	0	0	0	0	0
:Soil degradation	0	0	0	0	0	0	0	0	0	0
:Desertification	0	0	0	0	0	0	0	1	0	0
:Overgrazing	0	0	0	0	0	0	0	0	0	0
:Deforestation	1	0	0	1	1	0	0	0	0	0
Elevation: average (m)	300	20	135	1380	1010		0.9	316	71	10
:Highest point (m)	559	174		2880	3000	4100	0.3	1150	253	
:Lowest point (m)	130	0		3	37	0		22	2	
Timezone (GMT)	1	8	1	3	2	8	6	0	1	12
Tectonic plate: African	0	0	0	1	1	0	0	1	0	0
:Eurasian	1	1	1	0	0	1	0	0	1	0
:Indo-Australian	0	0	0	0	0	0	1	0	0	0
:Pacific	0	0	0	0	0	0	0	0	0	1
:American	0	0	0	0	0	0	0	0	0	0
:Nasca	0	0	0	0	0	0	0	0	0	0
:Caribbean	0	0	0	0	0	0	0	0	0	0
Biome: Desert (1=yes)	0	0	0	0	0	0	0	1	0	0
:Monsoon	0	1	0	0	0	0	0	0	0	0
:Tropical rain forest	0	0	0	1	0	1	1	0	0	1
:Savanna	0	0	0	1	1	0	0	1	0	0
:Mediterranean	0	0	0	0	0	0	0	0	1	0
:Temperate grassland	0	0	0	0	0	0	0	0	0	0
:Temperate forest	1	0	1	0	0	0	0	0	0	0
:Mountain	0	0	0	0	0	0	0	0	0	0
:Taiga	0	0	0	0	0	0	0	0	0	0
:Tundra	0	0	0	0	0	0	0	0	0	0
:Polar	0	0	0	0	0	0	0	0	0	0
Zoology: Neotropical	0	0	0	0	0	0	0	0	0	0
:Nearctic	0	0	0	0	0	0	0	0	0	0
:Ethiopian	0	0	0	1	1	0	0	1	0	0
:Oriental	0	1	0	0	0	1	1	0	0	1
:Paleartic	1	0	1	0	0	0	0	0	1	0
:Australian	0	0	0	0	0	0	0	0	0	0

Characteristics	Martinique	Mauritania	Mauritius	Mayotte	Mexico	Micronesia Federation	Moldova	Monaco	Mongolia	Montserrat
Land: Total Area (km sq)	1100	1030000	1860	375	1970000	702	33700	2	1570000	100
: Density (pop/km sq)	346	2	597	240	46	144	130	15300	1	118
: # of boundaries	0	4	0	0	3	0	2	1	2	0
: Total boundary (km)	0	5070	0	0	4540	0	1390	4	8110	0
: Terrain (3=mountains)	3	0	2	2	3	2	0	1	1	3
Land Usage: Arable %	10	0	54	0	12	0	50	0	0	20
: Permanent crops %	8	0	4	0	1	0	9	0	0	0
: Meadows & pastures %	30	38	4	0	39	0	0	0	79	0
: Forest & woodland %	26	15	31	0	24	0	0	0	9	40
: Other %	26	47	7	0	24	0	41	100	1	30
: Irrigated %	5	0.2	9	0	3	0	0	0	0	0
: % Protected	.	.	0.1	0	5	0	1	0	4	.
: % Partially Protected	0	0	0	0	4	0	0	0	0	.
Risks: Earthquake (1=high)	1	0	0	0	1	0	0	0	0	0
: Volcanism	0	0	0	0	1	0	0	0	0	0
: Soil degradation	0	1	0	0	1	0	1	0	0	0
: Desertification	0	0	0	0	0	0	0	0	0	0
: Overgrazing	0	0	0	0	1	0	0	0	0	0
: Deforestation	4	0	0	0	1	0	0	0	0	0
Elevation: average (m)	.	.	55	.	1320	.	179	55	1310	.
: Highest point (m)	.	915	828	5	5610	10	429	140	4360	40
: Lowest point (m)	.	-3	0	.	-8	.	0.2	0	553	.
Timezone (GMT)	-4	0	4	3	-7	11	2	1	8	-4
Tectonic plate: African	0	1	1	1	0	0	0	0	0	0
: Eurasian	0	0	0	0	0	0	1	1	1	0
: Indo-Australian	0	0	0	0	0	0	0	0	0	0
: Pacific	0	0	0	0	0	1	0	0	0	0
: American	0	0	0	0	1	0	0	0	0	0
: Nasca	0	0	0	0	0	0	0	0	0	0
: Caribbean	1	0	0	0	1	0	0	0	0	1
Biome: Desert (1=yes)	0	1	0	0	1	0	0	0	1	0
: Monsoon	0	0	0	0	0	0	0	0	0	0
: Tropical rain forest	1	0	1	1	1	1	0	0	0	1
: Savanna	0	0	0	0	0	0	0	0	0	0
: Mediterranean	0	0	0	0	0	0	0	1	0	0
: Temperate grassland	0	0	0	0	1	0	0	0	1	0
: Temperate forest	0	0	0	0	1	0	1	0	0	0
: Mountain	0	0	0	0	1	0	0	0	1	0
: Taiga	0	0	0	0	0	0	0	0	0	0
: Tundra	0	0	0	0	0	0	0	0	0	0
: Polar	0	0	0	0	0	0	0	0	0	0
Zoology: Neotropical	1	0	0	0	1	0	0	0	0	1
: Nearctic	0	0	0	0	1	0	0	0	0	0
: Ethiopian	0	1	1	1	0	0	0	0	0	0
: Oriental	0	0	0	0	0	0	0	0	0	0
: Palearctic	0	0	0	0	0	0	1	1	1	0
: Australian	0	0	0	0	0	1	0	0	0	0

Characteristics	Morocco	Mozam-bique	Namibia	Nauru	Nepal	Nether-lands	Nether-lands Antilles	New Caledonia	New Zealand	Nicaragua
Land: Total Area (km sq)	447000	802000	824000	20	141000	37300	960	19100	269000	129000
:Density (pop/km sq)	60	20	2	485	150	410	188	9	13	32
:# of boundaries	2	6	4	0	2	2	0	0	0	2
:Total boundary (km)	2000	4570	3940	0	2930	1030	0	0	0	1230
:Terrain (3=mountains)	3	2	2	0	4	1	2	1	2	2
Land Usage: Arable %	18	4	1	0	17	25	8	0	2	9
:Permanent crops %	1	0	0	0	0	1	0	0	0	1
:Meadows & pastures %	28	56	64	0	13	34	0	14	53	43
:Forest & woodland %	12	20	22	0	33	9	0	51	38	35
:Other %	41	20	13	100	37	31	92	35	7	12
:Irrigated %	1	0	0	0	2	15	0	0	1	1
:% Protected	0.8	0	13	0	8	3	0	0	11	2
:% Partially Protected	0.7	0	2	0	1		0	0	1	0.3
Risks: Earthquake (1=high)	1	0	0	0	1	0	0	0	1	1
:Volcanism	0	0	0	0	0	0	0	0	1	1
:Soil degradation	1	1	1	1	1	0	0	0	0	0
:Desertification	0	1	1	0	0	0	0	0	0	0
:Overgrazing	1	1	1	0	1	0	0	0	0	0
:Deforestation	0	1	0	0	1	0	0	0	0	1
Elevation: average (m)	57	35	1650	27	1340		23	3	66	56
:Highest point (m)	4170	2440	2580	64	8850	321		1630	3760	2110
:Lowest point (m)	-55	0			60	-7			0	
Timezone (GMT)	0	2	1	12	6	1	-4	11	12	-6
Tectonic plate: African	1	1	1	0	0	0	0	0	0	0
:Eurasian	1	0	0	0	1	1	0	0	0	0
:Indo-Australian	0	0	0	0	1	0	0	1	1	0
:Pacific	0	0	0	1	0	0	0	0	1	0
:American	0	0	0	0	0	0	0	0	0	1
:Nasca	0	0	0	0	0	0	0	0	0	0
:Caribbean	0	0	0	0	0	0	1	0	0	1
Biome: Desert (1=yes)	1	0	1	0	0	0	0	0	0	0
:Monsoon	0	0	0	0	1	0	0	0	0	0
:Tropical rain forest	0	1	0	1	0	0	1	1	0	1
:Savanna	0	1	1	0	0	0	0	0	0	0
:Mediterranean	1	0	0	0	0	0	0	0	0	0
:Temperate grassland	0	0	0	0	0	0	0	0	0	0
:Temperate forest	0	0	0	0	0	1	0	0	1	0
:Mountain	1	0	0	0	1	0	0	0	0	0
:Taiga	0	0	0	0	0	0	0	0	0	0
:Tundra	0	0	0	0	0	0	0	0	0	0
:Polar	0	0	0	0	0	0	0	0	0	0
Zoology: Neotropical	0	0	0	0	0	0	1	0	0	1
:Nearctic	0	0	0	0	0	0	0	0	0	0
:Ethiopian	0	1	1	0	0	0	0	0	0	0
:Oriental	0	0	0	0	1	0	0	0	0	0
:Palearctic	1	0	0	0	0	1	0	0	0	0
:Australian	0	0	0	1	0	0	0	1	1	0

Characteristics	Niger	Nigeria	Niue	Norfolk Island	North Korea	Northern Mariana Isl.	Norway	Oman	Pacific Isl. Trust	Pakistan
Land: Total Area (km sq)	1270000	924000	260	40	121000	477	324000	212000	458	804000
: Density (pop/km sq)	7	115	8	67	191	100	13	8	35	159
: # of boundaries	7	4	0	0	3	0	3	4	0	4
: Total boundary (km)	5700	4050	0	0	1670	0	2580	1370	0	6770
: Terrain (3=mountains)	1	2	1	3	3	3	3	2	2	3
Land Usage: Arable %	3	31	61	0	18	1	3	0	0	26
: Permanent crops %	0	3	4	0	1	0	0	0	0	0
: Meadows & pastures %	7	23	4	25	0	19	0	5	0	6
: Forest & woodland %	2	15	19	0	74	0	27	0	0	4
: Other %	88	28	12	75	7	0	70	95	0	64
: Irrigated %	0	0	0	0	9	0	13	0	0	19
: % Protected	8	3			0.5		1	0.2		5
: % Partially Protected	0	1			0.1		0	0		3
Risks: Earthquake (1=high)	0	0			0	0	0	0	0	1
: Volcanism	0	0	0	0	0	0	0	0	0	0
: Soil degradation	1	1	0	0	0	0	0	0	0	1
: Desertification	1	1	0	0	0	0	0	0	0	1
: Overgrazing	1	0	0	0	0	0	0	0	0	0
: Deforestation	0	1	1	0	0	0	0	0	0	0
Elevation: average (m)	222		2	9	29	206	96	6	3	277
: Highest point (m)	2020	2420			2740		2470	3030		8610
: Lowest point (m)	198	0	0	0	0	0	0	0	0	0
Timezone (GMT)	1	1	-12	11	9	9	1	4	9	5
Tectonic plate: African	1	1	0	0	0	0	0	0	0	0
: Eurasian	0	0	0	0	1	0	1	1	0	1
: Indo-Australian	0	0	0	0	0	0	0	0	0	1
: Pacific	0	0	1	1	0	1	0	0	1	0
: American	0	0	0	0	0	0	0	0	0	0
: Nasca	0	0	0	0	0	0	0	0	0	0
: Caribbean	0	0	0	0	0	0	0	0	0	0
Biome: Desert (1=yes)	1	0	0	0	0	0	0	1	0	1
: Monsoon	0	0	0	0	0	0	0	0	0	0
: Tropical rain forest	0	1	1	0	0	1	0	0	1	0
: Savanna	1	1	0	0	0	0	0	0	0	0
: Mediterranean	0	0	0	0	0	0	0	0	0	0
: Temperate grassland	0	0	0	0	0	0	0	0	0	0
: Temperate forest	0	0	0	1	0	0	1	0	0	0
: Mountain	0	0	0	0	1	0	1	0	0	1
: Taiga	0	0	0	0	0	0	0	0	0	0
: Tundra	0	0	0	0	0	0	1	0	0	0
: Polar	0	0	0	0	0	0	0	0	0	0
Zoology: Neotropical	0	0	0	0	0	0	0	0	0	0
: Nearctic	0	0	0	0	0	0	0	0	0	0
: Ethiopian	1	1	0	0	0	0	0	1	0	0
: Oriental	0	0	1	0	0	1	0	0	1	1
: Palearctic	0	0	0	0	1	0	1	0	0	1
: Australian	0	0	0	1	0	1	0	0	0	0

Characteristics	Panama	Papua New Guinea	Paraguay	Peru	Philippines	Pitcairn Islands	Poland	Portugal	Puerto Rico	Qatar
Land: Total Area (km sq)	78200	462000	407000	1290000	300000	47	313000	92100	9100	11000
: Density (pop/km sq)	33	9	11	18	222	0	123	107	409	44
: # of boundaries	2	1	3	5	0	0	3	1	0	2
: Total boundary (km)	555	820	3920	6940	0	0	2980	1210	0	60
: Terrain (3=mountains)	2	3	2	3	3	3	2	3	3	0
Land Usage: Arable %	6	0	20	3	26	0	48	32	8	0
: Permanent crops %	2	1	1	0	11	0	1	6	7	0
: Meadows & pastures %	15	0	39	21	4	0	13	6	38	5
: Forest & woodland %	54	71	35	55	40	3	29	40	21	0
: Other %	23	28	5	21	19	0	9	16	28	95
: Irrigated %	17	0	0	0	5	0	0	7	4	0
: % Protected	2	0	3	2	2	0	7	6	0	0
: % Partially Protected	0	0.1	0.1	0.1	1	0	0	1	0	0
Risks: Earthquake (1=high)	0	1	0	1	1	0	0	0	0	0
: Volcanism	0	1	0	1	1	0	0	0	0	0
: Soil degradation	0	0	0	1	0	0	0	0	0	0
: Desertification	0	0	0	0	0	0	0	0	0	0
: Overgrazing	0	0	0	0	0	0	0	0	0	0
: Deforestation	0	0	0	0	0	0	0	0	0	0
Elevation: average (m)	26	17	64	154	16	2	106	95	17	10
: Highest point (m)	3480	4510	800	6750	2950	0	2500	2350	1340	105
: Lowest point (m)	0	0	46	0	0	0	-2	0	0	0
Timezone (GMT)	-5	10	-3	-5	8	-9	1	0	-4	3
Tectonic plate: African	0	0	0	0	0	0	0	0	0	0
: Eurasian	0	0	0	0	1	0	1	1	0	1
: Indo-Australian	0	1	0	0	0	0	0	0	0	0
: Pacific	0	1	0	0	1	1	0	0	0	0
: American	1	0	1	1	0	0	0	0	1	0
: Nasca	1	0	0	1	0	0	0	0	0	0
Biome: Desert (1=yes)	0	0	0	1	0	0	0	0	0	1
: Monsoon	0	0	0	0	1	0	0	0	0	0
: Tropical rain forest	1	1	1	1	1	1	0	0	1	0
: Savanna	1	0	1	0	0	0	0	0	0	0
: Mediterranean	0	0	0	0	0	0	0	1	0	0
: Temperate grassland	0	0	1	0	0	0	0	0	0	0
: Temperate forest	0	0	0	0	0	0	1	0	0	0
: Mountain	0	0	0	1	0	0	0	0	0	0
: Taiga	0	0	0	0	0	0	0	0	0	0
: Tundra	0	0	0	0	0	0	0	0	0	0
: Polar	0	0	0	0	0	0	0	0	0	0
Zoology: Neotropical	1	0	1	1	0	1	0	0	1	0
: Nearctic	0	0	0	0	0	0	0	0	0	0
: Ethiopian	0	0	0	0	0	0	0	0	0	0
: Oriental	0	0	0	0	1	0	0	0	0	0
: Palearctic	0	0	0	0	0	0	1	1	0	1
: Australian	0	1	0	0	0	0	0	0	0	0

Characteristics	Reunion	Romania	Russia	Rwanda	San Marino	Sao Tome E Principe	Saudi Arabia	Senegal	Serbia & Monten.	Seychelles
Land: Total Area (km sq)	2510	238000	17100000	26300	60	960	2150000	196000	102000	455
::Density (pop/km sq)	256	98	9	295	375	132	8	40	103	155
::# of boundaries	0	4	15	4	1	0	9	5		0
::Total boundary (km)	0	2900	20100	893	39	0	4410	2640	2230	0
::Terrain (3=mountains)	3	2	2	2	3	3	1		2	1
Land Usage: Arable %	20	43	8	29	17	2	1	27	30	4
::Permanent crops %	2	3	0	11	0	36	0	0	5	18
::Meadows & pastures %	4	19	5	18	0	1	39	30	25	0
::Forest & woodland %	35	28	0	10	0	0	0	31	20	18
::Other %	39	7	0	32	83	62	59	12	20	60
::Irrigated %	2	11	1	0	0	0	0	3	3	0
::% Protected		5	0	12	0	0	0	11	0	95
::% Partially Protected		4	0	0	0	0	0	6	1	0
Risks: Earthquake (1=high)		1	0	0	0	0	0	1	1	0
::Volcanism	1	0	0	1	0	1	0	0	0	0
::Soil degradation	0	0	0	0	0	0	0	0	0	0
::Desertification	0	0	0	0	0	0	1	1	0	0
::Overgrazing	0	0	0	1	0	0	1	1	0	0
::Deforestation	0	0	0	1	0	0	0	0	0	0
Elevation: average (m)		82	156	1540		17	298	24	132	3
::Highest point (m)	3070	2540	5640	4510	739	2020	3210	581		905
::Lowest point (m)	0	0	-28	950	50	0	0	0	0	0
::Timezone (GMT)	4	2	3	2	1	0	3	0	1	4
Tectonic plate: African	1	0	0	1	0	1	0	1	0	1
::Eurasian	0	1	1	0	1	0	1	0	1	0
::Indo-Australian	0	0	0	0	0	0	0	0	0	0
::Pacific	0	0	0	0	0	0	0	0	0	0
::American	0	0	0	0	0	0	0	0	0	0
::Nasca	0	0	0	0	0	0	0	0	0	0
::Caribbean	0	0	0	0	0	0	0	0	0	0
Biome: Desert (1=yes)	0	0	0	0	0	0	1	0	0	0
::Monsoon	0	0	0	0	0	0	0	0	0	0
::Tropical rain forest	1	0	0	0	0	1	0	0	0	1
::Savanna	0	0	0	1	0	0	0	1	0	0
::Mediterranean	0	0	0	0	1	0	0	0	0	0
::Temperate grassland	0	0	1	0	0	0	0	0	0	0
::Temperate forest	0	1	1	0	0	0	0	0	1	0
::Mountain	0	0	0	0	0	0	0	0	0	0
::Taiga	0	0	1	0	0	0	0	0	0	0
::Tundra	0	0	1	0	0	0	0	0	0	0
::Polar	0	0	1	0	0	0	0	0	0	0
Zoology: Neotropical	0	0	0	0	0	0	0	0	0	0
::Nearctic	0	0	0	0	0	0	0	0	0	0
::Ethiopian	1	0	0	1	0	1	0	1	0	1
::Oriental	0	0	0	0	0	0	0	0	0	0
::Palearctic	0	1	1	0	1	0	1	0	1	0
::Australian	0	0	0	0	0	0	0	0	0	0

Characteristics	Sierra Leone	Singapore	Slovakia	Slovenia	Solomon Islands	Somalia	South Africa	South Korea	Spain	Sri Lanka
Land: Total Area (km sq)	71700	580	49500	20300	28500	638000	1220000	98500	505000	65600
: Density (pop/km sq)	63	4940	108	97	12	15	3	452	78	273
: # of boundaries	2	0	0	4	0	3	6	1	4	0
: Total boundary (km)	958	0	0	998	0	2340	4970	238	1900	0
: Terrain (3=mountains)	2	0	0	1	2	2	2	3	3	1
Land Usage: Arable %	23	4	0	10	1	2	10	21	31	16
: Permanent crops %	2	7	0	2	1	0	1	1	10	17
: Meadows & pastures %	31	0	0	20	1	46	65	1	21	7
: Forest & woodland %	29	5	0	45	93	14	3	67	31	37
: Other %	15	84	0	23	4	38	21	10	7	23
: Irrigated %	0	0	0	1	0	0.3	1	12	6	8
: % Protected	0	4	1	4	0	0	6	6	7	12
: % Partially Protected	1	0	0	0	1	0	4	7	0	4
Risks: Earthquake (1=high)	0	0	0	1	1	0	0	0	1	0
: Volcanism	0	0	0	0	1	1	0	0	0	0
: Soil degradation	1	0	0	0	0	1	0	0	1	1
: Desertification	0	0	0	0	0	1	1	0	0	0
: Overgrazing	0	0	0	0	0	1	1	0	0	0
: Deforestation	1	0	0	0	0	0	0	0	1	1
Elevation: average (m)	26	10		132	55	210		85	660	
: Highest point (m)	1940	166		2860	2450	2410	3450	1950	3400	2520
: Lowest point (m)	0	0		0	0	0	0	0	0	0
Timezone (GMT)	0	8	1	1	11	3	2	9	1	6
Tectonic plate: African	1	0	0	0	0	1	1	0	0	0
: Eurasian	0	1	1	1	0	0	0	1	1	0
: Indo-Australian	0	0	0	0	1	0	0	0	0	1
: Pacific	0	0	0	0	1	0	0	0	0	0
: American	0	0	0	0	0	0	0	0	0	0
: Nasca	0	0	0	0	0	0	0	0	0	0
: Caribbean	0	0	0	0	0	0	0	0	0	0
Biome: Desert (1=yes)	0	0	0	0	0	1	1	0	0	0
: Monsoon	0	0	0	0	0	0	0	1	0	1
: Tropical rain forest	1	1	0	0	1	0	0	0	0	0
: Savanna	0	0	0	0	0	1	1	0	0	0
: Mediterranean	0	0	0	0	0	0	1	0	1	0
: Temperate grassland	0	0	0	0	0	0	1	0	0	0
: Temperate forest	0	0	1	1	0	0	0	1	1	0
: Mountain	0	0	0	0	0	0	0	0	0	0
: Taiga	0	0	0	0	0	0	0	0	0	0
: Tundra	0	0	0	0	0	0	0	0	0	0
: Polar	0	0	0	0	0	0	0	0	0	0
Zoology: Neotropical	0	0	0	0	0	0	0	0	0	0
: Nearctic	0	0	0	0	0	0	0	0	0	0
: Ethiopian	1	0	0	0	0	1	1	0	0	0
: Oriental	0	1	0	0	0	0	0	0	0	1
: Paleartic	0	0	1	1	0	0	0	1	1	0
: Australian	0	0	0	0	1	0	0	0	0	0

Characteristics	St. Helena	St. Kitts & Nevis	St. Lucia	St. Pierre & Miquelon	St. Vincent & Grenad.	Sudan	Suriname	Swaziland	Sweden	Switzerland
Land: Total Area (km sq)	310	360	620	242	340	2510000	163000	17400	450000	41300
·Density (pop/km sq)	24	118	237	26	335	11	3	47	19	166
·# of boundaries	0	0	0	0	0	8	3	2	0	0
·Total boundary (km)	0	0	0	0	0	7700	1710	535	2190	1850
·Terrain (3=mountains)	3	3	2	1	3	3	1	3	2	4
Land Usage: Arable %	7	22	8	13	38	5	0	8	7	10
·Permanent crops %	0	17	20	0	12	0	0	0	0	1
·Meadows & pastures %	7	3	5	4	6	24	0	67	2	40
·Forest & woodland %	3	17	13	83	41	20	97	6	64	26
·Other %	83	41	54		3	51	3	19	27	23
·Irrigated %	0	0	2		3	1	0	2	0	
·% Protected		0	0		21	4	4	0	6	0
·% Partially Protected	0	0	2			0.3	0	3	5	18
Risks: Earthquake (1=high)	0	0	0	0	0	0	0	0	0	0
·Volcanism	0	0	1	0	1	0	0	1	0	0
·Soil degradation	0	0	0	0	0	1	0	0	0	0
·Desertification	0	0	0	0	0	1	0	1	0	0
·Overgrazing	0	0	0	0	0	0	0	0	0	0
·Deforestation	0	0	0	0	0	0	4	0	0	0
Elevation: average (m)	12	40	21	47	24	235	4	1160	34	521
·Highest point (m)		1160	950		1230	3190	1230	1860	2110	4630
·Lowest point (m)	0	0	0		0	2	0	21	0	193
Timezone (GMT)	0	-4	-4	-3	-4	2	-4	2	1	1
Tectonic plate: African	1	0	0	0	0	1	0	1	0	0
·Eurasian	0	0	0	0	0	0	0	0	1	1
·Indo-Australian	0	0	0	0	0	0	0	0	0	0
·Pacific	0	0	0	0	0	0	0	0	0	0
·American	0	0	0	1	0	0	1	0	0	0
·Nasca	0	0	0	0	0	0	0	0	0	0
·Caribbean	0	1	1	0	1	0	0	0	0	0
Biome: Desert (1=yes)	0	0	0	0	0	1	0	0	0	0
·Monsoon	0	0	0	0	0	0	0	0	0	0
·Tropical rain forest	0	0	0	0	0	0	1	0	0	0
·Savanna	0	0	0	0	0	1	0	1	0	0
·Mediterranean	0	0	0	0	0	0	0	0	0	0
·Temperate grassland	0	0	0	0	0	0	0	0	0	0
·Temperate forest	0	0	0	0	0	0	0	0	0	1
·Mountain	0	0	0	0	0	0	0	0	0	1
·Taiga	0	0	0	0	0	0	0	0	1	0
·Tundra	0	0	0	0	0	0	0	0	1	0
·Polar	0	0	0	0	0	0	0	0	0	0
Zoology: Neotropical	0	1	1	0	1	0	1	0	0	0
·Nearctic	0	0	0	1	0	0	0	0	0	0
·Ethiopian	1	0	0	0	0	1	0	1	0	0
·Oriental	0	0	0	0	0	0	0	0	0	0
·Paleartic	0	0	0	0	0	0	0	0	1	1
·Australian	0	0	0	0	0	0	0	0	0	0

Characteristics	Syrian Arab Rep.	Taiwan	Tajikistan	Tanzania	Thailand	Togo	Tokelau	Tonga	Trinidad & Tobago	Tunisia
Land: Total Area (km sq)	185000	36000	143000	945000	514000	56800	10	700	5130	164000
:Density (pop/km sq)	74	578	40	30	111	69	154	137	253	52
:# of boundaries	5	0	4	4	4	3	0	0	0	2
:Total boundary (km)	2250	0	3650	3400	4860	1650	0	0	0	1420
:Terrain (3=mountains)	2	2	3	3	3	2	0	2	1	2
Land Usage: Arable %	28	24	6	5	34	25	0	25	14	20
:Permanent crops %	3	1	0	1	4	1	0	55	17	10
:Meadows & pastures %	46	5	23	40	1	4	0	6	2	19
:Forest & woodland %	3	55	0	47	30	28	0	12	44	4
:Other %	20	15	71	7	31	42	100	2	23	47
:Irrigated %	0	14	1	0	11	0	0	0	4	4
:% Protected	0	8	0	14	15	11	0	0	3	0.3
:% Partially Protected	0	3	0	10	0	1	0	0	0	0
Risks: Earthquake (1=high)	1	1	1	0	0	0	0	1	0	0
:Volcanism	0	0	0	0	0	0	0	0	0	0
:Soil degradation	1	0	0	0	0	0	0	0	0	0
:Desertification	1	0	0	0	0	0	0	0	0	1
:Overgrazing	1	0	1	0	0	0	0	0	0	1
:Deforestation	0	0	0	1	1	1	0	0	0	0
Elevation: average (m)	394		478	14	8	20			20	36
:Highest point (m)	2810	4000	7500	5890	2600	986	73	1050	940	1540
:Lowest point (m)	-200	0	300	0	0	0	0	0	0	-17
Timezone (GMT)	2	8	5	3	7	0	-11	13	-4	1
Tectonic plate: African	0	0	0	1	0	1	0	0	0	1
:Eurasian	1	1	1	0	1	0	0	0	0	0
:Indo-Australian	0	0	0	0	0	0	0	1	0	0
:Pacific	0	0	0	0	0	0	1	0	0	0
:American	0	0	0	0	0	0	0	0	1	0
:Nasca	0	0	0	0	0	0	0	0	0	0
:Caribbean	0	0	0	0	0	0	0	0	0	0
Biome: Desert (1=yes)	1	0	1	0	0	0	0	0	0	1
:Monsoon	0	0	0	0	1	0	0	0	0	0
:Tropical rain forest	0	1	0	0	1	0	1	1	1	0
:Savanna	0	0	0	1	0	1	0	0	0	0
:Mediterranean	1	0	0	0	0	0	0	0	0	1
:Temperate grassland	0	0	0	0	0	0	0	0	0	0
:Temperate forest	0	0	0	0	0	0	0	0	0	0
:Mountain	1	1	1	1	1	0	0	0	0	0
:Taiga	0	0	0	0	0	0	0	0	0	0
:Tundra	0	0	0	0	0	0	0	0	0	0
:Polar	0	0	0	0	0	0	0	0	0	0
Zoology: Neotropical	0	0	0	0	0	0	0	0	1	0
:Nearctic	0	0	0	0	0	0	0	0	0	0
:Ethiopian	0	0	0	1	0	1	0	0	0	0
:Oriental	0	1	0	0	1	0	0	0	0	0
:Palearctic	1	0	1	0	0	0	0	0	0	1
:Australian	0	0	0	0	0	0	1	1	0	0

Characteristics	Turkey	Turkme-nistan	Turks & Caicos	Tuvalu	Uganda	Ukraine	United Arab Emir.	United Kingdom	United States	Uruguay
Land: Total Area (km sq)	781000	488000	430	26	236000	604000	83600	245000	9370000	176000
.. Density (pop/km sq)	76	8	32	425	82	86	22	236	28	18
.. # of boundaries	6	4	0	0	5	7	3	1	2	2
.. Total boundary (km)	2720	3740	0	0	2700	4560	1020	360	9770	1560
.. Terrain (3=mountains)	3	0	0	0	0	0	0	0	3	1
Land Usage: Arable %	30	3	2	0	23	56	0	29	20	8
.. Permanent crops %	4	0	0	0	9	2	0	0	0	0
.. Meadows & pastures %	12	69	0	0	25	12	2	48	26	78
.. Forest & woodland %	26	0	0	0	30	0	0	9	29	4
.. Other %	28	28	98	100	13	30	98	14	25	10
.. Irrigated %	0.4				0	0.8	0	1	2	0.2
.. % Protected	0.1				8			19	11	0.1
.. % Partially Protected	1				4				1	
Risks: Earthquake (1=high)	1	0	0	0	0	0	0	0	1	0
.. Volcanism	0	0	0	0	0	0	0	0	1	0
.. Soil degradation	0	1	0	0	0	0	0	0	0	0
.. Desertification	0	1	0	0	0	0	0	0	0	0
.. Overgrazing	0	1	0	0	0	0	0	0	0	0
.. Deforestation	0	0	0	0	1	0	0	0	0	0
Elevation: average (m)	466	21	4	2	1190	179		45	12	22
.. Highest point (m)	5120	3140		5	5100	2060	1930	1340	6190	514
.. Lowest point (m)	0	-81	-5	12	610	2	4	-3	-86	-3
Timezone (GMT)	3	5	-5	12	3	2	4	0	-7	-3
Tectonic plate: African	0	0	0	0	1	0	0	0	0	0
.. Eurasian	1	1	0	0	0	1	1	1	0	0
.. Indo-Australian	0	0	0	1	0	0	0	0	0	0
.. Pacific	0	0	0	0	0	0	0	0	0	0
.. American	0	0	1	0	0	0	0	0	1	1
.. Nasca	0	0	0	0	0	0	0	0	0	0
.. Caribbean	0	0	0	0	0	0	0	0	0	0
Biome: Desert (1=yes)	0	1	0	0	0	0	1	0	1	0
.. Monsoon	0	0	0	0	0	0	0	0	0	0
.. Tropical rain forest	0	0	0	1	1	0	0	0	0	0
.. Savanna	0	0	1	0	1	0	0	0	0	0
.. Mediterranean	1	0	0	0	0	0	0	0	0	0
.. Temperate grassland	0	0	0	0	0	1	0	0	1	1
.. Temperate forest	0	0	0	0	0	1	0	1	1	0
.. Mountain	0	0	0	0	0	0	0	0	1	0
.. Taiga	0	0	0	0	0	0	0	0	1	0
.. Tundra	0	0	0	0	0	0	0	0	1	0
.. Polar	0	0	0	0	0	0	0	0	0	0
Zoology: Neotropical	0	0	1	0	0	0	0	0	0	1
.. Nearctic	0	0	0	0	0	0	0	0	1	0
.. Ethiopian	0	0	0	0	1	0	0	0	0	0
.. Oriental	0	0	0	0	0	0	0	0	0	0
.. Palearctic	1	1	0	0	0	1	1	1	0	0
.. Australian	0	0	0	1	0	0	0	0	0	0

Characteristics	Uzbekis-tan	Vanuatu	Vatican City	Venezuela	Vietnam	Virgin Isl; US	Wallis & Futuna	West Bank	Western Samoa	Western Sahara
Land: Total Area (km sq)	447000	14800	0.4	912000	330000	352	274	5860	2860	266000
:Density (pop/km sq)	48	11	2050	23	213	293	51	240	77	0.8
:# of boundaries	5	0	3	3	3	0	0	2	0	3
:Total boundary (km)	6220	0	3	4990	3820	0	0	404	0	2050
:Terrain (3=mountains)	1	3	1	2	2	2	1	1	3	1
Land Usage: Arable %	10	1	0	3	22	15	5	27	19	0
:Permanent crops %	0	5	0	1	2	6	20	32	24	0
:Meadows & pastures %	47	2	0	20	1	26	0	1	0	19
:Forest & woodland %	1	1	0	39	40	47	0	0	47	0
:Other %	43	91	100	37	35		75	40	10	81
:Irrigated %		0	0	0	3					
:% Protected	0	0	0	31	3					
:% Partially Protected	0	0	0	16						
Risks: Earthquake (1=high)	0	1	0	0	0	1	0	0	1	0
:Volcanism	0	1	0	0	0	0	0	0	0	0
:Soil degradation	0	0	0	0	0	0	0	0	0	0
:Desertification	0	0	0	0	0	0	0	0	0	0
:Overgrazing	0	0	0	0	0	0	0	0	0	0
:Deforestation	0	0	0	0	0	0	0	0	0	0
Elevation: average (m)		20	17	830						42
:Highest point (m)	4640	1880		5010	3140		2	580	1860	805
:Lowest point (m)	-12			-4						
Timezone (GMT)	5	11	1	-4	7	-4	12	2	-11	0
Tectonic plate: African	0	0	0	0	0	0	0	0	0	1
:Eurasian	1	0	1	0	1	0	0	1	0	0
:Indo-Australian	0	1	0	0	0	0	0	0	0	0
:Pacific	0	1	0	0	0	0	1	0	1	0
:American	0	0	0	1	0	1	0	0	0	0
:Nasca	0	0	0	0	0	0	0	0	0	0
:Caribbean	0	0	0	1	0	1	0	0	0	0
Biome: Desert (1=yes)	1	0	0	0	0	0	0	0	0	1
:Monsoon	0	0	0	0	1	0	0	0	0	0
:Tropical rain forest	0	1	0	1	1	1	1	0	1	0
:Savanna	0	0	0	1	0	0	0	0	0	0
:Mediterranean	0	0	1	0	0	0	0	1	0	0
:Temperate grassland	1	0	0	0	0	0	0	0	0	0
:Temperate forest	0	0	0	0	0	0	0	0	0	0
:Mountain	0	0	0	1	0	0	0	0	0	0
:Taiga	0	0	0	0	0	0	0	0	0	0
:Tundra	0	0	0	0	0	0	0	0	0	0
:Polar	0	0	0	0	0	0	0	0	0	0
Zoology: Neotropical	0	0	0	1	0	1	0	0	0	0
:Nearctic	0	0	0	0	0	0	0	0	0	0
:Ethiopian	0	0	0	0	0	0	0	0	0	0
:Oriental	0	0	0	0	1	0	0	0	0	0
:Paleartic	1	0	1	0	0	0	0	1	0	1
:Australian	0	1	0	0	0	0	1	0	1	0

Characteristics	Yemen	Zaire	Zambia	Zimbabwe
Land: Total Area (km sq)	528000	2350000	753000	391000
Density (pop/km sq)	25	18	12	28
# of boundaries	2	7	7	4
Total boundary (km)	1210	8340	5660	3070
Terrain (3=mountains)	3	2	2	2
Land Usage: Arable %	14	3	7	7
Permanent crops %	0	0	0	0
Meadows & pastures %	36	4	47	12
Forest & woodland %	8	78	27	62
Other %	42	15	19	19
Irrigated %	1	0	0	0
% Protected	0	4	8	8
% Partially Protected	0	0	0	1
Risks: Earthquake (1=high)	0	0	0	0
Volcanism	1	0	0	0
Soil degradation	1	0	1	1
Desertification	1	0	0	0
Overgrazing	0	0	0	1
Deforestation	1	0	1	1
Elevation: average (m)		290	1280	1410
Highest point (m)	3660	5110	2160	2590
Lowest point (m)	0	0	329	162
Timezone (GMT)	3	2	2	2
Tectonic plate: African	1	1	1	1
Eurasian	0	0	0	0
Indo-Australian	0	0	0	0
Pacific	0	0	0	0
American	0	0	0	0
Nasca	0	0	0	0
Caribbean	0	0	0	0
Biome: Desert (1=yes)	1	0	0	0
Tropical rain forest	0	1	0	0
Monsoon	0	1	0	0
Savanna	0	0	1	1
Mediterranean	0	0	0	0
Temperate grassland	0	0	0	0
Temperate forest	0	0	0	0
Mountain	0	0	0	0
Taiga	0	0	0	0
Tundra	0	0	0	0
Polar	0	0	0	0
Zoology: Neotropical	0	0	0	0
Nearctic	0	0	0	0
Ethiopian	1	1	1	1
Oriental	0	0	0	0
Palearctic	0	0	0	0
Australian	0	0	0	0

8

MARINE RESOURCES ACROSS COUNTRIES

Many discussions of national cultures focus on the role of the seas, oceans and marine environments (see Chapter 2). This chapter provides comparative statistics for a variety of variables characterizing each country's marine-based resources. For a full discussion of the methodology used to generate these estimates, please refer to Chapter 1 which gives important caveats. This chapter first gives summary statistics of the variables reported: the number of countries for which each variable was available, weighted averages (by population) and simple averages; these averages can be used as benchmarks. Then a lengthy comparative table is presented which provides raw statistics across countries.

Most of the variables are self explanatory, though some merit commentary. All of the statistics should be considered as estimates which have undergone rounding and certain adjustments. Some are in their aggregate form; "Coastline", for example, measures the average length of coastline, in kilometers, per group. Others are given on a per capita basis; "Coastline/cap" measures the average length of coastline per capita for each group. Depending on the variable, "capita" may signify per person, per person, per 1000 persons, or per million persons. The aggregate measure reflects the total accessible resource to the population, whereas the per capita measure indicates the quantity available if the resource was uniquely divisible. The extent to which each country can be characterized by its marine biologic zone, and prevailing winds is also given. Some countries have multiple marine biologic and prevailing wind conditions (generated from ocean currents and topology).

Summary Statistics:
Marine Resources

Characteristics	Number of Countries Covered	Weighted Average by Pop 1994	Simple Average	Simple Standard Deviation
Coastline: length (km)	226	10510.60	3255.76	10710.14
: length km/capita	226	144.46	12882.91	92053.31
Zones: Sea territory	233	21.79	21.83	48.45
: Continental shelf (m)	229	98.33	84.93	98.69
: Exclusive fishing (nm)	228	20.20	36.77	76.00
: Extended economic zone (nm)	229	100.32	77.18	97.98
: 200-Mi EEZ, area	204	1295479.26	443679.80	1065010.71
: Contiguous zone (nm)	226	7.01	3.40	7.37
Inland waterways (km)	231	36110.98	2765.06	11913.83
Inland waterways/capita	231	0.12	0.22	0.97
Water area: (km sq)	231	202162.24	438322.37	5483994.12
: area/capita	231	18.18	253.23	2617.14
Access: Number of ports	204	10.38	4.41	6.42
: Natural Harbor (1=yes)	214	0.00	0.03	0.18
: Number of outlets	204	0.06	0.26	0.70
: Island (1=yes)	234	0.10	0.35	0.48
: Landlocked (1=yes)	232	0.04	0.14	0.35
Ships: Number/capita	190	6.12	122.69	606.99
: tonnage (dwt)/capita	190	112.55	2207.63	11169.37
Offshore Reserves: oil/capita	204	0.05	0.17	0.80
: gas/capita	204	0.18	2.71	32.09
Fish supply kgrm/year/capita	204	0.37	39.71	151.88
Marine Biology: Arctic	232	0.08	0.02	0.13
: North West American Boreal	232	0.05	0.01	0.09
: North Pacific, American	232	0.05	0.00	0.07
: Tropical East Pacific	232	0.06	0.15	0.35
: South Pacific	232	0.01	0.01	0.11
: Antiboreal	232	0.00	0.00	0.07
: Atlantic Boreal	232	0.10	0.06	0.25
: Atlantic Warm Temperature	232	0.19	0.22	0.65
: Tropical Indo-West-Pacific	232	0.55	0.19	0.39
: East Asia Boreal	232	0.05	0.01	0.09
: North Pacific, East Asia	232	0.25	0.02	0.13
: Indo-Australian	232	0.04	0.02	0.15
: Tropical Atlantic	232	0.15	0.26	0.44
Coral reef (1=yes)	233	0.32	0.31	0.46
Salinities	234	32.90	29.61	13.22
Ocean circulation	232	0.31	0.56	0.95
Prevailing Wind: Polar	232	0.01	0.01	0.11
: Westerlies Zone	232	0.13	0.13	0.34
: Subtropical	232	0.10	0.11	0.31
: Monsoon Zone	232	0.32	0.06	0.23
: Trades Zone	232	0.60	0.64	0.48
: Intertropical	232	0.08	0.18	0.38
: Transition	232	0.00	0.00	0.07
No oceans (1=yes)	232	0.07	0.12	0.33
Fresh water (cub/kil)	122	215.55	21.46	69.82

Characteristics	Afghan-istan	Albania	Algeria	American Samoa	Andorra	Angola	Anguilla	Antigua & Barbuda	Argentina	Armenia
Coastline: length (km)	0	362	1180	116	0	1600	61	153	4990	0
: length km/cap	0	114	41	1460	0	156	8130	2340	149	0
Zones: Sea territory	0	15	12	200	0	0	200	0	200	0
: Continental shelf (m)	0	0	10	200	0	200	200	200	200	0
: Excl. fish (nm)	0	0	0	0	0	0	0	0	0	0
: Extend. econ. zone (nm)	0	0	0	0	0	0	0	200	0	0
: 200-Mi EEZ, area	0	12300	137000	0	0	506000	0	0	1160000	0
: Contiguous zone (nm)	0	43	0	12	0	0	0	24	24	0
Inland waterways (km)	1200	0	0	0	0	0	0	0	11000	1400
Inland waterways/cap	0.1	0	0	0	0	0	0	0	0.3	0.4
Water area: (km sq)	0	1350	0	0	0	0	0	4730	30200	0
: area/cap	0	0.4	0	0	0	0	0	18500	0.9	0
Access: Number of ports	2	0.3	1	2	2	4	2	1	0.6	0
: Natural Harbour (1=yes)	0	0	1	0	0	0	1	1	0	0
: Number of outlets	1	0	1	1	1	0	0	1	0	0
: Island (1=yes)	0	0	0	0	0	0	1	1	0	0
: Landlocked (1=yes)	1	0	0	0	1	0	0	0	0	1
Ships: Number/cap	0	6	3	0	0	0	0	0	0	0
: tonnage (dwt)/cap	0	26	40	0	0	11	0	0	0	0
Offshore Reserves: oil/cap	0	0	0	0	0	0.3	0	0	0	0
: gas/cap	0	0	0	0	0	0.2	0	0	0	0
Fish supply kgrm/year/cap	0	0	0	0	0	0	0	468	0	0
Marine Biology: Arctic	0	0	0	0	0	0	0	0	0	0
: NW American Boreal	0	0	0	0	0	0	0	0	0	0
: N Pacific. American	0	0	0	0	0	0	0	0	0	0
: Tropical East Pacific	0	0	0	0	0	0	0	0	0	0
: South Pacific	0	0	0	1	0	0	0	0	0	0
: Antiboreal	0	0	0	0	0	0	0	0	1	0
: Atlantic Boreal	0	0	0	0	0	0	0	0	0	0
: Atlantic Warm Temp	0	1	1	0	0	0	0	0	0	0
: Tropical Indo-West-Pacif	0	0	0	0	0	0	0	0	0	0
: East Asia Boreal	0	0	0	0	0	0	0	0	0	0
: North Pacific, East Asia	0	0	0	0	0	0	0	0	0	0
: Indo-Australian	0	0	0	0	0	0	0	0	0	0
: Tropical Atlantic	0	0	0	0	0	1	1	1	0	0
Coral reef (1=yes)	0	0	0	1	0	1	1	1	1	2
Salinities	0	39	37	35	2	34	36	35	34	0
Ocean circulation	0	0	0	0	0	-1	0	0	-1	0
Prevailing Wind: Polar	0	0	0	0	0	0	0	0	0	0
: Westerlies Zone	0	1	0	0	0	0	0	0	1	0
: Subtropical	1	0	1	0	1	0	0	0	0	1
: Monsoon Zone	0	0	0	0	0	0	0	0	0	0
: Trades Zone	0	0	0	1	0	1	1	1	0	0
: Intertropical	0	0	0	0	0	0	0	0	0	0
: Transition	0	0	1	0	0	0	0	0	1	0
No oceans (1=yes)	1	0	0	0	1	0	0	0	0	1
Fresh water (cub/kil)	26	0.2	3	0	0	0.5	0	0	28	0

Characteristics	Aruba	Australia	Austria	Azerbaijan	Bahamas	Bahrain	Bangla-desh	Barbados	Belarus	Belgium
Coastline: length (km)	69	25800	0	0	3540	161	580	97	0	64
: length km/cap	737	1440	0	0	12400	303	5	346	0	6
Zones: Sea territory	12	3	0	0	3	0	12	12	0	12
: Continental shelf (m)	0	200	0	0	200	0	0	0	0	0
: Excl. fish (nm)	0	200	0	0	200	5150	0	200	0	200
Extend. econ. zone (nm)	0	0	0	500	0	0	200	200	0	0
200-Mi EEZ, area	0	7010000	0	0	759000	0	76800	167000	0	2740
Contiguous zone (nm)	0	12	0	0	0	0	18	0	0	0
Inland waterways (km)	0	8370	446	0	0	0	8240	0	0	1790
Inland waterways/cap	0	0.5	0.1	0.1	0	0	0.1	0	0	0.2
Water area: (km sq)	0	68900	1120	500	3870	0	10100	0	0	280
: area/cap	0	4	0.1	0.1	14	0	0.1	0	0	0
Access: Number of ports	2	13	0	0	2	4	2	1	1	5
: Natural Harbour (1=yes)	0	0	3	0	0	0	0	0	0	0
: Number of outlets	0	0	0	0	0	0	0	0	0	0
: Island (1=yes)	1	1	0	0	1	0	0	1	0	0
: Landlocked (1=yes)	0	0	1	1	0	0	0	0	1	0
Ships: Number/cap	0	7	3	0	0	0	0	1	0	3
: tonnage (dwt)/cap	.	199	27	0	3200	28	4	11	0	5
Offshore Reserves: oil/cap	0	0.1	0	0	114400	299	0	285	0	0
: gas/cap	0	0	0	0	0	3	0	0	0	0
Fish supply kgrm/year/cap	0	2	0	0	0	48	0	116	0	2
Marine Biology: Arctic	0	0	0	0	0	0	0	0	0	0
: NW American Boreal	0	0	0	0	0	0	0	0	0	0
: N Pacific, American	0	0	0	0	0	0	0	0	0	0
: Tropical East Pacific	0	0	0	0	0	0	0	0	0	0
: South Pacific	0	1	0	0	0	0	0	0	0	0
: Antiboreal	0	0	0	0	0	0	0	0	0	0
: Atlantic Boreal	0	0	0	0	0	0	0	0	0	8
: Atlantic Warm Temp	0	0	0	0	0	0	0	0	0	0
: Tropical Indo-West-Pacif	0	0	0	0	0	1	1	0	0	0
: East Asia Boreal	0	0	0	0	0	0	0	0	0	0
: North Pacific, East Asia	0	0	0	0	0	0	0	0	0	0
: Indo-Australian	0	1	0	0	0	0	0	0	0	0
: Tropical Atlantic	1	0	0	0	1	0	0	1	0	0
Coral reef (1=yes)	1	0	0	0	0	0	0	0	0	0
Salinities	36	35	2	40	36	38	30	36	0	34
Ocean circulation	1	0	0	1	1	1	1	1	0	1
Prevailing Wind: Polar	0	1	1	0	0	0	0	0	1	0
: Westerlies Zone	0	0	0	0	0	0	0	0	0	1
: Subtropical	0	1	0	0	0	0	0	0	0	0
: Monsoon Zone	0	0	0	0	0	0	1	0	0	0
: Trades Zone	1	1	0	0	1	1	0	1	0	0
: Intertropical	1	1	0	0	0	0	0	0	0	0
: Transition	0	0	0	0	0	0	0	0	0	0
No oceans (1=yes)	0	0	1	1	0	0	0	0	1	0
Fresh water (cub/kil)	.	18	3	1	0	0	23	0	.	9

Characteristics	Belize	Benin	Bermuda	Bhutan	Bolivia	Bosnia & Herzegov.	Botswana	Brazil	British Virgin Isl.	Brunei
Coastline: length (km)	386	121	103	0	0	.	0	7490	80	161
: length km/cap	1930	24	1670	0	0	12	0	48	5210	553
Zones: Sea territory	3	200	200	0	0	200	0	200	3	12
: Continental shelf (m)	0	0	200	0	0	200	0	200	200	200
: Excl. fish (nm)	0	0	200	0	0	12	0	200	200	0
: Extend. econ. zone (nm)	0	0	0	0	0	.	0	0	0	0
: 200-Mi EEZ, area	30900	1720	422000	0	0	.	0	3170000	0	24400
: Contiguous zone (nm)	0	0	0	0	14000	.	15000	0	0	0
Inland waterways (km)	825	0	0	0	2	0	11	50000	0	209
Inland waterways/cap	4	0	0	0	14200	0	0	0.3	0	0.7
Water area: (km sq)	160	2000	0	0	2	.	0	55500	0	500
: area/cap	0.8	0.4	0	0	2	.	0	0.4	0	2
Access: Number of ports	0.4	1	3	0	2	0	3	1	0	2
: Natural Harbour (1=yes)	0	0	0	1	0	.	0	1	1	0
: Number of outlets	0	0	0	1	1	.	1	0	0	0
: Island (1=yes)	0	0	1	0	0	0	0	0	1	0
: Landlocked (1=yes)	0	0	0	0	0.1	0	0	0	0	34
Ships: Number/cap	135	0	.	0	2	.	0	2	0	1180
: tonnage (dwt)/cap	242	0	0	0	0	.	0	54	0	5
Offshore Reserves: oil/cap	0	0.2	0	0	0	.	0	0	0	32
: gas/cap	0	0	2	0	0	.	0	0	0	170
Fish supply kgrm/year/cap	0	0	482	0	0	.	0	0	0	0
Marine Biology: Arctic	0	0	0	0	0	.	0	0	0	0
: NW American Boreal	0	0	0	0	0	.	0	0	0	0
: N Pacific, American	0	0	0	0	0	.	0	0	0	0
: Tropical East Pacific	0	0	0	0	0	.	0	0	0	0
: South Pacific	0	0	0	0	0	.	0	0	0	0
: Antiboreal	0	0	0	0	0	.	0	0	0	0
: Atlantic Boreal	0	0	0	0	0	.	0	0	0	0
: Atlantic Warm Temp	0	0	0	0	0	.	0	0	0	0
: Tropical Indo-West-Pacif	0	0	0	0	0	.	0	0	0	1
: East Asia Boreal	0	0	0	0	0	.	0	0	0	0
: North Pacific, East Asia	0	0	0	0	0	.	0	0	0	0
: Indo-Australian	0	0	0	0	0	.	0	0	0	0
: Tropical Atlantic	1	1	1	0	0	.	0	1	1	0
Coral reef (1=yes)	1	1	1	0	0	0	0	1	1	1
Salinities	35	33	36	30	2	0	2	37	36	34
Ocean circulation	0	1	1	2	0	.	0	0	1	-1
Prevailing Wind: Polar	0	0	0	0	0	.	0	0	0	0
: Westerlies Zone	0	0	0	0	0	.	0	0	0	0
: Subtropical	0	0	1	0	0	.	0	1	0	0
: Monsoon Zone	0	0	0	0	0	.	0	0	0	1
: Trades Zone	1	1	0	0	0	.	0	1	1	0
: Intertropical	0	0	0	0	0	.	0	0	0	1
: Transition	0	0	0	0	0	.	0	0	0	0
No oceans (1=yes)	0	0	0	1	0	0	0	0	0	0
Fresh water (cub/kil)	.	0.1	.	0	1	.	0.1	35	0	.

Characteristics	Bulgaria	Burkina Faso	Burma	Burundi	Cambodia	Cameroon	Canada	Cape Verde	Cayman Islands	Central Afric. Rep.
Coastline: length (km)	354	0	3060	0	443	402	58800	965	160	0
: length km/cap	40	0	46	0	49	32	4660	2390	3420	0
Zones: Sea territory	12	0	12	0	12	50	12	12	3	0
: Continental shelf (m)	0	0	200	0	200	0	200	0	0	0
: Excl. fish (nm)	0	0	0	0	0	0	200	0	0	0
: Extend. econ. zone (nm)	200	0	200	0	200	0	200	200	200	0
200-Mi EEZ, area	32900	0	0	0	55600	15400	4700000	790000	0	0
: Contiguous zone (nm)	0	0	24	0	24	0	0	0	0	0
Inland waterways (km)	470	0	3100	0	3700	2090	3000	0	0	800
Inland waterways/cap	0.1	0	0.1	0	0.4	0.2	0.1	0	0	0.2
Water area: (km sq)	360	400	18800	2180	4520	6000	755000	200	200	0
: area/cap	0	0	0.4	0.4	0.5	0.5	27	0	0	0
Access: Number of ports	6	0	3	0	2	0	7	2	2	0
: Natural Harbour (1=yes)	6	2	0	1	0	1	0	0	0	0
: Number of outlets	0	1	0	0	0	0	0	1	0	1
: Island (1=yes)	0	0	0	0	0	0	0	1	1	0
: Landlocked (1=yes)	0	1	0	1	0	0	0	0	0	1
Ships: Number/cap	14	0	2	0	0	0	6	42	0	0
: tonnage (dwt)/cap	211	0	30	0	0	0	18	64	922	0
Offshore Reserves: oil/cap	0	0	0	0	0.1	0.2	0.4	0	0	0
: gas/cap	0	0	0.1	0	0.2	0.3	0.9	0	0	0
Fish supply kgrm/year/cap	0	0	0	0	0	0.4	0	75	0	0.1
Marine Biology: Arctic	0	0	0	0	0	0	1	0	0	0
: NW American Boreal	0	0	0	0	0	0	0	0	0	0
: N Pacific, American	0	0	0	0	0	0	0	0	0	0
: Tropical East Pacific	0	0	0	0	0	0	0	0	0	0
: South Pacific	0	0	0	0	0	0	0	0	0	0
: Antiboreal	0	0	0	0	0	0	0	0	0	0
: Atlantic Boreal	0	0	0	0	0	0	0	0	0	0
: Atlantic Warm Temp	1	0	0	0	0	0	1	1	1	0
: Tropical Indo-West-Pacif	0	0	1	0	1	0	0	0	0	0
: East Asia Boreal	0	0	0	0	0	0	0	0	0	0
: North Pacific, East Asia	0	0	0	0	0	0	0	0	0	0
: Indo-Australian	0	0	0	0	0	0	0	0	0	0
: Tropical Atlantic	0	0	0	0	0	1	0	0	0	0
Coral reef (1=yes)	0	0	0	0	0	0	0	0	0	0
Salinities	39	2	30	2	31	33	32	35	36	2
Ocean circulation	1	0	1	0	-1	1	1	1	1	0
Prevailing Wind: Polar	0	0	0	0	0	0	0	0	0	0
: Westerlies Zone	1	0	0	0	0	0	1	1	0	0
: Subtropical	0	0	0	0	0	0	0	0	0	0
: Monsoon Zone	0	0	1	0	1	0	0	0	0	0
: Trades Zone	0	0	0	0	0	0	0	0	1	0
: Intertropical	0	1	0	1	0	1	0	1	0	1
: Transition	0	0	0	0	0	0	0	0	0	0
No oceans (1=yes)	0	1	0	1	0	0	0	1	0	1
Fresh water (cub/kil)	14	0.2	4	0.1	0.5	0.4	42	.	.	0.1

Characteristics	Chad	Chile	China	Christmas Island	Cocos (Keel.) Isl.	Colombia	Comoros	Congo	Cook Island	Costa Rica
Coastline: length (km)	0	6440	14500	54		2410	340	169	120	1290
·: length km/cap	0	466	8	32000		79	553	69	6680	394
Zones: Sea territory	0	12	12	3	3	12	12	200	12	12
··: Continental shelf (m)	0	200	0	200	200	200	0	0	200	200
··: Excl. fish (nm)	0	200	0	200	200		200	0		
··: Extend. econ. zone (nm)	0		0			200		0	200	200
··: 200-Mi EEZ, area	0	2290000				603000		24700		259000
··: Contiguous zone (nm)		24	0	12	12	6				
Inland waterways (km)	2000	725	110000	0	0	14300	0	4390	0	730
Inland waterways/cap	0.3	0.1	0.1	0	0	0.4	0		0	0.2
Water area: (km sq)	24800	8150	271000	0	0	100000	0	500	0	240
··: area/cap	4	0.6	0.2	0		3	0	0.2	0	0.1
Access: Number of ports		8	12	1	0	7	2	2	1	0.5
··: Natural Harbour (1=yes)	0	0	1	0	0	0	0	0	0	0.5
··: Number of outlets	2	0	0	1	1	0	0	0	1	0
··: Island (1=yes)	0	0	0	1		0	1	0	1	0
··: Landlocked (1=yes)	1	0	0	0	0	0	0	0	0	0
Ships: Number/cap		4	1	0	1	1	5	1	1	1
··: tonnage (dwt)/cap	0	53	17	0	0	11	4	19	0	0.8
Offshore Reserves: oil/cap	0	0.2	0	0	0	0	0	0	0	0
··: gas/cap	3	2	0	0	0	0	0	2	0	0
Fish supply kgrm/year/cap			0	0	0	0	0		0	0
Marine Biology: Arctic	0	0	0	0	0	0	0	0	0	0
··: NW American Boreal	0	0	0	0	0	0	0	0	0	0
··: N Pacific, American	0	0	0	0	0	0	0	0	0	0
··: Tropical East Pacific	0	0	0	0	0	0	0	0	0	1
··: South Pacific	0	1	0	0	0	0	0	0	1	0
··: Antiboreal	0	0	0	0	0	0	0	0	0	0
··: Atlantic Boreal	0	0	0	0	0	0	0	0	0	0
··: Atlantic Warm Temp.	0	0	0	0	0	0	0	0	0	0
··: Tropical Indo-West-Pacif	0	0	0	1	1	0	1	0	0	0
··: East Asia Boreal	0	0	0	0	0	0	0	0	0	0
··: North Pacific, East Asia	0	0	1	0	0	0	0	0	0	0
··: Indo-Australian	0	0	0	0	0	0	0	0	0	0
··: Tropical Atlantic	0	0	0	0	0	1	0	1	0	0
Coral reef (1=yes)	0	0	1	1	1	0	1	1	1	1
Salinities		35	34	35	35	30	35	32	35	32
Ocean circulation	0	-1	0	1	1	0	1	1	1	0
Prevailing Wind: Polar	2	0	0	0	0	0	0	0	0	0
··: Westerlies Zone	0	1	0	0	0	0	0	0	0	0
··: Subtropical	0	1	0	0	0	0	0	0	0	0
··: Monsoon Zone	0	0	1	0	0	0	0	0	0	0
··: Trades Zone	0	0	0	1	1	1	1	1	1	1
··: Intertropical	0	0	0	0	0	0	0	0	0	0
··: Transition	0	0	1	0	0	0	0	0	0	0
No oceans (1=yes)	1	0	0	0	0	0	0	0	0	0
Fresh water (cub/kil)	0.2	17	460	0	0	5	0	0	0	1

Characteristics	Croatia	Cuba	Cyprus	Czech Republic	Denmark	Djibouti	Dominica	Dominican Republic	Ecuador	Egypt
Coastline: length (km)	1780	3740	648		3380	314	148	1290	2240	2450
: length km/cap	367	343	902		651	631	1920	169	197	44
Zones: Sea territory	12	12	12		3	12	12		200	12
: Continental shelf (m)	200	200	200		200	200		6	200	200
: Excl. fish (nm)	12									
: Extend. econ. zone (nm)	12	200			200	200	200	200	200	200
: 200-Mi EEZ, area	0	363000	99500		68600	6170	19900	269000	1160000	174000
: Contiguous zone (nm)				303	4	24	24	24		18
Inland waterways (km)	393	240			417				1500	173
Inland waterways/cap	0.1	0			0.1				0.1	0
Water area: (km sq)	128		1		700	20	200	350	6720	6000
: area/cap	0	0	0	0	0.1	0	0	0	0.6	0.1
Access: Number of ports	7	12	5	0	5	1	2	4	4	5
: Natural Harbour (1=yes)	0	0	0		4	0	0	0	0	0
: Number of outlets	0	0	0	0	0	0	0	0	0	0
: Island (1=yes)	0	1	1		0	0	1	1	1	0
: Landlocked (1=yes)	0	0	0	1	0	0	0	0	0	0
Ships: Number/cap	18	8	1930	2	96	4	26	2	5	4
: tonnage (dwt)/cap	38	65	4950	43	1300	5	21	2	42	28
Offshore Reserves: oil/cap	0	0	0		0.7	0	0	0	0.1	0.1
: gas/cap	0	0	0		0.4	0	0	0	0	0.1
Fish supply kgrm/year/cap	0	0	0	0	0	0	0	0	0	0
Marine Biology: Arctic	0	0	0	0	0	0	0	0	0	0
: NW American Boreal	0	0	0	0	0	0	0	0	0	0
: N Pacific, American	0	0	0	0	0	0	0	0	0	0
: Tropical East Pacific	0	0	0	0	0	0	0	0	1	0
: South Pacific	0	0	0	0	0	0	0	0	0	0
: Antiboreal	0	0	0	0	0	0	0	0	0	0
: Atlantic Boreal	0	0	0	0	1	0	0	0	0	0
: Atlantic Warm Temp	1	0	1	0	0	0	0	0	0	0
: Tropical Indo-West-Pacif	0	0	0	0	0	1	0	0	0	1
: East Asia Boreal	0	0	0	0	0	0	0	0	0	0
: North Pacific, East Asia	0	0	0	0	0	0	0	0	0	0
: Indo-Australian	0	0	0	0	0	0	0	0	0	0
: Tropical Atlantic	0	1	0	0	0	0	1	1	0	0
Coral reef (1=yes)	0	1	0	0	0	1	1	1	1	1
Salinities	39	36	39		34	38	36	35	34	39
Ocean circulation	1	1	1	0	1	1	1	1	1	1
Prevailing Wind: Polar	0	0	0	0	0	0	0	0	0	0
: Westerlies Zone	1	0	0	0	1	0	0	0	0	0
: Subtropical	0	0	1	0	0	0	0	0	0	1
: Monsoon Zone	0	0	0	0	0	0	0	0	0	0
: Trades Zone	0	1	0	0	0	1	1	1	0	0
: Intertropical	0	0	0	0	0	0	0	0	1	0
: Transition	0	0	0	0	0	0	0	0	0	0
No oceans (1=yes)	0	0	0	1	0	0	0	0	0	0
Fresh water (cub/kil)	1		1		1	0	0	3	6	56

Characteristics	El Salvador	Equatorial Guinea	Eritrea	Estonia	Ethiopia	Falkland Islands	Faroe Islands	Fiji	Finland	France
Coastline: length (km)	307	296	112000	1390	1090	1290	764	1130	1130	3430
: length km/cap	56	750	32100	878	14	612000	16100	1550	224	60
Zones: Sea territory	200	12	0	0	12	3	3	12	4	12
: Continental shelf (m)	0	0	0	0		200	200	200	200	200
: Excl. fish (nm)	0	0		0	0	200	200	200	12	200
: Extend. econ. zone (nm)				0	0			200	200	200
: 200-Mi EEZ, area	91900	283000				513000		1130000	98100	341000
: Contiguous zone (nm)		0		0	0	0	4	163	6	12
Inland waterways (km)		0	0	250	0	0			6390	8500
Inland waterways/cap		0	0	0.2	0	0		0.2		0.1
Water area: (km sq)	320	0	82200000	1900	121000	0		163	31600	1400
: area/cap	0.1	2	23600	3	2	1	2	0.2	6	6
Access: Number of ports	2	0	0		0	0	0	4	11	54
: Natural Harbour (1=yes)	0	0		0	0	1	0	0	0	
: Number of outlets	0	0	0	0	0	0	2	0	1	
: Island (1=yes)	0	0	0	0	0	1	1	1	0	
: Landlocked (1=yes)	0	5	0	64	0	0		34	24	4
Ships: Number/cap	0	17	0	370	0.4	0		86	203	97
: tonnage (dwt)/cap	0	0	0	0	2	0	0	0	0	
Offshore Reserves: oil/cap	0	0		0	0	0	0	0	0	0.5
: gas/cap	0	0	0	0	0	0	0	60	0	0
Fish supply kgrm/year/cap		0	0	0	0	0	0	0	7	0
Marine Biology: Arctic	0	0	0	0	0	0	0	0	0	0
: NW American Boreal	0	0	0	0	0	0	0	0	0	0
: N Pacific. American	0	0	0	0	0	0	0	0	0	0
: Tropical East Pacific	1	0	0	0	0	0	0	0	0	0
: South Pacific	0	0	0	0	0	0	0	1	0	0
: Antiboreal	0	0	0	0	0	1	0	0	0	0
: Atlantic Boreal	0	0	0	1	0	0	1	0	1	1
: Atlantic Warm Temp	0	0	0	0	0	0	0	0	0	0
: Tropical Indo-West-Pacif	0	0	0	0	1	0	0	0	0	0
: East Asia Boreal	0	0	0	0	0	0	0	0	0	0
: North Pacific, East Asia	0	0	0	0	0	0	0	0	0	0
: Indo-Australian	0	0	0	0	0	0	0	0	0	0
: Tropical Atlantic	0	1	0	0	0	0	0	0	0	0
Coral reef (1=yes)	0	0	0	0	0	0	0	0	0	0
Salinities	33	32		34	38	34	35	35	34	34
Ocean circulation	-1	-1		-1	0	-1	-1	0	-1	-1
Prevailing Wind: Polar	0	0	0	0	0	0	0	0	0	0
: Westerlies Zone	0	0	0	1	0	1	1	0	1	1
: Subtropical	1	0	0	0	0	0	0	0	0	0
: Monsoon Zone	0	0	0	0	1	0	0	0	0	0
: Trades Zone	0	1	0	0	0	0	0	1	0	0
: Intertropical	0	0	0	0	0	0	0	0	0	0
: Transition	0	0	0	0	0	0	0	0	0	0
No oceans (1=yes)	0	0	0	0	1	0	0	0	0	0
Fresh water (cub/kil)	1	0		0	2	4			4	40

Characteristics	French Guiana	French Polynesia	Gabon	Gambia	Gaza Strip	Georgia	Germany	Ghana	Gibraltar	Greece
Coastline: length (km)	378	2630	885	80	40	310	1490	539	12	13700
: length km/cap	3090	12000	702	86	58	57	18	33	384	1340
Zones: Sea territory	12	12	100	200	0		3	200	3	6
: Continental shelf (m)	200	200			0		200		200	200
: Excl. fish (nm)			150	0			200	100		
: Extend. econ. zone (nm)	200	200	200	0	0	0				0
200-Mi EEZ, area	160000		214000	19600			218000	218000		505000
: Contiguous zone (nm)	12	12		0						0
Inland waterways (km)	230	0	1600	400	0	0	6700	155		80
Inland waterways/cap	2	1	1	0.4	0	0	0.1	1	0	1
Water area: (km sq)	1850	281	10000	1300	0	0	4300	8520	0	1140
: area/cap	15	1	8	1	0	0	0.1	0.5	0	0.1
Access: Number of ports	1	1	3	1	0	2	44	0.2	1	2
: Natural Harbour (1=yes)		2								
: Number of outlets	0	0	0	0	0	0	0	0	0	0
: Island (1=yes)	0	1	0	0	0	0	0	0	0	0
: Landlocked (1=yes)	0	0	0	0	0	0	0	0	0	0
Ships: Number/cap	0	0	6	0	0	0	9	0.7	0	138
: tonnage (dwt)/cap	0	0	22	0	0	0	77	0	0	4540
Offshore Reserves: oil/cap	0	0	0	0	0	0	0	0.5	0	0.1
: gas/cap	0	0	3	0	0	0	0	0	0	0
Fish supply kgrm/year/cap	359	170	24	22		184				
Marine Biology: Arctic	0	0	0	0	0	0	0	0	0	0
: NW American Boreal	0	0	0	0	0	0	0	0	0	0
: N Pacific. American	0	0	0	0	0	0	0	0	0	0
: Tropical East Pacific	0	0	0	0	0	0	0	0	0	0
: South Pacific	0	0	0	0	0	0	0	0	0	0
: Antiboreal	0	0	0	0	0	0	0	0	0	0
: Atlantic Boreal	0	0	0	0	0	0	0	0	0	0
: Atlantic Warm Temp	0	0	0	0	0	0	0	0	0	0
: Tropical Indo-West-Pacif	0	0	0	0	0	0	0	0	0	0
: East Asia Boreal	0	0	0	0	0	0	0	0	0	0
: North Pacific, East Asia	0	0	0	0	0	0	0	0	0	0
: Indo-Australian	0	0	0	0	0	0	0	0	0	0
: Tropical Atlantic	1	0	1	1	1	1	0	1	0	0
Coral reef (1=yes)	0	1	0	0	0	0	0	0	0	0
Salinities	35	35	32	35	39	40	35	35	36	35
Ocean circulation	0	0	0	0	0	0	0	0	0	0
Prevailing Wind: Polar	0	0	0	0	0	0	0	0	0	0
: Westerlies Zone	0	0	0	0	0	0	1	0	0	0
: Subtropical	1	0	0	0	1	1	0	0	1	1
: Monsoon Zone	0	0	0	0	0	0	0	0	0	0
: Trades Zone	0	1	0	1	0	0	0	0	0	0
: Intertropical	0	0	1	0	0	0	0	1	0	0
: Transition	0	0	0	0	0	0	0	0	0	1
No oceans (1=yes)	0	0	0	0	0	0	0	0	0	0
Fresh water (cub/kil)			0.1	0	1		41	0.3		7

Characteristics	Greenland	Grenada	Guade-loupe	Guam	Guatemala	Guernsey	Guinea	Guinea-Bissau	Guyana	Haiti
Coastline: length (km)	44100	121	306	126	400	50	346	274	459	1770
: length km/cap	770000	1380	735	3	40	793	54	292	565	256
Zones: Sea territory	3	12	12	3	12	3	12	12	12	12
: Continental shelf (m)	200		200	200		200			200	
: Excl. fish (nm)	200	200	200	200	200	200	200	200	200	200
: Extend. econ. zone (nm)	0	0	0	0	0	0	0	0		200
: 200-Mi EEZ, area	4	200	13100	12	99100	200	71000	151000	130000	161000
: Contiguous zone (nm)	0	0			625	0	1300		6007	24
Inland waterways (km)	0		20		0.1		0.2	8120	18100	50
Inland waterways/cap	1830000	0		12	460	0		8	22	190
Water area: (km sq)	32000									
: area/cap	7				3		2		0	2
Access: Number of ports	0	1	2	0	0	0	0	0	0	0
: Natural Harbour (1=yes)	0	0		1	0	2	0	1	0	1
: Number of outlets	1	1	2	0	0	1	0	0	0	
: Island (1=yes)	0	1	0	1	0		2	0	0	0
: Landlocked (1=yes)		0	0	0	0	1	0	0	0	0
Ships: Number/cap	0		1	1				0	14	
: tonnage (dwt)/cap							0.2		9	
Offshore Reserves: oil/cap	0									
: gas/cap	1550	274	146						48	
Fish supply kgrm/year/cap	1	0	0	0	0	0	0	0	0	0
Marine Biology: Arctic										
: NW American Boreal										
: N Pacific, American										
: Tropical East Pacific					1					
: South Pacific										
: Antiboreal										
: Atlantic Boreal										
: Atlantic Warm Temp						1				
: Tropical Indo-West-Pacif				1						
: East Asia Boreal										
: North Pacific, East Asia										
: Indo-Australian										
: Tropical Atlantic	1	1	1	1	1	1	1	1	1	1
Coral reef (1=yes)	0	1	1	1	0	0	0	0	0	0
Salinities	34	35	35	35	33	34	35	36	35	36
Ocean circulation	-1	-1	-1	-1	-1	-1	-1	-1	-1	
Prevailing Wind: Polar	1									
: Westerlies Zone	0					1				
: Subtropical	0									
: Monsoon Zone	0									
: Trades Zone	0	1	1	1	1	0	1	1	1	1
: Intertropical	0									
: Transition	0									
No oceans (1=yes)	0	0	0	0	0	0	0	0	0	0
Fresh water (cub/kil)	0	0	0		0.7	0	0.7	0	0	0

Characteristics	Honduras	Hong Kong	Hungary	Iceland	India	Indonesia	Iran	Iraq	Ireland	Isle of Man
Coastline: length (km)	820	733	0	4990	7000	54700	3180	58	1450	113
: length km/cap	145	83	0	17600	8	281	50	83	415	1610
Zones: Sea territory	12	3	0	12	12	12	12	12	3	
: Continental shelf (m)	200	200	0	200	200	0	0	200	0	200
: Excl. fish (nm)		0	0	0	0	200	50	0	0	200
: Extend. econ. zone (nm)	200	0	0	200	200	0	0	0	0	0
: 200-Mi EEZ, area	201000	0	0	867000	2020000	5410000	156000	686	380000	0
: Contiguous zone (nm)	24	0	0	0	24	0	0	573	0	0
Inland waterways (km)	465	0	1660	0	19100	21600	517	950	429	0
Inland waterways/cap	0.1	0	0.2	0	0	0.1	0	3	0.1	0
Water area: (km sq)	200	50	690	2750	314000	93000	12000	0	1390	3
: area/cap	0	0	0.1	10	0.4	0.5	0.2	0	0.4	
Access: Number of ports	3	1	0	7	7	8	0	3	4	
: Natural Harbour (1=yes)		1	1	0	0	0	0	0	0	1
: Number of outlets	0	0	2	1	0	1	3	0	1	0
: Island (1=yes)	0	1	0	1	0	4	0	0	0	1
: Landlocked (1=yes)	0	0	1	0	0	0	0	0	0	0
Ships: Number/cap	101	46	1	64	0	15	3	2	18	
: tonnage (dwt)/cap	250	2040	13	195	0.4	0	16	7	54	
Offshore Reserves: oil/cap	0	0	0	0	1	0.2	0.6	0	0.4	0
: gas/cap	0	0	0	0	0	0	0.5	0	0	0
Fish supply kgrm/year/cap	0	8	0	354	0	0	0	0	0	0
Marine Biology: Arctic	0	0	0	0	0	0	0	0	0	0
: NW American Boreal	0	0	0	0	0	0	0	0	0	0
: N Pacific, American	0	0	0	0	0	0	0	0	0	0
: Tropical East Pacific	1	0	0	0	0	0	0	0	0	0
: South Pacific	0	0	0	0	0	0	0	0	0	0
: Antiboreal	0	0	0	0	0	0	0	0	0	0
: Atlantic Boreal	0	0	0	1	0	0	0	0	1	1
: Atlantic Warm Temp	0	0	0	0	0	0	0	0	0	0
: Tropical Indo-West-Pacif	0	1	0	0	0	0	1	1	0	0
: East Asia Boreal	0	0	0	0	0	0	0	0	0	0
: North Pacific, East Asia	0	0	0	0	0	0	0	0	0	0
: Indo-Australian	0	0	0	0	1	1	0	0	0	0
: Tropical Atlantic	1	0	0	0	0	0	0	0	0	0
Coral reef (1=yes)	1	0	0	0	0	0	0	0	0	0
Salinities	33	34	5	35	34	35	38	38	35	35
Prevailing Wind: Polar	-1	-1		-1	1				-1	-1
: Westerlies Zone	0	0	0	1	0	0	0	0	1	0
: Subtropical	0	0	0	0	0	0	0	0	0	1
: Monsoon Zone	0	0	0	0	0	0	0	0	0	0
: Trades Zone	0	0	0	0	0	0	0	0	0	0
: Intertropical	1	1	1	1	1	1	1	1	1	1
: Transition	1	1	0	0	0	0	0	0	0	0
No oceans (1=yes)	0	0	0	0	0	0	0	0	0	0
Fresh water (cub/kil)	1	0	5	0	380	82	45	43	0.8	

Characteristics	Israel	Italy	Ivory Coast	Jamaica	Japan	Jersey	Jordan	Kazakhstan	Kenya	Kiribati
Coastline: length (km)	273	5000	515	1020	13700	70	26	0	536	1140
: length km/cap	50	86	38	407	110	819	6	0	21	15200
Zones: Sea territory	6	12	12	12	12	3	3		12	12
:Continental shelf (m)		200	200			200				
:Excl. fish (nm)	0	0	0	0	200	200	0	0	200	200
:Extend. econ. zone (nm)	0									
:200-Mi EEZ, area	0	552000	105000	298000	3860000		686		118000	0
:Contiguous zone (nm)	0	0	980	0	1770	0	0		0	0
Inland waterways (km)	0	2400								0.5
Inland waterways/cap			0.1							0.1
Water area: (km sq)	440	7210	4460	160	1280		340	47500	13400	
:area/cap	0.1	0.1	0.3	0.1	18	3	0.1	3	0.5	
Access: Number of ports	0	0	0	0	0		0		0	0
:Natural Harbour (1=yes)	0.2	0.9	0.2	2	1		0		0	2
:Number of outlets	0	0	0	1	0	1	0	0	0	0
:Island (1=yes)	0	0	0	1	1		0	0	0	1
:Landlocked (1=yes)	0	0	0	0	0		0	1	0	0
Ships: Number/cap	7	14	0.6	2	30		0.4		0.2	67
:tonnage (dwt)/cap	149	175	7	6	291		26		0.4	36
Offshore Reserves: oil/cap	0	0.1	0	0	0		0		0	0
:gas/cap	0	0.3	0	0	0.6		0		0	0
Fish supply kgrm/year/cap										
Marine Biology: Arctic	0	0	0	0	0	0	0	0	0	0
:NW American Boreal	0	0	0	0	0	0	0	0	0	0
:N Pacific, American	0	0	0	0	0	0	0	0	0	0
:Tropical East Pacific	0	0	0	0	0	0	0	0	0	0
:South Pacific	0	0	0	0	0	0	0	0	0	0
:Antiboreal	0	0	0	0	0	0	0	0	0	0
:Atlantic Boreal	0	0	0	0	0	1	0	0	0	0
:Atlantic Warm Temp	1	1	0	0	0	0	0	0	0	0
:Tropical Indo-West-Pacif	0	0	0	0	0	0	1	0	1	1
:East Asia Boreal	0	0	0	0	0	0	0	0	0	0
:North Pacific, East Asia	0	0	0	0	1	0	0	0	0	0
:Indo-Australian	0	0	0	0	0	0	0	0	0	0
:Tropical Atlantic	0	0	1	1	0	0	0	0	0	0
Coral reef (1=yes)	0	0	0	1	1	0	0	0	0	0
Salinities	39	38	35	36	33	34	41	40	35	35
Ocean circulation	0	0	0	0	0	1	0	1	0	0
Prevailing Wind: Polar	1	1	1	1	1	0	1	1	1	1
:Westerlies Zone	0	0	0	0	0	1	0	0	0	0
:Subtropical	0	0	0	0	0	0	0	0	0	0
:Monsoon Zone	0	0	0	0	0	0	0	0	0	0
:Trades Zone	0	0	0	0	0	0	0	0	0	0
:Intertropical	1	1	1	1	1	0	1	1	1	1
:Transition	0	0	0	0	0	0	0	0	0	0
No oceans (1=yes)	1	1	0	0	0		0	1	0	0
Fresh water (cub/kil)	2	56	0.7	0.3	108		0.4	1	1	

Characteristics	Kuwait	Kyrgyz-stan	Laos	Latvia	Lebanon	Lesotho	Liberia	Libya	Liechten-stein	Lithuania
Coastline: length (km)	499	0	0	531	225	0	579	1770	0	108
: length km/cap	263	0	0	198	78	0	278	350	0	29
Zones: Sea territory	12	0	0	12	12	0	200	12	0	12
: Continental shelf (m)	0	0	0		0	0	200	0	0	
: Excl. fish (nm)	0	0	0		0	0	0	0	0	0
: Extend. econ. zone (nm)	0	0	0	200	0	0	0	0	0	
: 200-Mi EEZ, area	12000	0	0	0	22600	0	230000	338000	0	0
: Contiguous zone (nm)	0	0	0	0	0	0	0	0	0	0
Inland waterways (km)	0	600	4590	300	170	0	15100	0	0	600
Inland waterways/cap	0	0.1	1	0.1	0.1	0	0	0	0	0.2
Water area: (km sq)	0	7200	6000	0	0	0	0	0	0	0
: area/cap	0	2	1	0	0	0	0	0	0	0
Access: Number of ports	3	0	0	4	7	0	4	6	0	2
: Natural Harbour (1=yes)	0	0	0	0	0	0	0	0	0	0
: Number of outlets	0	0	3	0	0	1	0	0	1	0
: Island (1=yes)	0	0	0	0	0	0	0	0	0	0
: Landlocked (1=yes)	0	1	1	0	0	1	0	0	1	0
Ships: Number/cap	33	0	0.2	49	48	0	539	8	0	18
: tonnage (dwt)/cap	2000	0	0.3	500	149	0	33400	239	0	124
Offshore Reserves: oil/cap	0	0	0	0	0	0	0	0.2	0	0
: gas/cap	0	0	0	0	0	0	0	0.4	0	0
Fish supply kgrm/year/cap	0	0	0	0	0	0	0	0	0	0
Marine Biology: Arctic	0	0	0	0	0	0	0	0	0	0
: NW American Boreal	0	0	0	0	0	0	0	0	0	0
: N Pacific American	0	0	0	0	0	0	0	0	0	0
: Tropical East Pacific	0	0	0	0	0	0	0	0	0	0
: South Pacific	0	0	0	0	0	0	0	0	0	0
: Antiboreal	0	0	0	0	0	0	0	0	0	0
: Atlantic Boreal	0	0	0	1	0	0	0	0	0	1
: Atlantic Warm Temp	0	0	0	0	1	0	0	1	0	0
: Tropical Indo-West-Pacif	1	0	0	0	0	0	0	0	0	0
: East Asia Boreal	0	0	0	0	0	0	0	0	0	0
: North Pacific, East Asia	0	0	0	0	0	0	0	0	0	0
: Indo-Australian	0	0	0	0	0	0	0	0	0	0
: Tropical Atlantic	0	0	0	0	0	0	1	0	0	0
Coral reef (1=yes)	0	0	0	0	0	0	0	0	0	0
Salinities	38	0	0	34	39	0	35	38	0	34
Ocean circulation	1	2	2	-1	1	2	-1	1	2	-1
Prevailing Wind: Polar	0	0	0	0	0	0	0	0	0	0
: Westerlies Zone	0	0	0	1	0	0	0	0	0	1
: Subtropical	0	0	0	0	1	0	0	1	0	0
: Monsoon Zone	1	0	0	0	0	0	0	0	0	0
: Trades Zone	0	0	0	0	0	0	0	0	0	0
: Intertropical	0	0	0	0	0	0	1	0	0	0
: Transition	0	0	0	0	0	0	0	0	0	0
No oceans (1=yes)	0	1	1	0	0	1	0	0	1	0
Fresh water (cub/kil)	0.5		1		0.8	0.1	0.1	3	0	

Characteristics	Luxembourg	Macau	Macedonia	Madagascar	Malawi	Malaysia	Maldives	Mali	Malta	Marshall Islands
Coastline: length (km)	0	40	·	4830	0	4680	644	0	140	·
: length km/cap	0	53	·	364	0	243	2780	0	389	·
Zones: Sea territory	0	·	0	50	0	12	55	0	12	12
: Continental shelf (m)	0	6	0	150	0	200		0	200	200
: Excl. fish (nm)	0	·	0	150	0	200	100	0	25	·
: Extend. econ. zone (nm)	0	12	0	150	0	200	300	0		200
: 200-Mi EEZ, area	0	0	·	1290000	0	476000	959000	0	66200	·
: Contiguous zone (nm)	0	0	·	0	0	0	0	0	24	12
Inland waterways (km)	37	0	0	566	144	3210	0	1820	0	0
Inland waterways/cap	0.1	0	0	0	0	0.2	0	0.2	0	0
Water area: (km sq)	0	0	0	5500	24400	1200	0	20000	0	0
: area/cap	0	0	·	0.4	4	0.1	0	2	0	0
Access: Number of ports	1	0	·	0	4	0	0	0	2	0
: Natural Harbour (1=yes)	0	1	0	1	0	0	2	0	1	1
: Number of outlets	1	0	·	0	2	8	0	2	0	
: Island (1=yes)	0	1	0	1	0	0	1	0	1	1
: Landlocked (1=yes)	1	0	·	0	1	0	0	1	0	0
Ships: Number/cap	133	0	0	1	0	16	121	0	2330	0
: tonnage (dwt)/cap	6670	68	0	3	0	151	319	0	49800	0
Offshore Reserves: oil/cap	0	·	·	0	0	0.1	0	0	0	·
: gas/cap	0	·	·	0	0	0.3	0	0	0	·
Fish supply kgrm/year/cap	0	·	·	0	0	2	221	0	0	·
Marine Biology: Arctic	0	0	·	0	0	0	0	0	0	0
: NW American Boreal	0	0	·	0	0	0	0	0	0	0
: N Pacific_American	0	0	·	0	0	0	0	0	0	0
: Tropical East Pacific	0	0	·	0	0	0	0	0	0	0
: South Pacific	0	0	·	0	0	0	0	0	0	1
: Antiboreal	0	0	·	0	0	0	0	0	0	0
: Atlantic Boreal	0	0	·	0	0	0	0	0	0	0
: Atlantic Warm Temp	0	0	·	0	0	0	0	0	1	0
: Tropical Indo-West-Pacif	0	0	·	1	0	1	1	0	0	0
: East Asia Boreal	0	0	·	0	0	0	0	0	0	0
: North Pacific, East Asia	0	1	·	0	0	0	0	0	0	0
: Indo-Australian	0	0	·	0	0	0	0	0	0	0
: Tropical Atlantic	0	0	·	0	0	0	0	0	0	0
Coral reef (1=yes)	0	0	·	1	0	1	1	0	0	1
Salinities	2	33	0	35	2	34	35	2	38	34
Ocean circulation	0	-1	·	1	0	0	1	0	1	0
Prevailing Wind: Polar	0	0	·	0	0	0	0	0	0	0
: Westerlies Zone	1	0	·	0	0	0	0	0	1	0
: Subtropical	0	0	·	0	0	0	0	1	0	0
: Monsoon Zone	0	1	·	0	0	1	1	0	0	0
: Trades Zone	0	0	·	1	1	0	0	0	0	1
: Intertropical	0	0	·	0	0	0	0	0	0	0
: Transition	0	0	·	0	0	0	0	0	0	0
No oceans (1=yes)	0	0	·	0	0	0	0	0	0	0
Fresh water (cub/kil)	·	·	·	16	0.2	9	0	1	1	0

Characteristics	Martinique	Mauritania	Mauritius	Mayotte	Mexico	Micronesia Federation	Moldova	Monaco	Mongolia	Montserrat
Coastline: length (km)	290	754	177	165	9330	6110	0	4	0	40
: length km/cap	761	345	159	1830	104	60500	0	140	0	3380
Zones: Sea territory	12	70	12	12	12	12	0	12	0	3
: Continental shelf (m)	200	200	200	200		200	0	0	0	
: Excl. fish (nm)				200			0	0	0	200
: Extend. econ. zone (nm)	200	200	200		200	200	0	0	0	
: 200-Mi EEZ, area	513000	154000	1180000	200	2850000	200	0	0	0	
: Contiguous zone (nm)						12	0	0	0	
Inland waterways (km)	0	0	0	0	2900	0	0	0	0	0
Inland waterways/cap							0	0	0	0
Water area: (km sq)	40	300	10		49500	0	0	0	199	0
: area/cap	0.1	0.1	1		0.5	0	0	0	0.1	0
Access: Number of ports	1	0	1	0	11	3	0	1	0	0
: Natural Harbour (1=yes)	0	2	0	0	1	0	0	1	0	0
: Number of outlets	0	0	0	0	0	0	2	0	2	0
: Island (1=yes)	1	0	1	1	0	1	0	0	0	1
: Landlocked (1=yes)	0	0	0	0	0	0	1	0	1	0
Ships: Number/cap		0.9	0	1	0.9	0	0	0	0	
: tonnage (dwt)/cap	0	1	7	0	13	0	0	0	0	0
Offshore Reserves: oil/cap	0	0			0.5	0	0	0	0	0
: gas/cap	0	0			0.6	0	0	0	0	0
Fish supply kgrm/year/cap	145	0	150	0	0	0	0	0	0	0
Marine Biology: Arctic	0	0	0	0	0	0	0	0	0	0
: NW American Boreal	0	0	0	0	0	0	0	0	0	0
: N Pacific American	0	0	0	0	0	0	0	0	0	0
: Tropical East Pacific	0	0	0	0	1	0	0	0	0	0
: South Pacific	0	0	0	0	0	0	0	0	0	0
: Antiboreal	0	0	0	0	0	0	0	0	0	0
: Atlantic Boreal	0	0	0	0	0	0	0	0	0	0
: Atlantic Warm Temp	0	0	0	0	0	0	0	1	0	0
: Tropical Indo-West-Pacif	0	0	1	1	0	1	0	0	0	0
: East Asia Boreal	0	0	0	0	0	0	0	0	0	0
: North Pacific, East Asia	0	0	0	0	0	0	0	0	0	0
: Indo-Australian	0	0	0	0	0	0	0	0	0	0
: Tropical Atlantic	1	1	0	0	1	0	0	0	0	1
Coral reef (1=yes)	1	0	1	1	1	1	0	0	0	1
Salinities	35	36	35	35	35	35	2	37	0	35
Ocean circulation	0	-1	0	0	0	0	0	0	0	0
Prevailing Wind: Polar	0	0	0	0	0	0	0	0	0	0
: Westerlies Zone	0	0	0	0	0	0	0	1	1	0
: Subtropical	0	1	0	0	1	0	0	0	0	0
: Monsoon Zone	0	0	0	0	0	0	0	0	0	0
: Trades Zone	1	0	1	1	0	1	0	0	0	1
: Intertropical	0	0	0	0	0	0	0	0	0	0
: Transition	0	0	0	0	0	0	0	0	0	0
No oceans (1=yes)	0	0	0	0	0	0	1	0	1	0
Fresh water (cub/kil)		0.7	0.4	0	54	0	0	1	0.6	

Characteristics	Morocco	Mozam-bique	Namibia	Nauru	Nepal	Nether-lands	Netherlands Antilles	New Caledonia	New Zealand	Nicaragua
Coastline: length (km)	1840	2470	1490	30	0	451	364	2250	15100	910
:length km/cap	68	155	950	2680	0	29	2020	12700	4310	200
Zones: Sea territory	12	12	6	12	0	12	12	12	12	200
:Continental shelf (m)	200	0	0	0	0	0	0	0	0	200
:Excl. fish (nm)	0	0	12	0	0	0	0	0	0	0
:Extend. econ. zone (nm)	200	200	200	200	0	200	0	200	200	200
:200-Mi EEZ, area	278000	562000	500000	431000	0	84700	0	1310000	4830000	160000
:Contiguous zone (nm)	24	0	0	0	0	12	0	0	0	0
Inland waterways (km)	0	3750	0	0	0	4610	0	0	1610	2220
Inland waterways/cap	0	0.2	0	0	0	0.3	0	0	0.5	0.5
Water area: (km sq)	250	17500	1000	0	4000	3370	0	300	10	924
:area/cap	0	0	0.6	0	0.2	0.2	0	0	5	2
Access: Number of ports	10	3	0	1	0	39	3	4	5	5
:Natural Harbour (1=yes)	0	0	0	0	0	0	0	0	1	0
:Number of outlets	0	0	0	0	1	0	0	0	0	0
:Island (1=yes)	0	0	0	1	0	0	1	1	0	0
:Landlocked (1=yes)	0	0	0	0	1	0	0	0	0	0
Ships: Number/cap	2	0	0	103	0	34	0	0	7	0
:tonnage (dwt)/cap	18	0	0	598	0	295	0	0	74	0
Offshore Reserves: oil/cap	0	0.9	0	0	0	0.1	0	0	0	0.2
:gas/cap	0	0.2	0.1	0	0	0.7	0	0	0	0.3
Fish supply kgrm/year/cap	0	0	16	0	0	4	102	125	2	0
Marine Biology: Arctic	0	0	0	0	0	0	0	0	0	0
:NW American Boreal	0	0	0	0	0	0	0	0	0	0
:N Pacific American	0	0	0	0	0	0	0	0	0	0
:Tropical East Pacific	0	0	0	0	0	0	0	0	0	1
:South Pacific	0	0	0	1	0	0	0	0	0	0
:Antiboreal	0	0	0	0	0	0	0	0	1	0
:Atlantic Boreal	0	0	0	0	0	1	0	0	0	0
:Atlantic Warm Temp	1	0	1	0	0	0	0	0	0	0
:Tropical Indo-West-Pacif	0	1	0	0	0	0	0	1	0	0
:East Asia Boreal	0	0	0	0	0	0	0	0	0	0
:North Pacific, East Asia	0	0	0	0	0	0	0	0	0	0
:Indo-Australian	0	0	0	0	0	0	0	0	0	0
:Tropical Atlantic	0	0	0	0	0	0	1	0	0	1
Coral reef (1=yes)	0	1	0	1	0	0	1	1	0	1
Salinities	36	35	35	35	0	34	36	35	34	33
Ocean circulation	-1	-1	-1	1	0	-1	-1	1	1	1
Prevailing Wind: Polar	0	0	0	0	0	0	0	0	0	0
:Westerlies Zone	0	0	1	0	0	1	0	0	1	0
:Subtropical	1	0	0	0	0	0	0	0	0	0
:Monsoon Zone	0	0	0	0	2	0	0	0	0	0
:Trades Zone	0	1	0	1	0	0	1	1	0	1
:Intertropical	1	0	0	0	0	0	0	0	0	0
:Transition	0	0	0	0	0	0	0	0	0	0
No oceans (1=yes)	0	0	0	0	1	0	0	0	0	0
Fresh water (cub/kil)	11	0.8	0.1		3	15			1	0.9

Characteristics	Niger	Nigeria	Niue	Norfolk Island	North Korea	Northern Mariana Isl.	Norway	Oman	Pacific Isl. Trust	Pakistan
Coastline: length (km)	0	853	64	32	2500	·	21900	2090	·	1050
: length km/cap	0	8	32200	12000	108	·	4630	1250	·	8
Zones: Sea territory	0	30	12	3	12	3	4	12	3	12
: Continental shelf (m)	0	200	0	200	200	200	200	200	200	200
: Excl. fish (nm)	0		0	200		200	200		200	0
: Extend. econ. zone (nm)	0	200	200	200	200	200	200		200	200
: 200-Mi EEZ, area	0	211000			130000		2030000	562000		319000
: Contiguous zone (nm)	0			12		12			12	24
Inland waterways (km)	300	8580	0	0	2250	0	1580	0	0	0
Inland waterways/cap	0	0.1	0	0	0.1	0	0.4	0	0	0
Water area: (km sq)	0	13000	0	0	130	0	16400	0	0	25200
: area/cap	0	0.1	0	0		0	4	0	0	0.2
Access: Number of ports	0	6	0	0	9	3	6	2	1	3
: Natural Harbour (1=yes)	·	0	·	·	0	0	0		0	0
: Number of outlets	2	0	0	0	0	0	0	5	0	0
: Island (1=yes)	0	0	1	0	0	1	0	0	1	0
: Landlocked (1=yes)	1	0	0	0	0	0	0	0	0	0
Ships: Number/cap	0	0.5	0	0	3	0	277	1	0	0.2
: tonnage (dwt)/cap	0	0.7	0	0	41	0	8460	25	0	4
Offshore Reserves: oil/cap	0	0.1	0	0	0	0	3	0	0	0
: gas/cap	0		0	0	0	0	24	0	0	0
Fish supply kgrm/year/cap	0		0	0	2	0	10	0	0	0
Marine Biology: Arctic	0	0	0	0	0	0	1	0	0	0
: NW American Boreal	0	0	0	0	0	0	0	0	0	0
: N Pacific, American	0	0	0	0	0	0	0	0	0	0
: Tropical East Pacific	0	0	0	0	0	0	0	0	0	0
: South Pacific	0	0	1	1	0	0	0	0	0	0
: Antiboreal	0	0	0	0	0	0	0	0	0	0
: Atlantic Boreal	0	0	0	0	0	0	1	0	0	0
: Atlantic Warm Temp	0	0	0	0	0	0	0	0	0	0
: Tropical Indo-West-Pacif	0	0	0	0	0	1	0	1	1	1
: East Asia Boreal	0	0	0	0	0	0	0	0	0	0
: North Pacific, East Asia	0	0	0	0	1	0	0	0	0	0
: Indo-Australian	0	0	0	0	0	0	0	0	0	0
: Tropical Atlantic	0	1	0	0	0	0	0	0	0	0
Coral reef (1=yes)	0	0	1	1	0	1	0	0	1	1
Salinities	2	33	35	35	32	35	34	37	34	37
Ocean circulation	0	0	0	0	-1	0	-1	1	0	1
Prevailing Wind: Polar	0	0	0	0	0	0	0	0	0	0
: Westerlies Zone	0	0	0	0	1	0	1	0	0	0
: Subtropical	0	0	0	1	0	0	0	0	0	0
: Monsoon Zone	0	0	0	0	0	0	0	1	0	1
: Trades Zone	0	0	1	0	0	1	0	0	1	0
: Intertropical	0	1	0	0	0	0	0	0	0	0
: Transition	0	0	0	0	0	0	0	0	0	0
No oceans (1=yes)	1	0	0	0	0	0	0	0	0	0
Fresh water (cub/kil)	0.3	4	0	0	0	0	2	0.4	0	153

Characteristics	Panama	Papua New Guinea	Paraguay	Peru	Philip-pines	Pitcairn Islands	Poland	Portugal	Puerto Rico	Qatar
Coastline: length (km)	2490	5150	0	2410	22500	51	491	1790	501	563
: length km/cap	974	1230	0	105	408	981000	13	150	0	1150
Zones: Sea territory	200	12	0	200	100	0	12	12	3	3
: Continental shelf (m)	0	200	0	200	0	200	0	200	200	0
: Excl. fish (nm)	0	0	0	0	0	0	0	0	200	0
: Extend. econ. zone (nm)		200	0	0	200	0	200	200	0	0
: 200-Mi EEZ, area	307000	2350000	0	787000	1890000	0	28500	1770000	0	24000
: Contiguous zone (nm)	0	0	0	0	0	0	0	0	12	0
Inland waterways (km)	800	10900	3100	8600	3220	0	4000	820	0	0
Inland waterways/cap	0.3	3	0.7	0.4	0	0	0.1	0.1	0	0
Water area: (km sq)	2210	9980	9450	5220	1830	0	8170	440	145	3
: area/cap	0.3	2	1	0.2		1	0.2		4	
Access: Number of ports	0	5	0	5	8		7	7	4	3
: Natural Harbour (1=yes)	0	0	1	0	0	1	0	0	1	0
: Number of outlets		0	0	0	0		0	0	0	0
: Island (1=yes)	0	0	1	0	1	1	0	0	1	0
: Landlocked (1=yes)	0	0	1	0	0	0	0	0	0	0
Ships: Number/cap	1490	9	3	2	13	0	7	7	0	47
: tonnage (dwt)/cap	31000	11	4	23	205		106	91	0	1210
Offshore Reserves: oil/cap			0	0.8	0.6		0.5			6
: gas/cap		5	0	0	0		0	0		457
Fish supply kgrm/year/cap	0	0	0	0	0	0	0	0	0	0
Marine Biology: Arctic	0	0	0	0	0	0	0	0	0	0
: NW American Boreal	0	0	0	0	0	0	0	0	0	0
: N Pacific_American	0	0	0	1	0	0	0	0	0	0
: Tropical East Pacific	1	0	0	1	0	1	0	0	0	0
: South Pacific	0	1	0	0	1	0	0	0	0	0
: Antiboreal	0	0	0	0	0	0	0	0	0	0
: Atlantic Boreal	0	0	0	0	0	0	0	0	0	0
: Atlantic Warm Temp	0	0	0	0	0	0	0	0	0	0
: Tropical Indo-West-Pacif	0	0	0	0	0	0	0	0	0	0
: East Asia Boreal	0	0	0	0	0	0	0	0	0	0
: North Pacific, East Asia	0	0	0	0	0	0	0	0	0	0
: Indo-Australian	0	1	0	0	1	0	0	0	0	0
: Tropical Atlantic	1	0	0	0	0	0	0	0	1	1
Coral reef (1=yes)	1	0	2	1	1	0	1	1	1	0
Salinities	32	35	0	35	34	35	34	35	36	38
Ocean circulation	0	0	0	-1	0	-1	-1	-1	0	-1
Prevailing Wind: Polar	0	0	0	0	0	0	0	0	0	0
: Westerlies Zone	0	0	1	0	0	0	1	1	0	0
: Subtropical	1	0	0	1	1	1	0	0	1	1
: Monsoon Zone	0	1	0	0	0	0	0	0	0	0
: Trades Zone	0	0	0	0	0	0	0	0	0	0
: Intertropical	0	0	0	0	0	0	0	0	0	0
: Transition	0	0	0	0	0	0	0	0	0	0
No oceans (1=yes)	0	0	1	0	0	1	0	0	1	1
Fresh water (cub/kil)	1	0.1	0.4	6	30		17	11	0	0

Characteristics	Reunion	Romania	Russia	Rwanda	San Marino	Sao Tome E Principe	Saudi Arabia	Senegal	Serbia & Monten.	Seychelles
Coastline: length (km)	201	225	37700	0	0	209	2510	531	.	491
: length km/cap	313	10	253	0	0	1650	152	67	.	6960
Zones: Sea territory	12	12	12	0	0	12	12	12	.	12
: Continental shelf (m)	200	200	200	0	0	0	0	200	.	200
: Excl. fish (nm)	200	200	200	0	0	200	0	200	.	200
: Extend. econ. zone (nm)	200									
: 200-Mi EEZ, area	0	31900	0	0	0	128000	1870000	206000	.	500000
: Contiguous zone (nm)	0	0	124000	0	0	0	18	24	0	0
Inland waterways (km)	0	1720	0.8	1390	0	0	0	899	0	0
Inland waterways/cap	10	0.1	79400	0.2	0	0	0	0.1	.	0
Water area: (km sq)	1	7160	0.5		0	0	0	4190	2	0
: area/cap	0	0.3	24		2	0	0	0.5	.	0
Access: Number of ports	1	0	0	2	0	2	7	4		1
: Natural Harbour (1=yes)	0	0	0	0	1	0	0	0	0	0
: Number of outlets	1	0	0	1	1	1	0	0	0	1
: Island (1=yes)	0	0	0	0	0	0	0	0	4	0
: Landlocked (1=yes)	1	0	0	0	0	0	0	0	142	1
Ships: Number/cap	.	11	11	0	0	16	7	0.8		0
: tonnage (dwt)/cap		177	94	0	0	10	76	0.2		0
Offshore Reserves: oil/cap	0	0	0	0	0	0	5	0	0	0
: gas/cap	0	0	1	0	0	0	4	0	0	0
Fish supply kgrm/year/cap	0	0	0	0	0	339	0	0	0	661
Marine Biology: Arctic	0	0	1	0	0	0	0	0	0	0
: NW American Boreal	0	0	0	0	0	0	0	0	0	0
: N Pacific, American	0	0	0	0	0	0	0	0	0	0
: Tropical East Pacific	0	0	0	0	0	0	0	0	0	0
: South Pacific	0	0	0	0	0	0	0	0	0	0
: Antiboreal	0	0	0	0	0	0	0	0	0	0
: Atlantic Boreal	0	0	1	0	0	0	0	0	0	0
: Atlantic Warm Temp	0	1	0	0	1	0	0	0	0	0
: Tropical Indo-West-Pacif	0	0	0	0	0	0	1	0	0	0
: East Asia Boreal	0	0	1	0	0	0	0	0	0	0
: North Pacific, East Asia	0	0	0	0	0	0	0	0	0	0
: Indo-Australian	0	0	0	0	0	0	0	0	0	0
: Tropical Atlantic	0	0	0	0	0	0	0	1	0	0
Coral reef (1=yes)	1	0	0	0	0	0	1	0	0	1
Salinities	35	39	32	2	39	33	41	36	39	35
Ocean circulation	0	1	-1	0	1	0	1	-1	1	1
Prevailing Wind: Polar	0	0	0	0	0	0	0	0	0	0
: Westerlies Zone	0	0	0	0	0	0	0	0	0	0
: Subtropical	0	0	0	0	0	0	0	0	0	0
: Monsoon Zone	0	0	1	0	0	0	0	0	0	0
: Trades Zone	1	1	1	0	1	1	1	1	1	1
: Intertropical	0	0	0	0	0	0	0	0	0	0
: Transition	0	0	0	0	0	0	0	0	0	0
No oceans (1=yes)	1	1	0	1	1	0	1	0	0	1
Fresh water (cub/kil)	0	25	.	0.2		0	4	1	1	0

Characteristics	Sierra Leone	Singapore	Slovakia	Slovenia	Solomon Islands	Somalia	South Africa	South Korea	Spain	Sri Lanka
Coastline: length (km)	402	193	45400	32	5310	3030	2880	2410	4960	1340
: length km/cap	89	67	8520	16	16000	318	73	54	127	75
Zones: Sea territory	200	3	0	12	12	200	12	12	12	12
: Continental shelf (m)	0	12	0	200	200	200	200	12		200
: Excl. fish (nm)	0	0					200		0	200
: Extend. econ. zone (nm)	0	0	0	0		0	200	12	200	200
: 200-Mi EEZ, area	156000	343	172	0	1570000	783000	1020000	348000	1220000	518000
: Contiguous zone (nm)	0	0	0	0	0	0	0			24
Inland waterways (km)	700	0	14100000	0	910	10300	0	1610	1050	215
Inland waterways/cap	0.2	0	2640	0	0	4	0	290		870
Water area: (km sq)	120	10	0	0	3	0	7	5	5350	2
: area/cap	0	1		0.1	2	0	0	14	0.1	1
Access: Number of ports	3		0	1	1	0	0	30	23	2
: Natural Harbour (1=yes)		1	0	0	6	0.5	0.2		8	24
: Number of outlets		0	0	0	2	1	0.5		102	
: Island (1=yes)	0	0	0	0	0	0	0	1	0	0
: Landlocked (1=yes)	0	0	0	0	0	0	0	0	0	0
Ships: Number/cap	0	210	0	0	0	0	0	0	0	0
: tonnage (dwt)/cap	0	5400	0	0	0	0	0	0	0	0
Offshore Reserves: oil/cap	0	12	0	0	200	0	0	0	0	0
: gas/cap	0	0	0	0	0	0	0	0	0	0
Fish supply kgrm/year/cap	0	0	0	0	0	0	0	0	0	0
Marine Biology: Arctic	0	0	0	0	0	0	0	0	0	0
: NW American Boreal	0	0	0	0	0	0	0	0	0	0
: N Pacific, American	0	0	0	0	0	0	0	0	0	0
: Tropical East Pacific	0	0	0	0	0	0	0	0	0	0
: South Pacific	0	0	0	0	0	0	0	0	0	0
: Antiboreal	0	0	0	0	0	0	0	0	0	0
: Atlantic Boreal	0	0	0	0	0	0	0	0	0	0
: Atlantic Warm Temp	0	0	0	1	0	0	1	0	1	0
: Tropical Indo-West-Pacif	0	1	0	0	1	1	0	0	0	1
: East Asia Boreal	0	0	0	0	0	0	0	0	0	0
: North Pacific, East Asia	0	0	0	0	0	0	0	1	0	0
: Indo-Australian	0	0	0	0	0	0	1	0	0	0
: Tropical Atlantic	1	0	0	0	0	0	0	0	0	0
Coral reef (1=yes)	0	0	0	0	1	0	0	0	0	0
Salinities	35	34	0	39	35	38	35	32	35	33
Ocean circulation	-1	-1	0	1	1	1	1	-1	-1	1
Prevailing Wind: Polar	0	0	0	0	0	0	0	0	0	0
: Westerlies Zone	0	0	0	0	0	0	1	1	1	0
: Subtropical	0	0	0	1	0	0	0	0	0	0
: Monsoon Zone	1	1	0	0	1	1	0	0	0	1
: Trades Zone	0	0	0	0	0	0	0	0	0	0
: Intertropical	0	0	0	0	0	1	1	0	0	0
: Transition	0	0	0	1	0	0	0	0	0	0
No oceans (1=yes)	0	0	0	0	0	0	0	0	0	0
Fresh water (cub/kil)	0.4	0.2		1		0.8	9	11	45	6

Characteristics	St. Helena	St. Kitts & Nevis	St. Lucia	St. Pierre & Miquelon	St. Vincent & Grenad.	Sudan	Suriname	Swaziland	Sweden	Switzerland
Coastline: length (km)	60	135	158	120	84	853	386	0	3220	0
: length km/cap	8150	2120	1070	19000	737	31	877	0	371	0
Zones: Sea territory	3	12	3	12	3	12	12	0	12	0
: Continental shelf (m)	0	0	12	200	7	200	0	0	200	0
: Excl. fish (nm)	0	200	0	200	12	0	200	0	200	0
: Extend. econ. zone (nm)										0
: 200-Mi EEZ, area		200		12		91600	101000		155000	0
: Contiguous zone (nm)		24				18				0
Inland waterways (km)						4070	5030		2050	1210
Inland waterways/cap						0.1	11		0.2	0
Water area: (km sq)						130000	1800	160	38300	1520
: area/cap			0.1			5	4	0.2	4	0.2
Access: Number of ports	2	2	1	1		2	2	0	7	0
: Natural Harbour (1=yes)										
: Number of outlets	1	2	1	0		0	0	1	0	4
: Island (1=yes)	1	1	1	1	1	0	0	0	0	0
: Landlocked (1=yes)	0	0	0	0	0	0	0	1	0	1
Ships: Number/cap		24	14				16		32	4
: tonnage (dwt)/cap		14	6				33		387	88
Offshore Reserves: oil/cap										
: gas/cap										
Fish supply kgrm/year/cap			121							
Marine Biology: Arctic										
: NW American Boreal										
: N Pacific American										
: Tropical East Pacific										
: South Pacific										
: Antiboreal										
: Atlantic Boreal										
: Atlantic Warm Temp										
: Tropical Indo-West-Pacif										
: East Asia Boreal										
: North Pacific, East Asia										
: Indo-Australian										
: Tropical Atlantic										
Coral reef (1=yes)	0	1	1	1	1	1	1	0	0	0
Salinities	36	35	35	34	35	40	35	0	35	
Ocean circulation	1	1	1	1	1	1	1	1	1	2
Prevailing Wind: Polar										
: Westerlies Zone				1					1	1
: Subtropical								1		
: Monsoon Zone										
: Trades Zone	1	1	1		1	1	1			
: Intertropical										
: Transition										
No oceans (1=yes)								1		1
Fresh water (cub/kil)		0	0			19			4	3

Characteristics	Syrian Arab Rep.	Taiwan	Tajikistan	Tanzania	Thailand	Togo	Tokelau	Tonga	Trinidad & Tobago	Tunisia
Coastline: length (km)	193	1450	0	1420	3220	56	101	419	362	1150
: length km/cap	14	46	0	49	57	14	65400	4360	279	144
Zones: Sea territory (m)	35	12	0	50	12	30	12	200	12	12
: Continental shelf (m)	200	200	0	0	200	0	0	0	200	0
: Excl. fish (nm)	0	0	0	0	0	0	0	0	200	0
: Extend. econ. zone (nm)	0	0	0	0	0	200	200	200	200	0
: 200-Mi EEZ, area	10300	200	0	223000	325000	1030	0	0	76800	85800
: Contiguous zone (nm)	0	0	0	0	0	0	0	0	0	0
Inland waterways (km)	672	0	200	0	3850	25	0	0	0	0
Inland waterways/cap	0	0	0	0	0.1	0	0	0	0	0
Water area: (km sq)	1130	3720	400	59100	2230	2400	0	30	0	8250
: area/cap	0.1	0.2	0.1	0	0	0.6	0	0.3	0	0
Access: Number of ports	3	1	0	6	5	2	1	3	3	7
: Natural Harbour (1=yes)	0	0	0	0	0	0	0	0	0	7
: Number of outlets	0	1	1	0	0	0	0	1	1	0
: Island (1=yes)	0	0	0	0	0	0	0	0	0	0
: Landlocked (1=yes)	0	0	1	0	0	0	0	0	0	0
Ships: Number/cap	7	11	0	0.5	0.5	5	0	83	8	3
: tonnage (dwt)/cap	17	429	0	0.2	23	5	0	138	9	27
Offshore Reserves: oil/cap	0	0.1	0	0.1	0.1	0	0	0	0.8	0
: gas/cap	0	0	0	0	0.4	0	0	0	0	0
Fish supply kgrm/year/cap	0	0	0	0	0	0	200	234	0	0
Marine Biology: Arctic	0	0	0	0	0	0	0	0	0	0
: NW American Boreal	0	0	0	0	0	0	0	0	0	0
: N Pacific American	0	0	0	0	0	0	0	0	0	0
: Tropical East Pacific	0	0	0	0	0	0	0	0	0	0
: South Pacific	0	0	0	0	0	0	1	1	0	0
: Antiboreal	0	0	0	0	0	0	0	0	0	0
: Atlantic Boreal	0	0	0	0	0	0	0	0	0	0
: Atlantic Warm Temp	1	0	0	0	0	0	0	0	0	1
: Tropical Indo-West-Pacif	0	0	0	1	1	0	0	0	0	0
: East Asia Boreal	0	1	0	0	0	0	0	0	0	0
: North Pacific, East Asia	0	0	0	0	0	0	0	0	0	0
: Indo-Australian	0	0	0	0	0	0	0	0	0	0
: Tropical Atlantic	0	0	0	0	0	1	0	0	1	0
Coral reef (1=yes)	0	0	0	1	1	1	1	1	1	0
Salinities	40	34	2	35	31	35	35	35	35	37
Ocean circulation	1	0	0	1	1	1	1	1	1	1
Prevailing Wind: Polar	0	0	0	0	0	0	0	0	0	0
: Westerlies Zone	0	0	1	0	0	0	0	0	0	0
: Subtropical	1	1	0	0	0	0	0	0	0	1
: Monsoon Zone	0	0	0	0	1	0	0	0	0	0
: Trades Zone	0	0	0	1	1	1	1	1	1	0
: Intertropical	0	0	0	0	0	0	0	0	0	0
: Transition	0	0	0	0	0	0	0	0	0	0
No oceans (1=yes)	0	0	1	0	0	0	0	0	0	1
Fresh water (cub/kil)	3	.	.	0.5	32	0.1		.	0.2	2

Characteristics	Turkey	Turkme-nistan	Turks & Caicos	Tuvalu	Uganda	Ukraine	United Arab Emir.	United Kingdom	United States	Uruguay
Coastline: length (km)	7200	0	300	24	0	2780	1450	12400	19900	660
; length km/cap	121	0	22100	2170	0	53	794	215	77	211
Zones: Sea territory	6	0	3	12	0		3	3	3	200
:: Continental shelf (m)	0	0	0	0	0		0	200	200	200
:: Excl. fish (nm)		0	200	200	0		0	200	200	0
:: Extend. econ. zone (nm)	200	0	200	200	0		200	200	200	0
:: 200-Mi EEZ, area	237000	0	0	725000	0	0	59300	943000	7620000	119000
:: Contiguous zone (nm)	0	0	0	0	0	0	0	0	12	0
Inland waterways (km)	1200	0	0	0	36300	4400	0	2750	41000	1430
Inland waterways/cap	0	0	0	0	2	0.1	0	0	0.2	0.5
Water area: (km sq)	9820	0	0	0	0	0	0	3230	206000	2600
:: area/cap	0.2	0	0	0	0	0	0	0.1	28	0.2
Access: Number of ports	4	0	4	2	0	9	7	7	8	5
:: Natural Harbour (1=yes)	0	1	0	0	0	0	0	0	0	0
:: Number of outlets	0	0	0	0	1	0	0	0	0	0
:: Island (1=yes)	0	0	1	1	0	0	0	1	0	0
:: Landlocked (1=yes)	0	1	0	0	1	0	0	0	0	0
Ships: Number/cap	2	0	0	452	0.1	0.1	50	114	87	48
:: tonnage (dwt)/cap	12	0	0	1430	0.3	0	691	0.7	0.3	0
Offshore Reserves: oil/cap	115	0	0	0	0	0	4	0.2	0.1	0
:: gas/cap	0	0	0	0	0	0	12	0.3	0	0
Fish supply kgrm/year/cap	0	0	0	0	0	0	16	0	0	0
Marine Biology: Arctic	0	0	0	0	0	0	0	0	0	0
:: NW American Boreal	0	0	0	0	0	0	0	0	0	0
:: N Pacific, American	0	0	0	0	0	0	0	0	0	0
:: Tropical East Pacific	0	0	0	0	0	0	0	0	0	0
:: South Pacific	0	0	0	0	0	0	0	0	0	0
:: Antiboreal	0	0	0	0	0	0	0	0	0	0
:: Atlantic Boreal	0	0	0	0	0	0	0	0	0	0
:: Atlantic Warm Temp	0	0	0	0	0	0	0	0	0	0
:: Tropical Indo-West-Pacif	0	0	1	1	0	0	1	0	0	0
:: East Asia Boreal	0	0	0	0	0	0	0	0	0	0
:: North Pacific, East Asia	0	0	0	0	0	0	0	0	0	0
:: Indo-Australian	0	0	0	0	0	0	0	0	0	0
:: Tropical Atlantic	0	0	0	0	0	0	0	0	0	0
Coral reef (1=yes)	0	0	1	1	0	0	1	0	1	0
Salinities	39	40	34	35	2	40	38	35	35	35
Ocean circulation	0	1	0	1	0	1	1	1	1	1
Prevailing Wind: Polar	1	0	0	0	0	1	0	0	0	0
:: Westerlies Zone	0	1	0	0	0	0	0	1	1	1
:: Subtropical	0	0	0	0	0	0	1	0	0	0
:: Monsoon Zone	0	0	0	0	2	0	0	0	0	0
:: Trades Zone	0	0	0	0	0	0	0	0	0	0
:: Intertropical	1	0	1	1	0	0	0	0	1	0
:: Transition	0	0	0	0	0	0	0	0	0	0
No oceans (1=yes)	1	1	0	0	0	1	0	0	0	1
Fresh water (cub/kil)	16	1	.	.	0.2	1	0.9	28	467	0.6

Characteristics	Uzbekistan	Vanuatu	Vatican City	Venezuela	Vietnam	Virgin Isl., US	Wallis & Futuna	West Bank	Western Samoa	Western Sahara
Coastline: length (km)	0	2530	0	2800	3440	0	129	0	403	1110
: length km/cap	0	15400	0	136	49	0	9160	0	1830	5370
Zones: Sea territory	0	12	0	12	12	3	12	0	12	0
: Continental shelf (m)	0	200	0	200	200	200	200	0	0	0
: Excl. fish (nm)	0	0	0	200	200	200	0	0	200	0
: Extend. econ. zone (nm)	0	200	0	200	200		200	0		0
: 200-Mi EEZ, area	0	617000	0	364000	723000		0	0	96000	0
: Contiguous zone (nm)	0	24	0	15	24	12		0		0
Inland waterways (km)	1100	0	0	7100	17700					
Inland waterways/cap	0.1			0.3	0.3					
Water area: (km sq)	22000	0	0	30000	4200			220		2
: area/cap	0	0	0		0.1			0.2		
Access: Number of ports	0	4	0	6		3	2	0	10	2
: Natural Harbour (1=yes)	0	0	0	0	0	0	0	0	0	0
: Number of outlets	0	0	2	0	0	6	0	0		0
: Island (1=yes)	0	1	0	0	0	1	1	0	1	0
: Landlocked (1=yes)	1	0	1	0	0	0	0	0	0	0
Ships: Number/cap	0	726	0	4	0	0	0	0	14	0
: tonnage (dwt)/cap	0	18000	0	59	0	0	0	0	26	0
Offshore Reserves: oil/cap	0	0	0	0.6	0	0	0	0	0	0
: gas/cap	0	0	0	0.2	0	0	0	0	0	0
Fish supply kgrm/year/cap	0	190	0					0	266	0
Marine Biology: Arctic	0	0	0	0	0	0	0	0	0	0
: NW American Boreal	0	0	0	0	0	0	0	0	0	0
: N Pacific, American	0	0	0	0	0	0	0	0	0	0
: Tropical East Pacific	0	0	0	0	0	0	0	0	0	0
: South Pacific	0	1	0	0	0	0	1	0	1	0
: Antiboreal	0	0	0	0	0	0	0	0	0	0
: Atlantic Boreal	0	0	0	0	0	0	0	0	0	0
: Atlantic Warm Temp	0	0	0	0	0	0	0	0	0	1
: Tropical Indo-West-Pacif	0	0	0	0	1	0	0	0	0	0
: East Asia Boreal	0	0	0	0	0	0	0	0	0	0
: North Pacific, East Asia	0	0	0	0	0	0	0	0	0	0
: Indo-Australian	0	0	0	0	0	0	0	0	0	0
: Tropical Atlantic	0	0	0	1	0	1	0	0	0	0
Coral reef (1=yes)	0	1	0	0	1	1	1	0	1	0
Salinities	40	35	38	35	33	36	35	39	35	36
Ocean circulation	1	1	1	1	-1	1	1	1	1	-1
Prevailing Wind: Polar	0	0	0	0	0	0	0	0	0	0
: Westerlies Zone	0	0	1	0	0	0	0	0	0	0
: Subtropical	0	0	0	0	0	0	0	1	0	0
: Monsoon Zone	0	0	0	0	1	0	0	0	0	0
: Trades Zone	0	1	0	1	0	1	1	0	1	1
: Intertropical	1	0	0	0	0	0	0	0	0	0
: Transition	0	0	0	0	0	0	0	0	0	0
No oceans (1=yes)	1	0	1	0	0	0	0	1	0	0
Fresh water (cub/kil)	1		0	4	5	0	0	1	0	0

Characteristics	Yemen	Zaire	Zambia	Zimbabwe
Coastline: length (km)	523	37	0	0
: length km/cap	40	0.9	0	0
Zones: Sea territory	12	12	0	0
: Continental shelf (m)	200	0	0	0
: Excl. fish (nm)	0	200	0	0
: Extend. econ. zone (nm)	0	0	0	0
: 200-Mi EEZ, area	0	1030	0	0
Contiguous zone (nm)	18	0	0	0
Inland waterways (km)	0	15100	2250	0
Inland waterways/cap	0	0.4	0.3	0
Water area: (km sq)	0	77800	11900	391
: area/cap	0	0	1	0.4
Access: Number of ports	7	2	0	0
: Natural Harbour (1=yes)	0	3	0	0
: Number of outlets	0	0	0	2
: Island (1=yes)	0	0	0	0
: Landlocked (1=yes)	0	0	1	1
Ships: Number/cap	0.5	0	0	0
: tonnage (dwt)/cap	0.7	0.4	0	0
Offshore Reserves: oil/cap	0	0	0	0
: gas/cap	0	0	0	0
Fish supply kgrm/year/cap	0	0	0	0
Marine Biology: Arctic	0	0	0	0
: NW American Boreal	0	0	0	0
: N Pacific, American	0	0	0	0
: Tropical East Pacific	0	0	0	0
: South Pacific	0	0	0	0
: Antiboreal	0	0	0	0
: Atlantic Boreal	0	0	0	0
: Atlantic Warm Temp	0	0	0	0
: Tropical Indo-West-Pacif	0	0	0	0
: East Asia Boreal	0	0	0	0
: North Pacific, East Asia	0	0	0	0
: Indo-Australian	0	0	0	0
: Tropical Atlantic	0	1	0	0
Coral reef (1=yes)	0	0	0	0
Salinities	0	33	2	2
Ocean circulation	0	0	0	0
Prevailing Wind: Polar	0	0	0	0
: Westerlies Zone	0	0	0	0
: Subtropical	0	0	0	0
: Monsoon Zone	0	0	0	0
: Trades Zone	0	0	0	0
: Intertropical	0	1	1	1
: Transition	0	0	0	0
No oceans (1=yes)	0	0	1	0
Fresh water (cub/kil)	2	0.7	0.4	1

9

CLIMATIC RESOURCES ACROSS COUNTRIES

Many of the authors cited in Chapter 1 have noted the effects of climate on various national cultures. This chapter provides comparative statistics for a variety of climatic variables across national cultures. For a full discussion of the methodology used to generate these estimates, please refer to Chapter 1 which gives important caveats. This chapter first gives summary statistics of the variables reported: the number of countries for which each variable was available, weighted averages (by population) and simple averages; these averages can be used as benchmarks. Then a lengthy comparative table is presented which provides raw statistics across countries.

Most of the variables are self explanatory, though some merit commentary. All of the statistics should be considered as estimates which have undergone rounding and certain adjustments. Meteorological estimates are averages recorded over a 30-year or similar period. For example, "Temp monthly high (min C)" records the lowest level of monthly high temperatures, in Celsius; "Temp monthly high (max C)" measures the highest recorded level of monthly high temperatures. Some of the variables represent interactions. For example, the variable "High temp @ max humidity" is the estimate for the highest temperature during the month when average afternoon humidity is at its highest (a proxy for physiological heat/humidity stress). Similarly, the variable "High humid @ max temp" estimates the maximum humidity level during the month having the highest temperature. Other variables measure the extent to which certain climatic events (e.g. snowfall) are likely to occur where a culture resides. "Flooding risk (10=high)" and other risk variables estimate whether these are a common occurrence. Finally, climatic types are given across groups based on Trewartha's modification of Koppen's classification scheme. A given country can be exposed to more than one climatic type.

Summary Statistics:
Climatic Resources

Characteristics	Number of Countries Covered	Weighted Average by Pop 1994	Simple Average	Simple Standard Deviation
Latitude (absolute degrees)	234	28.59	25.27	16.62
Temperature: degrees (C)	234	17.46	19.96	7.86
: monthly high (minimum C)	234	22.10	25.23	8.76
: monthly high (maximum C)	234	40.81	37.45	4.93
: monthly low (minimum C)	234	-8.06	0.78	16.23
: monthly low (maximum C)	234	15.57	15.23	6.63
Humidity: morning minimum (%)	234	57.74	69.42	14.37
: morning maximum (%)	234	82.09	85.25	7.15
: afternoon minimum (%)	234	42.46	53.92	16.35
: afternoon maximum (%)	234	70.52	74.24	9.29
High temperature @ maximum humidity	234	23.60	20.97	11.37
High humidity @ maximum temperature	234	52.08	59.27	16.92
Rain: monthly minimum (mm)	234	17.07	33.09	38.22
: monthly maximum (mm)	234	201.71	199.98	162.91
: days/month minimum	234	3.33	4.87	4.49
: days/month maximum	234	13.47	15.22	6.08
Snow: persistent (1=yes)	234	0.44	0.19	0.39
: intermittent (1=yes)	234	0.50	0.28	0.45
Frost present (1=yes)	234	0.61	0.51	0.50
Evaporation (1=low)	234	0.35	-0.16	0.91
Barometric pressure: July	234	1008.19	1012.18	4.70
: January	234	1018.27	1014.91	4.51
Risks: Typhoon (10=high)	234	2.54	0.90	2.86
: Flooding (10=high)	234	5.53	1.32	3.40
: Tropical storm (10=high)	234	0.09	1.11	3.15
: Windstorm (10=high)	234	2.10	1.15	3.20
: Drought (10=high)	234	3.03	1.03	3.04
Climate Type: Tropical wet	234	0.08	0.21	0.41
: Tropical monsoon	234	0.21	0.14	0.35
: Tropical wet & dry	234	0.38	0.22	0.41
: Steppe, low latitude	234	0.35	0.15	0.35
: Desert, low latitude	234	0.17	0.15	0.36
: Steppe, middle latitude	234	0.30	0.04	0.20
: Desert, middle latitude	234	0.25	0.02	0.13
: Subtropical, humid	234	0.52	0.08	0.27
: Mediterranean	234	0.05	0.10	0.30
: Marine, west coast	234	0.10	0.11	0.31
: Continental humid hot summer	234	0.33	0.04	0.20
: Continental humid cool summer	234	0.35	0.07	0.26
: Subarctic	234	0.03	0.02	0.13
: Tundra	234	0.03	0.02	0.13
: Ice cap	234	0.00	0.00	0.07
: Dry steppe wasteland	234	0.03	0.03	0.16
: Temperate highland	234	0.04	0.01	0.09
: Temperature desert dry summer	234	0.00	0.01	0.11
: Temperature desert dry winter	234	0.01	0.01	0.09
: Highland	234	0.40	0.09	0.29

Characteristics	Afghan-istan	Albania	Algeria	American Samoa	Andorra	Angola	Anguilla	Antigua & Barbuda	Argentina	Armenia
Latitude (abs degrees)	33	41	36	14	42	8	18	17	39	40
Temperature: degrees (C)	10	16	21	27	9	26	26	27	17	8
: monthly high (min C)	14	19	24	32	13	28	28	32	25	12
: monthly high (max C)	40	40	42	34	36	37	37	37	40	40
: monthly low (min C)	-21	-8	0	17	-18	14	15	15	-6	-27
: monthly low (max C)	-11	-1	1	21	-5	21	21	21	6	-10
Humidity: morning min (%)	51	72	67	75	78	77	62	62	81	62
: morning max (%)	80	86	75	82	87	84	70	70	92	91
: afternoon min (%)	22	39	57	73	55	74	59	59	60	36
: afternoon max (%)	70	63	66	79	79	78	68	68	79	75
High temp @ max humidity	2	17	15	30	11	28	29	29	14	3
High humidity @ max temp	23	42	60	79	48	77	61	61	61	36
Rain: monthly min (mm)	0			81	34		61	61	56	8
: monthly max (mm)	102	211	137	455	105	117	196	196	109	53
: days/month min	0.1	4	0.4	7	4	0	8	8	6	2
: days/month max	0.7	16	12	22	15	8	16	16	9	1
Snow: persistent (1=yes)					1					
: intermittent (1=yes)	1	1			1				1	1
Frost present (1=yes)	1	1			1				1	1
Evaporation (1=low)	1				-1	-1	-1	-1	-1	
Barometric pressure: July	999	1010	1010	1010	1020	1020	1020	1010	1010	1010
: January	1020	1020	1020	1010	1020	1010	1020	1020	1000	1020
Risks: Typhoon (10=high)	0	0	0	0	0	0	0	0	0	0
: Flooding (10=high)	0	0	0	0	0	0	0	0	0	0
: Tropical storm (10=high)	0	0	0	1	0	0	1	1	0	0
: Windstorm (10=high)	0	0	0	0	0	0	0	0	0	0
: Drought (10=high)	1	0	1	0	0	1	0	0	0	0
Climate Type: Tropical wet	0	0	0	1	0	0	0	0	0	0
: Tropical monsoon	0	0	0	0	0	0	0	0	0	0
: Tropical wet & dry	0	0	0	0	0	0	1	1	0	0
: Steppe, low latitude	0	0	0	0	0	1	0	0	0	0
: Desert, low latitude	0	0	0	0	0	0	0	0	0	0
: Steppe, middle latitude	1	0	0	0	0	0	0	0	0	0
: Desert, middle latitude	0	0	0	0	0	0	0	0	0	0
: Subtropical, humid	0	0	0	0	0	0	0	0	1	0
: Mediterranean	0	1	1	0	0	0	0	0	0	0
: Marine, west coast	0	0	0	0	0	0	0	0	0	0
: Cont humid hot summer	0	0	0	0	0	0	0	0	0	0
: Cont humid cool summer	0	0	0	0	0	0	0	0	0	0
: Subarctic	0	0	0	0	0	0	0	0	0	0
: Tundra	0	0	0	0	0	0	0	0	0	0
: Ice cap	0	0	0	0	0	0	0	0	0	0
: Dry steppe wasteland	0	0	0	0	0	0	0	0	0	0
: Temperate highland	0	0	0	0	1	0	0	0	0	0
: Temp desert dry summer	0	0	0	0	0	0	0	0	0	0
: Temp desert dry winterte	0	0	0	0	0	0	0	0	0	0
: Highland	0	0	0	0	0	0	0	0	0	1

Characteristics	Aruba	Australia	Austria	Azerbaijan	Bahamas	Bahrain	Bangla-desh	Barbados	Belarus	Belgium
Latitude (abs degrees)	12	28	47	40	25	26	23	13	54	51
Temperature: degrees (C)	29	17	8	14	25	25	25	26	4	10
: monthly high (min C)	31	18	13	12	29	29	29	31	2	13
: monthly high (max C)	36	43	38	40	34	45	42	33	32	37
: monthly low (min C)	17	-10	-23	-27	5	5	7	16	-32	-17
: monthly low (max C)	22	3	9	10	19	24	24	21	5	6
Humidity: morning min (%)	76	56	72	62	79	69	37	67	58	87
: morning max (%)	79	85	86	91	84	85	74	79	87	94
: afternoon min (%)	66	35	49	36	62	63	37	64	43	65
: afternoon max (%)	72	64	76	75	73	77	74	78	83	86
High temp @ max humidity	30	12	3	3	31	22	31	29	-5	6
High humidity @ max temp	67	39	54	36	70	65	42	73	54	68
Rain: monthly min (mm)	20	41	39	8	33	0	16	28	36	53
: monthly max (mm)	112	56	84	53	175	18	437	206	88	95
: days/month min	4	7	10	2	5	0	1	7	12	13
: days/month max	16	11	15	11	15	2	16	18	23	21
Snow: persistent (1=yes)	0	0	1	0	0	0	0	0	0	0
: intermittent (1=yes)	0	1	1	1	0	0	0	0	1	1
Frost present (1=yes)	0	1	1	1	0	0	0	0	1	1
Evaporation (1=low)	-1	1	-1	-1	1	-1	-1	-1	-1	1
Barometric pressure: July	1010	1020	1010	1010	1020	999	1000	1020	1010	1020
: January	1010	1010	1020	1020	1020	1020	1020	1020	1020	1010
Risks: Typhoon (10=high)	0	0	0	0	0	0	0	0	0	0
: Flooding (10=high)	0	0	0	0	0	0	0	0	0	0
: Tropical storm (10=high)	0	0	0	0	0	0	0	0	0	0
: Windstorm (10=high)	1	1	0	0	1	0	0	1	0	0
: Drought (10=high)	0	1	0	1	0	1	1	0	0	0
Climate Type: Tropical wet	0	0	0	0	0	0	0	0	0	0
: Tropical monsoon	0	0	0	0	0	0	1	0	0	0
: Tropical wet & dry	0	0	0	0	1	0	0	1	0	0
: Steppe, low latitude	1	0	0	0	0	0	0	0	0	0
: Desert, low latitude	0	1	0	0	0	1	0	0	0	0
: Steppe, middle latitude	0	0	0	0	0	0	0	0	0	0
: Desert, middle latitude	0	0	0	0	0	0	0	0	0	0
: Subtropical, humid	0	0	0	0	0	0	0	0	0	0
: Mediterranean	0	0	0	0	0	0	0	0	0	0
: Marine, west coast	0	0	1	0	0	0	0	0	0	1
: Cont humid hot summer	0	0	0	0	0	0	0	0	0	0
: Cont humid cool summer	0	0	0	0	0	0	0	0	1	0
: Subarctic	0	0	0	0	0	0	0	0	0	0
: Tundra	0	0	0	0	0	0	0	0	0	0
: Ice cap	0	0	0	0	0	0	0	0	0	0
: Dry steppe wasteland	0	0	0	0	0	0	0	0	0	0
: Temperate highland	0	0	0	0	0	0	0	0	0	0
: Temp desert dry summer	0	0	0	0	0	0	0	0	0	0
: Temp desert dry winter	0	0	0	0	0	0	0	0	0	0
: Highland	0	0	0	1	0	0	0	0	0	0

Characteristics	Belize	Benin	Bermuda	Bhutan	Bolivia	Bosnia & Herzegov.	Botswana	Brazil	British Virgin Isl.	Brunei
Latitude (abs degrees)	17	6	32	27	18	45	24	16	18	5
Temperature: degrees (C)	26	27	22	17	12	10	20	25	26	27
: monthly high (min C)	32	31	27	24	21	20	31	32	32	29
: monthly high (max C)	36	35	37	36	27	41	42	39	37	33
: monthly low (min C)	9	18	4	-2	-3	-22	-4	10	15	16
: monthly low (max C)	18	22	17	18	2	7	10	18	21	22
Humidity: morning min (%)	90	83	76	68	77	70	55	87	62	84
: morning max (%)	94	91	82	90	93	93	74	87	70	90
: afternoon min (%)	86	68	69	53	49	40	55	68	59	70
: afternoon max (%)	91	78	75	84	74	77	74	74	68	76
High temp @ max humidity	28	26	24	28	30	7	29	28	29	29
High humidity @ max temp	87	74	64	61	61	42	63	71	61	72
Rain: monthly min (mm)	56	13	104	3	8	33	107	41	86	132
: monthly max (mm)	305	366	147	373	114	87	0.1	137	196	231
: days/month min	4	1	9	0.2	2	8	8	14	8	9
: days/month max	16	13	15	21	21	14	0	0	16	15
Snow: persistent (1=yes)	0	0	0	1	0	0	0	0	0	0
: intermittent (1=yes)	0	0	0	1	1	1	0	0	0	0
Frost present (1=yes)	0	0	0	1	1	1	1	0	0	0
Evaporation (1=low)	-1	0	-1	0	0	-1	-1	0	-1	-1
Barometric pressure: July	1010	1010	1020	1000	1020	1010	1020	1020	1020	1010
: January	1020	1010	1020	1020	1010	1020	1010	1010	1020	1010
Risks: Typhoon (10=high)	10	0	0	0	0	0	0	0	0	0
: Flooding (10=high)	10	0	0	0	0	0	0	10	10	0
: Tropical storm (10=high)	10	0	1	0	0	0	0	0	0	0
: Windstorm (10=high)	0	10	0	0	0	0	10	0	0	0
: Drought (10=high)	0	0	0	1	1	1	1	0	0	1
Climate Type: Tropical wet	0	0	0	0	0	0	0	0	0	0
: Tropical monsoon	0	1	0	0	1	0	0	1	1	0
: Tropical wet & dry	1	1	0	0	0	0	0	1	0	0
: Steppe, low latitude	0	0	0	0	0	0	1	0	0	0
: Desert, low latitude	0	0	0	0	0	0	0	0	0	0
: Steppe, middle latitude	0	0	0	0	0	0	0	0	0	0
: Desert, middle latitude	0	0	0	0	0	0	0	0	0	0
: Subtropical, humid	0	0	1	0	0	0	0	1	0	0
: Mediterranean	0	0	0	0	0	0	0	0	0	0
: Marine, west coast	0	0	0	0	0	0	0	0	0	0
: Cont humid hot summer	0	0	0	0	0	1	0	0	0	0
: Cont humid cool summer	0	0	0	0	0	0	0	0	0	0
: Subarctic	0	0	0	0	0	0	0	0	0	0
: Tundra	0	0	0	0	0	0	0	0	0	0
: Ice cap	0	0	0	0	0	0	0	0	0	0
: Dry steppe wasteland	0	0	0	0	0	0	0	0	0	0
: Temperate highland	0	0	0	0	0	0	0	0	0	0
: Temp desert dry summer	0	0	0	0	0	0	0	0	0	0
: Temp desert dry winter	0	0	0	0	0	0	0	0	0	0
: Highland	0	0	0	0	1	0	0	0	0	1

Characteristics	Bulgaria	Burkina Faso	Burma	Burundi	Cambodia	Cameroon	Canada	Cape Verde	Cayman Islands	Central Afric. Rep.
Latitude (abs degrees)	43	12	19	16	11	4	53	15	19	4
Temperature: degrees (C)	9	29	28	24	28	25	4	25	26	27
:monthly high (min C)	16	38	28	28	28	31	12	30	33	34
:monthly high (max C)	37	48	41	31	34	36	39	34	36	38
:monthly low (min C)	-21	9	13	17	14	14	-37	13	14	14
:monthly low (max C)	8	19	22	20	22	17	7	22	20	18
Humidity: morning min (%)	71	38	71	55	71	97	76	58	77	90
:morning max (%)	90	81	89	82	85	98	90	74	88	96
:afternoon min (%)	46	19	52	55	71	62	40	54	61	49
:afternoon max (%)	78	67	88	82	85	75	76	73	73	72
High temp @ max humidity	46	31	29	28	31	27	-6	29	31	29
High humidity @ max temp	28	20	64	59	73	67	53	73	70	49
Rain: monthly min (mm)		0	3		7	23	56	0	15	5
:monthly max (mm)	87	277	582	125	257	295	89	114	180	226
:days/month min	7	0	0	5	1	3	14	0	2	2
:days/month max	13	14	26	19	19	24		8	9	19
Snow: persistent (1=yes)	0	0	0	0	0	0	1	0	0	0
:intermittent (1=yes)	1	0	0	0	0	0	1	0	0	0
Frost present (1=yes)	1	0	0	0	0	0	1	0	0	0
Evaporation (1=low)	1	0	1	1	1	1	1	1	1	1
Barometric pressure: July	1010	1010	1010	1010	1010	1010	1010	1010	1010	1010
:January	1020	1010	1020	1010	1010	1010	1020	1010	1020	1010
Risks: Typhoon (10=high)	0	0	0	0	0	0	0	0	0	0
:Flooding (10=high)	0	0	0	0	0	0	0	0	0	0
:Tropical storm (10=high)	0	0	0	0	0	0	0	0	0	0
:Windstorm (10=high)	0	0	0	0	0	0	0	0	0	0
:Drought (10=high)	0	0	0	0	0	0	0	0	0	0
Climate Type: Tropical wet	0	0	0	0	0	1	0	0	0	0
:Tropical monsoon	0	0	1	0	1	0	0	0	0	0
:Tropical wet & dry	0	0	0	1	0	0	0	0	1	1
:Steppe, low latitude	0	1	0	0	0	0	0	1	0	0
:Desert, low latitude	0	0	0	0	0	0	0	0	0	0
:Steppe, middle latitude	0	0	0	0	0	0	1	0	0	0
:Desert, middle latitude	0	0	0	0	0	0	0	0	0	0
:Subtropical, humid	0	0	0	0	0	0	0	0	0	0
:Mediterranean	0	0	0	0	0	0	0	0	0	0
:Marine, west coast	0	0	0	0	0	0	1	0	0	0
:Cont humid hot summer	1	0	0	0	0	0	0	0	0	0
:Cont humid cool summer	0	0	0	0	0	0	1	0	0	0
:Subarctic	0	0	0	0	0	0	1	0	0	0
:Tundra	0	0	0	0	0	0	1	0	0	0
:Ice cap	0	0	0	0	0	0	0	0	0	0
:Dry steppe wasteland	0	0	0	0	0	0	0	0	0	0
:Temperate highland	0	0	0	0	0	0	0	0	0	0
:Temp desert dry summer	0	0	0	0	0	0	0	0	0	0
:Temp desert dry winter	0	0	0	0	0	0	0	0	0	0
:Highland	0	0	0	0	0	0	1	0	0	0

Characteristics	Chad	Chile	China	Christmas Island	Cocos (Keel.) Isl.	Colombia	Comoros	Congo	Cook Island	Costa Rica
Latitude (abs degrees)	12	36	35	10	11	6	11	4	15	10
Temperature: degrees (C)	28	17	11	27	26	14	26	25	26	21
: monthly high (min C)	36	27	13	34	32	22	30	32	32	29
: monthly high (max C)	46	37	43	35	34	24	33	37	34	33
: monthly low (min C)	8	-4	-23	19	17	4	19	12	17	9
: monthly low (max C)	19	6	15	21	21	7	22	19	21	14
Humidity: morning min (%)	32	70	46	68	75	82	74	77	75	80
: morning max (%)	93	93	74	75	82	88	79	89	82	92
: afternoon min (%)	10	38	46	68	73	51	74	54	73	55
: afternoon max (%)	72	64	74	74	79	64	78	71	79	78
High temp @ max humidity	31	14	30	31	30	19	28	31	30	25
High humidity @ max temp	13	40	72	73	79	53	74	65	79	70
Rain: monthly min (mm)	0	3	2	94	81	51	69	0	81	5
: monthly max (mm)	320	84	243	315	455	160	386	292	455	305
: days/month min	0	0	2	1	0	2	7	0	2	1
: days/month max	22	6	13	15	22	20	15	9	22	25
Snow: persistent (1=yes)	0	0	1	0	0	0	0	0	0	0
: intermittent (1=yes)	0	0	1	0	0	0	0	0	0	0
Frost present (1=yes)	1	1	1	0	0	0	0	0	0	0
Evaporation (1=low)	0	0	1	-1	-1	-1	-1	0	-1	-1
Barometric pressure: July	1010	1010	1010	1010	1010	1010	1020	1020	1010	1010
: January	1010	1010	1030	1010	1010	1010	1010	1010	1010	1010
Risks: Typhoon (10=high)	0	0	0	0	0	0	0	0	0	0
: Flooding (10=high)	0	0	0	0	0	0	0	0	0	0
: Tropical storm (10=high)	0	0	0	0	0	0	0	0	0	0
: Windstorm (10=high)	0	0	0	0	0	0	0	0	0	0
: Drought (10=high)	1	0	0	0	0	0	0	0	0	0
Climate Type: Tropical wet	0	0	0	1	1	1	1	1	1	1
: Tropical monsoon	0	0	0	0	0	0	0	0	0	0
: Tropical wet & dry	0	0	0	0	0	0	0	0	0	0
: Steppe, low latitude	0	0	0	0	0	0	0	0	0	0
: Desert, low latitude	1	0	0	0	0	0	0	0	0	0
: Steppe, middle latitude	0	0	1	0	0	0	0	0	0	0
: Desert, middle latitude	0	0	0	0	0	0	0	0	0	0
: Subtropical, humid	0	0	0	0	0	0	0	0	0	0
: Mediterranean	0	1	0	0	0	0	0	0	0	0
: Marine, west coast	0	0	0	0	0	0	0	0	0	0
: Cont humid hot summer	0	0	0	0	0	0	0	0	0	0
: Cont humid cool summer	0	0	1	0	0	0	0	0	0	0
: Subarctic	0	0	0	0	0	0	0	0	0	0
: Tundra	0	0	0	0	0	0	0	0	0	0
: Ice cap	0	0	0	0	0	0	0	0	0	0
: Dry steppe wasteland	0	0	0	0	0	0	0	0	0	0
: Temperate highland	0	0	0	0	0	0	0	0	0	0
: Temp desert dry summer	0	0	0	0	0	0	0	0	0	0
: Temp desert dry winter	0	0	0	0	0	0	0	0	0	0
: Highland	0	0	1	0	0	0	0	0	0	0

Characteristics	Croatia	Cuba	Cyprus	Czech Republic	Denmark	Djibouti	Dominica	Dominican Republic	Ecuador	Egypt
Latitude (abs degrees)	45	22	35	50	56	11	15	19	2	28
Temperature: degrees (C)	12	25	19	5	8	32	27	26	15	24
: monthly high (min C)	20	32	22	13	10	34	33	33	26	31
: monthly high (max C)	42	36	44	38	33	47	37	37	30	47
: monthly low (min C)	-25	10	-6	-28	-24	17	16	15	0	1
: monthly low (max C)	8	20	15	6	8	23	20	20	4	17
Humidity: morning min (%)	71	83	51	74	70	57	66	88	80	50
: morning max (%)	85	89	83	87	89	84	78	92	94	70
: afternoon min (%)	46	58	34	45	59	43	59	58	40	18
: afternoon max (%)	76	68	66	78	87	74		66	60	41
High temp @ max humidity	4	29	15	1	4	32	32	31	21	20
High humidity @ max temp	47	64	35	49	62	43	70	66	44	24
Rain: monthly min (mm)	46	46	0	18	32	0	61	36	20	0
: monthly max (mm)	96	173	76	68	71	25	274	185	175	5
: days/month min	8	4	0	0	11	0.3	10	5	7	0
: days/month max	14	11	14	13	17	3	22	12	22	1
Snow: persistent (1=yes)	0	0	0	0	0	0	0	0	0	0
: intermittent (1=yes)	-1	0	-1	-1	-1	-1	0	0	-1	0
Frost present (1=yes)	-1	0	-1	-1	-1	0	0	0	0	0
Evaporation (1=low)	-1	-1	-1	-1	-1	-1	-1	-1	-1	-1
Barometric pressure: July	1010	1020	1010	1010	1010	1010	1020	1020	1010	1010
: January	1020	1020	1020	1020	1010	1010	1020	1020	1010	1020
Risks: Typhoon (10=high)	0	0	0	0	0	0	0	0	0	0
: Flooding (10=high)	0	0	0	0	0	0	0	0	1	0
: Tropical storm (10=high)	0	1	0	0	0	0	1	1	0	0
: Windstorm (10=high)	0	0	0	0	0	0	0	0	0	0
: Drought (10=high)	0	0	0	0	0	1	0	0	0	0
Climate Type: Tropical wet	0	0	0	0	0	0	1	0	1	0
: Tropical monsoon	0	0	0	0	0	0	0	0	0	0
: Tropical wet & dry	0	1	0	0	0	0	0	1	0	0
: Steppe, low latitude	0	0	0	0	0	0	0	0	0	0
: Desert, low latitude	0	0	0	0	0	1	0	0	0	1
: Steppe, middle latitude	0	0	0	0	0	0	0	0	0	0
: Desert, middle latitude	0	0	0	0	0	0	0	0	0	0
: Subtropical, humid	0	0	0	0	0	0	0	0	0	0
: Mediterranean	0	0	1	0	0	0	0	0	0	0
: Marine, west coast	0	0	0	0	1	0	0	0	0	0
: Cont humid hot summer	1	0	0	0	0	0	0	0	0	0
: Cont humid cool summer	0	0	0	1	0	0	0	0	0	0
: Subarctic	0	0	0	0	0	0	0	0	0	0
: Tundra	0	0	0	0	0	0	0	0	0	0
: Ice cap	0	0	0	0	0	0	0	0	0	0
: Dry steppe wasteland	0	0	0	0	0	0	0	0	0	0
: Temperate highland	0	0	0	0	0	0	0	0	0	0
: Temp desert dry summer	0	0	0	0	0	0	0	0	0	0
: Temp desert dry winter	0	0	0	0	0	0	0	0	0	0
: Highland	0	0	0	0	0	0	0	0	1	0

Characteristics	El Salvador	Equatorial Guinea	Eritrea	Estonia	Ethiopia	Falkland Islands	Faroe Islands	Fiji	Finland	France
Latitude (abs degrees)	13	3	15	59	12	51	62	18	62	46
Temperature: degrees (C)	24	26	31	5	17	7	6	25	5	13
: monthly high (min C)	37	29	33	7	27	10	12	32	7	15
: monthly high (max C)	41	32	44	33	34	24	22	37	33	40
: monthly low (min C)	7	17	17	-33	0	-11	-10	13	-33	-15
: monthly low (max C)	16	19	23	5	7	-1	3	19	5	9
Humidity: morning min (%)	79	85	56	70	56	75	81	76	70	82
: morning max (%)	91	95	83	91	86	89	87	82	91	91
: afternoon min (%)	43	85	44	58	33	75	80	73	58	54
: afternoon max (%)	69	95	74	89	73	89	84	79	89	82
High temp @ max humidity	31	30	31	-1	21	5	14	28	-1	7
High humidity @ max temp	50	89	43	63	44	79	84	77	63	57
Rain: monthly min (mm)			0	36	5	38	67	125	36	35
: monthly max (mm)	328	302	23	73	300	71	167	368	73	64
: days/month min			0.1	12		11	16	13	12	12
: days/month max	20	24	3	20	28	17	26	21	20	17
Snow: persistent (1=yes)	0	0	0	0	0	0	0	0	0	0
: intermittent (1=yes)	0	0	0	1	0	1	1	0	1	1
Frost present (1=yes)	0	0	0	1	0	1	1	0	1	1
Evaporation (1=low)	-1	-1	-1	1	-1	1	1	0	1	
Barometric pressure: July	1010	1010	1010	1010	1010	1000	1010	1010	1010	1010
: January	1020	1020	1020	1020	1020	999	1000	1010	1010	1020
Risks: Typhoon (10=high)	0	0	0	0	0	0	0	0	0	0
: Flooding (10=high)	0	0	0	0	0	0	0	0	0	0
: Tropical storm (10=high)	0	0	0	0	0	0	0	1	0	0
: Windstorm (10=high)	0	1	0	0	0	0	0	0	0	0
: Drought (10=high)	0	0	0	0	0	0	0	0	0	0
Climate Type: Tropical wet	0	1	0	0	0	0	0	1	0	0
: Tropical monsoon	0	0	0	0	0	0	0	0	0	0
: Tropical wet & dry	1	0	0	0	0	0	0	0	0	0
: Steppe, low latitude	0	0	0	0	0	0	0	0	0	0
: Desert, low latitude	0	0	1	0	0	0	0	0	0	0
: Steppe, middle latitude	0	0	0	0	0	0	0	0	0	0
: Desert, middle latitude	0	0	0	0	0	0	0	0	0	0
: Subtropical, humid	0	0	0	0	0	0	0	0	0	0
: Mediterranean	0	0	0	0	0	0	0	0	0	0
: Marine, west coast	0	0	0	0	0	1	1	0	0	1
: Cont humid hot summer	0	0	0	0	0	0	0	0	0	0
: Cont humid cool summer	0	0	0	1	0	0	0	0	1	0
: Subarctic	0	0	0	0	0	0	0	0	0	0
: Tundra	0	0	0	0	0	0	0	0	0	0
: Ice cap	0	0	0	0	0	0	0	0	0	0
: Dry steppe wasteland	0	0	0	0	0	0	0	0	0	0
: Temperate highland	0	0	0	0	0	0	0	0	0	0
: Temp desert dry summer	0	0	0	0	0	0	0	0	0	0
: Temp desert dry winter	0	0	0	0	0	0	0	0	0	0
: Highland	0	0	1	0	1	0	0	0	0	0

Characteristics	French Guiana	French Polynesia	Gabon	Gambia	Gaza Strip	Georgia	Germany	Ghana	Gibraltar	Greece
Latitude (abs degrees)	5	17	0.2	13	31	41	51	7	36	38
Temperature: degrees (C)	27	26	27	24	20	13	8	27	20	19
: monthly high (min C)	33	32	33	33	25	20	14	32	23	21
: monthly high (max C)	36	34	37	41	42	40	38	38	38	43
: monthly low (min C)	18	17	17	7	-3	-15	-24	15	1	-6
: monthly low (max C)	21	21	19	21	11	14	8	21	14	16
Humidity: morning min (%)	73	75	85	66	47	57	78	95	72	47
: morning max (%)	86	82	95	95	77	80	91	97	81	78
: afternoon min (%)	69	73	69	26	32	40	50	61	60	34
: afternoon max (%)	83	79	79	78	66	65	81	77	72	63
High temp @ max humidity	29	30	30	29	13	9	4	27	19	15
High humidity @ max temp	69	79	75	29	36	40	53	68	60	34
Rain: monthly min (mm)	31	81		0	0	15	38	15	1	6
: monthly max (mm)	551	455	373	500	132	75	76	178	152	71
: days/month min	4	7	0.7	0	0	1	12	1	2	2
: days/month max	26	22	19	19	11	12	17	10	10	16
Snow: persistent (1=yes)	0	0	0	0	0	0	0	0	0	0
: intermittent (1=yes)	0	0	0	0	0	1	1	0	0	0
Frost present (1=yes)	0	0	0	0	0	1	1	0	0	1
Evaporation (1=low)	-1	0	-1	-1	-1	-1	-1	0	-1	-1
Barometric pressure: July	1010	1020	1010	1010	1010	1010	1010	1010	1020	1010
: January	1010	1010	1020	1010	1020	1020	1010	1010	1020	1020
Risks: Typhoon (10=high)	0	0	0	0	0	0	0	0	0	0
: Flooding (10=high)	0	0	0	0	0	0	0	0	0	0
: Tropical storm (10=high)	0	0	0	0	0	0	0	0	0	0
: Windstorm (10=high)	0	0	0	0	0	0	0	0	0	0
: Drought (10=high)	0	0	0	0	0	0	0	0	0	0
Climate Type: Tropical wet	1	1	1	0	0	0	0	0	0	0
: Tropical monsoon	0	0	0	0	0	0	0	0	0	0
: Tropical wet & dry	0	0	0	1	0	0	0	1	0	0
: Steppe, low latitude	0	0	0	0	0	0	0	0	0	0
: Desert, low latitude	0	0	0	0	0	0	0	0	0	0
: Steppe, middle latitude	0	0	0	0	0	0	0	0	0	0
: Desert, middle latitude	0	0	0	0	0	0	0	0	0	0
: Subtropical, humid	0	0	0	0	0	1	0	0	0	0
: Mediterranean	0	0	0	0	1	0	0	0	1	1
: Marine, west coast	0	0	0	0	0	0	1	0	0	0
: Cont humid hot summer	0	0	0	0	0	0	0	0	0	0
: Cont humid cool summer	0	0	0	0	0	0	1	0	0	0
: Subarctic	0	0	0	0	0	0	0	0	0	0
: Tundra	0	0	0	0	0	0	0	0	0	0
: Ice cap	0	0	0	0	0	0	0	0	0	0
: Dry steppe wasteland	0	0	0	0	0	0	0	0	0	0
: Temperate highland	0	0	0	0	0	0	0	0	0	0
: Temp desert dry summer	0	0	0	0	0	0	0	0	0	0
: Temp desert dry winter	0	0	0	0	0	0	0	0	0	0
: Highland	0	0	0	0	0	1	0	0	0	0

Characteristics	Greenland	Grenada	Guadeloupe	Guam	Guatemala	Guernsey	Guinea	Guinea-Bissau	Guyana	Haiti
Latitude (abs degrees)	64	12	16	13	14	50	10	12	6	19
Temperature: degrees (C)	-2	28	23	27	19	12	27	28	27	27
: monthly high (min C)	11	31	29	29	28	14	31	35	31	34
: monthly high (max C)	-24	36	33	32	32	34	36	43	34	38
: monthly low (min C)	-29	14	12	19	5	-10	17	13	20	16
: monthly low (max C)	-2	21	17	22	12		21	21	22	20
Humidity: morning min (%)	83	86	82	85	81	70	83	70	83	68
: morning max (%)	92	92	85	91	92	87	94	87	93	79
: afternoon min (%)	83	64	75	69	51	56	63	45	69	43
: afternoon max (%)	92	75	81	79	72	81	87	74	77	56
High temp @ max humidity	8	29	27	28	26	7	28	31	29	32
High humidity @ max temp	86	71	78	77	55	59	70	72	69	49
Rain: monthly min (mm)	31	91	155	69	3	37	3	0	76	3
: monthly max (mm)	84	269	447	338	274	64	1300	254	302	231
: days/month min	10	10	18	11	2	11	0	0	0	3
: days/month max	13	23	27	23	23	15	29	13	24	13
Snow: persistent (1=yes)	1	0	0	0	0	0	0	0	0	0
: intermittent (1=yes)	0	0	0	0	0	1	0	0	0	0
Frost present (1=yes)	1	0	0	0	0	1	0	0	0	0
Evaporation (1=low)	1	-1	-1	-1	-1	-1	-1	-1	-1	-1
Barometric pressure: July	1010	1010	1010	1010	1010	1010	1010	1010	1010	1020
: January	996	1010	1010	1010	1020	1020	1010	1010	1010	1020
Risks: Typhoon (10=high)	0	0	0	10	0	0	0	0	0	0
: Flooding (10=high)	0	0	0	0	0	0	0	0	0	0
: Tropical storm (10=high)	0	1	1	1	1	0	0	0	0	1
: Windstorm (10=high)	0	0	0	0	0	1	0	0	0	0
: Drought (10=high)	0	0	0	0	0	0	0	0	0	0
Climate Type: Tropical wet	0	0	0	1	0	0	0	0	1	0
: Tropical monsoon	0	0	0	0	0	0	0	0	0	0
: Tropical wet & dry	0	1	1	0	1	0	1	1	0	1
: Steppe, low latitude	0	0	0	0	0	0	0	0	0	0
: Desert, low latitude	0	0	0	0	0	0	0	0	0	0
: Steppe, middle latitude	0	0	0	0	0	0	0	0	0	0
: Desert, middle latitude	0	0	0	0	0	0	0	0	0	0
: Subtropical, humid	0	0	0	0	0	0	0	0	0	0
: Mediterranean	0	0	0	0	0	0	0	0	0	0
: Marine, west coast	0	0	0	0	0	1	0	0	0	0
: Cont humid hot summer	0	0	0	0	0	0	0	0	0	0
: Cont humid cool summer	0	0	0	0	0	0	0	0	0	0
: Subarctic	0	0	0	0	0	0	0	0	0	0
: Tundra	1	0	0	0	0	0	0	0	0	0
: Ice cap	1	0	0	0	0	0	0	0	0	0
: Dry steppe wasteland	0	0	0	0	0	0	0	0	0	0
: Temperate highland	0	0	0	0	0	0	0	0	0	0
: Temp desert dry summer	0	0	0	0	0	0	0	0	0	0
: Temp desert dry winter	0	0	0	0	0	0	0	0	0	0
: Highland	0	0	0	0	1	0	0	0	0	0

Characteristics	Honduras	Hong Kong	Hungary	Iceland	India	Indonesia	Iran	Iraq	Ireland	Isle of Man
Latitude (abs degrees)	15	22	47	64	21	5	33	33	52	54
Temperature: degrees (C)	22	21	9	5	24	28	15	21	9	12
: monthly high (min C)	25	26	14	10	28	33	18	25	14	14
: monthly high (max C)	30	36	39	23	46	37	43	49	30	34
: monthly low (min C)	14		-23	-17	-1	19	-21	-8	-12	-10
: monthly low (max C)	18	22	8	-1	22	21	15	18	-3	-7
Humidity: morning min (%)	79	73	71	75	35	90	47	32	75	70
: morning max (%)	91	87	88	83	80	95	77	84	88	87
: afternoon min (%)	43	60	47	67	19	61	39	12	75	56
: afternoon max (%)	70	78	81	80	64	75	75	52	88	81
High temp @ max humidity	26	28	4	4	34	29	11	18	10	7
High humidity @ max temp	60	77	47	72	20	71	41	13	78	59
Rain: monthly min (mm)	1	31	33	42	3	43	3	0	45	37
: monthly max (mm)	180	394	72	94	180	300	46	28	74	64
: days/month min	2	2	2	15	0.2	4	0.2	0	10	11
: days/month max	16	18	14	21	8	18	4	5	14	15
Snow: persistent (1=yes)	0	0	0	0	0	0	0	0	0	0
: intermittent (1=yes)	0	0	1	1	0	0	1	0	1	1
Frost present (1=yes)	0	0	1	1	0	0	1	1	1	1
Evaporation (1=low)	-1	0	1	1	0	0	1	-1	1	1
Barometric pressure: July	1010	1010	1010	1010	1000	1010	999	1010	1010	1010
: January	1020	1020	1010	999	1020	1010	1020	1020	1010	1010
Risks: Typhoon (10=high)	0	0	0	0	0	0	0	0	0	0
: Flooding (10=high)	0	0	1	0	1	1	0	0	0	0
: Tropical storm (10=high)	1	0	0	0	0	0	0	1	0	0
: Windstorm (10=high)	0	0	0	0	0	0	0	0	0	0
: Drought (10=high)	0	0	0	0	0	0	0	0	0	0
Climate Type: Tropical wet	0	0	0	0	0	1	0	0	0	0
: Tropical monsoon	0	0	0	0	1	0	0	0	0	0
: Tropical wet & dry	1	0	0	0	0	0	0	0	0	0
: Steppe, low latitude	0	0	0	0	1	0	0	0	0	0
: Desert, low latitude	0	0	0	0	0	0	0	1	0	0
: Steppe, middle latitude	0	0	0	0	0	0	1	0	0	0
: Desert, middle latitude	0	0	0	0	0	0	1	0	0	0
: Subtropical, humid	0	1	0	0	0	0	0	0	0	0
: Mediterranean	0	0	0	0	0	0	0	0	0	0
: Marine, west coast	0	0	0	0	0	0	0	0	1	1
: Cont humid hot summer	0	0	1	0	0	0	0	0	0	0
: Cont humid cool summer	0	0	0	0	0	0	0	0	0	0
: Subarctic	0	0	0	1	0	0	0	0	0	0
: Tundra	0	0	0	0	0	0	0	0	0	0
: Ice cap	0	0	0	0	0	0	0	0	0	0
: Dry steppe wasteland	0	0	0	0	0	0	0	0	0	0
: Temperate highland	0	0	0	0	0	0	0	0	0	0
: Temp desert dry summer	0	0	0	0	0	0	0	0	0	0
: Temp desert dry winter	0	0	0	0	0	0	0	0	0	0
: Highland	0	0	0	0	1	1	1	0	0	0

Characteristics	Israel	Italy	Ivory Coast	Jamaica	Japan	Jersey	Jordan	Kazakhstan	Kenya	Kiribati
Latitude (abs degrees)	32	42	6	18	37	49	32	43	2	1
Temperature: degrees (C)	20	17	26	26	15	12	19	5	18	28
: monthly high (min C)	25	19	31	33	22	14	24	5	26	34
: monthly high (max C)	42	40	36	36	38	34	43	42	31	35
: monthly low (min C)	-3	-6	15	14	-8	-10	-6	-33	5	19
: monthly low (max C)	11	12	20	20	16	7	13	-10	11	21
Humidity: morning min (%)	47	70	93	77	71	70	39	58	74	68
: morning max (%)	77	87	96	88	92	87	80	91	89	75
: afternoon min (%)	32	42	71	61	48	56	28	34	40	68
: afternoon max (%)	66	70	82	73	69	81	56	80	62	74
High temp @ max humidity	13	13	29	31	28	7	12	-4	22	31
High humidity @ max temp	36	43	72	70	66	59	30	37	40	73
Rain: monthly min (mm)	0	15	41	15	48	37	0	5	15	94
: monthly max (mm)	132	129	495	180	234	64	74	15	211	315
: days/month min	0	1	3	2	5	11	0	2	5	5
: days/month max	11	11	18	9	12	15	8	6	17	15
Snow: persistent (1=yes)	0	0	0	0	1	0	0	1	0	0
: intermittent (1=yes)	1	1	0	0	1	1	0	1	0	0
Frost present (1=yes)	1	1	0	1	1	1	0	1	0	0
Evaporation (1=low)	0	-1	0	-1	1	1	-1	1	0	1
Barometric pressure: July	1010	1010	1010	1010	1010	1010	1010	1010	1010	1010
: January	1020	1020	1010	1020	1020	1020	1020	1030	1010	1010
Risks: Typhoon (10=high)	0	0	0	0	0	0	0	0	0	10
: Flooding (10=high)	0	1	1	1	0	0	0	0	0	0
: Tropical storm (10=high)	0	0	0	0	0	0	0	0	0	0
: Windstorm (10=high)	0	0	0	0	0	1	0	0	0	0
: Drought (10=high)	1	0	0	0	0	0	1	1	0	0
Climate Type: Tropical wet	0	0	0	1	0	0	0	0	0	1
: Tropical monsoon	0	0	0	0	0	0	0	0	0	0
: Tropical wet & dry	0	0	1	0	0	0	0	0	0	0
: Steppe, low latitude	0	0	0	0	0	0	0	0	0	0
: Desert, low latitude	0	0	0	0	0	0	1	0	0	0
: Steppe, middle latitude	0	0	0	0	0	0	0	0	0	0
: Desert, middle latitude	0	0	0	0	0	0	0	0	0	0
: Subtropical, humid	0	0	0	0	0	0	0	0	0	0
: Mediterranean	1	1	0	0	0	0	0	0	0	0
: Marine, west coast	0	0	0	0	0	1	0	0	0	0
: Cont humid hot summer	0	0	0	0	1	0	0	0	0	0
: Cont humid cool summer	0	0	0	0	0	0	0	0	0	0
: Tundra	0	0	0	0	0	0	0	0	0	0
: Ice cap	0	0	0	0	0	0	0	0	0	0
: Dry steppe wasteland	0	0	0	0	0	0	0	0	0	0
: Temperate highland	0	0	0	0	0	0	0	0	0	0
: Temp desert dry summer	0	0	0	0	0	0	0	0	0	0
: Temp desert dry winter	0	0	0	0	0	0	0	0	0	0
: Highland	0	0	0	0	0	0	0	0	1	0

Characteristics	Kuwait	Kyrgyz-stan	Laos	Latvia	Lebanon	Lesotho	Liberia	Libya	Liechten-stein	Lithuania
Latitude (abs degrees)	29	43	18	57	34	29	6	32	47	54
Temperature: degrees (C)	25	2	26	4	21	16	25	24	8	5
: monthly high (min C)	26	12	33	7	25	23	29	28	15	7
: monthly high (max C)	48	38	40	33	42	38	34	46	38	33
: monthly low (min C)	1	-34	4	-33	-1	-9	13	-1	-23	-33
: monthly low (max C)	26	7	21	5	18	6	20	17	7	5
Humidity: morning min (%)	45	65	71	70	64	51	87	54	80	70
: morning max (%)	77	87	87	91	72	75	95	72	92	91
: afternoon min (%)	41	39	71	58	57	25	76	53	51	58
: afternoon max (%)	65	72	87	89	70	42	86	72	76	89
High temp @ max humidity	18	-2	31	-1	17	28	27	29	3	-1
High humidity @ max temp	46	48	74	63	57	33	80	69	52	63
Rain: monthly min (mm)	0	23	3	36	0	8	31	0	64	36
: monthly max (mm)	28	102	302	73	191	91	996	94	136	73
: days/month min	0	6	0	12	0	0	5	0.2	12	12
: days/month max	3	12	18	20	15	9	26	11	15	20
Snow: persistent (1=yes)	0	0	0	1	0	0	0	0	1	1
: intermittent (1=yes)	0	0	0	0	0	1	0	0	0	0
Frost present (1=yes)	0	0	0	0	0	0	0	0	0	0
Evaporation (1=low)	-1	-1	-1	-1	-1	-1	-1	-1	-1	-1
Barometric pressure: July	999	1000	1010	1010	1010	1020	1010	1010	1010	1010
: January	1020	1020	1010	1020	1020	1010	1010	1020	1010	1020
Risks: Typhoon (10=high)	0	0	0	0	0	0	0	0	0	0
: Flooding (10=high)	0	0	1	0	0	0	1	0	0	0
: Tropical storm (10=high)	0	0	0	0	0	0	0	0	0	0
: Windstorm (10=high)	0	0	0	0	0	0	0	0	0	0
: Drought (10=high)	0	0	0	0	0	0	0	1	0	0
Climate Type: Tropical wet	0	0	0	0	0	0	1	0	0	0
: Tropical monsoon	0	0	1	0	0	0	1	0	0	0
: Tropical wet & dry	0	0	0	0	0	0	0	0	0	0
: Steppe, low latitude	0	0	0	0	0	0	0	0	0	0
: Desert, low latitude	1	0	0	0	0	0	0	1	0	0
: Steppe, middle latitude	0	1	0	0	0	0	0	0	0	0
: Desert, middle latitude	0	0	0	0	0	0	0	0	0	0
: Subtropical, humid	0	0	0	0	0	0	0	0	0	0
: Mediterranean	0	0	0	0	1	0	0	0	0	0
: Marine, west coast	0	0	0	0	0	0	0	0	0	0
: Cont humid hot summer	0	0	0	0	0	0	0	0	0	0
: Cont humid cool summer	0	0	0	1	0	0	0	0	0	1
: Subarctic	0	0	0	0	0	0	0	0	0	0
: Tundra	0	0	0	0	0	0	0	0	0	0
: Ice cap	0	0	0	0	0	0	0	0	0	0
: Dry steppe wasteland	0	0	0	0	0	0	0	0	0	0
: Temperate highland	0	1	0	0	0	0	0	0	0	0
: Temp desert dry summer	0	0	0	0	0	0	0	0	0	0
: Temp desert dry winter	0	0	0	0	0	0	0	0	0	0
: Highland	0	0	0	0	0	1	0	0	1	0

Characteristics	Luxem-bourg	Macau	Macedonia	Madagas-car	Malawi	Malaysia	Maldives	Mali	Malta	Marshall Islands
Latitude (abs degrees)	49	22	45	19	15	4	4	14	36	10
Temperature: degrees (C)	9	23	10	18	19	28	28	29	23	29
: monthly high (min C)	11	26	20	27	28	35	32	36	22	32
: monthly high (max C)	37	36	41	35	34	37	37	47	40	35
: monthly low (min C)	-20	0	-22	1	-1	18	17	8	5	22
: monthly low (max C)	5	22	0	12	13	21	22	19	18	23
Humidity: morning min (%)	85	73	70	85	50	95	72	33	71	81
: morning max (%)	95	87	94	94	89	97	81	94	78	87
: afternoon min (%)	58	60	46	49	28	58	73	18	59	76
: afternoon max (%)	91	78	76	71	66	66	82	73	68	80
High temp @ max humidity	4	28	6	26	27	33	29	31	16	31
High humidity @ max temp	61	77	42	64	28	99	77	40	62	80
Rain: monthly min (mm)	42	31	32	8	0		18	0	0	46
: monthly max (mm)	84	394	61	300	218	292	295	348	110	264
: days/month min	13	2	4	0	0		1	0	0	12
: days/month max	20	18	12	21	19	20	17	17	13	24
Snow: persistent (1=yes)	0	0	0	0	0	0	0	0	0	0
: intermittent (1=yes)	1	0	1	0	0	0	0	0	0	0
Frost present (1=yes)	1	0	1	0	0	0	0	0	0	0
Evaporation (1=low)	1	0	-1	-1	0	-1	-1	-1	-1	-1
Barometric pressure: July	1010	1010	1010	1020	1020	1010	1010	1010	1010	1010
: January	1020	1020	1020	1010	1010	1010	1010	1010	1020	1010
Risks: Typhoon (10=high)	0	0	0	0	0	1	0	0	0	1
: Flooding (10=high)	0	0	0	0	0	0	0	0	0	0
: Tropical storm (10=high)	0	0	0	0	0	0	0	0	0	0
: Windstorm (10=high)	0	0	0	0	0	0	0	0	0	0
: Drought (10=high)	0	0	0	0	0	0	0	0	0	0
Climate Type: Tropical wet	0	0	0	0	0	1	0	0	0	1
: Tropical monsoon	0	0	0	0	0	0	1	0	0	0
: Tropical wet & dry	0	0	0	1	1	0	0	0	0	0
: Steppe, low latitude	0	0	0	0	0	0	0	1	0	0
: Desert, low latitude	0	0	0	0	0	0	0	1	0	0
: Steppe, middle latitude	0	0	0	0	0	0	0	0	0	0
: Desert, middle latitude	0	0	0	0	0	0	0	0	0	0
: Subtropical, humid	0	1	0	0	0	0	0	0	0	0
: Mediterranean	0	0	1	0	0	0	0	0	1	0
: Marine, west coast	1	0	0	0	0	0	0	0	0	0
: Cont humid hot summer	0	0	0	0	0	0	0	0	0	0
: Cont humid cool summer	0	0	0	0	0	0	0	0	0	0
: Subarctic	0	0	0	0	0	0	0	0	0	0
: Tundra	0	0	0	0	0	0	0	0	0	0
: Ice cap	0	0	0	0	0	0	0	0	0	0
: Dry steppe wasteland	0	0	0	0	0	0	0	0	0	0
: Temperate highland	0	0	0	0	0	0	0	0	0	0
: Temp desert dry summer	0	0	0	0	0	0	0	0	0	0
: Temp desert dry winter	0	0	0	0	0	0	0	0	0	0
: Highland	0	0	0	0	0	0	0	0	0	0

Characteristics	Martinique	Mauritania	Mauritius	Mayotte	Mexico	Micronesia Federation	Moldova	Monaco	Mongolia	Montserrat
Latitude (abs degrees)	14	18	20	13	24	5	47	43	48	17
Temperature: degrees (C)										
: monthly high (min C)	26	27	23	26	16	29	10	17	-4	26
: monthly high (max C)	32	36	27	30	23	32	8	19	8	32
: monthly low (min C)	34	46	35	33	32	35	35	34	-36	37
: monthly low (max C)	15	7	10	19	-3	22	-25	-1	-44	15
Humidity: morning min (%)	20	22	18	22	9	23	9	14	1	21
: morning max (%)	88	51	80	74	66	81	69	67	64	62
: afternoon min (%)	92	88	90	79	86	87	92	79	88	70
: afternoon max (%)	71	30	56	74	26	76	50	67	40	59
High temp @ max humidity	80	69	74	78	54	80	84	75	75	68
High humidity @ max temp	31	32	22	28	23	31	-1	72	-16	29
Rain: monthly min (mm)	80	0	0	69	5	46	30	21	0	86
: monthly max (mm)	262	104	20	386	170	264	91	123	76	196
: days/month min	13	0	0	7	4	12	8	7	1	8
: days/month max	29	3	8	15	27	24	13	7	10	16
Snow: persistent (1=yes)	0	0	0	0	0	0	0	0	1	0
: intermittent (1=yes)	0	0	0	0	0	0	1	1	1	0
Frost present (1=yes)	0				0					
Evaporation (1=low)	-1	-1	-1	-1		-1	-1	-1	-1	-1
Barometric pressure: July	1010	1010	1020	1020	1010	1010	1010	1010	1010	1020
: January	1020	1020	1010	1010	1020	1010	1020	1020	1030	1020
Risks: Typhoon (10=high)	10					10				10
: Flooding (10=high)	10									
: Tropical storm (10=high)										
: Windstorm (10=high)										
: Drought (10=high)										
Climate Type: Tropical wet	0	0	0	0	0	1	0	0	0	0
: Tropical monsoon	0	0	0	0	0	0	0	0	0	0
: Tropical wet & dry	1	0	0	1	0	0	0	0	0	1
: Steppe, low latitude	0	0	0	0	1	0	0	0	0	0
: Desert, low latitude	0	1	0	0	0	0	0	0	0	0
: Steppe, middle latitude	0	0	0	0	0	0	0	0	1	0
: Desert, middle latitude	0	0	0	0	0	0	0	0	0	0
: Subtropical, humid	0	0	1	0	0	0	0	0	0	0
: Mediterranean	0	0	0	0	0	0	0	1	0	0
: Marine, west coast	0	0	0	0	0	0	0	0	0	0
: Cont humid hot summer	0	0	0	0	0	0	0	0	0	0
: Cont humid cool summer	0	0	0	0	0	0	1	0	0	0
: Subarctic	0	0	0	0	0	0	0	0	0	0
: Tundra	0	0	0	0	0	0	0	0	0	0
: Ice cap	0	0	0	0	0	0	0	0	0	0
: Dry steppe wasteland	0	0	0	0	0	0	0	0	0	0
: Temperate highland	0	0	0	0	0	0	0	0	0	0
: Temp desert dry summer	0	0	0	0	0	0	0	0	0	0
: Temp desert dry winter	0	0	0	0	0	0	0	0	0	0
: Highland	0	0	0	0	1	0	0	0	0	0

Characteristics	Morocco	Mozam-bique	Namibia	Nauru	Nepal	Nether-lands	Netherlands Antilles	New Caledonia	New Zealand	Nicaragua
Latitude (abs degrees)	33	23	24	0.3	27	52	12	22	41	12
Temperature: degrees (C)										
: monthly high (min C)	24	27	18	28	17	9	27	24	15	27
: monthly high (max C)	27	34	25	34	24	15	31	29	19	31
: monthly low (min C)	48	46	36	35	36	34	36	37	31	34
: monthly low (max C)	0	7	-4	19	-2	-20	17	11	-2	20
Humidity: morning min (%)	12	17	9	21	18	6	22	18	5	23
: morning max (%)	87	65	27	68	68	78	68	68	73	80
: afternoon min (%)	92	75	62	75	90	89	79	76	73	92
: afternoon max (%)	59	57	11	68	53	65	66	66	67	44
High temp @ max humidity	17	67	35	74	84	85	72	74	78	70
High humidity @ max temp	17	29	28	31	28	68	30	28	13	27
Rain: monthly min (mm)	61	65	23	73	61	40	67	70	71	73
: monthly max (mm)	86	13	79	94	373	71	20	51	81	1
: days/month min	0.3	130	0.1	315	0.2	72	112	145	137	296
: days/month max	10	2	8	15	21	12	4	6	9	1
Snow: persistent (1=yes)		9				20			18	21
: intermittent (1=yes)										
Frost present (1=yes)	1				1	1			1	
Evaporation (1=low)	-1	-1	-1	-1	-1	-1	-1	-1	-1	-1
Barometric pressure: July	1010	1020	1020	1010	1000	1010	1010	1020	1010	1010
: January	1020	1010	1010	1010	1020	1020	1010	1010	1010	1010
Risks: Typhoon (10=high)	0	0	0	0	0	0	0	0	0	0
: Flooding (10=high)	0	1	0	0	0	0	0	0	0	0
: Tropical storm (10=high)	0	0	0	0	0	0	0	0	0	0
: Windstorm (10=high)	0	1	0	1	0	0	0	0	0	0
: Drought (10=high)	0	0	0	0	0	0	1	0	0	0
Climate Type: Tropical wet	0	0	0	0	0	0	0	0	0	0
: Tropical monsoon	0	0	0	1	0	0	0	0	0	0
: Tropical wet & dry	0	1	0	0	0	0	1	1	0	1
: Steppe, low latitude	0	0	1	0	0	0	0	0	0	0
: Desert, low latitude	1	0	1	0	1	0	0	0	0	0
: Steppe, middle latitude	0	0	0	0	0	0	0	0	0	0
: Desert, middle latitude	0	0	0	0	0	0	0	0	0	0
: Subtropical, humid	0	0	0	0	0	0	0	0	0	0
: Mediterranean	1	0	0	0	0	0	0	0	0	0
: Marine, west coast	0	0	0	0	0	1	0	0	1	0
: Cont humid hot summer	0	0	0	0	0	0	0	0	0	0
: Cont humid cool summer	0	0	0	0	0	0	0	0	0	0
: Subarctic	0	0	0	0	0	0	0	0	0	0
: Tundra	0	0	0	0	0	0	0	0	0	0
: Ice cap	0	0	0	0	0	0	0	0	0	0
: Dry steppe wasteland	0	0	0	0	0	0	0	0	0	0
: Temperate highland	0	0	0	0	0	0	0	0	0	0
: Temp desert dry summer	0	0	0	0	0	0	0	0	0	0
: Temp desert dry winter	0	0	0	0	0	0	0	0	0	0
: Highland	0	0	0	0	1	0	0	0	0	0

Characteristics	Niger	Nigeria	Niue	Norfolk Island	North Korea	Northern Mariana Isl.	Norway	Oman	Pacific Isl. Trust	Pakistan
Latitude (abs degrees)	13	9	19	29	39	17	64	23	15	29
Temperature: degrees (C)										
: monthly high (min C)	29	28	26	24	9	26	5	29	29	22
: monthly high (max C)	38	34	32	24	-3	29	11	31	32	24
: monthly low (min C)	46	40	34	37	29	32	-34	47	35	48
: monthly low (max C)	8	16	17	11	-13	19	-26	11	22	-4
Humidity: morning min (%)	19	21	21	18	-20	22	4	26	23	17
: morning max (%)	26	81	75	68	63	85	68	58	81	19
: afternoon min (%)	91	87	82	76	80	91	88	82	87	54
: afternoon max (%)	11	65	73	66	63	69	52	60	76	19
High temp @ max humidity	68	80	79	74	80	79	85	80	80	54
High humidity @ max temp	32	29	30	28	29	28	0	33	31	34
Rain: monthly min (mm)	18	72	79	70	80	77	59	72	80	23
: monthly max (mm)	0	25	81	51	11	69	26	0	46	12
: days/month min	188	460	455	145	237	338	95	28	264	258
: days/month max	0	2	7	6	3	11	9	0	12	
Snow: persistent (1=yes)	12	20	22	16	12	23	14	2	24	1
: intermittent (1=yes)	0	0	0	0	0	0	1	0	0	13
Frost present (1=yes)	0	0	0	0	1	0	1	0	0	1
Evaporation (1=low)	1	0	1	1	1	1	1	1	1	1
Barometric pressure: July	-1	0	0	-1	0	0	0	-1	0	-1
: January	1010	1010	1010	1020	1010	1010	1010	1000	1010	999
Risks: Typhoon (10=high)	1010	1010	1010	1010	1030	1010	1010	1020	1010	1020
: Flooding (10=high)	0	0	0	0	0	0	0	0	0	0
: Tropical storm (10=high)	0	0	1	0	1	1	0	0	1	1
: Windstorm (10=high)	0	0	0	0	0	0	0	0	0	0
: Drought (10=high)	0	0	1	1	1	1	1	1	1	1
Climate Type: Tropical wet	1	1	0	0	0	0	0	1	0	1
: Tropical monsoon	0	0	1	0	0	1	0	0	1	0
: Tropical wet & dry	0	1	0	0	0	0	0	0	0	0
: Steppe, low latitude	0	0	0	0	0	0	0	0	0	0
: Desert, low latitude	1	0	0	0	0	0	0	1	0	1
: Steppe, middle latitude	0	0	0	0	0	0	0	0	0	0
: Desert, middle latitude	0	0	0	0	0	0	0	0	0	0
: Subtropical, humid	0	0	0	1	0	0	0	0	0	0
: Mediterranean	0	0	0	0	0	0	0	0	0	0
: Marine, west coast	0	0	0	0	0	0	1	0	0	0
: Cont humid hot summer	0	0	0	0	0	0	0	0	0	0
: Cont humid cool summer	0	0	0	0	1	0	0	0	0	0
: Subarctic	0	0	0	0	0	0	0	0	0	0
: Tundra	0	0	0	0	0	0	0	0	0	0
: Ice cap	0	0	0	0	0	0	0	0	0	0
: Dry steppe wasteland	0	0	0	0	0	0	0	0	0	0
: Temperate highland	0	0	0	0	0	0	0	0	0	0
: Temp desert dry summer	0	0	0	0	0	0	0	0	0	0
: Temp desert dry winter	0	0	0	0	0	0	0	1	0	0
: Highland	0	0	0	0	0	0	0	0	0	0

Characteristics	Panama	Papua New Guinea	Paraguay	Peru	Philip- pines	Pitcairn Islands	Poland	Portugal	Puerto Rico	Qatar
Latitude (abs degrees)	9	7	25	10	11	25	52	39	18	25
Temperature: degrees (C)										
: monthly high (min C)	27	28	22	22	27	26	6	20	26	26
: monthly high (max C)	34	32	37	26	34	32	11	21	31	29
: monthly low (min C)	36	37	43	34	38	34	35	40	34	48
: monthly low (max C)	17	18	-2	9	14	17	-29	-1	17	3
Humidity: morning min (%)	81	72	73	92	85	75	80	62	75	61
: morning max (%)	91	78	89	95	93	82	93	85	81	82
: afternoon min (%)	78	69	48	64	55	79	56	48	74	59
: afternoon max (%)	92	78	62	80	74	79	87	72	78	65
High temp @ max humidity	29	28	25	20	31	30	2	15	29	36
High humidity @ max temp	91	69	56	69	61	81	63	49	77	64
Rain: monthly min (mm)	10	18	38	0	13	81	31	3	69	0
: monthly max (mm)	259	193	158	8	432	455	96	111	160	36
: days/month min	1	8	4	0.1	3	2	11	1	14	2
: days/month max	18	16	8	0.2	24	22	16	15	21	0
Snow: persistent (1=yes)	0	0	0	0	0	0	0	0	0	0
: intermittent (1=yes)	0	0	0	1	0	0	1	0	0	0
Frost present (1=yes)	0	0	0	1	0	0	1	1	0	0
Evaporation (1=low)	-1	-1	-1	-1	-1	-1	1	-1	-1	-1
Barometric pressure: July	1010	1010	1020	1020	1010	1010	1010	1020	1020	999
: January	1010	1010	1010	1010	1020	1010	1020	1020	1020	1020
Risks: Typhoon (10=high)	0	0	0	0	0	0	0	0	0	0
: Flooding (10=high)	0	0	0	0	0	0	0	0	0	0
: Tropical storm (10=high)	0	0	0	0	0	0	0	0	0	0
: Windstorm (10=high)	0	0	0	0	0	0	0	0	0	0
: Drought (10=high)	0	0	0	1	0	0	0	0	0	0
Climate Type: Tropical wet	1	1	0	0	1	0	0	0	0	0
: Tropical monsoon	0	0	0	0	0	0	0	0	0	0
: Tropical wet & dry	0	0	1	0	0	1	0	0	1	0
: Steppe, low latitude	0	0	0	0	0	0	0	0	0	0
: Desert, low latitude	0	0	0	1	0	0	0	0	0	1
: Steppe, middle latitude	0	0	0	0	0	0	0	0	0	0
: Desert, middle latitude	0	0	0	0	0	0	0	0	0	0
: Subtropical, humid	0	0	0	0	0	0	0	0	0	0
: Mediterranean	0	0	0	0	0	0	0	1	0	0
: Marine, west coast	0	0	0	0	0	0	0	0	0	0
: Cont humid hot summer	0	0	0	0	0	0	0	0	0	0
: Cont humid cool summer	0	0	0	0	0	0	1	0	0	0
: Subarctic	0	0	0	0	0	0	0	0	0	0
: Tundra	0	0	0	0	0	0	0	0	0	0
: Ice cap	0	0	0	0	0	0	0	0	0	0
: Dry steppe wasteland	0	0	0	0	0	0	0	0	0	0
: Temperate highland	0	0	0	0	0	0	0	0	0	0
: Temp desert dry summer	0	0	0	0	0	0	0	0	0	1
: Temp desert dry winter	0	0	0	0	0	0	0	0	0	0
: Highland	0	0	0	1	0	0	0	0	0	0

Characteristics	Reunion	Romania	Russia	Rwanda	San Marino	Sao Tome E Principe	Saudi Arabia	Senegal	Serbia & Monten.	Seychel-les
Latitude (abs degrees)	21	45	55	2	44	0.2	24	14	44	4
Temperature: degrees (C)										
: monthly high (min C)	24	8	3	20	17	25	23	28	9	27
: monthly high (max C)	27	16	2	24	19	31	30	35	20	30
: monthly low (min C)	35	41	32	27	40	33	45	43	42	33
: monthly low (max C)	10	-32	-32	12	-6	13	-7	12	-25	19
Humidity: morning min (%)	18	8	5	14	12	20	19	21	8	22
: morning max (%)	80	58	58	59	70	73	33	70	71	74
: afternoon min (%)	90	89	87	83	87	83	65	88	85	79
: afternoon max (%)	56	58	43	59	42	70	19	45	46	74
High temp @ max humidity	74	89	83	83	70	79	44	74	76	78
High humidity @ max temp	22	4	-5	25	13	29	21	31	5	28
Rain: monthly min (mm)	61	59	54	60	43	76	31	72	47	74
: monthly max (mm)	0	0	36	7	15	0	0	0	46	69
: days/month min	20	26	88	183	129	150	25	254	96	386
: days/month max	20	121	12	2	1	0	0	0	8	7
Snow: persistent (1=yes)	8	13	23	22	11	10	4	13	14	15
: intermittent (1=yes)	0	1	1	0	0	0	0	0	0	0
Frost present (1=yes)	0	1	1	0	1	0	0	0	1	0
Evaporation (1=low)	0	1	1	1	1	1	1	1	1	1
Barometric pressure: July	-1	1	0	1	-1	-1	-1	-1	-1	1
: January	1020	1010	1010	1010	1010	1020	1010	1010	1010	1020
Risks: Typhoon (10=high)	1010	1020	1020	1020	1020	1010	1020	1010	1020	1010
: Flooding (10=high)	0	0	0	0	0	0	0	0	0	0
: Tropical storm (10=high)	0	0	0	0	0	0	0	0	0	0
: Windstorm (10=high)	1	0	0	0	0	0	0	0	0	0
: Drought (10=high)	0	0	0	1	0	0	0	0	0	0
Climate Type: Tropical wet	1	0	0	0	0	0	0	0	0	1
: Tropical monsoon	0	0	0	0	0	0	0	0	0	0
: Tropical wet & dry	0	0	0	0	0	0	0	1	0	0
: Steppe, low latitude	0	0	0	0	0	0	0	0	0	0
: Desert, low latitude	0	0	0	0	0	0	1	0	0	0
: Steppe, middle latitude	0	0	0	0	0	0	0	0	0	0
: Desert, middle latitude	0	0	0	0	0	0	0	0	0	0
: Subtropical, humid	0	0	0	0	0	0	0	0	0	0
: Mediterranean	0	0	0	0	1	0	0	0	0	0
: Marine, west coast	0	0	0	0	0	0	0	0	0	0
: Cont humid hot summer	0	1	1	0	1	0	0	0	1	0
: Cont humid cool summer	0	0	1	0	0	0	0	0	0	0
: Subarctic	0	0	1	0	0	0	0	0	0	0
: Tundra	0	0	1	0	0	0	0	0	0	0
: Ice cap	0	0	1	0	0	0	0	0	0	0
: Dry steppe wasteland	0	0	0	0	0	0	0	0	0	0
: Temperate highland	0	0	1	0	0	0	0	0	0	0
: Temp desert dry summer	0	0	0	0	0	0	0	0	0	0
: Temp desert dry winter	0	0	0	0	0	0	0	0	0	0
: Highland	0	0	1	1	0	0	0	0	0	0

Characteristics	Sierra Leone	Singapore	Slovakia	Slovenia	Solomon Islands	Somalia	South Africa	South Korea	Spain	Sri Lanka
Latitude (abs degrees)	8	1	48	46	9	5	30	36	40	8
Temperature: degrees (C)	27	28	6	9	27	28	19	11	15	27
: monthly high (min C)	31	33	10	20	33	30	29	12	16	31
: monthly high (max C)	35	36	39	42	36	36	39	37	39	36
: monthly low (min C)	19	19	-27	-25	18	15	-2	-24	-10	15
: monthly low (max C)	21	21	4	8	22	21	4	14	8	22
Humidity: morning min (%)	80	76	74	71	75	78	71	77	58	71
: morning max (%)	91	82	90	85	82	85	91	91	86	80
: afternoon min (%)	67	70	51	46	76	75	54	46	33	66
: afternoon max (%)	82	78	82	76	81	80	67	67	71	78
High temp @ max humidity	28	31	3	5	30	29	17	29	9	29
High humidity @ max temp	71	73	53	47	80	70	54	62	33	76
Rain: monthly min (mm)	3	170	26	46	203	0	8	20	11	69
: monthly max (mm)	902	257	84	96	297	97	89	376	53	371
: days/month min	0.7	11	9	8	12	0.3	2	6	2	6
: days/month max	28	19	15	14	15	20	10	16	10	19
Snow: persistent (1=yes)	0	0	1	0	0	0	0	1	0	0
: intermittent (1=yes)	0	0	1	1	0	0	1	1	1	0
Frost present (1=yes)	0	0	1	1	0	0	1	1	1	0
Evaporation (1=low)	-1	0	1	1	-1	-1	-1	1	-1	-1
Barometric pressure: July	1010	1010	1010	1010	1010	1010	1010	1010	1020	1010
: January	1010	1010	1020	1020	1010	1010	1010	1020	1020	1010
Risks: Typhoon (10=high)	0	0	0	0	0	0	0	0	0	0
: Flooding (10=high)	0	0	0	1	0	0	0	0	0	0
: Tropical storm (10=high)	0	0	0	0	0	0	0	0	0	0
: Windstorm (10=high)	0	0	0	0	0	0	0	0	0	1
: Drought (10=high)	0	0	0	0	0	1	1	0	0	0
Climate Type: Tropical wet	1	1	0	0	1	0	0	0	0	1
: Tropical monsoon	0	0	0	0	0	0	0	0	0	0
: Tropical wet & dry	0	0	0	0	0	0	0	0	0	0
: Steppe, low latitude	0	0	0	0	0	1	1	0	0	0
: Desert, low latitude	0	0	0	0	0	0	0	0	0	0
: Steppe, middle latitude	0	0	0	0	0	0	0	0	0	0
: Desert, middle latitude	0	0	0	0	0	0	0	0	0	0
: Subtropical, humid	0	0	0	0	0	0	1	0	0	0
: Mediterranean	0	0	0	0	0	0	0	0	1	0
: Marine, west coast	0	0	0	0	0	0	1	0	0	0
: Cont humid hot summer	0	0	1	1	0	0	0	1	0	0
: Cont humid cool summer	0	0	0	0	0	0	0	0	0	0
: Subarctic	0	0	0	0	0	0	0	0	0	0
: Tundra	0	0	0	0	0	0	0	0	0	0
: Ice cap	0	0	0	0	0	0	0	0	0	0
: Dry steppe wasteland	0	0	0	0	0	0	0	0	0	0
: Temperate highland	0	0	0	0	0	0	0	0	0	0
: Temp desert dry summer	0	0	0	0	0	0	0	0	0	0
: Temp desert dry winter	0	0	0	0	0	0	0	0	0	0
: Highland	0	0	0	0	0	0	0	0	0	0

Characteristics	St. Helena	St. Kitts & Nevis	St. Lucia	St. Pierre & Miquelon	St. Vincent & Grenad.	Sudan	Suriname	Swaziland	Sweden	Switzer-land
Latitude (abs degrees)	15	17	14	47	13	12	6	26	59	47
Temperature: degrees (C)	24	27	26	9	26	29	27	17	6	9
: monthly high (min C)	26	32	31	14	31	40	33	27	10	15
: monthly high (max C)	34	37	36	30	36	48	37	37	35	38
: monthly low (min C)	14	15	14	-12	14	5	17	-5	-28	-23
: monthly low (max C)	19	21	21	14	21	19	19	9	8	8
Humidity: morning min (%)	63	62	86	75	86	18	87	59	66	80
: morning max (%)	76	70	92	88	92	67	92	81	89	92
: afternoon min (%)	61	59	64	75	64	41	66	59	53	51
: afternoon max (%)	74	68	75	88	75	37	80	81	86	76
High temp @ max humidity	22	29	29	10	29	13	30	24	2	3
High humidity @ max temp	61	61	71	78	71	70	67	79	59	52
Rain: monthly min (mm)	0	0	91	45	91	0	76	0	25	64
: monthly max (mm)	20	196	269	70	269	71	310	254	76	136
: days/month min	8	8	10	14	10	0	9	3	10	12
: days/month max	0	16	23	14	23	6	23	16	17	15
Snow: persistent (1=yes)	0	0	0	1	0	0	0	0	1	1
: intermittent (1=yes)	0	0	0	0	0	0	0	0	1	0
Frost present (1=yes)	0	0	0	1	0	0	0	0	1	1
Evaporation (1=low)	-1	-1	-1	-1	-1	-1	-1	-1	-1	-1
Barometric pressure: July	1020	1020	1020	1010	1020	1010	1010	1020	1010	1010
: January	1010	1020	1020	1010	1020	1010	1010	1010	1010	1020
Risks: Typhoon (10=high)	0	0	0	0	0	0	0	0	0	0
: Flooding (10=high)	0	0	0	0	0	0	0	0	0	0
: Tropical storm (10=high)	0	0	1	0	1	0	0	0	0	0
: Windstorm (10=high)	0	0	0	0	0	0	0	0	0	0
: Drought (10=high)	0	0	0	0	0	1	0	0	0	0
Climate Type: Tropical wet	0	0	0	0	0	0	1	0	0	0
: Tropical monsoon	0	0	1	0	1	0	0	0	0	0
: Tropical wet & dry	0	1	0	0	0	0	0	0	0	0
: Steppe, low latitude	0	0	0	0	0	0	0	0	0	0
: Desert, low latitude	0	0	0	0	0	1	0	0	0	0
: Steppe, middle latitude	0	0	0	0	0	0	0	0	0	0
: Desert, middle latitude	0	0	0	0	0	0	0	0	0	0
: Subtropical, humid	0	0	0	0	0	0	0	1	0	0
: Mediterranean	0	0	0	0	0	0	0	0	0	0
: Marine, west coast	1	0	0	0	0	0	0	0	0	0
: Cont humid hot summer	0	0	0	0	0	0	0	0	0	0
: Cont humid cool summer	0	0	0	1	0	0	0	0	1	1
: Subarctic	0	0	0	0	0	0	0	0	1	0
: Tundra	0	0	0	0	0	0	0	0	0	0
: Ice cap	0	0	0	0	0	0	0	0	0	0
: Dry steppe wasteland	0	0	0	0	0	0	0	0	0	0
: Temperate highland	0	0	0	0	0	0	0	1	0	0
: Temp desert dry summer	0	0	0	0	0	0	0	0	0	0
: Temp desert dry winter	0	0	0	0	0	0	0	0	0	0
: Highland	0	0	0	0	0	0	0	0	0	1

Characteristics	Syrian Arab Rep.	Taiwan	Tajikistan	Tanzania	Thailand	Togo	Tokelau	Tonga	Trinidad & Tobago	Tunisia
Latitude (abs degrees)	35	24	38	4	13	6	9	21	10	36
Temperature: degrees (C)	20	21	13	22	28	27	27	27	26	24
: monthly high (min C)	21	30	19	31	37	32	33	32	35	25
: monthly high (max C)	45	38	41	36	41	38	36	34	38	48
: monthly low (min C)	-6	9	-28	8	11	15	18	17	11	-1
: monthly low (max C)	13	19	9	16	22	21	22	21	16	11
Humidity: morning min (%)	43	90	59	70	90	95	75	75	83	72
: morning max (%)	81	93	82	84	94	97	82	82	89	86
: afternoon min (%)	19	62	34	36	53	61	76	73	61	40
: afternoon max (%)	59	75	63	56	70	77	81	79	76	64
High temp @ max humidity	13	18	3	28	32	27	30	30	32	14
High humidity @ max temp	21	64	34	48	58	68	80	79	76	47
Rain: monthly min (mm)	0	66	3	0	5	15	203	81	41	3
: monthly max (mm)	43	305	66	152	305	178	297	455	246	64
: days/month min	0	7	1	0	1	1	12	7	9	2
: days/month max	7	14	12	12	15	0	15	22	23	14
Snow: persistent (1=yes)	0	0	0	0	0	0	0	0	0	0
: intermittent (1=yes)	0	0	0	0	0	0	0	0	0	0
Frost present (1=yes)	1	0	1	0	0	0	0	0	0	0
Evaporation (1=low)	0	1	0	1	1	1	1	1	1	1
Barometric pressure: July	1010	1010	999	1020	1010	1010	1010	1010	1010	1010
: January	1020	1020	1020	1010	1010	1010	1010	1010	1010	1020
Risks: Typhoon (10=high)	0	10	0	0	0	0	0	0	0	0
: Flooding (10=high)	0	0	0	0	1	0	0	0	1	0
: Tropical storm (10=high)	0	0	0	0	0	0	0	0	0	0
: Windstorm (10=high)	0	0	0	0	0	0	0	0	0	0
: Drought (10=high)	0	0	0	1	0	1	0	0	0	0
Climate Type: Tropical wet	0	0	0	0	0	0	1	1	0	0
: Tropical monsoon	0	0	0	0	1	0	0	0	1	0
: Tropical wet & dry	0	0	0	1	0	1	0	0	0	0
: Steppe, low latitude	0	0	0	0	0	0	0	0	0	0
: Desert, low latitude	0	0	0	0	0	0	0	0	0	0
: Steppe, middle latitude	0	0	0	0	0	0	0	0	0	0
: Desert, middle latitude	0	0	0	0	0	0	0	0	0	0
: Subtropical, humid	0	1	0	0	0	0	0	0	0	0
: Mediterranean	1	0	0	0	0	0	0	0	0	1
: Marine, west coast	0	0	0	0	0	0	0	0	0	0
: Cont humid hot summer	0	0	0	0	0	0	0	0	0	0
: Cont humid cool summer	0	0	0	0	0	0	0	0	0	0
: Subarctic	0	0	0	0	0	0	0	0	0	0
: Tundra	0	0	0	0	0	0	0	0	0	0
: Ice cap	0	0	0	0	0	0	0	0	0	0
: Dry steppe wasteland	0	0	0	0	0	0	0	0	0	0
: Temperate highland	0	0	0	0	0	0	0	0	0	0
: Temp desert dry summer	0	0	0	0	0	0	0	0	0	0
: Temp desert dry winter	0	0	0	0	0	0	0	0	0	0
: Highland	0	0	1	0	0	0	0	0	0	0

Characteristics	Turkey	Turkme-nistan	Turks & Caicos	Tuvalu	Uganda	Ukraine	United Arab Emir.	United Kingdom	United States	Uruguay
Latitude (abs degrees)	39	38	21	8	0.2	50	25	53	44	34
Temperature: degrees (C)	9	14	20	28	24	5	26	12	12	20
: monthly high (min C)	15	16	29	33	29	8	29	14	23	26
: monthly high (max C)	38	42	34	36	36	35	48	34	41	43
: monthly low (min C)	-25	-17	5	18	12	-25	3	-10	-26	-4
: monthly low (max C)	7	14	19	22	15	9	23	7	11	8
Humidity: morning min (%)	54	52	79	75	78	69	61	70	68	73
: morning max (%)	86	77	84	82	89	92	82	87	81	89
: afternoon min (%)	25	41	62	76	54	50	59	56	45	52
: afternoon max (%)	71	69	73	81	72	84	65	81	56	69
High temp @ max humidity			31	30	25	-1	36			14
High humidity @ max temp	25	42	70	80	56	55	64	59	53	55
Rain: monthly min (mm)	10	5	33	203	46	30	0	37	66	66
: monthly max (mm)	48	23	175	297	175	91	36	64	112	99
: days/month min	1	1	5	12	9	8	0	11		5
: days/month max	9	5	15	15	19	13	2	15	12	7
Snow: persistent (1=yes)	1	0	0	0	0	1	0	0	1	0
: intermittent (1=yes)	1	1	0	0	1	1	0	1	1	0
Frost present (1=yes)	1	0	0	0	1	1	0	1	1	0
Evaporation (1=low)		-1	-1	1	1	1	-1	-1	1	-1
Barometric pressure: July	1010	1010	1010	1010	1010	1010	999	1010	1010	1020
: January	1020	1020	1010	1010	1010	1020	1020	1010	1020	1010
Risks: Typhoon (10=high)	0	0	0	0	0	0	0	0	0	0
: Flooding (10=high)	0	0	0	0	0	0	0	0	0	1
: Tropical storm (10=high)	0	0	0	0	0	0	0	0	0	0
: Windstorm (10=high)	0	0	0	0	0	0	0	0	0	0
: Drought (10=high)	0	0	0	0	0	0	1	0	0	0
Climate Type: Tropical wet	0	0	0	1	0	0	0	0	0	0
: Tropical monsoon	0	0	0	0	0	0	0	0	0	0
: Tropical wet & dry	0	0	1	0	1	0	0	0	0	0
: Steppe, low latitude	1	0	0	0	0	0	0	0	0	0
: Desert, low latitude	0	1	0	0	0	0	1	0	0	0
: Steppe, middle latitude	0	0	0	0	0	0	0	0	0	0
: Desert, middle latitude	0	0	0	0	0	0	0	0	0	0
: Subtropical, humid	0	0	0	0	0	0	0	0	0	1
: Mediterranean	1	0	0	0	0	0	0	0	0	0
: Marine, west coast	0	0	0	0	0	0	0	1	1	0
: Cont humid hot summer	0	0	0	0	0	0	0	0	1	0
: Cont humid cool summer	0	0	0	0	0	1	0	0	0	0
: Subarctic	0	0	0	0	0	0	0	0	0	0
: Tundra	0	0	0	0	0	0	0	0	0	0
: Ice cap	0	0	0	0	0	0	0	0	0	0
: Dry steppe wasteland	1	0	0	0	0	0	0	0	0	0
: Temperate highland	0	0	0	0	0	0	0	0	0	0
: Temp desert dry summer	1	0	0	0	0	0	0	0	0	0
: Temp desert dry winter	0	0	0	0	0	0	0	0	1	0
: Highland	0	0	0	0	1	0	0	0	0	0

Characteristics	Uzbekistan	Vanuatu	Vatican City	Venezuela	Vietnam	Virgin Isl. US	Wallis & Futuna	West Bank	Western Samoa	Western Sahara
Latitude (abs degrees)	41	17	42	9	15	18	14	32	14	27
Temperature: degrees (C)	13	25	17	20	25	27	26	20	26	26
: monthly high (min C)	16	32	19	28	33	32	32	25	32	27
: monthly high (max C)	42	37	40	33	43	37	34	42	34	49
: monthly low (min C)	-17	13	-6	7	6	15	17	-3	17	-3
: monthly low (max C)	14	19	12	12	22	21	21	11	21	14
Humidity: morning min (%)	52	76	70	78	74	62	75	47	75	69
: morning max (%)	77	82	87	84	83	70	82	77	82	90
: afternoon min (%)	41	73	42	60	67	59	73	32	73	36
: afternoon max (%)	69	79	70	63	76	68	79	66	79	63
High temp @ max humidity	3	28	13	33	23	29	30	13	30	18
High humidity @ max temp	42	77	43	60	72	61	79	36	79	37
Rain: monthly min (mm)	5	125	15	0	18	86	81	0	81	0
: monthly max (mm)	23	368	129	109	343	196	455	132	455	33
: days/month min	1	13	1	2	7	8	27	11	7	1
: days/month max	5	21	11	15	16	16	22		22	7
Snow: persistent (1=yes)	0	0	0	0	0	0	0	0	0	0
: intermittent (1=yes)	1	0	1	0	0	0	0	1	0	0
Frost present (1=yes)	1	0	1	0	0	0	0	1	0	0
Evaporation (1=low)	1	0	1	1	1	1	0	1	0	1
Barometric pressure: July	1010	1020	1010	1010	1010	1020	1010	1010	1010	1010
: January	1020	1010	1020	1010	1010	1020	1010	1020	1010	1020
Risks: Typhoon (10=high)	0	1	0	0	1	1	1	0	1	0
: Flooding (10=high)	0	0	0	1	1	0	0	0	0	0
: Tropical storm (10=high)	0	1	0	0	1	1	1	0	1	0
: Windstorm (10=high)	0	0	0	0	0	1	0	0	0	1
: Drought (10=high)	1	0	0	1	1	0	0	1	0	1
Climate Type: Tropical wet	0	1	0	0	0	0	1	0	1	0
: Tropical monsoon	0	0	0	0	1	0	0	0	0	0
: Tropical wet & dry	0	0	0	1	0	1	0	0	0	0
: Steppe, low latitude	0	0	0	0	0	0	0	0	0	0
: Desert, low latitude	0	0	0	0	0	0	0	0	0	1
: Steppe, middle latitude	0	0	0	0	0	0	0	0	0	0
: Desert, middle latitude	0	0	0	0	0	0	0	0	0	0
: Subtropical, humid	0	0	0	0	0	0	0	0	0	0
: Mediterranean	0	0	1	0	0	0	0	1	0	0
: Marine, west coast	0	0	0	0	0	0	0	0	0	0
: Cont humid hot summer	0	0	0	0	0	0	0	0	0	0
: Cont humid cool summer	0	0	0	0	0	0	0	0	0	0
: Subarctic	0	0	0	0	0	0	0	0	0	0
: Tundra	0	0	0	0	0	0	0	0	0	0
: Ice cap	0	0	0	0	0	0	0	0	0	0
: Dry steppe wasteland	0	0	0	0	0	0	0	0	0	0
: Temperate highland	0	0	0	0	0	0	0	0	0	0
: Temp desert dry summer	0	0	0	0	0	0	0	0	0	0
: Temp desert dry winter	1	0	0	0	0	0	0	0	0	0
: Highland	0	0	0	0	0	0	0	0	0	0

Characteristics	Yemen	Zaire	Zambia	Zimbabwe
Latitude (abs degrees)	15	7	20	19
Temperature: degrees (C)	30	25	21	18
: monthly high (min C)	31	32	28	26
: monthly high (max C)	41	36	38	35
: monthly low (min C)	19	14	4	9
: monthly low (max C)	24	19	14	9
Humidity: morning min (%)	63	88	39	43
: morning max (%)	79	95	85	77
: afternoon min (%)	52	61	19	26
: afternoon max (%)	69	73	71	57
High temp @ max humidity	28	31	26	26
High humidity @ max temp	52	71	23	26
Rain: monthly min (mm)	0	3	0	0
: monthly max (mm)	23	222	231	196
: days/month min	0.1	0.1	0.1	0.6
: days/month max	2	16	21	18
Snow: persistent (1=yes)	0	0	0	0
: intermittent (1=yes)	0	0	0	0
Frost present (1=yes)	0	0	0	0
Evaporation (1=low)	0	1	0	-1
Barometric pressure: July	1010	1010	1020	1020
: January	1020	1010	1010	1010
Risks: Typhoon (10=high)	0	0	0	0
: Flooding (10=high)	0	0	0	0
: Tropical storm (10=high)	0	0	0	1
: Windstorm (10=high)	1	1	1	0
: Drought (10=high)	0	1	1	0
Climate Type: Tropical wet	0	1	0	1
: Tropical monsoon	0	0	0	0
: Tropical wet & dry	0	1	1	0
: Steppe, low latitude	0	0	0	0
: Desert, low latitude	0	0	0	0
: Steppe, middle latitude	0	0	0	1
: Desert, middle latitude	0	0	0	1
: Subtropical, humid	0	0	0	0
: Mediterranean	0	0	0	0
: Marine, west coast	0	0	0	0
: Cont humid hot summer	0	0	0	0
: Cont humid cool summer	0	0	0	0
: Subarctic	0	0	0	0
: Tundra	0	0	0	0
: Ice cap	0	0	0	0
: Dry steppe wasteland	0	0	0	0
: Temperate highland	0	0	0	0
: Temp desert dry summer	0	0	0	0
: Temp desert dry winter	0	0	0	0
: Highland	0	1	0	0

10

SELECT BIBLIOGRAPHY

This chapter provides a bibliography of research works focusing on the relationship between cultures and civilizations and physioeconomic factors, especially climate. The bibliography does not specifically treat national cultures per se but rather considers aspects associated with all cultures, including linguistic cultures, civilization & history, culture and ethnology (the latter two cover a miscellany of topics). This chapter is drawn from a larger bibliography of over 3000 citations which cover a far broader range of physioeconomic effects on physiological, psychological, social and economic behaviors.[1] The bibliography given here is biased toward more recent publications because of the extensive use of computer databases which tend to index the more recent literature streams. Nevertheless, a special effort was made to include the more cited references published from the mid-18th century to the mid-20th century, and recent publications not readily available from databases. The usual disclaimer applies, however, as certain works may have been regrettably overlooked. Every effort has been made to avoid a particular regional bias by the extensive use of international databases and libraries, with their networks, in North America, Asia, and Europe. Furthermore, no reporting bias is introduced in the bibliography to the extent that the results reported were not used as a criteria for inclusion. Citations from various schools of thought, including those showing a lack of physioeconomic effect on a particular behavior, are represented.

In addition to original works, a number of databases were consulted including general on-line systems.[2] Readers will note that the citations include a brief run-in annotation of subjects discussed in the reference which have been drawn from the keywords, text, abstracts, or descriptors of the works in question.

---

[1] See Parker (1995) *Climatic Effects on Individual, Social and Economic Behavior: A Physioeconomic Review of Research Across Disciplines*. Bibliographies and Indexes in Geography, Number 2. Westport, Connecticut; London: Greenwood Press, (ISBN: 0-313-29400-3).

[2] These include DIALOG, Internet connections to libraries, MELVYL and specific databases (MEDLINE, NTIS, Dissertation Abstracts, SOICOFILE, Social Science Index, Social Science Citation Index, General Science Index, General Science Citation Index, Applied Science and Technology Index, GEOREF, Books in Print, AGRICOLA, PSYCHLIT, ECONLIT, Life Sciences Index and BIO Abstracts, among others). All of the journal abbreviations are those used by the National Library of Medicine (MEDLINE, MEDLARS onLINE) and provide sufficient information for complete identification. These abbreviations are indexed in "List of Serial Index for Online Services", available from the National Technical Information Service (NTIS), U.S. Department of Commerce, 5285 Port Royal Road, Springfield, VA 22161 (tel.: 703-487-4650, 4640). For further information on cited dissertations, the reader is referred to Dissertation Abstracts. For further information on reports, see NTIS.

CIVILIZATION & HISTORY

Allen, R. O. "Impact of the environment on Egyptian civilization before the Pharaohs." *Analytical Chemistry* 65 (January 1993): 32A-34A. Topics discussed include: rivers, sediments, the Nile, Egypt, civilization, archeology, climatic changes.

Allen, W. D. "Music history in five five-hundred-year cycles (Greek-Early Christian-Gregorian-Medieval-Modern); conditioned by the parallel climatic-cultural cycles." 41 pages. Weather Science Foundation. *Journal of Human Ecology,* 1 no. 13 (1951); Crystal Lake, Illinois: Published for the Weather Science Foundation by Weather Forecasts, 1951. Topics discussed include: history, physiology.

Anderson, E. *Latvia-past and present ... 1918-1968. Historical past in pictures, climate, fauna and flora, the country and its cities, people and their culture.* 2d. rev. ed. Waverly, IA: Latvju Gramata, 1969. Topics discussed include: Latvia.

Barrell, J. "Probable Relations of Climatic Changes to the Origin of the Tertiary Ape-Man." *Scientific Monthly* (1917). Topics discussed include: climate, history, anthropology, archeology.

Basu, A. "High Altitude Hypoxia, Culture, and Human Fecundity, Fertility." *American Anthropologist* 86 (December 1984): 994-996.

Beals, K. L. "Brain size, cranial morphology, climate, and time machines." *Current Anthropology* 25, no. 3 (June 1984): 301-330. Topics discussed include: head measures, ethnic groups, environment, morphology, evolution.

Bishop, C. W. "The Geographical Factor in the Development of Chinese Civilisation." *Geographical Review* (1922): 7. Topics discussed include: geography, civilisation, history, culture.

Boyden, S. "Cultural Adaptation to Ecological Maladjustment." in *The Impact of Civilization on the Biology of Man,* 190-218. editor S. Boyden. Canberra: Australian National University Press, 1970. Topics discussed include: culture, environment, society, behavior, biology.

Brown, N. "Climate-change and human history - some indications from Europe, AD400-1400." *Environmental Pollution* 83, no. 1-2 (1994): 37-43. Topics discussed include: history, science.

Bryson, R. A. "Climatic Change and the Mill Creek Culture of Iowa." *Journal of the Iowa Archeological Society* 15-16 (1968): 1-358. Topics discussed include: history.

---. "Some cultural and economic consequences of climate change." University of Wisconsin, Madison. Center for Climatic Research. Institute for Environmental Studies, 1975. Topics discussed include: crops, weather, mental illness, physiology, man.

Buchner, A. P. "Cultural responses to Altithermal (Atlantic) climate along the eastern margins of the North American grasslands, 5500 to 3000 B.C." Ph.D. diss., University of Calgary, National Museums of Canada, 1980. Topics discussed include: paleoclimatology, North America, Indians, antiquities, paleoecology.

Budyko, M. I. "Anthropogenic Climatic Changes." *Climate and development: Climatic change and variability and the resulting social, economic and technological implications,* 270-284. eds H. J. Otten, D. Trinidade, S. C. Karpe. New York; Berlin; London and Tokyo: Springer in cooperation with the United Nations, 1990. Topics discussed include: natural resources, climatic effects.

Bullen, A. K. ed. "Development of high civilizations in hot climates." 101-149. Florida Academy of Science. *Florida anthropologist* 6, no. 4 (December 1953) Gainesville, FL: Florida Anthropological Society, 1953.

Butzer, K. "Environment, culture, and human evolution." *Am Sci* 65, no. 5 (September 1977): 572-584. Topics discussed include: climate, fossils, history, medicine, ancient civilizations, culture, evolution.

Carter, G. F. *Man and the Land: A Cultural Geography*. New York: Holt, Rinehart and Winston, 1964. Topics discussed include: culture, geography, behavior.

Chaunu, P. "Le Climat et l'Histoire, à Propos d'un Livre Récent." *Rev Historique* (October 1967). Topics discussed include: climate, history, civilization.

Claiborne, R. *Climate, man and history*. 444 pages. London: Angus & Robertson, 1973. Topics discussed include: civilization, culture.

Condon, R. G. *Inuit behavior and seasonal change in the Canadian Arctic*. 228 pages. Studies in cultural anthropology; no. 2, Ann Arbor, Mich.: UMI Research Press, 1983. Topics discussed include: Eskimos, physical measures, psychology, arctic medicine, disease, seasonality, Indians of North America, man.

---. "Seasonal Variation and Interpersonal Conflict in the Central Canadian Arctic." *Ethnology* 21, no. 2 (April 1982): 151-164. Topics discussed include: sociology, Canada.

Custer, J. F. "Cultural ecology and archaeology in the Middle Atlantic: Are people really more than what they eat: Part I: A short history of studies of past environments in Middle Atlantic archaeology." *Pennsylvania Archaeologist* 57, no. 1 (1987): 47-51. Topics discussed include: Indians, culture, prehistory, ecology, archeology.

de Vries, J. "Measuring the Impact of Climate on History: The Search for Appropriate Methodologies." *Journal of Interdisciplinary History* 10 (1980): 599-630. Topics discussed include: history.

Edgerton, R. "Cultural vs. Ecological Factors in the Expression of Values, Attitudes, and Personality Characteristics." *American Anthropologist* 67 (1965): 442-447. Topics discussed include: culture, climatic effects, ecology, environment, behaviour, psychology.

Ekiguchi, K. *Japanese Craft & Customs: A Seasonal Approach*. New York: Kodansha America, 1993. Topics discussed include: sociology, anthropology, archeology, social life, customs, arts.

Feldman, D. A. "The history of the relationship between environment and culture in ethnological thought: An overview." *J of the Hist of the Behavioral Sci* 11, no. 1 (1975): 67-81. Topics discussed include: ethnology, cultural ecology.

Fischer, D. H. "Climate and History: Priorities for Research." *Journal of Interdisciplinary History* 10 (1980): 821-831. Topics discussed include: history.

Fournol, A. *Climats et Habitation*, Paris, 1956. Topics discussed include: climate, civilization, building.

Friedman, R. M. "Appropriating the weather." *Technology and Culture* 31 no. 31 (October 1990): 251, 888-889.

Gates, D. M. *Man and his environment: climate*. 175 pages. Man and his environment series, New York: Harper & Row, 1971. Topics discussed include: climatology, environment, policy.

George, H. B. *The Relations of Geography and History.* Oxford University Press: 1901. Topics discussed include: climate, culture, geography, history.

Gourou, P. "Civilisations et Malchance Geographique." *Annales Economies Societes Civilisations* 4 (1949): 445-450. Topics discussed include: climate, geography, history, economy, society, culture.

Gribbin, J. R. *Climate and mankind.* 56 pages. World Climate Conference (Geneva, Switzerland). London: Earthscan, 1979. Topics discussed include: climatic changes.

Griffin, J. B. "Some Correlations of Climatic and Cultural Change in Eastern American Prehistory." *Annals of the New York Academy of Sciences* 95, no. 1 (1961): 710-717. Topics discussed include: climate, culture, history, archeology.

Guterbock, T. M. "The Effect of Snow on Urban Density Patterns in the United States." *Environment and Behavior* 22, no. 3 (May 1990): 358-386. Topics discussed include: weather, population density.

Hadlow, L. *Climate, vegetation and man.* 288 pages. Fundamental geography, book 3, London: University of London Press, 1964. Topics discussed include: bioclimatology, crops, agricultural zones.

Hardy, J. D. "Measurement of the radiant heat load on man in summer and winter Alaskan climates." 43 pages. United States. Arctic Aeromedical Laboratory, Ladd Air Force, Alaska Special report, Ladd Air Force Base, Alaska: 1953. Topics discussed include: Alaska, climatic effects, temperature, physiology.

Harris, M. *Culture, Man and Nature.* New York: Crowell, 1971. Topics discussed include: culture, civilization, environment.

Hippocrates. *Airs, Waters and Places.* 460 B.C. Topics discussed include: weather, climatic effects, mortality, health.

Hoch, I. "Wages, Climate and the Quality of Life." *Journal of Environmental Economics and Management* 1 (1974): 268-295. Topics discussed include: environment, economy, society, culture.

Huntington, E. "Changes of Climate and History." *Am Hist Rev* 18 (1913): 213-232. Topics discussed include: history, society, culture.

---. *Mainsprings of Civilization.* New York: Wiley, 1945. Topics discussed include: theory, culture, history, society, geography, climate.

---. "Maya Civilization and Climatic Changes." Proc 19th Intern Congr Americanists, 150-164. Washington, 1917. Topics discussed include: climate, civilization, culture, history, environment.

---. "Physical Environment as a Factor in the Present Conditions of Turkey." *J Race Development* I (1911): 460-481. Topics discussed include: environment, geography, society, history, anthropolgy.

---. *The Character of Races As Influenced by Physical Environment, Natural Selection and Historical Development.* New York: Charles Scribner's Sons, 1924. Topics discussed include: climate, geography, biology, history, society, culture.

---. *Civilization and climate.* 453 pages. 3d ed., New Haven: Yale University Press, 1924. Topics discussed include: man, geography.

---. "Climate and the Evolution of Civilization." in *The Evolution of Earth and its Inhabitants*, editor R. S. Lull. New Haven: Yale University Press, 1919. Topics discussed include: civilization, culture.

---. "Death Valley and our future climate." Harper's Monthly Magazine (May 1916). Topics discussed include: climate.

Jones, A. M. "Exploiting a Marginal European Environment: Population Control and Resource Management under the Ancien Regime." *Journal of Family History* 16, no. 4 (October 1991): 363-379. Topics discussed include: resources, demography, France, Malthus.

Junior League of McAllen, Inc. Staff. *Some Like It Hot: The Climate, Culture & Cuisine of South Texas*. McAllen, TX: Junior League of McAllen, 1992. Topics discussed include: social life, customs, cookery, Texas.

Lamb, H. H. "Climate and history: Report on the international conference on Climate and history: Climatic research unit, University of East Anglia, Norwich, England, 8-14 July 1979." *Past & Present* 88 (1980): 136-141. Topics discussed include: methodology, history.

---. *Climatic History & the Modern World*. New York, NY: Routledge, Chapman & Hall, 1982. Topics discussed include: weather, meteorology.

---. *Climatic History & the Future*. Princeton, NJ: Princeton University Press, 1985. Topics discussed include: weather, meteorology.

Laudien, H. *Temperature relations in animals and man*. 229 pages. Biona report; 4. Schriftenreihe der Akademie der Wissenschaften und der Literatur, Mainz, Kommission für Biologische Kybernetik, Mainz, Stuttgart ; New York: Akademie der Wissenschaften und der Literatur ; G. Fischer, 1986. Topics discussed include: animals, heat.

Le Roy Ladurie, E. "Histoire et Climat." *Annales: Economies, Societes, Civilisations* 14 (1959): 3-34. Topics discussed include: climate, economy, society, weather, culture.

Lee, D. "Culture and climatology." *Int J Biometeorol* 12, no. 4 (December 1968): 317-319. Topics discussed include: acclimation, culture.

Leff, D. N. "Biology, Behavior and Environment in Human Evolution." *Mosaic* 10, no. 2 (March 1979): 2-12. Topics discussed include: evolution, biology, behavior, history.

Ludlum, D. M. *The Weather Factor: Fascinating Accounts of How Weather Shaped America's Battles, Sports, & History*. Boston, MA: Houghton Mifflin Company, 1984. Topics discussed include: history, sports.

Mackey, W. C. "A Statistical Analysis of Whiting's Effects of Climate on Certain Cultural Practices' with Special Reference to Galton's Problem." *Southeastern Review* 1, no. 1 (December 1973): 64-87. Topics discussed include: climates, culture, anthropology, Africa, ecology, diffusion.

Meggers, B. "Environmental Limitations on the Development of Culture." *American Anthropologist* 56 (1954): 801-824. Topics discussed include: environment, geography, culture, economy, history, society.

Melichar, F. "Civilization diseases in tropical climate." *Med Welt* 11 (13 March 1971): 431-433. Topics discussed include: civilization, Vietnam, arteriosclerosis epidemiology, diabetes mellitus epidemiology, hypertension epidemiology, tropical medicine.

---. "Changes in the Seasonality of Human Mortality: A Medico-Geographical Study." *Social Science and Medicine* 12, no. 1D (March 1978): 29-42. Topics discussed include: death, disease, civilization, biometeorology, Europe, North America, Japan.

Mills, C. A. *Climate makes the man*. 320 pages. [1st ed.] ed. New York, London: Harper & Brothers, 1942. Topics discussed include: weather, mental illness, physiology, climatology, medicine.

Milov, L. V. "Natural and Climatic Factors and Peculiarities of Russian Historic Process." *Historical Social Research, Historische Sozialforschung* 16, no. 2(58) (1991): 40-59. Topics discussed include: USSR, history, Russia, nature, climatic effects.

Monge M. *Acclimatization in the Andes; historical confirmations of climatic aggression in the development of Andean man*, 130 pages. Baltimore: Johns Hopkins Press, 1948. Topics discussed include: altitude, mountain sickness.

Montesquieu, C. d. S. d. *The Spirit of Laws*. Anne M. Cohler, Basia Carolyn Miller and Harold Samuel Stone, translators, Cambridge; New York: Cambridge University Press, 1989; original 1748. Topics discussed include: climate, culture, civilization, mortality, fertility, alcohol, labor, laws, economics.

Nelles, H. V. "Commerce in a Cold Climate: Bliss on Canadian Business History." *Business History Review* 62, no. 2 (June 1988): 310-316. Topics discussed include: economics, history, Canada.

Newman, R. W. "The Relation of Climate and Body Size in U. S. males." *Am J Phys Anthropol N S* 13 (1955): 1-17. Topics discussed include: biology, physiology.

Numata, K. "Fudo, or climate and culture." *Shakaigaku Hyoron, Japanese Sociological Review* 25, no. 3 (December 1974): 99, 113-119. Topics discussed include: culture, climate, national character.

Nuttonson, M. Y. *Rice culture and rice-climate relationships with special reference to the United States rice areas and their latitudinal and thermal analogues in other countries*. 555 pages. American Institute of Crop Ecology, and United States. Weather Bureau. Washington: American Institute of Crop Ecology, 1965. Topics discussed include: rice, climatic effects.

Ogum, G. E. O. "Seasonality of Births in South-Eastern Nigeria." *Journal of Biosocial Science* 11, no. 2 (April 1979): 209-217. Topics discussed include: Nigeria, birth, season, culture.

Pain, S. "Rigid cultures caught out by climate-change." *New Scientist* 141, no. 1915 (5 March 1994): 13.

Global dermatology: diagnosis and management according to geography, climate, and culture, eds Lawrence Charles Parish, Larry E. Millikan, and Mohamed Amer. New York: Springer-Verlag, 1994. Topics discussed include: medicine, geography, skin disease, epidemiology, dermatology, cross-cultural analysis, diagnosis, treatment, anthropology.

Parker, P.M. *Climatic Effects on Individual, Social and Economic Behavior: A Physioeconomic Review of Research Across Disciplines*, Bibliographies and Indexes in Geography, Number 2, Westport, Connecticut; London: Greenwood Press, 1995 (ISBN: 0-313-29400-3).

Pearce, F. "Climate and man." *New Scientist* 125 (13 January 1990): 67.

Peattie, R. *Geography in Human Destiny*. New York: George W. Stewart, 1940. Topics discussed include: geography, history, behavior, biology.

Petersen, W. F. *Man, weather, sun.* 463 pages. [1st ed.] ed. Springfield, IL.: C. C. Thomas, 1947. Topics discussed include: environment, climatology, medicine.

Pfister, C. "Climate and Economy in Eighteenth-Century Switzerland." *Journal of Interdisciplinary History* 9, no. 2 (1978): 223-243. Topics discussed include: Switzerland, history, climatic effects, economy, demography, eighteenth century.

Post, J. D. "The Impact of Climate on Political, Social, and Economic Change: A Comment." *Journal of Interdisciplinary History* 10, no. 4 (March 1980): 719-723. Topics discussed include: demography, economics, cycles, climatic variation.

---. "A Study in Meteorological and Trade Cycle History: The Economic Crisis Following the Napoleonic Wars." *Journal of Economic History* 34, no. 2 (June 1974): 315-349. Topics discussed include: history, fluctuations.

"Proceedings of the World Climate Conference : a conference of experts on climate and mankind, Geneva, 12-23 February 1979." World Climate Conference (1979 : Geneva, Switzerland), and World Meteorological Organization. Secretariat of the World Meteorological Organization, Geneva, 1979. Topics discussed include: climatology, climatic changes.

Rentsch, J. R. "Climate and culture: interaction and qualitative differences in organizational meanings." *Journal of Applied Psychology* 75 (December 1990): 668-681. Topics discussed include: sociology, interpersonal interaction, psychology.

Robbins, M. C. "Climate and Behavior: A Biocultural Study." *Journal of Cross Cultural Psychology* 3 (1972): 331-344. Topics discussed include: behavior, biology, culture.

---. "Explorations in Psychocultural Bioclimatology." Ph.D. diss., University of Minnesota, 1966. Topics discussed include: anthropology, bioclimatology; available from UMI.

Roberts, D. F. "Body Weight, Race and Climate." *Am JPhys Anthropol* II (1953): 533-558. Topics discussed include: biology, physionomy, anthropology.

---. *Climate and human variability.* 123 pages. 2d ed ed. Cummings modular program in anthropology, Menlo Park, CA.: Cummings Pub. Co., 1978.

Ross, A. *Strange weather : culture, science, and technology in the age of limits,* 1956 Andrew Ross. London; New York: Verso, 1991. Topics discussed include: science, philosophy, sociology, technology, change in society.

Rotberg, R. L. *Climate & History.* 1981. Topics discussed include: history.

Semple, E. Ch. *American History and Its Geographic Conditions.* 1903. Topics discussed include: history, geography, environment, climate.

---. *Influences of Geographic Environment.* New York: Holt, Rinehart & Winston, 1911. Topics discussed include: history, geography, climate, economy.

Shapley, H. *Climate and Civilization.* Cambridge: Harvard University Press, 1953. Topics discussed include: culture, society, history.

Silverberg, R. *The challenge of climate: man and his environment.* 326 pages. [1st ed.] ed. New York: Meredith Press, 1969.

Stahl, P. "On climate and occupation of the Santa Elena Peninsula: implications of documents for Andean prehistory." *Current Anthropology* 25 (June 1984): 351-352. Topics discussed include: geography, Ecuador, history, social forces.

Upham, S. "Smallpox and Climate in the American Southwest." *American Anthropologist* 88, no. 1 (March 1986): 115-128. Topics discussed include: culture, interpersonal contact, epidemics, diseases, weather, American Indians, Spanish exploration, climatic effects.

Valentine, J. H. "Human Crises and the Physical Environment." *Man Environment Systems* 5, no. 1 (January 1975): 23-28. Topics discussed include: weather, crisis, news, pollution, a literature review.

Walker, E. G. *The Gowen Sites: Cultural Responses to Climatic Warming on the Northern Plains, 7500 500 BP*. Chicago, IL: University of Chicago Press, 1993. Topics discussed include: sociology, anthropology, archeology, history, Canada, British Columbia.

Walker, T. S. *Village and household economies in Indi's semi-arid tropics*. 394 pages. Baltimore and London: Johns Hopkins University Press, 1990. Topics discussed include: rural areas, economics.

Wallis, W. "Geographical Environment and Culture." *Social Forces* 4 (1926): 702-708. Topics discussed include: geography, culture, society.

Watsuji, T. *Climate and culture : a philosophical study*. 235 pages. Classics of modern Japanese thought and culture, New York: Greenwood Press, 1988. Topics discussed include: monsoons, ecology, Japan, philosophy.

Whitebeck, R. H. "The Influence of Geographical Environment upon Religious Belief." *The Geographical Review* 5 (1918): 316-324. Topics discussed include: geography, behavior, religion, culture.

Whiting, J. "Effects of Climate on Certain Cultural Practices." *Explorations in Cultural Anthropology*, W. Goodenough. New York: McGraw-Hill, 1964.

Wigley, T. M. L. *Climate and history : studies in past climates and their impact on man*. 530 pages. Cambridge ; New York: Cambridge University Press, 1981. Topics discussed include: climatic change, sociology, paleoclimatology.

Woodbury, R. "Climatic Changes and Prehistoric Agriculture in the South-Western United States." *N Y A S* 95, no. art I (5 October 1961): 705-709. Topics discussed include: climate, history, civilization.

Wulsin, F. R. "Adaptations to Climate Among Non-European Peoples." in *Physiology of Heat Regulation*, editor L. N. Newburgh. Philadelphia: Saunders, 1949. Topics discussed include: anthropology, biology, environment, temperature.

CULTURE, MISCELLANEOUS

Abelson, A. "Altitude and fertility." *Anthropological studies of human fertility*, 83-91. ed B. A. Kaplan. Detroit: Wayne State Univ Press, 1976. Topics discussed include: anoxia, culture, Peru.

Aronin, J. *Climate and Architecture*. New York: Van Nostrand Reinhold, 1984. Topics discussed include: meteorology, science.

Bach, W. *Carbon dioxide : current views and developments in energy, climate research: 2nd course of the International School of Climatology, Ettore Majorana Centre for Scientific Culture, Erice, Italy, July 16-26, 1982*. 525 pages. International School of Climatology. Dordrecht; Boston; Hingham, MA: D. Reidel; Sold and distributed in the U.S.A. and Canada by Kluwer Academic Publishers, 1983. Topics discussed include: atmospheric carbon dioxide.

Bahel, V. et al. "A computer study for estimation of seasonal energy consumption and selection of air-conditioner in six Saudi Arabian cities." *Energy Conversion and Management* 28, no. 1 (1988): 27-33. Topics discussed include: electricity, air conditioning, buildings, Saudi Arabia, climate.

Barnett, G. A. "Seasonality in Television Viewing: A Mathematical Model of Cultural Processes." *Communication Research* 18, no. 6 (December 1991): 755-772. Topics discussed include: programming, production, sociocultural factors, television ratings.

Binford, L. R. "Mobility, Housing and Environment: A Comparative Study." *Journal of Anthropological Research* 46, no. 2 (June 1990): 119-152. Topics discussed include: hunting, gathering cultures, sociology, mobility, seasonality, cross-cultural effects.

Building Research Advisory Board. "Weather and Building Industry." Proceedings of B R A B Conference, Washington, 1950. Washington DC: U. S. National Academy of Sciences, 1950. Topics discussed include: climate, economy, society, culture.

Caldwell, J. C. et al. "Periodic high risk as a cause of fertility decline in a changing rural environment: survival strategies in the 1980-1983 south Indian drought." *Economic Development and Cultural Change* 34 (July 1986): 677-701. Topics discussed include: India, rural areas, food supply.

Campbell, M. "Sudden infant death syndrome and environmental temperature: further evidence for a time lagged relationship." *Med J Aust* 151, no. 7 (2 October 1989): 365-367. Topics discussed include: age effects, body regulation, culture, risks, epidemiology, timing, etiology.

Cecil, R. G. et al. "The Caribbean Migrant Farm Worker Programme in Ontario: Seasonal Expansion of West Indian Economic Spaces." *International Migration, Migrations Internationales, Migraciones Internationales* 30, no. 1 (March 1992): 19-37. Topics discussed include: Caribbean, culture, agriculture, workers, employment, Canada.

Collins, J. L. "Seasonal migration as a cultural response to energy scarcity at high altitude." *Current Anthropology* 24 (February 1983): 103-104. Topics discussed include: Peru, adaptation, culture.

Condon, R. G. et al. "The ecology of human birth seasonality." *Human Ecology* 10 (December 1982): 495-511. Topics discussed include: Papua New Guinea, culture, customs, Eskimos, sociology, sex customs, primitive cultures, fertility.

Coon, C. S. "Some Problems of Human Variability and Natural Selection in Climate and Culture." *Am Naturalist* 89 (1955): 257-280. Topics discussed include: culture, biology, mortality.

Dutt, J. et al. "Environment, migration and health in southern Peru." *Soc Sci Med* 12, no. 1B (January 1978): 29-38. Topics discussed include: age effects, altitude, culture, gender effects, health issues, transients.

Edgerton, R. "Cultural vs. Ecological Factors in the Expression of Values, Attitudes, and Personality Characteristics." *American Anthropologist* 67 (1965): 442-447. Topics discussed include: culture, climatic effects, ecology, environment, behaviour, psychology.

Farrington, M. K. "The Seasonality of Pathology: A Sociological Analysis." Ph.D. diss., University of New Hampshire, 1980. Topics discussed include: sociology, social welfare, suicide, mortality, disease, behavior, culture, economy, climatic effects; available from UMI.

---. "Geophysical variables and behavior: XXXVI. Regional variation in suicide and homicide: Controls for weather and southern culture." *Perceptual and Motor Skills* 64, no. 2 (April 1987): 430. Topics discussed include: geography, epidemiology, atmospheric effects.

Goldstein, M. C. et al. "High altitude hypoxia, culture, and human fecundity, fertility: a comparative study." *American Anthropologist* 85 (March 1983): 28-49. Topics discussed include: anoxemia, Ladakh India, anthropometry.

Guendelman, S. et al. "Migration Tradeoffs: Men's Experiences with Seasonal Lifestyles." *International Migration Review* 21, no. 3 (September 1987): 709-727. Topics discussed include: migrants, workers, family issues, California, Latin America, culture, Mexico, work, health issues.

Hertz, D. G. "Psychosomatic and psychosocial implications of environmental changes on migrants: A review of contemporary theories and findings." *Israel Journal of Psychiatry and Related Sciences* 19, no. 4 (1982): 329-338. Topics discussed include: environment, culture, overcrowding, migrant populations.

Holland, B. "Seasonality of Births: Stability and Change in a Developing Country." *Human Biology* 61, no. 4 (August 1989): 591-598. Topics discussed include: Malaysia, fertility, urban population, religious cultural groups, demographic characteristics, Muslims, residential patterns, socioeconomic determinants.

Housing and Home Finance Agency. *Application of Climatic Data to Home Design.* Washington, DC: U.S. Government Printing Office, 1954. Topics discussed include: climate, weather, society, culture.

Ito, A. et al. "Prevalence of seasonal mood changes in low latitude area: Seasonal Pattern Assessment Questionnaire score of Quezon City workers." *Jpn J Psychiatry Neurol* 46, no. 1 (March 1992): 249. Topics discussed include: cross-sectional analysis, Philippines, epidemiology, seasonal affective disorder, diagnosis, psychology, cross-cultural analysis.

Kamo, T. et al. "Fifty young women's seasonal changes in mood and behavior in Tokyo." *Jpn J Psychiatry Neurol* 46, no. 1 (March 1992): 246-248. Topics discussed include: cross-sectional analysis, Hong Kong, seasonal affective disorder, diagnosis, psychology, cross-cultural analysis, epidemiology.

Kanekar, S. et al. "Intelligence, extraversion, and neuroticism in relation to season of birth." *J Soc Psychol* 86, no. 2 (April 1972): 309-310. Topics discussed include: cross-cultural analysis, extraversion psychology, India, intelligence, neurotic disorders, personality, delivery, personality.

Kok, L. "Season, climate and suicide in Singapore." *Med Sci Law* 33, no. 3 (July 1993): 247-252. Topics discussed include: Singapore, epidemiology, psychology, cross-cultural issues.

---. "Geophysical variables and behavior: XLVIII. Climate and personal violence (suicide and homicide): a cross cultural study." *Percept Mot Skills* 66, no. 2 (April 1988): 602. Topics discussed include: cross-cultural issues, homicide, epidemiology.

---. "The seasonal variation of suicide in Zimbabwe." *Percept Mot Skills* 73, no. 1 (August 1991): 18. Topics discussed include: epidemiology, Zimbabwe, cross-cultural issues.

---. "The seasonal variation in suicide in urban and rural areas: comment on Micciolo, Zimmerman Tansella, Williams and Tansella." *J Affect Disord* 19, no. 3 (July 1990): 171. Topics discussed include: cross-sectional analysis, Italy, epidemiology, cross-cultural issues.

Lam, D. et al. "Seasonality of births in human populations." *Social Biology* 38 (March 1991): 51-78. Topics discussed include: seasonality, fertility, cross-cultural analysis.

Lanier, S. *Florida: its scenery, climate, and history*, 336 pages. Philadelphia: J. B. Lippincott & co., 1876. Topics discussed include: agriculture, Florida, fruit culture.

Lantis, M. "Environmental stresses on human behavior. Summary and suggestions." *Arch Environ Health* 17, no. 4 (October 1968): 578-585. Topics discussed include: acclimation, acculturation, alcoholism, epidemiology, arctic regions, cold climates, communication, culture, disease propagation, Eskimos, personality.

Loftness, V. "Climate and Architecture." *Weatherwise* 31 (December 1978): 212-217. Topics discussed include: industry, culture, housing.

Miller, M. "Industrialization, ecology and health in the tropics." *J Occup Med* 15, no. 4 (April 1973): 365-368. Topics discussed include: Africa, agriculture, Asia, culture, pollution, malaria, work-related medicine, South America, urbanization, water supply, developing countries.

Mosher, S. W. "Birth Seasonality among Peasant Cultivators: The Interrelationship of Workload, Diet, and Fertility." *Human Ecology* 7, no. 2 (June 1979): 151-181. Topics discussed include: Taiwan, nutrition, fishermen, nutritional cycles, labor, fishing, culture.

Nadkarni, M. V. et al. "Socio-economic conditions in drought-prone areas." *Economic Development and Cultural Change* 36 (April 1988): 609-613.

Parkes, A. "Environmental influences on human fertility." *J Biosoc Sci Suppl* no. 3 (June 1971): 13-28. Topics discussed include: altitude, birth rate, climate, coitus, culture, infants, light, marriage, population growth, pregnancy, seasonality, temperature, twins.

Paul, A. H. "Weather and the Daily Use of Outdoor Recreation Areas in Canada." in *Weather Forecasting for Agriculture and Industry*, editor J. A. Taylor. Newton Abbot, UK: David and Charles, 1972. Topics discussed include: culture, society, behavior.

Perry, A. H. "Weather, Climate, and Tourism." *Weather* 27 (1972): 199-203. Topics discussed include: economy, society, culture, behavior.

Planalp, J. M. *Heat stress and culture in North India.* 557 pages. United States. Army Medical Research and Development Command. United States Army Medical Research and Development Commmand Special technical report, Washington: U.S. Army Medical Research and Development Command, 1971. Topics discussed include: India, ethnology, physiology.

Rotton, J. "Determinism redux: Climate and cultural correlates of violence." *Environment and Behavior* 18, no. 3 (May 1986): 346-368. Topics discussed include: sociology, suicide, homicide, atmospheric effects.

Sankar, D. V. S. "Demographic studies on childhood schizophrenia: preliminary report on season of birth, diagnosis, sex, I.Q. and race distribution." *In: Sankar, D, Schizophrenia: current concepts and research Hicksville, N Y, PJD Publications, 1969 944 p* (1969): 450-469. Topics discussed include: children, intelligence, cross-cultural analysis, neurosciences, demography.

Shapiro, A. "Heat, ethnic differences, and creativity in the Negev desert." *J Educ Psychol* 67, no. 2 (April 1975): 183-187. Topics discussed include: cross-cultural analysis, Europe, heart rate, intelligence, Israel, Morocco ethnology, creativity, desert climates, ethnic groups.

Tembon, A. "Seasonality of births in the North West Province, Cameroon: implications for family planning programme." *Cent Afr J Med* 36, no. 4 (April 1990): 90-93. Topics discussed include: Cameroon, culture, infants, birth rates, family planning.

Witkowski, S. R. et al. "Climate, clothing, and body-part nomenclature." *Ethnology* 24 (July 1985): 197-214. Topics discussed include: anatomy, terminology, language, culture, dress.

Wong, M. "Sudden unexplained death syndrome. A review and update." *Trop Geogr Med* 44, no. 4 (October 1992): S1-19. Topics discussed include: Asia, autopsy, causality, culture, pathology, ethnic groups, risk, seasonality, gender effects, Singapore, socioeconomics.

ETHNOLOGY, MISCELLANEOUS

Abel, E. L. et al. "Seasonal, monthly, and day of week trends in homicide as affected by alcohol and race." *Alcoholism Clinical and Experimental Research* 9, no. 3 (May 1985): 281-283. Topics discussed include: consumption, victims, ethnic differences, drinking patterns.

Abelson, A. et al. "Altitude, migration, and fertility in the Andes." *Soc Biol* 21, no. 1 (March 1974): 12-27. Topics discussed include: Caucasoid race, ethnic groups, Indians, South America, transients, migrants.

Bangham, C. et al. "Fertility of Nepalese Sherpas at moderate altitudes: comparison with high altitude data." *Ann Hum Biol* 7, no. 4 (July 1980): 323-330. Topics discussed include: China ethnology, marriage, menarche, Nepal, sex ratio.

Bradbury, T. N. "Racial factors and season of birth in schizophrenia: A reinterpretation of Gallagher, McFalls, and Jones." *Journal of Abnormal Psychology* 95, no. 2 (May 1986): 187-188. Topics discussed include: methodology, ethnic differences.

Cabezas, G. M. et al. "The nutritional status of the Kung population (the Kalahari Desert)." *Rev Enferm* 16, no. 175 (March 1993): 81-84. Topics discussed include: Angola, Botswana, diet, food supply, Namibia, water supply, desert climates, ethnic groups, nutrition.

Cervinka, R. "Psychosocial aspects of fitness for employment in the tropics." *Offentl Gesundheitswes* 45, no. 4 (April 1983): 180-182. Topics discussed include: Germany, ethnology, Nigeria, timing, personality, personnel management, personnel selection.

Chance, N. "Implications of environmental stress. Strategies of developmental change in the North." *Arch Environ Health* 17, no. 4 (October 1968): 571-577. Topics discussed include: acclimation, acculturation, arctic regions, cold climates, crowding, Indians, North America, religion, psychology, social behavior, social welfare.

Cohen, P. "The influence on survival of season of onset of childhood acute lymphoblastic leukemia." *Chronobiol Int* 4, no. 2 (1987): 291-297. Topics discussed include: ethnic groups, Israel, epidemiology, mortality, cycles.

Erhardt, C. L. et al. "Seasonal patterns of conception in New York City." *Am J Public Health* 61, no. 11 (November 1971): 2246-2258. Topics discussed include: birth, death, ethnic groups, illegitimacy, income, maternal age, menstruation, pregnancy, Puerto Rico, gender effects, timing, fertilization.

Fox, R. et al. "A study of temperature regulation in New Guinea people." *Philos Trans R Soc Lond Biol* 268, no. 893 (1 August 1974): 375-391. Topics discussed include: acclimation, body constitution, chlorides analysis, blood supply, effects on heart beat, tropical climates, thermoregulation, ethnic groups.

Frazen, E. "Medical aspects of work in tropical countries." *Z Arztl Fortbild Jena* 72, no. 19 (1 October 1978): 950-955. Topics discussed include: aerospace medicine, development, Europe, ethnology, malaria, tropical climates, work-related medicine.

Grivetti, L. E. "Geographical location, climate and weather, and magic: Aspects of agricultural success in the Eastern Kalahari, Botswana." *Social Science Information* 20, no. 3 (1981): 509-536. Topics discussed include: magic ritual, success, Botswana, Africa, ethnic groups, environment effects, geography, rites, workers.

Hanhart, E. "Contribution of genetic factors in suicide based on temporary increase in the rate of familial suicides in Swiss isolates." *Arch Julius Klaus Stift Vererbungsforsch Sozialanthropol Rassenhyg* 43-44, (1968): 305-376. Topics discussed include: depression, pregnancy, religion, psychology, schizophrenia, seasonality, twins.

Hayes, J. "Emphysema in a non industrialized tropical island." *Thorax* 24, no. 5 (September 1969): 623-625. Topics discussed include: age effects, air pollution, ethnic groups, Jamaica, lung pathology, pulmonary emphysema, pathology, epidemiology, gender effects.

Hunter, J. "The summer disease. Some field evidence on seasonality in childhood lead poisoning." *Soc Sci Med* 12, no. 2D (June 1978): 85-94. Topics discussed include: preschool children, ethnic groups, blood, mass screening, maternal fetal exchange, Michigan, pregnancy, risk, skin pigmentation, epidemiology.

Jaremin, B. "Acute non inflammatory chemical diarrhoeas among employees of Polish building enterprise in a tropical country." *Bull Inst Marit Trop Med Gdynia* 37, no. 3-4 (1986): 229-237. Topics discussed include: acute disease, epidemiology, diarrhea treatment, Iraq, ethnology, seasonality, water supply.

---. "Limited, intragroup epidemics of acute infectious diseases of the upper respiratory tracts and throat among workers of a Polish construction site in a tropical country." *Bull Inst Marit Trop Med Gdynia* 38, no. 1-2 (1987): 42-49. Topics discussed include: Iraq, work-related drug treatment, ethnology, respiratory tract infections, seasonality, tropical climates, propagation.

Korochkin, I. "Adaptation and morbidity among Soviet engineers in tropical countries." *Sov Med* no. 8 (1990): 56-59. Topics discussed include: Nigeria, work-related diseases, etiology, seasonality, USSR, ethnology, acclimation, physiology, epidemiology, transients, migrants.

Krylov, V. et al. "Metabolic indicators in children depending on their national ethnic background and climatic geographical zones of residence." *Lab Delo* no. 1 (1978): 25-28. Topics discussed include: arctic regions, Siberia, amino acids, blood, glucose analysis, cold climates, electrolytes, lipids.

Macdonald, E. "Demographic variation in cancer in relation to industrial and environmental influence." *Environ Health Perspect* 17 (October 1976): 153-166. Topics discussed include: age effects, air analysis, pollution, climatic effects, ethnic groups, neoplasms mortality, gender effects, Texas, exposure, industry.

Mann, I. C. *Culture, race, climate, and eye disease; an introduction to the study of geographical ophthalmology.* 580 pages. Springfield, Ill.: C. C. Thomas, 1966. Topics discussed include: geography, ethnology, culture.

Marshall, R. "An analysis of the seasonal variation of coronary heart disease and respiratory disease mortality in New Zealand." *Int J Epidemiol* 17, no. 2 (June 1988): 325-331. Topics discussed include: age effects, ethnology, etiology, epidemiology, New Zealand, gender effects.

Mason, E. et al. "Variations in basal metabolic rate responses to changes between tropical and temperate climates." *Hum Biol* 44, no. 1 (February 1972): 141-172. Topics discussed include: age effects, calorimetry, ethnic groups, India, oxygen consumption, residential mobility, timing, acclimation.

Massey, D. et al. "A demonstration of the effect of seasonal migration on fertility." *Demography* 21, no. 4 (November 1984): 501-517. Topics discussed include: preschool, marriage, Mexico, rural areas, population, socioeconomics, timing, ethnology, transients, migrants.

Mavlanov, K. et al. "Seasonal dynamics of the indices of humoral immunity in children aged 3 months to 1 year in relation to nutrition in an arid zone." *Vopr Pitan 1992* no. 4 (July 1992): 26-29. Topics discussed include: Caucasoid race, Mongoloid race, Turkmenistan ethnology, desert climates.

Mueller, W. et al. "A multinational Andean genetic and health program. VIII. Lung function changes with migration between altitudes." *Am J Phys Anthropol* 51, no. 2 (August 1979): 183-195. Topics discussed include: adaptation, Chile, ethnic groups, Indians, South America, development, occupations, gender effects, Spain, ethnology, histology, travel.

Nelson, E. et al. "Climatic and social associations with postneonatal mortality rates within New Zealand." *N Z Med J* 101, no. 849 (13 July 1988): 443-446. Topics discussed include: ethnic groups, New Zealand, socioeconomics, temperature, sudden infant death.

Nonaka, K. et al. "Effects of maternal birth season on birth seasonality in the Canadian population during the seventeenth and eighteenth centuries." *Hum Biol* 62, no. 5 (October 1990): 701-717. Topics discussed include: Canada, fertility, France, ethnology, history, medicine, marriage, childbearing age.

Odinaev, F. "The characteristics of the development and course of pneumoconiosis under the conditions of a mountain climate." *Gig Tr Prof Zabol no. 7* (1992): 13-14. Topics discussed include: mining, epidemiology, silicosis, ethnology, etiology, Tajikistan epidemiology, altitude, pneumoconiosis.

Pasternak, B. "Seasonality in Childbirth and Marriage: A Chinese Case." *Bulletin of the Institute of Ethnology, Academia Sinica* 41 (1976): 25-45. Topics discussed include: birth, fertility, behavior, society, demography.

Paulozzi, L. "The seasonality of mortality in Alaska." *Soc Sci Med D* 15, no. 3 (August 1981): 335-339. Topics discussed include: Alaska, demography, Eskimos, ethnic groups, infants, sociology, medicine.

Ricketts, T. et al. "An evaluation of subsidized rural primary care programs: II. The environmental contexts." *Am J Public Health* 73, no. 4 (April 1983): 406-413. Topics discussed include: health, services, economics, ethnic groups, labor, supply, distribution, rural areas.

Scaglion, R. "Seasonal births in a Western Abelam village, Papua New Guinea." *Hum Biol* 50, no. 3 (September 1978): 313-323. Topics discussed include: agriculture, ethnic groups, New Guinea, birth rate.

Sharma, V. M. et al. "Ethnic variations in psychological performance under altitude stress." *Aviation, Space, and Environmental Medicine* 47 (March 1976): 248-251. Topics discussed include: stress, ethnic groups, variations, depression, anxiety, concentration, eye coordination, India.

Underwood, J. "Seasonality of vital events in a Pacific Island population." *Soc Biol* 38, no. 1-2 (March 1991): 113-126. Topics discussed include: delivery, Guam, history, medicine, infant mortality, trends, marriage, religion, weather.

Vallery, M. J. et al. "Can a protracted stay in the tropics permanently lower basal metabolic rates of European expatriates?" *Ann Hum Biol* 7, no. 3 (May 1980): 267-271. Topics discussed include: Africa, Asia, Caucasoid race, France, ethnology, timing, adaptation, basal metabolism, tropical climate.

Velcek, F. et al. "Traumatic death in urban children." *J Pediatr Surg* 12, no. 3 (June 1977): 375-384. Topics discussed include: accidents, traffic, ethnic groups, fires, New York City, seasonality, gender effects, socioeconomics, population, wounds, injuries, mortality.

Visscher, B. et al. "Latitude, migration, and the prevalence of multiple sclerosis." *Am J Epidemiol* 106, no. 6 (December 1977): 470-475. Topics discussed include: California, China, ethnology, Europe, genetics, medicine, Israel, Japan, diagnosis, South Africa, Washington, demography, epidemiology, transients, migrants.

Whitebeck, R. H. "The Influence of Geographical Environment upon Religious Belief." *The Geographical Review* 5 (1918): 316-324. Topics discussed include: geography, behavior, religion, culture.

Zunnunov, Z. "Physical work capacity as a criterion of human resistance under the hot climatic conditions of an arid zone." *Fiziol Zh SSSR* 78, no. 6 (June 1992): 18-24. Topics discussed include: acclimatization physiology, ethnic groups, exercise test, Uzbekistan, desert climate, exercise physiology, physical endurance physiology, tropical climates.

11

INDEXES

INDEX OF COUNTRIES

INDEX OF SUBJECTS

About the Author

PHILIP M. PARKER is an Associate Professor at the European Institute of Business Administration (INSEAD) in Fontainebleau, France, where he teaches graduate courses in multivariate statistics, research methodology, and international marketing. He holds undergraduate degrees in biology and economics, and graduate degrees in finance and managerial economics. He received his Ph.D. in Business Economics from the Wharton School of the University of Pennsylvania in 1988. His research interests include evaluating cross-national effects of physical environment on human behavior and the resulting implications for business and economic policy. Dr. Parker has consulted on various projects with international development agencies and has conducted field research and training with private concerns in Europe, Africa, the Middle East, Asia, Latin America and North America. He has recently published articles in academic and industry journals on various economic and business topics, including the diffusion of innovations, marketing and industrial organization.

ISBN 0-313-29770-3

HARDCOVER BAR CODE

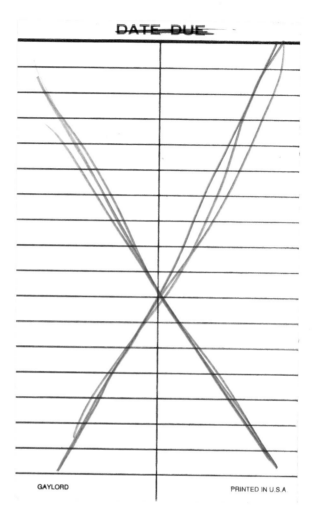